Music in American Life

Bluegrass Breakdown

BLUEGRASS

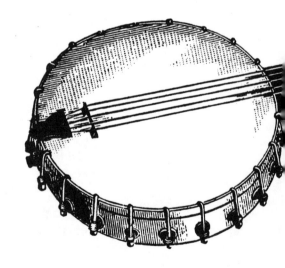

Volumes in the series
Music in American Life
are listed at the end of this book.

Robert Cantwell

BREAKDOWN

The Making of the Old

Southern Sound

University of Illinois Press

Urbana & Chicago

This book is printed on acid-free paper.

Portions of this book first appeared, in a slightly different
form, in the *Journal of Popular Culture* and the *Kenyon
Review*. The author wishes to express his gratitude to the
editors of these journals for permission to reprint.

Library of Congress Cataloging in Publication Data

Cantwell, Robert, 1945-
  Bluegrass breakdown.

  (Music in American Life)
  Bibliography: p.
  1. Bluegrass music—United States—History and
criticism. I. Title. II. Series.
  ML3520.C36 1984   784.5′2′00973   83-4861
  ISBN 0-252-01054-X

To Rose Schulman Cantwell, 1912-81

Contents

O for the gentleness of old Romance,
The simple plaining of a minstrel's song!
                                    —Keats

Preface

Bluegrass music is an original characterization, what I call simply a "representation," of traditional Appalachian music in its social form: what Bill Monroe, the acknowledged "Father of Bluegrass Music," calls "the old southern sound." It was played first in 1946, on the famous radio barn dance the Grand Ole Opry, by Bill Monroe and his Blue Grass Boys, a hillbilly string band, and has since been widely imitated by amateurs and professionals in America, Canada, England, France, Germany, Sweden, and Japan. Like jazz, bluegrass is the fruit of a union of Afro-American musical ideas with the European, especially the Celtic, on the folk and popular levels, and its roots are to be found in the popular culture of nineteenth- and early twentieth-century America, in blackface minstrelsy in particular, transformed by its sojourn in Appalachian folklife. In time bluegrass has become an emblem of our folk tradition in much the same way that Dixieland jazz was at one point in our history an emblem of our popular culture.

Bluegrass Breakdown is an essay, along the lines of art or literary criticism, into the imaginative world of bluegrass music. In order to develop its theme, which is the meeting of African and European musical ideas in America, and to achieve its purpose, which is to say what bluegrass music is, the book expands outward from its center, Bill Monroe, to its circumference, which is the great minstrel tradition extending from medieval folklife through the blackfaced clowns of antebellum America to our own popular music and grounded in age-old comic archetypes. After portraying Monroe both as a country music star and as a child of the Kentucky hills, we trace his career as a hillbilly musician to the moment at which bluegrass music coalesced in his newly formed string band. Here we widen our perspective to embrace the many influences that worked in and upon his music at that moment—an embrace which takes in the history of the banjo in America, the evolution of jazz rhythms out of minstrelsy and ragtime, and the development of the famous three-finger banjo style pioneered by Earl Scruggs of North Carolina. Incorporated into Monroe's string band, these rhythms became the matrix of a musical synthesis in which diverse folk and popular traditions, sacred and secular, black and white, urban and rural, combined to form an altogether new strain of American music which epitomized what Monroe calls the "old southern sound."

Having described the background of bluegrass and its musical features, we widen our perspective again to interpret its aural and visual symbols, lyric and narrative songs, and vocal sounds in light of the imaginative traditions surrounding them, particularly the recurrent American dreams of an edenic Old South and boundless West which have shaped our thought since the earliest European accounts of the New World. Bluegrass, we discover, belongs to a long-standing and widespread folk revival movement, both learned and popular, that is bound up with these ideas and, in this century, with the power of radio and phonograph to inspire them. The strong social character of this movement provides the basis of our closing discussion, which places Bill Monroe, alongside Daniel Decatur Emmett and Joel Walker Sweeney, among the pioneers of American minstrelsy, an art which transforms social tensions into the imaginative forces through which a dynamic and diverse civilization realizes itself.

Having taken up this volume you have certainly noticed the lengthy bibliography at the back, which records my enormous debt to the many scholars and writers who have gone over this ground, or passed very near to it, before me. Anyone who has attempted a book of this kind must feel, as I do, that any claim of originality is specious in light of the fact that knowledge is a human production and as such a social one. I bow at once, then, to the names which bibliographical convention dictates I place at the end of my text but which to my way of thinking belong at the beginning.

My debts are not of course limited to authors of books. My own writing embodies the ideas of many friends and acquaintances, some, I fear, whom I have failed to acknowledge out of sheer forgetfulness, perhaps representing someone else's thought as my own. Most neglected in this respect is my wife, Marion Cantwell, who has given her thought and her idiom to virtually every passage in the text and who ought to be considered as one of its authors.

To folklorist Archie Green I am deeply indebted for many particular ideas and suggestions, and even more for his continual guidance, encouragement, and inspiration. To Ralph Rinzler, of the Smithsonian, I am indebted for helping me to better appreciate Bill Monroe's achievement and for making it possible for me to know Bill Monroe personally. I am indebted, too, to the many thoughtful and interested people I encountered while teaching at Exeter University, England, whose excellent library in American music proved my most valuable resource. My conversations with American music bibliographer David Horn, of the Exeter University library, vastly increased my comprehension of the subject and opened up many lines of enquiry of which I had been ignorant. Through David I was fortunate to meet English folksong collector Peter Kennedy, who very generously spent an afternoon with me in his tape library, helping me to complete many then half-formed comparisons between British and American folk traditions.

To the staff of the John Edwards Memorial Foundation, where I began my research, I am grateful for much patient assistance, and to the people who very kindly consented to read the manuscript, including Nolan Porterfield, Robert Winans, Neil Rosenberg, and Judy Sacks, who helped me to work out some organizational difficulties, I am indebted for many useful and important suggestions and corrections. To the musician who taught me, by example, what bluegrass is, fiddler Alan Murphy, my debt is immeasurable. Finally I wish to thank Joel and Mary Thomas, without whose friendship and hospitality I could not have finished my revisions in time to meet the publisher's schedule.

But a book may perhaps best be known by the company it keeps. Naturally I hope that *Bluegrass Breakdown* will have readers with many different motives and interests, and that a few bluegrass musicians will be among them to pass judgment upon it. In truth, though, I have addressed myself, with great assiduousness and constancy, to a former academic colleague, a tepid, retiring gentleman who, with gentlemanly indirectness, through a third party who conveyed the idea to me in a letter, suggested that if I wished to advance in the academic world I should probably not write about bluegrass at all.

BLUEGRASS
BREAKDOWN

All sounds, all colours, all forms, either because of their preordained energies or because of long association, evoke indefinable and yet precise emotions, or, as I prefer to think, call down among us certain disembodied powers, whose footsteps over our hearts we call emotions; and when sound, and colour, and form are in a musical relation, are beautiful in relation to one another, they become, as it were, one sound, one colour, one form, and evoke an emotion that is made out of their distinct evocations and yet is one emotion.

–W. B. Yeats, "The Symbolism of Poetry"

Prologue

A New Grand Ole Opry
Bill Monroe at Capitol Center

*I thought bluegrass music would never
get no further than the farmer.*—Bill Monroe

In April 1977, when he was sixty-five years of age, Bill Monroe, the Father of Bluegrass Music, appeared with Roy Acuff, Minnie Pearl, Grandpa Jones, and other stars of the Grand Ole Opry at the Capitol Center in Largo, Maryland, near Washington. The Capitol Center is a giant convention hall comparable in size to Madison Square Garden or the Cow Palace, with a floor spacious enough for hockey and basketball games, three-ring circuses, ice pageants, and rodeos, and a seating capacity running to nearly twenty thousand—approximately the population of Batavia, New York.

For the country music show a high platform has been erected at one end of the arena. In near darkness the performer ascends to the platform by a narrow flight of raw plank stairs. Ahead of him he sees a human multitude diabolized by a lurid red glow reflecting from the stage and drifting upwards toward the huge outcroppings of darkness at the back of the hall; glacial shafts of concentrated light converge upon him from above, out of a kind of counterfeit night. Beyond the glare of the spots he can just make out, along the topmost tier of seats, like passengers high on the deck of some departing ocean liner, a filament of tiny human heads and the pale yellow lamps of the concourse behind them. Though his voice in the gigantic loudspeakers may have the amplitude of a tidal wave, to the spectators he can be little more than a diminutive mechanical doll who, with a few disproportionate gestures curiously remote from his song, which seems to come from some other source, presents a bizarre, spectral, and inconclusive manifestation of himself. Seen in silhouette from under the scaffolding backstage, he might be some terror-stricken mortal, standing at the gates of a world built on a different scale and a darker principle than this one, strumming his guitar.

The Grand Ole Opry, with its roots in the minstrel and medicine shows which persisted in the rural South until the 1930s, was originally a radio barn dance first broadcast in 1925 from a hotel room in Nashville to the rural audiences of middle Tennessee. The success of the show's first performer, an eighty-year-old fiddler called Uncle Jimmy Thompson, accompanied on the piano by his niece, Eva, inspired amateur musicians from all over the region to bring their banjos, fiddles, and guitars to the WSM studio on a Saturday night, so that in a matter of weeks the program became a kind of informal country music festival implicitly dedicated, through the influence of its producer, George D. Hay, to the preservation of old-fashioned rural music, especially southern music. Most of the musicians were artisans, tradesmen, or farmers, though a physician from Sumner County, Dr. Humphrey Bate, along with five or six of his neighbors brought the first string band to the program, Dr. Humphrey Bate and the Possum Hunters. They were soon joined by other bands: the Crook Brothers, the Gully Jumpers, the Fruit Jar Drinkers.

When Bill Monroe joined the Opry fourteen years later, in 1939, the show had acquired network status and a national reputation, having embraced the entire southern tier of the country with a fifty-thousand-watt, clear-channel transmitter and a travelling caravan of Opry performers.[1] But its emphasis was still upon the old-fashioned rural music, what most people knew then as hillbilly music, represented on the program not only by the original string bands but by accomplished and colorful professional and semiprofessional musicians such as Uncle Dave Macon, Fiddlin' Arthur Smith, Sam and Kirk McGee, and the Delmore Brothers, and by comedians such as Lazy Jim Day and Minnie Pearl. Hillbilly music was the social and domestic music of the rural South, of Appalachia particularly, drawn out of its native setting by some technological device such as radio or phonograph and offered for sale commercially. It was an Americanized strain of English, Irish, and Scots-Irish traditional music, shaped by Afro-American rhythms and tonalities and rich with deposits of nineteenth-century popular songs, especially those of blackface minstrels. Though not yet fully

evolved into the driving and brilliant form which came ultimately to
be called bluegrass, Monroe's new music, with its high pitches, speedy
tempos, and athletic instrumental breaks, its eclectic use of traditional,
gospel, sentimental, and blues songs, must have seemed somehow to
epitomize hillbilly music, almost to the point of parody—as if preservation of the old rural music for some reason demanded, in 1939, that
it be grasped more firmly and pursued more aggressively than it had
been when Uncle Jimmy Thompson sat on a cushion and fiddled into
a carbon mike, accompanied by his niece, Eva, on the piano.

Bluegrass music, characterized now by the same tight discipline and
careful integration that Bill Monroe brought to the Opry forty years
ago and identified by most of us with the three-finger syncopated banjo
style named for Earl Scruggs, who introduced it into Monroe's band,
the Bluegrass Boys, in 1946, remains a kind of musical icon which
somehow embodies traditional southern music, though it is not itself
traditional. Indeed bluegrass seems to have absorbed the immense
variety of hillbilly music into itself, maintaining at a high intensity its
signifying features such as pinched nasal tones and sentimental lyrics,
while obliterating under its sheer technical power and strict economy
some of the delicate richness of the traditional southern music that
commercial record companies discovered when they made their first
forays into the hills in the 1920s. Of the old string bands and hoedown
fiddlers, the blues guitar pickers such as Sam McGee and medicine
show raconteurs such as Uncle Dave Macon, little besides bluegrass
remains on the Grand Ole Opry, while commercial country music has
become the gleaming and uniform corporate product typified by the
crooning, mellifluous voices, undulating pedal steel guitars, and professional songwriters of Nashville. This music belongs no longer to a
region, though the South is still the major contributor to it, but to an
economic class, the industrial working class, which can appreciate both
the vulgar glamor of the music and its mercurial capacity to treat
subjects of immediate social and personal significance. Loneliness, betrayal, heartbreak, and vice were not of course unknown either to
hillbilly music or to Anglo-Irish traditional song, nor are they problems
peculiar to postwar working-class life; but hillbilly music, with its gaze
fixed wistfully upon old times, rarely turned, except by innuendo, to
face the realities of adultery, divorce, and alcoholism which since World
War II have been the staple subject matter of commercial country
music. Though it makes habitual reference both in song and in style
to the rural and traditional influences out of which it grew, modern
country music is dominated by an unerring, though often perfunctory,
professional musicianship which carries it frequently to the boundaries

of popular music, with its complex studio arrangements and bloated orchestration. It is the perfect expression of an economically ascendant, but culturally uprooted, people, reinterpreting the rural ethos, to which it has no intrinsic connection, in politically and socially conservative terms more typical of the suburban tract than of the coal company town or mountain farm.

In the vast parking lot surrounding the Capitol Center, where the sun is blazing with a ferocity unusual for an April afternoon, spreading its brightness uniformly over the high concrete battlements of the arena, the motorcoaches of the Grand Ole Opry stars stand in an imposing regimental row, engines gruffly idling and air conditioners laboring, steel roofs crawling with the light like small rectangular lakes; radiating waves of heat redolent of road tar, diesel fuel, and boiling motor oil suggest recent turnpike travel. The musicians' names, or rather, their titles—Little Jimmy Dickens, Wilma Lee Cooper, Jim Ed Brown, Jack Greene, and Jeannie Seeley—speak grandiloquently in paint from the burnished side panels of the coaches, almost as if the buses themselves were the celebrities, while the faces hidden inside them, framed disappointingly on the human scale and only imperfectly resembling the faces that look back at us from album covers and fan magazines, belong to mere interlopers, shamelessly squatting in their own huge fame.

On Monroe's bus, which Bill himself has outfitted with cowhide upholstery, a tangled shag rug creeping up the wall, and spruce panelling, there is a kind of expert idleness: the idleness of men who have grown completely accustomed to the interminable waiting that belongs to a musician's life on the road. For when he is not actually performing, the country musician's existence is a tedious succession of mile markers, road maps, rest stops, restaurant counters and cups of coffee, lackluster motels, and derelict industrial towns, a sequence periodically arrested by the prolonged intervals of anticipation that precede show times. Monroe's men have learned to accept and even to relish the empty hours, strengthened against tension, boredom, and restlessness by a persistent consciousness, perhaps, of the alternatives: a day job in a coal mine or a cotton mill, or on an assembly line in Dayton or Detroit. Probably they are conscious, too, that a bluegrass performance under the most uncompromising bandleader in country music calls upon all the strength required by an ordinary hard day's work, so that there is little point in squandering one's energy uselessly offstage.

In over fifty years as a professional musician, Monroe himself has engineered an almost fantastic taciturnity, one which contrasts eerily with, and certainly anticipates, the astounding power of his performances. This afternoon he is sitting, relaxed but alert, motionless as a Buddha, on one of his cowhide benches, his heavy white hands folded complacently in his lap. His eyes float in the glycerine-like lenses of his glasses, and, with his white hair curled thickly about his ears, the long melancholy lines of his mouth, and the faintly scowling, effeminate, and puritanical lips of an old divine, he has, surprisingly, an unmistakably elderly look. For people who know bluegrass, Monroe is an august, even an awesome, presence in whom age figures as a moral trait, not a physical affliction. It is not only that he has ascended to eminence as the founder of a music with respectable folk ancestors, an ardent and cohesive following, and an incipient classical form, or even that he carries himself with the natural patriarchal elegance of a man who expects, by experience, to be admired. It is that he is simply a great musician and that, like all great musicians and poets, he lives in closer communion with the tyrannies of imagination than people less understanding, less reckless, or less innocent than himself. Although at times his personal presence may seem oddly brittle or chimerical, or his personal conduct, seen in the harsh light of conventional morality, not entirely spotless, he inspires a certain leisurely reverence even in his professional colleagues of many years' standing.

There isn't much point in trying to talk to Monroe when he is in this state of repose: one might as well address a gardenia. No one attempts it. On the other side of the aisle Monroe's fiddler, Kenny Baker, a rugged, homely man of about fifty with the stern expression of a mountaineer fixed into the bones of his face, is sitting at his ease with one of Bill's mandolins in his hands. It is an antique Gibson F-5 in mint condition, light as the ribcage of a hawk, gleaming as a doubloon, carrying on a label in its sound box the graceful authenticating signature of Lloyd Loar, the acoustic engineer from Ohio who in 1919 or 1920 designed the instrument for use in the then-popular mandolin orchestras. Bill has recently been offered, Kenny reports, the unheard of sum of $7500 for it. Baker, a thoroughly expert musician, is dabbling on its tiny fingerboard, and a cold trickle of notes issues from it. Next to him a burly young man with a villainous-looking black mustache, Monroe's driver, is bowing his head over a folded section of a newspaper someone has just dropped off at the bus. He is reading an article from today's *New York Times* on Monroe, who will appear, after a hiatus of several years, at New York University tomorrow night. "Mr.

Baker," the young man reads aloud in the syncopated accent of central Kentucky, "is considered by many the leading fiddler in bluegrass, even if he still considers himself a Kentucky coal miner—his original occupation";[2] He delivers the concluding phrase to Baker in the imperious tone of a criminal lawyer.

"Let me see thet thang," Baker says, snatching the paper from the other man's hands and scanning the page himself. As he reads, another young man of about thirty emerges through a pair of curtains from the sleeping quarters at the back of the bus, buttoning up his shirt. This is Monroe's current lead singer-guitarist, Wayne Lewis, an earnest, moody, and well-mannered son of an evangelist preacher, formerly a lead singer with an obscure bluegrass gospel group. Though not, by his own testimony, a religious man, but an unrepentant and contented sinner, he has nevertheless something of the evangelist's dandified charm; with his tense and dusky tenor voice, his ingratiating vanity and virile good looks that might belong to a professional water-skier, he is in some respects an ideal lead singer for Bill Monroe, who in the autumnal phase of his career arouses a veneration not unmixed with a certain religious awe. Though his timing, as Kenny complains, is not always perfect, Wayne is likely to prove a retainer loyal to the end.

"Kenny," Wayne says, noting the fiddler's dour concentration as he seats himself beside him, "you're gonna read them words right off the page. How'd you expect me to read it?"

"Bill Monroe," Baker responds dryly from the newspaper, "is to bluegrass what Charles DeGaulle was to the Fifth Republic. . . ."

"Now whut's *that* supposed to mean?" the mustachioed driver demands. The mandolin has meanwhile passed, like a Pekingese, into his hands, where it rests at an awkwardly unprofessional angle while his puffy fingers probe irritably at it without any appreciable musical effect.

". . . he wrote the script."

"That's right, man!" says Bill Monroe, who you would have thought had been paying no attention whatever to the conversation. The paper is handed over to him and he reads, circumspectly as a philologist through his massive bifocals, with a faint avuncular smile. "When he comes to the big city," Bill reads to himself, his lips whispering the words, "Mr. Monroe is very much aware of presenting an art form, and he treats it with just such dignity. . . . At 65 with his jutting jaw, his long mane of white hair, and his solid colored western-cut suits, Mr. Monroe still presents a very imposing figure."

"Now that feller writes the truth, don't he?" asks Bill.

Strange, that this venerated figure, who can silence even Gotham City journalists with a look, whom one is likely to treat at this close proximity as if he were some crepey old document like the Constitution of the United States, is only a hayseed after all—and he probably doesn't even read music.

At this juncture a fourth man appears, leaping into the bus like a Doberman, his fingers in his lank brown hair which is clipped neatly over his ears in a style apparently inspired by the football helmet. This is Monroe's bass player, Randy Davis, an urchin-like lad with rosy cheeks who at twenty is the youngest member of the band. An accountant by training, Randy can be relied upon not only to play a steady and supple bass line so much more animated than the diurnal thump-thump of the typical Saturday-afternoon bassist, but to keep careful account of routes and itineraries, show times and places, promoters' names and addresses, telephone numbers, minutes on stage—he is never without his digital watch. He has come to announce that the band is expected backstage in exactly one-half hour.

Across the burning asphalt lot, between the Opry buses and the service entrance to the stadium, which opens at the bottom of a long ramp descending on a gentle incline one story below the pavement, increasingly heavy pedestrian traffic is gathering. Most of the people are the musicians themselves, dressed in the nifty, garish, and at times outlandish costumes typical of country-western musicians. A few, though, are only Grand Ole Opry fans who have lost their way or who may believe they have found a way into the stadium without a ticket. Some are an ambiguous class of men and women connected in various obscure ways to the performers but without visible functions, who descend the ramp with impunity, contemptuous of uniformed guards and indifferent parking attendants with their white flightsuits and ribbons of plastic tape.

One group particularly attracts attention: not musicians, apparently, or lackeys of some kind, but a band of hoodlums—if that is the right name for them—who hope to enter the arena through the back door by the authority of number alone and by the intimidating effect of their brawling laughter and loud talk. One has a can of Budweiser in his fist—are they drunk? All the more dangerous, then. Their scruffy jowls, unruly black and grey beards, threadbare jeans, square-toed boots, and especially their straw hats—a peculiar high-crowned variety of rodeo hat whose brim curls down impudently in front to shade the brow—identify them as "outlaws": a class of bohemianized men who style themselves after Willie Nelson, the country-western singer who went to Austin to establish an outpost of a rough, resourceful, and

arrogant new country music galvanized by the relentless mood of sixties' rock. Their costumes, inspired by Hollywood, recall the displaced
rebel soldiers who sought out the moral vagaries of the frontier after
the Civil War.

This particular band of outlaws—five or six of them, some as men-
acingly skinny as starving mules—is dominated by a large, unkempt
man whose florid polyester shirt clings sensuously to his cumbersome
beer belly. With him is a small, voluptuous woman with platinum
blonde hair that hangs stiffly to her waist, whose crisp new levis and
undersized Jeanie Seeley T-shirt conspicuously display her peach-like
rump and insistent breasts. The men surround her with a sort of
proprietary zeal, as if they had just won her from a gumball machine.

With the congenial assent of a guard who pretends not to notice
them, this group enters the performers' gate without incident. A small
crowd of show people has already assembled in the vast room backstage
which might be a skating rink or warehouse. Here most of the stadium
equipment—scaffolding, collapsible bleachers and folding chairs,
macabre-looking light fixtures, huge drums of wax and cleaning fluid,
slabs of flooring and the like—is stored. Everything looks brand new.
Jim Ed Brown, slightly more endomorphic than his photographs reveal, wearing a snazzy Mexican outfit with sequins flashing in several
colors along his arms and legs, is speaking, as if into a telephone, into
a tangled pile of hair the color and texture of black shoe polish. This
mass has a hollow-faced, middle-aged woman under it, whose immod-
estly short skirt reveals a pair of shapely legs in net stockings. Brown
and the woman are holding styrofoam cups of coffee, dispensed at a
nearby folding table by a hostess in chambermaid's uniform. Grandpa
Jones, who has already completed his part of the show, is strolling
towards the back door, drawing the palm of his hand compulsively
over the top of his bald head. He has exchanged his suspenders and
flannel shirt for a dapper white leisure suit, which makes him look
something like the manager of a Palm Beach hotel. Wilma Lee Cooper,
whose husband, Stoney, the fiddler with whom she has performed these
twenty-five years, has recently died of a heart attack, is posing with
a family of four girls for somebody's photograph album. Her rigorous,
mechanical smile, breaking through her weariness and recent troubles,
betrays her long experience with admirers, autographs—she is signing
one now—and snapshots. She and her husband once received an award
from Harvard folksong enthusiasts for the authenticity of their music.
This afternoon the bluegrass fiddler and corporate mathematician, Tex
Logan, who with his rakish black mustache oddly resembles Stoney,
is taking his place. Perhaps Wilma Lee will sing "Poor Ellen Smith"

today, in the heart-rending way that makes you think she knew the murdered girl personally.

At the far end of the room, where a lofty burgundy-colored curtain has been drawn to form a backdrop in the darkened arena beyond it, Little Jimmy Dickens is preparing to go on. His gorgeous black and white cowboy suit with its double row of silver buttons and his enormous ten-gallon white hat suggest thundering hooves, blazing sixguns, desert sunsets. Really, Little Jimmy is astonishingly short—not more than five feet high, it seems, with the quick, darting movements of a dwarf. His Gibson guitar seems disproportionately huge, while the three grave men standing an arm's length away from him; the producers of today's show, look like professional wrestlers in business suits. With urgent gesticulations they are conferring with Opry stars Roy Acuff and Minnie Pearl, whose act will conclude the show. In a conservative blue suit instead of her crinolines, straw hat, and Mary Janes, Minnie has the reassuring respectability of Eleanor Roosevelt; Acuff, too—his presence is as vivid as an ex-President's, his head, with seventy-four years upon it, having already assumed the indomitability of a rough-hewn bronze bust. Roy and Minnie belong to an aristocracy of fame which, by assuming their personal debts to time, makes of their mortality something selfish or impertinent, as if they'd grown old deliberately, out of luxuriousness or spite. Acuff, in fact, looks alarmingly tired and weatherbeaten, no doubt because it has been only a matter of days since he was released from the cardiac unit of a Nashville hospital. And when Little Jimmy Dickens, just before disappearing through the velvet curtain, momentarily doffs his hat to reveal on his boyish frame the bald head of a man in late middle age, the effect, however fleeting, is grotesque.

From all this one takes the unhappy impression that in spite of its gargant..an new popularity the Grand Ole Opry is a gaseous expanding star in the concluding stages of its existence. These aging country performers, helpless before the power of an industry impersonal as a utility company to prolong their public lives are, like the tiny holographic figures they become under the spotlights of the Capitol Center, illusions begotten out of the impure ethers of show business. Yet Uncle Jimmy Thompson, Dr. Humprey Bate, and the rest—they were phantoms too, generated on an empty, unsurveyed plane of the electromagnetic spectrum, ubiquitous, ineffable, and as immune to change as Yoknapatawpha County, where a fading way of life could resurrect itself imaginatively. Hillbilly music has never been anything but entrepreneurial and commercial, prospering in the one commodity which in America is ever in short supply—the past.

On a stack of boards in a remote corner of the huge room, Kenny
Baker is intently fiddling. He is wearing that poker face that comes
to him involuntarily when the fiddle goes to his chin, and his head is
cocked slightly, his ear trained to the breeze. All sorts of things come
out: a waltz, an elegant rag, a few bars of a mountain breakdown, a
sinuous lick from a smokey Paris jazz club. Nearby, Larry Beasley, a
tall, raw-boned young banjo player, whose cobalt blue suit seems several sizes too large for him, is pacing about cracking his knuckles.
Monroe has just hired him, and his stage fright, coupled with natural
shyness, has nearly paralyzed him; on stage only his fingers move,
thrusting out ingenious diagrammatic riffs from his low-slung banjo,
while the sweat stands out on his brow and courses down the sides of
his face. Wayne Lewis, though far from a novice, seems restless too.
He has staked out an empty expanse of floor, where he and his guitar
are in private consultation with one another, as if he had temporarily
forgotten how to play.

Bill Monroe has been moving commandingly about in a cream-colored
suit, conversing with a number of friends and acquaintances. Big Howdy Forrester, a fiddler who played with the Blue Grass Boys in the
old days, now a florid, red-faced man with abundant iron grey hair,
greets Bill with a few words about Stoney Cooper, whose death seems
to have rattled him a little. Three portly matrons with giant handbags
take Howdy's place and commandeer his attention, with his cheerful
acquiescence, for the better part of an hour. He seems to have known
them for years, and probably he has. After they depart to see the rest
of the show, a pretty young lady in a gingham dress takes Bill by the
hand and draws him towards a group of fifteen or twenty girls like
herself, who applaud her bold and decisive action. They are a clogging
team, whom Bill rewards with a few minutes of square dancing, displaying a vigor which in most men his age would seem merely dangerous. There's no doubt that Monroe has a winning way with the
ladies, however old or young. But the cloggers are called to the stage,
leaving Bill vulnerable to a pale, bespectacled young reporter from the
Baltimore *Sun*, whose quick, economical, uncompromising questions
stimulate Monroe to emphasize today the *decency* of bluegrass music.
It's something the whole family can listen to, Bill observes, implying
that most of the rest of country music is not fit for the whole family.
And just what *is* bluegrass? the reporter asks obligingly, sensing that
Monroe is forming an idea of it he has not advanced before. "Bluegrass," Monroe discloses, "is the old southern sound, that was heard
years ago, many, many years ago in the backwoods, at country
dances. . . ." But his sense today of its antiquity is strong, and he is

not quite satisfied. "Blue grass brings out the old tones," he adds, "ancient tones."

Ancient, the reporter writes in his notebook, with a bold underline, *ancient tones*.

The interview ends abruptly, as if by a prearranged signal, and Monroe strolls back towards the corner where his musicians are warming up. At sixty-five Monroe seems closer than he has been at any other period of his life to realizing the idea of himself which has grown in him, subject to innumerable influences, over the years. Each step he takes, delicate, cautious, even ladylike, the step, perhaps, of a man whose eyesight is not altogether reliable, seems to lead him towards a predestined meeting with that ideal conception, an incarnation at once glorious and deeply mortifying. Its power seems to have steadied him, placed him beyond his own arrogance and pride, restoring the old forgotten dignity of a lineage that reaches back to President James Monroe. In the circus-like atmosphere of a Grand Ole Opry Road Show, where he has performed these thirty-eight years, he now seems curiously misplaced, more a historical than an actual figure, and yet far less theatrical—or perhaps only more finely so—than the gaudy Opry stars of today.

The show at Capitol Center has been running late, and to pass the time Monroe takes out his mandolin, the famous battered old F-5 he found in a Miami barbershop window and bought for $125. He slings it over his shoulder, tunes it with a few bright bursts of notes, and in a moment a familiar old dance tune is streaming out of it, modulating almost imperceptibly into a less familiar piece, perhaps one of Bill's variations. Gradually the melody changes again, like refracted light, and the shadow of a minor key rolls over it. This one, too, is vaguely familiar—or is it one that Monroe has composed on the spot? Still another variation bursts forth, sunnier than the last, and then another . . . before long Bill has posted himself in front of Kenny Baker, stripping the new tunes from his mandolin like dispatches from the wire service, in hopes of establishing them in Baker's memory, where they will gestate and perhaps be born onto the bands of a record album, with evocative titles such as "Wheel Hoss" or "Crossing the Cumberlands" supplied by Bill or his friends. Baker has recently recorded an entire album of Monroe's inventions, twelve or fifteen tunes which represent only a tiny detail of an ever-evolving musical mural.[3] In Baker, Monroe has found the fiddler into whose imagination he is willing to commit his melodies—for such a commitment means a kind of abandonment—on behalf of their survival in the transpersonal realm where traditional music resides. Why, one might ask, does Monroe not record the tunes himself, on the mandolin? He does, sometimes; but Monroe has a fiddler's imagination, and it is to the fiddle that certain tunes must go.

Bill Monroe is what folklorists call a tradition bearer. Though bluegrass music, like other kinds of popular music, reflects the various social and commercial influences that worked upon it during its formative period, it stands securely upon a traditional foundation which, if we could somehow uncover it, would show itself to be as abstract as a grammar, and just as mysteriously linked on the one hand to the values of a culture and on the other to the structure of human thought. That is what distinguishes the true tradition bearer from the mere collector or antiquarian, whose very existence may imply the morbidity of a tradition. A traditional fiddler recalls the melodies he has heard around him, offering his own elaborations, combinations, and variations upon them; he finds that the circle of his memory intersects others', so that something independent reveals itself—the "tradition"—which compels his loyalty because it is apparently so much larger and more enduring than he is. What he has discovered, in fact, is sure evidence of an otherwise imperceptible interconnectedness in the human community, a community without which there would be no "tradition." But a tradition has its internal laws as well, and it is to this deeper level that the tradition bearer penetrates: to the hidden principle, in effect, of which all particular tunes are an expression and out of which can emerge new tunes which are, in the familiar folklorists' paradox, at once traditional and original. It is as possible for the tradition bearer to emerge from a corrupted tradition as from a rich, flourishing one, since the imagination requires only a handful of particular examples from which to make its hypothesis: only what a Pen Vandiver—Monroe's fiddling uncle—for instance, might have had in his repertoire. Perhaps the evolution of a tradition ought to be compared not to the original arts but to the sciences, in which an inherited idea rules the work of a community of scientists, until out of some anomalous case, or out of some new perspective or circumstances impinging from without, a new vision, more efficient, more powerful, or simply more expedient, displaces the old.

In the crowd of performers gathered backstage at the Capitol Center this afternoon, Bill Monroe may be only one who is at this moment playing music for its own sake, or for that matter, the only one playing music at all. He *likes* to play music, and, given his acknowledged brilliance at it, it is perhaps more than a mere impertinence that the young woman in the Jeannie Seely T-shirt, who has just entered the hall with her hairy entourage, should see fit to intrude herself into

Bill's presence. She strides forward ebulliently, her slender white arm extended towards him, and warbles, "I jest wanted to say howdy, Bill, how *are* you-all?"

There are few men on earth, probably, who would not be made at least a little uncomfortable by the close proximity of this woman, who has made it practically impossible to regard her without a certain vague apprehension. Bill returns her greeting cordially, if a bit stiffly; he seems not to know her as well as her neighborliness might suggest— in fact, he seems not to know her at all. The Blue Grass Boys, like pastured cows, look on impassively. She'd like to stay and *visit*, she says, but she and the boys are *fixin'* to go on.

Go on?

She *is* Jeannie Seeley, it turns out, and the shaggy one with the spare tire is her singing companion, Jack Greene, with his band, the Renegades. Or was it the Rustlers?

"Ah luv ever damn one uv ya," Greene drawls into the mike, practically vomiting up the words, once the troupe has established itself on stage. He might as well be addressing himself to a cavern full of sleeping bats. It is heartening to discover that both have fine singing voices, Jeannie's as strong as steel, Jack's as hearty as beef, though their songs, full of barstools, motel rooms, and adulterers' jargon, seem to have come out of divorce-court testimony. The honky-tonk, it seems, has drifted from the Texas oilfields to the panelled rec-rooms of suburban Tulsa or Phoenix. In the shadows below stage, where Bill Monroe and the Blue Grass Boys are milling about among a throng of technicians, managers, sidemen, and other half-shrouded figures, the music is little more than a hollow din which mingles confusedly with the vast dull rattle of applause when Jeannie and Jack quit the stage.

Monroe opens his set by unbinding a handful of twisted notes from his mandolin, opening "Muleskinner Blues" and releasing a bright chill wind upon which Baker launches his fiddle, circling about with a wild, melancholy cry that descends towards earth in reiterated patterns. The words of the old Jimmie Rodgers song, which Rodgers pieced together sixty years ago in Mississippi out of the lingo of black teamsters, spills out of Monroe's mouth like the ecstatic claptrap of a cultist speaking in tongues. He rides the jetstream with his tenor voice, gathering up the snowdrop-like notes that flourish in the purer air above the timberline. A kind of frontier opens before us, shimmering half-visible in the mind's eye where sound flows out into light—boundless, lonely, and ethereal—where a man has ventured forth behind a muleteam, leaving behind the unearthly laugh Monroe has made out of Rodgers's supple and sad blue yodel.

That country is a country of imagination, the only region from which country music has ever really come. It is situated in a historical fastness that prolonged national meditation has engendered out of the old rural South, where traditional music, whose very nature is to assimilate and transfigure, according to its own slow-changing aesthetic, the sounds of the civilization around it, had freed the past from Time, setting it forth into an imaginary country in which innumerable epochs and ways of life thrive together. Country music is a popular form of the American historical imagination, and bluegrass is a pure form of country music.

I think we need a new Grand Ole Opry, one which might return to us the vast inheritance that lies in "the old southern sound," bearing us to the moral interior of the old romantic America in remembrance of which the Grand Old Opry was founded.

ɔck around him, and if the concert has been held in the South it
nes apparent that Monroe's audience constitutes one of the last
nely rural classes in America, with traits that recall now largely
tten stereotypes that used to distinguish the rube from the city
r. What precisely characterizes this audience, or why it is so
ctively itself, why it is, in a word, so vividly Appalachian, I am
ɔss to explain. Perhaps it is the effect of poverty, whose marks
verywhere—poverty of the endemic kind, I mean, that over a
·ation or so has become a principle of life, in evidence even when
sy new prosperity of wages has diverted its course. Good nutrition
ental care are apparently among the casualties of mountain folk-
Ɔverweight in varying degrees is a general blight. Faces are
·, sometimes coarse or picturesque, often interesting, seldom
iful. Gestures are large, unprepossessing, at times child-like,
s warm and animated, relations among people convivial and en-
ɪstic. There is pride in fashionable grooming and dress, though
m are they the fashions that rule the day elsewhere: Appalachian
, like other aspects of Appalachian culture, salvages the scraps
· past. Everyone's hair is done up, men and women, in sometimes
ɪ or foppish ways that may suggest either the antebellum ballroom
e ducktails and teases we used to see around the soda fountain
g the Eisenhower era. Both men and women dress to emphasize
sex, men favoring the bulging bicep, perhaps a tatoo, some va-
of western boot; women, tight fitting blouses and pants and fem-
frills, though only a few—the most sexually conspicuous—wear
up: perhaps the old church sanction against it remains silently in
, Older men and women, more simply and conventionally groomed
ɪressed, apparently less buffeted about by social change than the
ger people, represent the rural folk of a generation or so ago, Bill
ɪoe's generation; Monroe himself, apparently immune to these
ges, has transcended the times and stands out like a lighthouse
g his people.

th this audience Monroe is warm, often witty, but rarely familiar.
·illingly poses with admirers for photographs and never fails to
·nd politely to compliments. It is astonishing how frequently a
ɔr woman will recall to Bill having seen him at another show ten,
n, even *thirty* years ago: his fans are loyal, and Monroe often
rds them with some honest recollection of the time and place, and
times with some mutually familiar name. I have never seen him
e a person soliciting his attention, though he may behave coolly
rds one or another of whom he disapproves—particularly those
seem to have no pride or self-respect: for Monroe, certain coun-

Chapter 1

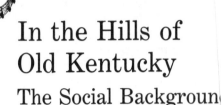

In the Hills of
Old Kentucky
The Social Backgroun

Whoever has seen Bill Monr
especially in these late yea
remember that he carries
of austere majesty, as if ti
selled him, like his presidential ancestor, from a
whatever art it is that a man conveys his character
to the world, Monroe seems to continue a lineage
almost to Lexington, the heart of the Blue Grass
the West. He is a striking figure, dashing and pa
that peculiar vividness and clarity that we associa
or movie stars. Even now Monroe is an extraordinar
whose face, with a jutting jaw and acquiline nose
structed and whose expression, enigmatically con
gance, sorrow, and humor, is perilously easy to
mouth, with its pouting lower lip and faint sneer
corner that opens slightly with the effort of playin
drawn tight with a kind of vigilant mistrust, the
ancestor; the eyes are a pioneer's. Whatever may
recesses of Monroe's personality, this public image
of vanity, pomposity, vulgarity, or corruption, thou
reserved each of these traits might easily blossom o
subtly theatrical poise Monroe's image demands.

Monroe has the rugged dignity one sees, for insta
daguerrotypes of Lincoln; and when this impressive
from the stage, in a Western-cut, cream-colored, ta
Stetson hat, he is predictably an object of veneration.

ers
bec
gen
for
slic
dis
at
are
ge
a f
an
lif
sh
b
v
t
s
d
o
l

tercultural types fall into this class, as well as the inevitable thug or drunk.

Bill Monroe is no teen-age idol, but something far more durable—a patriarch, whose dedication to his sprawling, incoherent family is never more apparent than when he has occasion to lead them in song at one of his bluegrass festivals or pays them tribute to writers and reporters. Asked recently if he had thought of retiring, having dashed back to the Opry stage after major surgery, he answered—honestly, I think—that he didn't want to let his fans down. His leadership in fact has the character of spiritual guidance, with special attention given to the young and to the solidarity of the bluegrass community; his public pronouncements are implicitly or explicitly affirmations of the wholesomeness, honesty, and decency of bluegrass music. Though not an eloquent man, Monroe is thoughtful, with the habit of reflection upon matters of principle deeply established in him; it seems there is virtually nothing in the way of music or conduct that has escaped his consideration.

Monroe's patriarchal aspect is more than impersonation. It is a reality formed from the conjunction of his sense of himself and the growing public recognition of his achievement. The famous photographs of him by David Gahr and Carl Fleischhauer, and the graphic art they have inspired, illustrate the contribution of Monroe's admirers to his identity. These portraits, shot in performance, employ dramatic angles, high contrasts, and a shallow depth of field in order to isolate the subject and bring out the marks of character in his face. One of Fleischhauer's is mostly black; Monroe's great hands emerge from the shadows, cradling the mandolin, whose shape we see only as a kind of sketch in light. Monroe's hat and profile glow with bright phosphorescence. He is set slightly above us; behind him, in the lower right corner of the picture, a spectral face, lean, almost haggard—one of the Blue Grass Boys—looks on solemnly.

Monroe has always been especially photogenic. In early photographs of the Blue Grass Boys he doesn't distinguish himself in any obvious way from the others. Dressed in jodphers, riding boots, and Stetsons, the younger men address themselves and their instruments to a microphone, or they put their heads together fraternally for a gospel quartet, or they kneel like scouts behind their instruments, whose necks are crossed like banners in front of them. Occasionally Monroe styles himself the leader, with some slight difference of pose or costume; this tendency becomes more pronounced after the dissolution of the original Blue Grass Boys, and as the years go by the band recedes into the background, ultimately disappearing altogether in record-jacket photos. Pride, no doubt, has maintained Monroe's reserve and fixed his ever-businesslike, sometimes mournful, sometimes impatient expression; the man has smiled, but never, I think, for a photographer. Pride, too, allowed him to garnish his mid-career successes with a showmanlike touch of pomposity; once we find him in the fringed leathers of a Hollywood cowboy, his hat held high over his head in a deadpan salute. Or he is mounted atop his sumptuous gelding, King Wilke, as fit for the range as Gene Autry. In 1954, in his early middle age, he smirks at us from a Decca album cover, looking as smug and self-satisfied in his starched collar, necktie, and white hat as any Rotarian—and even a little menacing, as if he had just been elected sheriff.

A photograph, though, will sometimes show the heart. A memorable early photograph of Bill Monroe pictures a man of about thirty, in a dark jacket and modest dark hat, standing with a guitar behind the WSM mike. He is staring with an arresting directness at the camera, not with the familiar arrogance, but with the sad, beseeching look of a pure but wounded heart, out of which the ferocity that would redeem his early sorrows is about to be born.

Buck Monroe, Bill's father, owned a 600-acre farm outside Rosine in central Kentucky.[1] Buck farmed, cut and hauled timber, and mined coal on his land; his wife, Malissa, tended house, farmyard, garden, and a family of ten children, of whom Bill was the youngest, born in the nineteenth year of the marriage and in his mother's forty-second year. Like most rural people the Monroes experienced lean years, but theirs was not the desperately impoverished life that has more recently characterized the Cumberland region. Though not, strictly speaking, mountaineers, having settled farther west in the Pennyroyal region of the state, they shared the Scots heritage that formed the nucleus of the great migration into Appalachia begun early in the eighteenth century. Historically these people, the Presbyterian Scots-Irish, have a reputation for clannishness, aggressiveness, and, at times, primitiveness; they were the stock of the frontiersman, in whose character lay the raw materials for an American archetype—the hardy, fearless, proud, durable, and independent Crockett or Boone who led the westward expansion.

History does little, however, to help us conceive of a childhood as remote in place and time as Bill Monroe's, particularly when history itself, as well as Monroe's own recollections, is dyed deeply with myth. As a backdrop, then, to the few important details Monroe has so far recalled for his potential biographers, let us look briefly at a small but enlightening book, *Children of the Cumberland*, by a young Manhattan private school teacher, Claudia Lewis, who in the 1940s accepted a position in a remote Tennessee settlement school, in part to discover what differences in upbringing might contribute to the capacity of children to adapt to the competitive, complex, and swiftly changing modern world—a capacity well developed in the privileged children she had left behind in New York.

What Ms. Lewis found in her new situation, though almost thirty years later than the period of Monroe's childhood, cannot have been vastly different from what a visitor to Rosine would have encountered in 1925 or 1930. "There are still mountain wives," she reports, "who scarcely stir out of their homes and are too shy to talk to callers; grandmothers who still speak an Elizabethan language; young folks who carry on their courtin' by means of secret trysts and notes left under the stone by the gate." Nearly every family, she found, had some kinship ties to its neighbors, so that for each person the surrounding community was a network of uncles, aunts, cousins, and grandparents, many of whom could be counted upon to care for a child whose own household was crowded with brothers and sisters.[2] This situation obtained in Rosine, where Buck Monroe's farm joined his brothers' farms, the entire neighborhood belonging in effect to the Monroes.[3] And in the casual conversation of mountain people Ms. Lewis found abundant evidence of the idiomatic and musical vivacity of speech which so many other Appalachian travelers have remarked:

> "Howdy, Ernest, how are you?"
> "On top of the world, and you?"
> "Oh, I'm able to get to the table."[4]

If in bluegrass and hillbilly music we frequently meet expressions of intense longing for home and for the childhood Eden often linked in song to the resplendent Paradise of evangelical religion, it may be because for many mountain children existence is, by Ms. Lewis's account, simply paradisical: "The baby is sure to find himself immediately the loved darling of his own family and his host of relatives. He will seldom be out of his mother's arms. And when he is, his sisters and even his brothers will grab him up and cuddle him, for these boys have never heard it suggested that it might be sissy for them to fondle and care for babies." Unlike the child of busy urbanites, "he is not left at home when his parents go out; he does not have to be torn away and tucked into bed before he feels sleepy; he is present when guests come; even as a small baby it is right and proper that he should participate in life's fundamental solemnities, such as buryings . . . he is dressed as a baby, and nursed and cuddled, for a good long time, with no one expecting him or wanting him to grow up. He is surrounded by protective, adoring brothers and sisters, and in many cases there are several 'mothers' available at almost any time for care and comfort."[5]

"Back in them days," Bill Monroe remembers, "a kid was babied and patted more than they are today."[6]

Discipline, Ms. Lewis notes, "is theoretically of the old 'authoritative' kind, yet the actual routine of living is far from a strictly regulated one." The child's life "is still in many ways very much the stronghold of delight and comfort that it was when he was still a small baby. . . ." It is a life, apparently, that differs little in practical respects from adult life and involves few restrictions. "Children . . . for the most part do not find themselves in constant conflict with adults and with the routine of living that is expected of them." The child "has a whole world of his own where he is free to do as he likes—the barn lot and adjoining woods. He calls grown men by their first names, and is rarely shielded from the realities of drunkenness, violence and death; he sees his parents at work, at play, and may see them get 'converted' at the revival meeting. By the time he is six he has absorbed a good deal of the traditional attitude toward what is right and wrong, good and bad. He has a vague concept of a powerful Jesus up there in the sky somewhere. He learns early that he should look down on colored people. . . ."[7]

Sexual differentiation begins very early, as the children begin to imitate their parent of the same sex and assist in their duties: cooking, baking, sewing, gardening, and baby-tending for the women; ploughing, hauling stovewood, tending the dogs, and the like for the men. Bill Monroe recalls as a very young boy digging potatoes, carrying firewood and water, and egg-gathering.[8] A boy is encouraged to fight as viciously as he needs to defend his own rights and protect himself. By age ten the children are "small adults," deeply involved with adult life, so deeply that it is not unusual for them to drop out of school, education being simply irrelevant to what for most of them is life. The one thing from which the children are carefully protected, Ms. Lewis notes, is the sexual relation itself.

The relative simplicity and innocence of this world, apparently so picturesque, rarely fails to arouse tender sentiments not only in people who have never experienced it but in those who have—and who have been broken from it. But for Claudia Lewis, who saw some advantage in the more rigorous way of child rearing in urban society, with its restrictions, schedules, its orientation towards growth, achievement, and competition, the picture was not ultimately so altogether unspotted. "One wonders," she remarks, "why so many drop out of high

school, why so many girls find themselves with babies to care for and
no husbands to support them, why so many who have tried the outside
world choose to return to the hopeless poverty of the mountain. . . . One looks around at the adults, too, even those who grew
up under much less trying economic conditions, and though greatly
admiring their militant, independent spirit, wonders why so many of
them are so hot-tempered, so quick to flare up and become involved
in petty disagreements, why they are so frequently at bickering odds
with their neighbors. . . . For it begins to appear that the placidity of
childhood, with its limited experience of conflict and contact and its
comparatively easy-going, indulgent routine, may not have given these
adolescents a foundation of sufficient strength and breadth and elasticity to sustain them."[9]

However justified or not Claudia Lewis's conclusions, it is obvious
that the people she describes, long after the advent of radio, phonograph, popular music, honky-tonks, and hair spray, are still the deeply
parochial mountain people of history and legend. In Bill Monroe's day,
the "outside" world, by his own account, was still more remote, and
the familiar world much like what Ms. Lewis describes. This is plain
not only from the substance of Bill's recollections and those of his elder
brother, Birch, but from the elegaic, often plaintive *tone* of those
recollections and from the peculiarly archaic attitudes towards such
matters as sex and race that both men express. Yet Bill Monroe's
childhood, not surprisingly, was in a few respects profoundly exceptional; though the community may have been bound by blood, and the
family by filial affection, Bill found himself at least partially isolated
from community and family, and in a matter of a few years, while he
was still a boy, both community and family had dissolved.

Monroe was born to parents who were well into their middle age,
and was separated from the nearest sibling, Charlie, by eight years.
That childbearing often begins early and ends late in mountain culture
almost certainly contributes to its strong traditionality, for the family
and its imaginative life can span a century in two or three generations.
When Bill was ten, his mother died; when he was thirteen, his older
brothers left home for the North, and a few years later, in 1927, his
father died, at seventy. After his father's death, Bill went to live first
with his uncle Jack Monroe and then with uncle Pen Vandiver, his
mother's brother, who for a brief period had lived with the Monroes,
while his sister Malissa was still alive, after separating from his wife.[10]
Pen had been a farmer and a family man with two children; during
young Bill's tenure with him he was a trader, circling the countryside
on muleback, a dance fiddler and bachelor. After breaking his hip in

a fall from horseback, he went about on crutches until his death in 1933. By the time Bill had established himself in Chicago, the Monroe family in Rosine, with the death of old uncle Birch, had dwindled to a few cousins.[11]

Bill's late arrival into the life of his family placed him in a world of habits and attitudes belonging to a grandparents' generation—almost as if he had been born in the 1880s. Monroe's extraordinarily melodic and elastic "snapping" speech may record part of the vast indelible impression a parent makes upon a child—the impression, in this instance, of a speech formed in the middle of the nineteenth century. It is certain, in any case, that the superabundant warmth Claudia Lewis describes cannot have been Bill's lot, especially after his mother's death, and the declining of feminine influences that ran out finally during his sojourn with Pen Vandiver. "He done the cooking for the two of us," Monroe recalls. "We had fat back, sorghum molasses, and hoecakes for breakfast followed by black-eyed peas with fat back, and cornbread and sorghum for dinner and supper."[12] Monroe recently revisited the scene of this adventure with a magazine reporter, whose photograph discovers Uncle Pen's house to have been little more than a two-room shack, a chickenhouse, in fact, now covered with peeling tarpaper. That life, Birch Monroe recalls, was "pretty rough . . . there wasn't no women there, you know."[13]

Monroe's loneliness as a child was exacerbated by what Ralph Rinzler calls a "leitmotif" in his life, his seriously impaired eyesight. Bill's eyes as a child were badly crossed, a misfortune that often made him, he says, an object of curiosity or ridicule. He remembers shrinking under the morbid gaze of strangers or at the thoughtless remarks of visitors to the farm, which was on the wagon road into Rosine. Frequently he would escape such situations by hiding in the barn or losing himself in the open fields, where, he tells us, he first began to sing.

On account of his eyesight Monroe was excluded from most of the normal occupations and pastimes, especially from the most popular local sport, baseball. This is especially significant when we remember that the original Blue Grass Boys traveled both as a bluegrass band and as a baseball team, and that in Bill's vocabulary many metaphors move over from the baseball diamond to the bluegrass band, where a fiddler, for example, "comes up to bat" or to "pinch hit" for another musician. Moreover the "Blue Grass Boys" might easily have been the name of a nineteenth-century baseball team, which were often called "Boys"; bluegrass seems even to have some formal resemblance to baseball, sharing its emphasis upon individual distinction and its interplay between rigidly structured procedures and unbounded aims.[14]

"I'd have liked to be a baseball player. I love baseball. But you have to have good eyes to play baseball and my eyes never was good. I could hit good and could've been a fair player."[15]

It is possible that Bill's impaired eyesight contributed to his musical ability. At church singing school he had to learn by ear the harmony parts which others could read in the shape-note hymnals. The blind singer or poet is of course an ancient figure, in whom two simple facts converge: impaired vision is frequently accompanied by a concomitant auditory acuteness and is a condition which is likely to exclude the sufferer from ordinary occupations and open him to those which call upon his special strength. Bill Monroe is not blind, but in an illuminating study of a congenitally blind musician, Melvin Borstein suggests that it is not blindness itself which engenders musical ability but its psychological effects, beginning with the infant's or child's need for sounds to assure him of his mother's presence.[16] By means of music, Borstein writes, the musician sustains the equilibrium of the senses threatened by visual impairment; it is a "mirroring" activity, by which he extends himself into the world and maintains his autonomy in it. In Borstein's subject, a jazz trumpeter, there are some interesting parallels to Bill Monroe. Like Monroe, the trumpeter claims to be able to assess a musician's character from the way he plays, and, like Monroe, he avoids alcohol or drugs—fearing, Borstein suggests, far more than the normal person, the states of disorganization induced by them. In the rural South, furthermore, it has been common for the blind or handicapped child, black or white, to find himself early on with a musical instrument in his hands, for music might promote, if not actually assure, his survival and provide him with a degree of independence. The list of blind musicians in traditional music is a long one, including the revered Kentucky fiddler Ed Hailey, singer-guitarist Riley Puckett, blues singer Lemon Jefferson, hillbilly duet Mac and Bob, street singer Reverend Gary Davis, our contemporary flat-picker Doc Watson.

All this lends credence to Bill's insistence that he never actually chose a musician's career; he can't recall ever having been anything else. As a very young boy he played with his brothers for visitors to his house and tried his voice in the open fields. Indeed the scheme of Bill's boyhood reflects and reveals the important place of music in Appalachian rural society. Claudia Lewis tells us of a five year old girl who rocked her doll to sleep with an Elizabethan ballad, in a "loud, clear, mountain voice," and when the other children had gathered around her followed the ballad with several more, in the "nasal twang" Ms. Lewis tried in vain to imitate. She notes that the mountain children

not only sang traditional songs and ballads but regularly made up
original variations upon them. Their ears, too, seemed unusually keen:
one child compared the squeak of a tricycle to the "rooster crowin' in
the mornin'," and another heard the windshield wiper saying "chip-
chop, chip-chop," and the water spilling onto the hot stove saying
"hush!"[17] Often the children made up games based upon the sounds of
words, in which they took immense delight. Ms. Lewis observes that
such pleasures come readily to children who do not have artist's materials, mechanical toys, or a great many books at their disposal.

Yet, as the fable of the grasshopper and the ant tells us, music does
not produce; a dedication to it, particularly in a rural economy whose
basis is materially productive work, may be a sign of alienation. Never
has the musician in the rural South been entirely "respectable," however much he may be admired, however essential to social and psychic
life his music may be, however much pleasure, solace, and joy it may
bring. Music has its place on the margins of life, in children's games,
songs, and lullabys, in hearthside pastimes, at Saturday night dances;
but come Sunday morning, the ballads and the fiddle must go. In the
Old Regular Baptist church and in other rural fundamentalist churches,
"music," meaning musical instruments, is prohibited entry into the
meetinghouse, while "fiddling" is traditionally regarded by the pious
as a form of idleness. The Kentucky minstrel, an "itinerant, wandering,
shiftless fiddler or banjo picker, who makes a specialty of seeking out
all 'parties' and dances," has earned a reputation akin to that of his
medieval counterpart, and like him has won the contempt of people in
authority, like this mountain judge: "Gentlemen! Whenever you see a
great big overgrown buck sitting at the mouth of some holler, or at
the fork of some road, with a big slouch hat on, a blue celluloid collar,
a celluloid, artificial, red rose in his coat lapel, a banjo strung across
his breast, and a pickin' of 'Sourwood Mountain,' fine that man, gentlemen, fine him! For if he hasn't already done something, he's a goin'
to!"[18] Like the camp meeting of old, the country dance was the scene
of a spectrum of evils ranging from smoking, swearing, and drinking
to brawling, fornication, and murder. Alan Lomax, returning to the
mountains in the 1930s, found that square dancing had nearly disappeared on account of the number of killings which had occurred at
Saturday night "blowouts."[19] Even the bluegrass festival has been
occasionally marred by a shooting, and at least one well-regarded singer, Roy Lee Centers, was shot to death in a drunken brawl. These
associations are difficult to dislodge, and it is not unreasonable that a
blues guitar picker such as Mose Rager should give up the instrument

later in life, or that Wade Mainer and Molly O'Day, both mountain banjo players in their youth, should restrict themselves now to gospel songs, or that A. P. Carter's father, whose brother Jim owned a banjo but kept it hidden, would give up the instrument after being "saved"[20]—one of hundreds, black and white, who have done so. The musician lingers on the moral edge of rural society not only because he is an idler, then, or because he may be strange in some way—blind, perhaps, or vaguely effeminate—but because his music opens a door onto unacted desires and may be a sign in him of daemonic energies which can also find an outlet in destructive or antisocial conduct, energies which it is the business of morality to subdue or of religion to harness.

I am always a bit surprised at the willingness with which certain bluegrass musicians of my acquaintance pronounce themselves sinners—that is, unhesitatingly, and without the slightest hint of remorse. When I asked Bill Monroe whether he considered himself a religious man I expected *at least* some reflection on his part: to hear him sing "Walkin' in Jerusalem" or "Lord Protect My Soul" you'd think he'd gone to heaven already. He simply said, "No." As Katherine Anne Porter once pointed out, southern rural religion often means little more in practice than refraining from smoking, drinking, fighting, swearing, fornicating, and so on—sins which carry an approximately equal moral weight. You are either wicked or you are saved; the religious feeling itself, which may have saved you, works in other departments of life as well, and most powerfully in music.

If the fiddle is the instrument of the devil, it may be because its music makes the same incursion into the soul as the preacher's far-flung oratory or the resonant hymn, and establishes sacramental habits every bit as persistent as the habit of purity, and is consequently in competition with religion for the heart's allegiance. A folk religion such as the Old Regular Baptist mediates between spirit and man by the same avenue that Nature follows—the passions—exciting them to catharsis, from which follows the transient emotional repose that has all the features of a spiritual infusion. How does the wild exultation of a fiddle breakdown differ from the unearthly cries of grief and joy that erupt during an Old Regular Baptist sermon, itself formed out of a pattern of stylized sobs and a high-pitched whine? Only a sense of sanction distinguishes them. A rural society whose religion is also a stronghold of its economic values, which prohibits all those practices whose only aim is personal gratification, cannot tolerate an art which works its effects by the same methods as religion but seems to re-

pudiate its values, unless that art completely acknowledges its sub-
servience to religion and eschews all connection to the secular: precisely
what bluegrass gospel groups have done.

There is another alternative, of course—to make a religion of the
music. If bluegrass is what Ralph Rinzler calls a "musical gospel," it
is one born out of the moral ambivalence that surrounds the old mountain music. Monroe recalls:

> There's a long ridge back home called Jerusalem Ridge, and I
> remember we had to cross that and go on down about a mile to
> where we come to this real old house called the Lizer place,
> and this man, Clea Baze that played the fiddle, he lived there.
> We'd walk back there with a coal oil lantern, and we got there
> that night and there was a good many people in the room
> listening to them play and they sat in the middle of the room
> and I thought that was awful pretty music . . . numbers like
> "Turkey in the Straw" . . . It was something to go knowing
> you was going to hear some music that night.[21]

The dark mountain ridge, the lantern's glow, the old house and the
roomful of people—do I detect something exotic, perhaps something
faintly illicit, in this recollection? Perhaps I am thinking of Bill's wild
and beautiful A-minor fiddle tune "Jerusalem Ridge," whose gothic
strains are a musical reflection upon the same occasion. "Me and him"
Monroe recalls, alluding to Arnold Shultz, a black fiddler and guitar
player who worked for a time in Rosine, "played for a dance there one
night and he played the fiddle and we started at sundown and the next
morning at daylight we was still playing music—all night long. And,
of course, that automatically made you be dancing on Sunday. . . ."[22]

Bill's first musical influence was his mother, who played fiddle and
accordion; but his predilection for music took him to the remoter corners
of Rosine society, far from the household from which circumstances
and events had already partly estranged him. That Bill and his uncle
Pen spent their last days in Kentucky together may suggest the extent
of the young man's alienation. "Might have been a bad life for alot of
people, I guess."[23] But Monroe took pride in his gaunt, mustachioed,
fiddling uncle, whom he followed about the countryside on muleback,
guitar over his shoulder, to play at square dances six or ten miles out
in the country. Pen had, Bill recalls, "the prettiest shuffle on the bow
you ever saw."

Still more telling, perhaps, is the young Monroe's association with
Arnold Shultz, an important Kentucky tradition bearer whose influence
reached not only Monroe but Ike Everly—the Everly Brothers' fa-

ther—Mose Rager, and, through Rager, Merle Travis. Folklorist William Lightfoot has discovered in interviews some of the important details of Schultz's otherwise obscure life: that he was born in 1886 in Ohio County, Kentucky, the son of a man who had been born into slavery and who had taken his name from his owner, a Revolutionary War soldier who had moved to Ohio County before the turn of the eighteenth century.[24] Shultz's whole family played stringed instruments and toured Ohio County as a family band; his cousin remembers him playing "Waggoner" and "Old Hen Cackle" on the fiddle. His most important contribution was known then as "thumb-style" guitar, the instrument which Schultz took up first in 1900, taking lessons from his uncle. From this style grew the regional guitar-picking style now most associated with Merle Travis and Chet Atkins, characterized by a syncopated melody, a steady, damped bass heavily accented, walking bass runs, melodic ornaments, a swinging or bouncing tempo, and, in contrast to other country styles, sophisticated chording up the neck of the guitar, with all the strings stopped. In other words, the guitar style which Arnold Shultz apparently introduced into central Kentucky had all the earmarks of jazz, if it was not actually a jazz style. Shultz died in 1931, leaving behind him a number of legends: that he had played showboats on the Green River, that he had played with Louis Armstrong, that he had been poisoned at the end by a jealous white musician.

Being as thoroughly familiar as we are now with all forms of Afro-American music, it may be difficult for us to catch the significance of a young rural white in the 1920s taking up what the late Birch Monroe called "them old nigger blues." To seek out the black bluesman was usually a literal journey to the nether regions of society—shantytown, railroad depot, honky-tonk—but more significantly, a social descent which, like the descents of mythology and folklore, was made on behalf of the special powers conferred by secret knowledge. It was not until rather late in his career, under the influence of the new self-consciousness aroused by the folk revival, that Bill Monroe explicitly acknowledged the black influence upon his music and named the man to whom that influence could be attributed. Yet throughout his career Monroe has shown an interest in and an admiration for the black musician far more typical of country musicians than is generally acknowledged or even understood. The popular tent show which Monroe ran in the early forties included the Opry's black harmonica player, Deford Bailey, with whom Monroe developed a close friendship, taking it upon himself to find lodgings for Bailey in the many southern towns in which blacks were not offered hospitality.[25]

I don't know how close Bill Monroe was to Arnold Shultz, and I'm
sure it would be useless to ask him. I should perhaps take Birch Monroe
at his word when he insists that outside of music there was no association whatever between Shultz and the young Bill Monroe. Whatever
the truth is, there is little doubt about Monroe's depth of feeling for
the black Kentucky bluesman:

> I used to listen to him talk and he would tell us about contests
> that he had been in and how tough they was . . . I admired
> him that much that I never forgot alot of the things that he
> would say. There's things in my music, you know, that come
> from Arnold Shultz—runs that I use alot in my music, I don't
> say that I make them the same way that he could make them
> 'cause he was powerful with it. In following a fiddle piece or
> a breakdown, he used a pick and he could just run from one
> chord to another the prettiest you've ever heard. There's no
> guitar picker today that could do that. . . . I believe it was the
> next day about ten o'clock there was a passing train come
> down through and stopped at Rosine and I believe he caught
> that train and went back home and that was about the last time
> I ever saw him. I believe if there's ever an old gentleman that
> passed away and is resting in peace, it was Arnold Shultz—
> I really believe that.[26]

Monroe asserts that had circumstances not led him to the mandolin
he would have become a blues guitar player, "the way Arnold Shultz
played it, with a straight pick."[27] As psychologist Erik Erikson observes, in his idols a child is often poignantly judicious. The idol must
be someone who has won his respect by affirming, through his own
character and place in the adult world, the child's sense of what he is
himself; and it must be someone who inspires his love by accepting
him as he is, without a parent's expectations, hopes, and fears.[28] Where
a child goes to find his idol, how far above or below the station of life
into which he was born, will depend not only upon his family's judgment
of him, but his of them; and in his association with Arnold Shultz,
however fleeting or superficial it may have been, I believe we can
detect the germ of the identity which Bill Monroe has in time formed
for himself.

According to Erikson, identity is "the successful alignment of the
individual's basic drives with his endowment and his opportunities."
"The growing child must . . . derive a vitalizing sense of reality from
the awareness that his individual way of mastering experience is a
successful variant" of the ways of others.[29] There is little in Monroe's

childhood to suggest that his eventual achievement was in any way inevitable. It is certain that throughout the rural South, with its rich musical heritage, many youngsters have shown propensities like his— his own brothers among them—who have not developed so strikingly, having found their backgrounds as much a barrier to success, in the outside world especially, as a foundation for it. Few of us emerge from childhood unscathed; many of us as a consequence of early pain or deprivation emerge emotionally crippled, our lives damaged or misdirected by fugitive longings and irrational beliefs about ourselves and the world, the lesson of psychology being that the laws of personality are dictated in childhood.

The self, however, is not a fateful equation of psychic wounds and the effort to heal them, but a creative act, an act of imagination that resolves conflict by baffling it. Always in the psyche there is an inviolable and secret womb of originality, deeper than personality, inaccessible to others and perhaps even to ourselves, though we may nevertheless in mysterious ways draw upon it. And, like an art, its activities demand a field of action, a theater of operations in which the transformation of the raw materials of personality into a genuine identity may take place; like an art, it demands an audience, a community, in whom it may find recognition and affirmation.

For Bill Monroe bluegrass music has been such a psychic theater— one perplexingly akin to theater itself, the life of a musician, with its road schedules and stage appearances forming a skein of fresh encounters out of which identity may be fashioned and refashioned, and finally brought to completion as artist and audience, individual and community, come mutually to acknowledge and reaffirm one another. If in recent years Monroe's identity has emerged with greater clarity and force than in the early years of his career, it is because he has become more sensitive to his expanding roles as man and as musician. We have already observed him as a public figure—an aristocrat, landowner or planter, the blood of the frontiersman and statesman in his veins; the prototype of this figure can perhaps still be seen in the halls of Congress, but its essence is in fable. As Monroe's childhood carried him to the farther reaches of Rosine society and to the floor of the social hierarchy, so has his music symbolically thrust him to the zenith of an imagined community ambiguously situated in the "years ago" and in the emblematic "hills of Old Kentucky," whose embodiments in bluegrass music have by sheer emotional magnetism caused an actual community to coalesce around it. Thus it has been necessary for Monroe to compound his ideal role with a more familiar one better suited to the actual demands of leadership.

What must an aristocrat (considering the ideal figure first) have that the rest of us do not? A name, perhaps, traditions, good breeding, land or wealth, but above all, a past, upon which all the rest depends. Traditional music, of course, has been Monroe's avenue into the past, a past neither personal nor historical but fabulous:

> I told you about writing the old fiddle number called "Land of Lincoln". . . . Take Abraham Lincoln when he was a young man, and say there was a fiddler there seventy, seventy-five years older than he was—you know that it was bound to have been a long ways back; and they was bound to have been some of the oldest tones and ideas in the world that old man would be playing. I made "Land of Lincoln" go the way I thought Abraham Lincoln might have heard it—a tune like he might have heard when he was a boy from some old-time fiddler. . . .[30]

Of another instrumental which he wrote one evening at his home in Tennessee, Bill said it was "bound to be about a hundred years old."[31] Monroe's sense of the antiquity of his music has, it seems, a specific reference point in the past associated with an historical figure, but that reference point itself is not historical; the "old fiddler," in Bill's reflection on the scene, is a survivor of a still remoter time which, like the "once upon a time" of fairy tales or the wildernesses of romance, is beyond history and in fact not connected to time at all. Rather it is the original womb of reality from which all things emerge uncorrupted, located in the web of laws it is the purpose of fairytale, legend, and myth to reveal. Monroe seems to identify himself both with the old fiddler *and* with the young Lincoln: with the fiddler by making the "old"—that is, traditional—fiddle tune, and with Lincoln by listening to it "the way I thought Abraham Lincoln might have heard it." It is amusing, perhaps, that Bill can claim to have written an old fiddle tune; but in the paradox is an insight into traditional music, which is simply that on account of its thoroughgoing conventionality its location in time, which cannot be reliably fixed on the basis of internal evidence, has no effect upon its meaning: we might as well attempt to write a history of cloud formations. For Monroe, "old" is simply a metaphor for the quality of mystery, majesty, or simplicity no strictly original work—if there is such a thing—can achieve, such as we encounter in traditional English ballads and Irish reels. To compose an "old" tune or song, Monroe employs devices very like those which the romantic poets employed to the same purpose: a narrative frame, an archaic language, a wild or picturesque setting, mysterious or magical events,

and a careful exclusion of particularizing or historicizing detail in favor
of the general and universal. The bluegrass style itself is the distancing
device or frame, a way of *re*presenting the traditional song or tune.
We find "archaic language" not only in the bluegrass instruments and
vocal style but in certain themes and phrases and occasionally in the
use of a modal scale or mode-like chord progression. A minor key may
supply a sense of mystery, though the symbolic landscape of bluegrass
songs—a dreamworld of highways, graveyards, mountain cabins,
waifs, wayfarers, maidens, and rogues—is inherently mysterious;
some bluegrass songs, such as Monroe's "Walls of Time," written with
Peter Rowan, are essentially ghost stories. Through his music, then,
Monroe seems to take the past into himself, drawing upon, or acting
as the agent of, a kind of power which has the psychological status of
a minor diety. For his audiences, this power enhances his personal
reality, his *charisma*—using the word in its strict religious sense; for
Monroe himself, it works inwardly as a conviction of special destiny.

It is mere coincidence that Monroe was born less than forty miles
from Lincoln's birthplace in central Kentucky; but in his picture of the
young Lincoln and the old fiddler there is, perhaps, an element of
personal recollection, young Abe and the fiddler being the elogated
shadows of young Bill and his Uncle Pen, whom Bill has celebrated
with a record album of his tunes and a song about him:

> He'd play an old piece he called Soldier's Joy,
> And one he wrote called the Boston Boy;
> But the greatest of all was Jenny Lynn [Lind],
> To me that's where the fiddle begins.

Chorus: Late in the evening about sundown,
       High on the hill above the town,
       Uncle Pen played the fiddle, oh how it would ring,
       You could hear it talk, you could hear it sing.[32]

I have heard that the railroad whistle that Casey Jones used to blow
now stands on a boiler somewhere in Jackson, Tennessee; this is a bit
like hearing that an arrow shot from the bow of Robin Hood lies in a
case at the British Museum. The point is that "Uncle Pen" elevates
Pen Vandiver to a certain fabulous status, though the singer and composer of the song, alive and real, descends directly from him. With a
phrase—"to me that's where the fiddle begins"—he links his own origins to those of the music itself; the brief catalogue of fiddle tunes
corroborates the relationship and identifies the tradition, evoking an
epoch with the name of Jenny Lind; the occasion of the first verse,

"the people would come from miles away, and dance all night 'til the break of day," the mountain-top locale and the evening backdrop, "about sundown," evoke, in the picturesque shorthand of a sheet-music cover, the region and the era, while the concluding verse—

> I'll never forget that lonesome day
> When Uncle Pen was called away;
> He hung up his fiddle, he hung up his bow,
> He said it was time for him to go.

—suggests that Uncle Pen, with his magical fiddle that can talk and sing, was a sojourner from a better world and that the era he embodies has passed away with him.

Symbolically, then, Monroe's career recapitulates Lincoln's, the career of an original American hero, born in Old Kentucky, that primal garden of fecundity and strength, expelled from it but dedicated to the preservation of its values, an aristocrat more by virtue of natural gifts than by inherited privilege. Let me note in passing that the first private opinion I ever heard Monroe express—he had recently returned from a tour in England—was a thoroughly traditional contempt for the English: "Yeah, it's terrible, man. They think they're better than you."[33]

Yet Monroe is a man, as well as a manifestation, and has not entirely freed himself from the personality which for most people constitutes the immediate mental environment; it remains with us, a fossil or vestigal organ, even if only as traces of a larval stage of our growth. Monroe's personal life has not been free of the ordinary human failures and distress: a long and mysterious estrangement from his brother Charlie, which persisted through Charlie's last illness and about which many lurid stories have grown up; a disabled but not entirely dissolved first marriage and a child who suffered crippling emotional difficulties; a love affair which ended in a lawsuit after twenty years, as Monroe entered late middle age; in this private dimension, Monroe is simply a man like other men, neither better nor worse, whose weaknesses may stand out more vividly, and perhaps have more devastating effects, in the general amplitude of his character. "I guess if I hadn't left Rosine and gone up North," he told a reporter, "I'd probably be just like the other folks who live here now, farming and raising a family. I probably wouldn't have gone through seven, ten, fifteen women."[34]

One side of Monroe quite probably is the issue of childhood privations. All who know him, as we've already noted, recall his many years of isolation, when his intense concentration on his work seemed to exclude most ordinary social intercourse. Even now there are periods when he will sink into a taciturnity so profound—almost a kind of trance—which the most urgent business cannot draw him out of; yet he is also, at times, highly animated and voluable. He shows little eagerness to fraternize with other musicians, though old friends and young admirers constantly seek him out. Among these he is passive and may seem remote or forgetful, though he never forgets a request made of him, a favor owed or favor granted, an insult or injury, real or imagined, done. Until the influences of the folk revival began to work upon him, his fierce competitiveness at least partially blinded him to the achievements of other bluegrass musicians and, more importantly, to his own immense contribution to others' achievements. Against some people he has harbored resentments of a most durable and intransigent kind; his readiness to believe he has been deliberately slighted or wounded is probably connected to his tempestuous love life, which for some people contrasts sharply with the rigorous standards of decency he holds up to others. What Rinzler calls his "savage, arrogant, intransigent spirit," so impressive in his music, cannot but trespass somewhat upon the laws that govern ordinary personal conduct, from which as an artist Monroe has won a certain limited immunity.[35] He lives, like a poet, in a moral universe of his own making which, though it may not touch ours at every point, has the integrity and wholeness that is the heart of morality.

Among his friends Monroe is relaxed and affable, and though his authority, especially over band members, is always implicit, he never exercises it in a wanton or arbitrary way. He inspires allegiance, and his friends take it upon themselves to protect and defend him. For there is something infinitely delicate and terribly vulnerable in Monroe. One hears it in his speech, which is quaint, lilting, sometimes so musical that he seems more to sing than to speak; delicately articulated words fall from his lips with a quickness and liquidity which suggests he has formed them from light. Sometimes he walks delicately, too, as if he were afraid of falling—perhaps because his vision is poor—and will unconsciously extend his hand for aid. In some of his habits, too, there is a boy-like charm. He reads with high scrutiny, moving his lips whisperingly as he goes, sometimes annotating the text—I have heard of a copy of Woody Guthrie's *Bound for Glory* whose margins are black with Bill's comments. He is excessively fond of sweets, rarely failing to order the chocolate sundae or wedge of cake at roadside cafes along his route, his love of sugar being his only obvious vice, one he shares with other conservative rural people such as the Amish. His life on the farm in Goodlettsville, Tennessee, where he raises cattle, quarter horses, fox hounds, and game hens, is like theirs, deliberately conservative and antiquarian in spirit. Most of the work on the farm is done by draught horses and mules, for Bill believes that tractors are too dangerous.

Kentucky planter, then, and Tennessee farmer—but what identity has Bill Monroe adopted for his *offstage* public role, the one which has come upon him in the final quarter of his career, as the "Father of Bluegrass Music?" Monroe's speech and gestures, his oblique and steady grace that is almost womanly, his alert and agile hands massively framed, his careful dress and finger rings, the silver hair that curls behind his ears—I see in Monroe the dandified rural evangelist, the man risen out of his station in response to a call compounded equally of spirit and of flesh, who perhaps has won fame for himself, as they did in the old days, "in proportion to the carrying power of their voices in the open air. . . ."[36]

Bluegrass music, particularly the summertime outdoor bluegrass festival, with its potluck supper, jam session, gospel sings and the like, has swept into the social and psychic space occupied a century ago by religion and by religious revivals and camp meetings. Thus it is a kind of religious leadership that Monroe exercises, appropriately paternal, mannerly, reverent, and, when he is in his musical pulpit, fired by the Holy Spirit. As Arthur Moore reminds us, the old religious revivals and camp meetings "were social no less than religious events; while the meek and pious listened to the preaching, the more spirited habitually engaged in decidedly secular activity, including gambling, drinking, shooting and brawling."[37]

All the diversions of Cane Ridge were in evidence at the last bluegrass festival I attended, in Shade Gap, Pennsylvania, in the summer of 1978. I had gone to consult with Bill Monroe about what has become this book; Shade Gap was a few hours' drive from my home in Ohio, and Bill was to make an appearance there. When we arrived late in the afternoon we found not the usual groups of parking-lot pickers and families cooking over charcoal or kerosene fires before their tents and campers, but a different sort of crowd, mostly young, many with portable record players, tape machines, and radios, a crowd dominated by the presence of a motorcycle gang from, I think, Baltimore, called the Pagans, who, with their oiled denims, leather vests, chains, clubs, sheath knives, and tatooed bare arms, were patrolling the festival grounds with a frightening determination to avenge some nameless wrong by recourse to arbitrary cruelty or violence. Not ten minutes after we arrived a delerious biker naked to the waist drove his huge Harley chopper directly into a group of people standing under the trees near the music pavilion, scattering them in every direction and throwing dust and grit into the faces of my little girls, one only a toddler, who screamed together in terror.

I ought to have left at once. But I had paid my money at the gate; I wanted to see Monroe; and I was unable, so accustomed was I to the wholesome scenes of Bean Blossom and other bluegrass festivals, to interpret the sinister signs at Shade Gap. I did see him the next day, early in an afternoon already oppressively humid and hot. I was gratified to discover that Monroe, sequestered in the silent shadows of his new motor coach, was actually pleased to see me, even though, after a sleepless night with sleepless children and a frightened wife in a tent surrounded by roaring cycle engines, a blood-curdling scream which, we supposed, could only have been inspired by a rape, rude curses and drunken laughter, distant shouts, an oddly recurrent rebel yell which sounded as if it were being produced at regular intervals by a machine, and hour upon hour of acid rock spilling out of somebody's dashboard tape deck, I must have appeared to him something other than the bespectacled "bookrhater" who had travelled with him the previous spring. I was glad, genuinely glad, to see him, too; he had shown me much warmth, kindness, and generosity, treating me to more than one good supper, answering my questions thoughtfully and patiently, permitting me to name, or try to name, one of his mandolin tunes (I'm still looking for my title, "Campfire," on one of his record albums), and one night in the wee hours, as we rolled out of New York City back into the South and I dozed fitfully on one of the bench seats at the front of the bus, my clothes twisted about me, stuffing a pillow under my head with a stiff, truncated gesture that did entirely conceal the affection that was in it.

"Is it hot out there?" he asked as we shook hands. I felt as if we were in the upper reaches of some girdered skyscraper, in the inner sanctum from which one man guided the operations of a multinational corporation.

It was hot, I said, and as we sat down at a small cardtable Bill glanced out the window towards the nearby pavilion and discharged an audible groan. The bus was air-conditioned and cool, quieted by the steady hum of the conditioner itself. It happened, though, that there was to be no interview today, never mind how many miles I had come; we would have to arrange another time. So our business was soon concluded, after some cautionary words about another writer's book, of which Monroe could not approve. As I left, gathering up my recorder and notepad, I expressed my hope that I might see him again soon and was nearly out the door when he called out to me: "Say, if you and your wife and kids want to come on into the bus and cool off, you're welcome anytime." It is better left unsaid, perhaps; but I felt these were the words of a man to whom the lesson of charity had come rather late in life, under the shadow of his own mortality.

Bill's show that afternoon was magnificent, one of the best I've ever seen, and his audience wildly appreciative. His mandolin churned like the waters under a hydroelectric dam, and I learned that day what Bill Monroe's mandolin playing is, and why there is nothing anywhere like it. It wasn't until the next morning, long after Bill and his band had pulled out, that a man, a Pagan, was killed by four or five pistol shots not ten yards from where we were standing. The biker, who had a slavering Doberman at the end of a rope, had been provoked to strike a young woman over the head with his long black club, for her white dog, a Malamute or something like it, had snapped at his; as she gripped her crown and screamed, the young man who had accompanied her appeared from within their VW bus to fire the retributory shots. It was an appalling scene, and the people around us trembled and wept as the Pagans, massing together in a matter of moments, mounted their cycles to pursue the young man, who had fled into the surrounding cornfields. We left, of course, without hesitation, full of fear; later in the day, after retrieving my tent and cookstove, finding the park occupied by over a thousand bikers and staked out by fifty police cars, we departed Shape Gap, well pleased—if I may borrow the words of a nineteenth-century visitor to the Kentucky wilderness—" to turn my back on all the spitting, gouging, drinking, duelling, swearing and staring, of old Kentucky."[38]

Chapter 2

Hillbilly Music
The Commercial Background

Whiting, Indiana, and the other municipalities surrounding the southern shore of Lake Michigan—East Chicago, Gary, Hammond, Calumet City—make up the grim landscape of one of the most heavily industrialized regions in the world, where railroad trunk lines from the East and South converge with Great Lakes shipping in Calumet Harbor at what has been since early in the century a capitol of iron, steel, and chemical manufacture, oil refining, grain and ore transport. United States Steel was firmly established in its own city of 10,000 inhabitants, Gary, by 1906; it was soon joined in East Chicago and Whiting by Inland Steel, which had built in Chicago Heights in the 1880s, by Youngstown Sheet and Tube, and by the refineries of Standard and Sinclair oils, all clustered at Indiana Harbor.[1] By the 1920s the southern shore of the lake had become a continuous midway of thundering foundries and rolling mills, blast furnaces, foul-smelling chemical plants and oil refineries, fields of stockpiled ore, coal, and stone, gantry cranes and giant grain elevators standing in rows like the inscrutable monoliths of antiquity.

Bill Monroe came to Whiting from rural Kentucky in 1929, when he was eighteen, following scores of immigrants, black and white, who flowed from Appalachia and from the deep South after World War I.[2] A labor force had been growing steadily in the region since 1900, supplied in roughly equal numbers from the rural Midwest and South and from Eastern Europe; after the war, which closed off European emigration, labor agents were sent into the South to recruit workers from among blacks and poor whites. In the twenties the black population of Chicago nearly tripled, while the great preponderance of the white labor force emigrated from the middle South, particularly from

Kentucky and Tennessee. In Lake County, Indiana, the black population remained comparatively small; but the white population, like
the black population a few miles to the west and north, was comprehensively southern and rural.[3]

Monroe left Kentucky for the same reasons as his brothers before
him: farming in Kentucky seemed to offer little prospect for success,
especially in a rural economy sporadically depressed, increasingly
mechanized, and largely reliant upon capital. "I reckon my people
figured I would never make anything there," Bill says, "and that they
should try and get me out of there to where I could make a decent
living." He spent five years at the Sinclair refinery, unloading barrels
from a freight car and washing them with gasoline, sometimes as many
as two thousand barrels a day. The work was steady, but the Depression had arrived, and because Bill's older brothers, Birch and Charlie,
were out of work for extended periods, the family—which included a
sister and some cousins in the neighborhood—could not prosper: Bill's
income of twenty-five dollars a week or so was often its sole support.
"At that time you couldn't hardly get a job playing music that paid
any money."[4]

It was music, nevertheless, that delivered Monroe from the refinery
and from menial labor forever. Industry had engendered in the Calumet region a southern rural community more dense and variegated
than it had ever been or could be in Kentucky itself, a community
which was in a sense cosmopolitan. The vitality and coherence of the
Appalachian community in the Calumet region was in part sustained
by industry itself, which drew large numbers of people into a common
economic system. It is likely that the Chicago plants, like their counterparts in Detroit and Cincinnati, sought to encourage stability in the
work force by preserving kinship ties within the plant; but if the Monroe Brothers' early professional career provides any clue, one of the
most powerful binding influences was the radio.

The three brothers—Charlie on guitar, Birch on fiddle, Bill on mandolin—entertained at local dances and house parties, just as they had
in their native Rosine. This work could hardly have been called professional, since it merely repeated the social practice of rural Kentucky;
three, four, or perhaps five dollars was the most a musician could
expect from such an appearance. But at a square dance in Hammond,
Indiana, the band was approached by an agent of radio station WLS
in Chicago, which in 1928 had been purchased by the *Prairie Farmer*
newspaper and whose audience was chiefly in the rural Midwest. Its
Saturday night Barn Dance, initiated in 1924 in part by George D.
Hay, who later conceived the Grand Ole Opry, was one of the first

hillbilly music jamborees and the first to acquire a national reputation. WLS had recently inaugurated a road show in which it wished to include, along with prominent names from the Barn Dance such as Arkie the Arkansas Woodchopper, a troupe of exhibition square dancers such as the one performing at the WLS theater downtown. The Monroe Brothers, with their girlfriends, and another man named Moore and his wife, accepted this offer. For the two years between 1932 and 1934 they travelled for two-week periods in a Packard through northern Indiana and Illinois, or occasionally to Wisconsin and Michigan, the WLS listening area. In 1933 they performed at the Chicago World's Fair, where Bill took on the fiddle while Charlie, for a comedy routine, played the banjo. For a six-month period they played a brief spot at station WAE in Hammond, six days a week, and later took a weekly show over WJKS in Gary, earning only enough money to pay their car fare back and forth to the studio. Radio, they saw at once, made excellent advertising, and they used it to attract audiences to their personal appearances. Monroe took periodic leaves from his refinery job, finding that the travelling life was much more to his liking; moreover he found that on the WLS tour a wage came far more easily than at Sinclair: the station paid each man twenty-two dollars a week, at a time, as Bill points out, when a steak cost thirty-five cents and a good hotel room seventy-five.[5]

Radio has the power to transmit its message over geographical and cultural boundaries which even the most intrepid folklorist would hardly dare to cross; concomitantly it has the capacity, particularly on large commercial stations such as WLS, to gather together messages of widely diverse origins and kinds, presenting them as emanations from a common source in repeated juxtaposition with one another. As such it is a syncretic influence, drawing scattered elements of culture, attitude, or opinion into consensus—witness the political role of radio in the 1930s—amplifying the audience's consciousness of its own identity, or even defining it. In the days of live radio, the station might serve a social function similar to that of a marketplace, keeping the community informed of its own activities, but in a way more immediate and accessible than, say, a newspaper: everyone has experienced the sensation of keeping "in touch" by means of radio.

Yet, while particular programs addressed to particular local audiences may consolidate and define that audience, the radio itself, as an electronic device, transcends particular audiences, and may arouse in the individual listener far afield of the broadcasting studio an awareness of, and perhaps a yearning for, places distant from and ways of life markedly different from his own. That the radio brought the sounds

of urban life into rural America is well known; but the evocative and
often archaic sounds of rural music and rural voices also made their
way into the urban imagination, where, catapulted over vast distances
and decisively severed from its cultural setting, it could evoke a fresh
response, one which might partake of the listener's own desires and
fancies, and permit him to accept and even relish what he might otherwise reject. The early programming of station WBAP in Fort Worth,
for example, quite typically consisted of popular music, jazz, sacred
and semiclassical music; but the station's hour-and-a-half program of
square dance music in January 1923 provoked more telegrams and
phone calls than the station had received since its opening, and may
have been, as Bill Malone suggests, the beginning of hillbilly music on
radio.[6] Its audience was far from local and parochial, however, and
certainly not exclusively rural: WBAP had listeners in New York,
Canada, Haiti, and Hawaii. Before the pervasive influence of network
broadcasting, federal regulation, and commercial homogenization, the
radio dial was an instrument of fantastic sweep and power, which could
convey the listener aurally from region to region, city to city, and voice
to voice, and even in effect move him about in time at the speed of
light, establishing in his imagination far more effectively than a geography or history book a sense of the larger society to which he
belonged, with its ceaseless activity, prodigious strength and variety,
even its fleetingly perceptible form. In this audial Baghdad the traditional imagination, with its ready ability to adapt new modes of
expression to its own aesthetic laws and thus assimilate them, ought
to experience a renaissance, so long as those laws are not washed away
in the flood of new sounds. For the radio nearly brought to completion
during the two decades between the wars the emancipation of popular
culture from time and place, which the mobility and heterogeneity of
American society could only partly accomplish.

A kind of imaginative synthesis, based upon the variegated character
of the rural midwestern audience, had already begun, for instance, on
the WLS Barn Dance, to which the Monroes frequently listened, whose
performers influenced their own style, and of which they themselves
became members.[7] As Malone points out, the Barn Dance had from
its outset a "broader musical perspective" than most hillbilly music
shows.[8] By presenting southern, rural, and traditional music in conjunction with old-fashioned sentimental and popular songs—what had
become, in effect, the "folksongs" of the urban north—the Barn Dance
seemed to reconstitute the rural music as a popular or national form,
while at the same time effacing under its influence the bourgeois quality
of the old popular songs and bestowing upon them a faintly rustic or

bucolic character. In this sense the program recapitulated the folk process itself. A few titles from the disc and sheet-music offerings of the 1910 Sears catalogue will illustrate that such an amalgamation was in a sense natural: the very sentimentality of many popular songs consisted in their evocation not only of young love but of rural, rustic, or sylvan scenes, often called up by the names of southern states or by the mere mention of the South. One would think, indeed, that every person in America had spent his youth in the South: "On the Farm in Old Missouri," "My Old Kentucky Home," "In the Heart of the Kentucky Hills," "In the Shadow of the Carolina Hills," "Mid the Green Fields of Virginia," "When the Birds of Georgia Sing of Tennessee," "Way Down South in Dixie," "Memories of the South," "'Cross the Mason and Dixon Line."[9] The South had already become, through blackface minstrelry and vaudeville, an image ambiguously bound up with an agrarian past. The rustic motif was often carried out in graphic art on sheet music, in record catalogues, and on record jackets beginning in the 1890s.[10] These songs have survived in school and camp songbooks, in music lesson books, in countless piano anthologies and the like and can be said to belong, in some fragment of lyric or melody, to nearly everyone: "Old Folks at Home," "Shine on Harvest Moon," "Silver threads among the Gold," "Old Black Joe," "When You and I Were Young, Maggie," "After the Ball," "Alexander's Ragtime Band," "By the Light of the Silvery Moon," "Down by the Old Mill Stream," "In the Good Old Summertime," "I Wonder How the Old Folks Are at Home," "In the Shade of the Old Apple Tree," "Let Me Call you Sweetheart," "Row, Row, Row Your Boat." The prominence of Stephen Foster's minstrel songs in this list ought to remind us that America's popular song tradition, like its hillbilly music, has its roots in the South, but at an earlier period, and in the association of black and white. And it ought to alert us to the fact that a synoptic form such as bluegrass will retain vivid traces of the popular element; not only have many of the old popular tunes survived intact or been revived in bluegrass, but several of the old titles—"When the Golden Leaves Are Falling," "In the Far Off Golden West," "Memories of the South," "There's a Light in the Window"—anticipate the titles of, or pivotal lines from, several of Monroe's original compositions: "When the Golden Leaves Begin to Fall" "The Golden West," "Memories of Mother and Dad," "Memories of You," and "There's no light at the window," a line from the chorus of "I'm On My Way Back to the Old Home."

This is not to say that the organist Ralph Waldo Emerson, or the Irish tenor Bill O'Connor, or the Maple City Four Quartet, or the contralto Grace Wilson dominated the WLS Barn Dance with their nostalgic and sentimental popular songs; but between their cultivated styles and those of the program's rural southern musicians there was no rude contrast, as there might have been, say, on the Grand Ole Opry, had trained singers appeared there beside Uncle Dave Macon and the McGee brothers. Though many of them came from the Cumberland Foothills in east central Kentucky—a fact emphasized in the station's promotional material—the southern musicians on the Barn Dance were chiefly "folksingers" in a sense akin to the contemporary folk revivalist, that is, more collectors of songs than representatives of some archaic or traditional vocal or instrumental style. Through these musicians, whose styles were generally smoother and more polished than is typical of mountain music in its native setting, the program offered an anthology-like variety of traditional ballads, mountain, cowboy, comic, and heart songs, in a milieu of agreeable caricature enforced by the performers' costumes, as they appeared in photographs, and their stage names: Walter Peterson, the "Kentucky Wonder Bean"; banjoist Chubby Parker, "The Stern Old Bachelor"; Luther Ossenbrink, "the Arkansas Woodchopper"; Bradley Kincaid, "the Kentucky Mountain Boy." Mac and Bob, a guitar-mandolin duet, provided the prototype of the many such duets popular in hillbilly music during the thirties, including the Monroe Brothers, with close tenor harmonies and mandolin instrumental leads, though Mac and Bob's style was more studied and formal than that of either the Monroe Brothers or the equally popular Blue Sky Boys. Still another guitar-mandolin duet, Karl and Harty, formed the core of a string band, the Cumberland Ridge Runners, whose instrumentation, if not their sound, prefigured that of bluegrass: guitar, mandolin, five-string banjo, fiddle, and bass. The band's leader, John Lair, was a folksong authority who later founded a Barn Dance in his hometown of Renfro Valley, Kentucky, still a center for traditional music and bluegrass, where his library of old-time music is housed.

But perhaps the most important bands, with respect to bluegrass music, on the WLS Barn Dance were the Prairie Ramblers and Clayton McMichen and the Georgia Wildcats, both of which were strongly jazz-influenced and which, as Birch Monroe reported to Neil Rosenberg, deeply impressed the young Bill Monroe—especially McMichen's.[11] It is perhaps worth mentioning that during the 1920s New Orleans jazz had flourished on the south side of Chicago, attracting a group of young white musicians, many of them second-generation immigrants, who, in attempting to play the revolutionary new black music, helped to develop a particular ensemble style now known as Dixieland or the "Chicago" style. What distinguishes the Chicago style is the emergence of the soloist and the individual improvisatory tour de force; the New Orleans style, until the spectacular leadership of Louis Armstrong, had consisted chiefly of a continuous collective improvisation following in the wake of the lead instrument. Armstrong's brilliance introduced a dynamic element which allowed the white musician to engineer an overall shape to a jazz piece on the basis of changing levels of intensity—what Mezz Mezzrow, who played tenor sax with the Chicago Rhythm Kings, called the "flare-up," the "explosion," the "break," and the "rideout."[12]

It is this succession of instrumental solos or "breaks," sometimes improvisatory and sometimes not, which structurally distinguishes bluegrass from the traditional string band styles that preceded it, and it is this aspect of bluegrass which has led to the instrumental virtuosity now so emphasized, sometimes to the exclusion of other elements, by bluegrass musicians. And just as the emergence of the Chicago style largely depended upon the unprecedented individual musicianship of Louis Armstrong, so has the bluegrass style grown out of the extraordinary efforts of Bill Monroe on the mandolin, which before Monroe had rarely been anything more in hillbilly music than an accompaniment to singing, occasionally used, as Lester McFarland of Mac and Bob used it, for polite solo verses "sung" instrumentally. That Bill Monroe has heard Louis Armstrong is of course certain: everybody has heard Louis Armstrong. That Monroe heard Armstrong or any of the other Chicago jazz musicians, either live, on radio, or on phonograph, while he lived in Chicago, seems likely. In 1976 Monroe recorded a mandolin instrumental he called "Milenberg Joy," of which he says, quoted on the back of the record jacket, "an old instrumental I kept for 46 years"—since 1930, that is—"before recording it."[13] The tune in fact is an accelerated version of the Jelly Roll Morton composition "Milneburg Joys," which Louis Armstrong and Morton recorded with the New Orleans Rhythm Kings in 1923, and which became a popular ballroom standard.[14].

The radio, then, not only formed the basis of Monroe's early professional career, but on the Barn Dance, a program which only partook of a national mood, gathered together the audial images of that past which lay in the opposite shore of a history divided by world war, swift industrialization, and rural to urban migration. Monroe entered professional music at a juncture in his life at which his personal past had slipped irretrievably behind him, into the rural world which was itself in decay and to which he could not return except in his music. But Monroe's personal experience repeated the experience of thousands of people like him, his audiences, who had left Appalachia for the indus-

trial North, an experience which literally reiterated what in effect was
a kind of national myth, expressed in popular music, of an expulsion
from an idyllic South into an urban and technological wilderness in the
North. We should repeat in passing that popular song has assimilated
this motif directly from blackface minstrelsy during the nineteenth
century, and perhaps from black folk and spiritual song itself, which
had fused secular history with Biblical themes.[15] Monroe entered
professional music, too, at a time when the hillbilly musician was valued
for his power to represent and evoke the past, so that the musician's
very purpose was to explore and in some measure recover his own
tradition; in Monroe's case, that recovery extended years later to his
personal experience, particularly that of his early youth, transfigured
by time and distance, and especially to his earliest musical influences,
which became for him quasi-sacred prototypes. The structure of live
broadcasting and personal appearances built on the radio provided the
hillbilly musician with a haven—not, admittedly, a perfectly secure
one—from the Great Depression, while at the same time bringing him
into regular and immediate contact with audiences far more demanding
than the old rural society. He was, in other words, commercially exploited, a situation which pulled him in contrary directions: it required
that he remain alert to changes in popular taste; but it required, too,
that he concentrate with a new intensity upon his own music, seeking
to cultivate it in ways directed by its own character which now, having
always taken it for granted, he must set out to discover. A musical
style may be secure, even in the presence of many outside influences;
but a traditional musician offering his music commercially *as* traditional
music cannot hope to supply his commercial repertoire from his own
background alone, unless he has the encyclopedic memory of a Huddie
Ledbetter or the prodigious inventiveness of a Woody Guthrie. He
must find other resources, and unless he has a folklorist to guide him
into songbooks, field recordings, and academic collections, as did many
of the traditional musicians brought into the public eye by the folk
revival of the 1960s, his repertoire will reflect some conscious or unconscious principle of selection.

In 1934 the Monroe Brothers, a duet, accepted the offer of full-time
radio work under the sponsorship of Texas Crystals, a cathartic.[16] This
connection between the hillbilly musician and patent medicine whose
market is chiefly rural is of course an old one, stretching back to the
rural medicine show with its comedian, its banjo player, often in min-
strel-show-inspired blackface, and its "doctor" and his array of salves,
linaments, tonics, elixirs, nostrums, soaps, and candies.[17] As the Monroe brothers correctly perceived, hillbilly music was for the manufac-

turer essentially a mode of advertising, by which the product could be aurally associated with its market just as it was visually linked in newspapers, magazines, and mail-order catalogues. This fact certainly influenced both the Monroe Brothers repertoire and their style. While Birch Monroe stayed behind to support his sister, Bill and Charlie left the Chicago area permanently, moving first to Shenandoah, Iowa, to Omaha, and finally to the Carolinas, where with daily radio shows and frequent personal appearances they became one of the best known and most imitated duets in country music.[18]

The Monroe Brothers' music, like that of the many hillbilly brother duets popular on the radio during the thirties, including the Delmores, the Mainers, the Bolicks, the Morrises, the Dixons, the Carlisles, and the Callahans, was ideally suited to the less than perfect reproductive powers of early radio. It was a music so elegantly simple that its simplicity and purity, its rigorous leveling of auditory textures, of dissonance of almost any kind, can scarcely have been arrived at except by conscious contrivance. It communicated to the airwaves only what the receiving set could be relied upon to reproduce with perfect accuracy: simple melodic lines and parallel harmonies in thirds or fifths, high-pitched but effortless singing, a steady and unaccented rolling rhythm. What distinguished the Monroe Brothers' music from the rest was perhaps that it best exploited the medium of radio by discovering ways to excel within its narrow auditory confines. Like the other duets, their harmonies were straightforward and their voices agile, cool, and clear; Bill's harmony lines, however, often stood out, almost to the extent of becoming a secondary melody. Their pace, too, was steady and swift, often conscientiously accelerated. Coupled to that light, dancing tempo, or perhaps demanded by it, was the unique feature of the duet, Bill's athletic mandolin playing. Other mandolin players had confined themselves to single-noting—that is, to one fretted string struck independently of the other strings in a sequence of notes from which a melody, usually the lead part, would be constructed; Bill's playing was somehow more textured and resonant, more dynamic, and though rarely as melodically complex as it ultimately became in later years, certainly more inventive and plastic rhythmically than any hillbilly instrument save the fiddle. Bill seemed to play not with the beat, but *within* it, as later he would play around and against it, like a jazz musician. The older mandolin technique was one largely dictated by the physical properties of the instrument: the mandolin is a tiny fretted instrument with a short neck and double strings which offer more resistance to the flat pick than, say, a guitar or banjo string, and which cannot sustain a tone as a guitar or banjo string except through the

tremolo as practiced in classical mandolin. The shallow, metallic, and
sometimes toylike sound characteristic of the mandolin, a tone which
had confined the expressiveness of the instrument and restricted it to
the background, arises from the simple difficulty of striking the double
string accurately and with enough concentrated force to arouse the
tones of which the string is capable. This is the problem that Monroe
solved by abandoning the effort to produce discrete, pure tones. Monroe's tones are not discrete; they come at us like meteors trailing the
smoke and flames of a multitude of sounds compounded of tones, overtones, and sheer noise. "He concentrates strictly on his sound," says
Kenny Baker; "the sound is one thing, the melody is another."[19]

To begin with, Monroe's style is far more aggressive and forceful
than anything that had been heard before in country music; he strikes,
or rather, *scrapes* the string, or several strings in a chord or combination, with the combined strength of wrist and forearm, which like
a fiddler's wrist and forearm remain flexible, subject to many complex
articulations. This causes the string to vibrate openly and the whole
body of the mandolin to resonate sympathetically—playing, in a word,
as loudly as he can and rarely, except when necessary in a run or
melodic line, limiting himself to single-noting. One might suppose that
his inimitable technique was born in the effort simply to be heard. The
well known rough or "grainy"[20] sound of Monroe's mandolin is the sound
of the flat pick moving back and forth over a series of double or triple
stops built upon the melody or a variation of it; its texture arises in
part from the undercurrent of noise made by the washboarding of the
pick itself on the strings and from the many complex overtones in the
mandolin string: the two strands of the double string can never be
tuned to precisely the same pitch. Like the jazz horn player's "dirty"
tones, Monroe's raw materials are both acoustic and musical; but
whereas the jazz trumpet seems to take the smoke of the caberet into
its throat, the mandolin's sound, like that of a distant engine, is a noise
that seems to resolve itself into a tone.

But the effort to be heard is more than a matter of volume and tone.
Even while playing with Charlie, Bill displayed the jazzman's abhorrence of silence, introducing brief mandolin runs into conventionally
silent intervals between vocal or instrumental phrases, "hot licks" from
which the lively polyphony of bluegrass would ultimately develop. In
the Monroe Brothers' music there was little jazz influence, though Bill's
intrusive licks often set him apart from the beat, so that they had a
parenthetical or argumentative quality similar to the responsive ex-
temporizing of a jazz trumpet or a bluegrass fiddle or banjo.

It is apparent, then, that Monroe's early mandolin style had already travelled much of the distance toward bluegrass. He had redefined the role of the instrument, liberating it somewhat from the musical line and giving it a sort of proprietary role, darting in and out of the music, forging tough little links that bound its separate elements together, welling up into it to interpret it. In doing so he had begun to redefine the music itself, although a thorough redefinition would require further experiments with rhythm. The sources of Monroe's mandolin technique have of course been a subject of much discussion. Monroe himself has cited the importance of the fiddle, calling it the "king instrument" in string music;[21] indeed there is a strong affinity between Monroe's textured sound and that of the traditional Kentucky fiddler, who strives to nest the melody note in a rich texture of chordal stops, vibrating open strings, and bowing *finesse*.[22] It has been suggested, too, that Monroe handles the flat pick as a blues guitar player might—perhaps due to the influence of the black guitarist Shultz. But there are no blues guitar players, black or white, whose guitar styles sound anything like Monroe's mandolin style, though there are, of course, points of resemblance. My own rather naive observations of several traditional jazz bands in San Francisco, and of recordings in traditional jazz collections, strongly incline me to believe that Monroe's mandolin technique, in both the right and left hands and in its various functions as an ensemble instrument, is essentially that of the plectrum banjo player in a Dixieland jazz band.

The Monroe Brothers' repertoire, assembled in what we have seen was an atmosphere of folk and folk-like songs, consisted not of originally composed songs but of songs learned from WLS broadcasts and, significantly, from phonograph records. To call up the spirit of home in East Chicago, the boys bought records which, were they to survive today on the dusty shelves of some chaotic junk shop, would constitute for the collector a major strike: Gid Tanner and the Skillet Lickers, Charlie Poole and the North Carolina Ramblers, Jimmie Rodgers, the Carter Family, and Bradley Kincaid, among others.[23] Perhaps there was some jazz in their collection. It is always a bit of a shock to realize that the human career, which seems so brief from within, can embrace spans of time which have become historical. It is not only that these recordings are rare, and can be found now only in folklore and country music archives or reissued on esoteric labels catering to the hillbilly and old-time music enthusiast, but that they represent what we now regard as the high-water marks of old-time music, the best achievements of what is often called the "golden age" of hillbilly recording, which began early in the twenties and ended, for all practical purposes, with the descent of the Great Depression. It is clear, then, that the Monroe Brothers stood squarely at the center of that tradition, not by virtue of the retrospect that we enjoy, but by virtue of the unique convergence in their lives of rural background, radical dislocation, still wider social change, and the entrepreneurial energy of the early record companies.

And it is only at the center, I think, that the radicle of Bill Monroe's music could have taken root. The great musicians of the golden age had each discovered and cultivated some one aspect of hillbilly music of which bluegrass would later make use. In the Skillet Lickers, a short-lived Georgia string band whose outstanding figures were fiddler Clayton McMichen and the blind guitarist Rily Puckett, we hear the raucous, brilliant, and spontaneous sound of southern mountain dance music played by men who understood that in the recording studio they were at liberty to play as they might after the dancers had gone home—that is, with a heightened vitality and energy, taking immense pleasure in their own music, communicating that pleasure to an audience who could attend more closely to the music than actual dancers and who could *imagine* a dance more gay and wonderful than is usually possible for ordinary self-conscious mortals, even in the north Georgia hills. The Skillet Lickers, in other words, exploited their new medium, translating for their dispersed audience a social experience into a personal one which might imaginatively become social again, but on a different plane, powerfully dramatic and essentially fictive. Listen, for instance, to their joyous recording of "Soldier's Joy," which Gid Tanner introduces in his musical, auctioneer-like patois: "Well, folks, here we are again, the Skillet Lickers, red hot an' rarin' to go—gonna play you another little tune this mornin' wantcha to *grab that gal* an' shake a foot. C'*mon*! Don't you let 'em dance on your new carpet—you make 'em roll it up."[24] Neither Tanner's rhythmic fiddle style nor Fate Norris's clawhammer banjo style, both of which are strongly black-influenced and date back well into the nineteenth century, survive in bluegrass; but the two instruments, which were joined in minstrelsy and formed the core of the old mountain dance bands, have been given special emphasis in bluegrass through new techniques designed specifically for the new music. Puckett's stout bass runs on the guitar, though we do not hear precisely the same kind of run in bluegrass, helped to establish that instrument in the string band tradition and, derived as they are from blues guitar—Riley sometimes played with a bottleneck in the fashion of black bluesmen—introduced an unmistakable strain of jazz into string band music.[25] Listen to his duet with

McMichen, "Paddy, Won't You Drink Some Cider," in which McMichen calls twice for "that run," with which he has obviously been impressed before the session. Riley answers with three runs of three measures each which, like the bass line of a ragtime pianist, assign one note to each beat, all equally accented, including a flatted seventh typical of blues, and ends with a witty syncopation that allows the expected fourth measure to sneak wholly into the third.[26]

In Charlie Poole and the North Carolina Ramblers we have a very different kind of string band, modified by more obvious contemporary and popular influences such as vaudeville, and still more explicitly addressed to a listening, rather than a participating, audience, though the band began its career in 1918 playing for dances, cornhuskings, and other social occasions. While the Skillet Lickers sounded wild and carefree, Poole's delivery was crisply articulated and scrupulously metrical, nearly as rigid rhythmically and as free of dynamic changes as a player piano. It was a style that somehow objectified his subject matter, allowing him to present songs of many different kinds, ranging from mountain breakdowns to ragtime tunes such as "Whitehouse Blues" and "Dont' Let Your Deal Go Down," now bluegrass standards, which Poole set forth in a mid-range nasal bark reminiscent of radio politicians such as John L. Lewis or Herbert Hoover. Though the Ramblers' recordings sometimes included crackerbarrel dialogue—

> (railroad whistle in the distance)
> "Say, that man sure does blow a wicked whistle, don't he? Sounds like that old feller that used to run on the Southern, between Monroe and Spencer, pulled that Crescent Limited— what *was* his name, Charlie?"
> "Why, you thinkin' about Bill Mason."
> "Oh, yeah. What ever become of him?"
> "Uh, he got married here awhile back."
> "Married? I thought he got *sick*, that's what's the matter with him, I thought."[27]

—they did not represent themselves as rude mountaineers "red hot and rarin' to go," but, in a well-known photograph, as a genteel trio of afficianados in dark suits, Poole seated in the center as stiffly as if he were demonstrating finger positions for an instruction booklet, Posey Rorer and Roy Harvey behind him, the one holding his fiddle under his arm, the other, sporting a pair of scholarly horn-rims, his fingers poised on an torturous-looking chord on his guitar: altogether a photo fit for a college yearbook.

The band's most memorable and most influential element, however, was Charlie Poole's three-finger banjo picking, a style derived from late nineteenth-century classical and parlor banjo method but modified by Poole into a raggy, percussive style whose prominent upbeat, expressed by tight, stiff chords snatched often from positions high on the banjo neck, echoed the rhythmic pulse of the older mountain clawhammer or frailing styles.[28] Unlike the classical banjoists, Poole picked with his fingernails, his right hand having been crooked in a childhood accident; but he showed a professional musician's diligence by practicing two hours a day and learning every key on the fingerboard.[29] His was not a bluegrass style, but banjo did not figure so prominently again in country music until Earl Scruggs, also from North Carolina, joined Bill Monroe in 1945.

Once a song of whatever origin has been recorded, it is in a sense exhausted, since a single disc can be played again and again. As Anne and Norm Cohen point out, rural musicians who had become "recording artists" became, of necessity, de facto song collectors, since if a new record was to be sold a new song had to be recorded.[30] Of the hillbilly musicians who collected songs, none were more fertile in their offerings than the Carter Family. As Archie Green notes, A. P. Carter, though hardly a scholar, was in effect a collector of folksongs every time he recorded a song or published it in folio;[31] his methods, too, resembled those of the folklorist: whenever the trio arrived in a new town for a show, A. P. would seek out the *old people* in the neighborhood from whom to collect new material.[32] Once their very considerable fame was established, the Carter Family began to receive unsolicited material from throughout the South, in the form of song sheets, hymnals, "poetry"—words without music—and "ballets," or the written verses of narrative songs, ballads, whose melodies were traditional. Consequently the Carters would be called upon to compose new melodies for old songs whose melodies had been lost and for originally composed verses without melodies; they composed many of their own songs as well, a talent A. P. Carter had begun to nurture in 1910, prompted by a deep nostalgia for his home in Scott County, Virginia, during a year spent working on the railroad in Indiana—hear "My Old Clinch Mountain Home."[33] Thus the Carter Family offered songs of nearly every kind congenial to the southern rural imagination: hymns old and new; gospel songs; ballads and saga songs; songs of unrequited love, of outlaws, bandits, cowboys, hobos, and railroaders; topical songs, and finally many of the sentimental or maudlin Victorian popular or "parlor" songs which had drifted into the South and survived there long after the rest of the world had forgotten them. Altogether the

Carter Family recorded over 300 songs on fourteen different record labels, songs which represent, perhaps better than any merely scholarly collection, the essential spirit of southern rural music. Because they were in continuous communication with their audience from whom much of their material came, and because that audience was certainly the widest and most varied any hillbilly performer had ever commanded, gathered into the wide embrace of several radio stations and ultimately of a fifty-thousand watt Mexican border station in 1938, saturated by a continuous output of recorded songs in which its own traditions were preserved, the Carter Family's music is a kind of Olduvai Gorge of southern rural life. From the Elizabethan ballad to a Cheasapeake and Ohio railroad disaster, traces of southern culture are fixed in the diction, imagery, characters, and situations of the Carter family's repertoire, which has a unity of style and outlook. They had learned their harmonies in church singing schools, and with their voices buried piously in their breasts—it was a music that came physiologically, as well as emotionally, from the heart—sang with the brave innocence of schoolchildren as well as the conviction of a gospel choir. It was a style replete with tension and underwritten by a deep reluctance born of a kind of ambivalence: one feels that the music, wholesome and even domestic as it is, has been forcibly displayed to, rather than openly and freely given to, its public audience. It was a style, in other words, which perfectly embodied the universe of values for which the Carter Family and their songs stood: the sanctity of home, hearth, and mother's love, sexual innocence, the necessity of a firm religion, the purity of the grave, and the durable hope of a better world beyond it, whose earthly colony was the church. This is a familiar "rural" morality, perhaps; but we find it also in middle-class Victorian England, where, with its concentration upon the security of the home and family, and upon personal faith, it was a fortress set against a world newly dominated by tradition-shattering industry and a religion-ruining natural science.

A brief list of Carter Family songs will show the large proportion that have survived in bluegrass and in our own folk-revivalist practice: "Wildwood Flower," "Worried Man Blues," "Lonesome Valley," "Keep on the Sunny Side," "Gathering Flowers from the Hillside," "My Old Cottage Home," "Poor Little Orphan Boy," "On the Sea of Galilee," "Little Moses," "Gospel Ship," "Little Darling, Pal of Mine," "Jimmy Brown the Newsboy," "You Are My Flower," "On the Rock Where Moses Stood," "Will the Circle Be Unbroken," "John Hardy," "Will You Miss Me," "Wabash Cannonball." But have so many survived merely because they are charming, quaint, or only simple? A word

must be added about the Carter Family's rhythm. It was a spacious
4/4 time, usually in a peppy tempo, founded upon Maybelle Carter's
famous guitar "lick," which was, it appears, an adaptation of the old
banjo frailing style, which she also played, since it included, after the
base or melody note played on the down beat, a sharp downward brush
stroke played with the back of the fingernail of the index or first finger,
on the upbeat. Consequently most Carter Family songs moved against
a steady upbeat or "backbeat," the characteristic rhythm of Afro-
American music and, as we'll see in a later chapter, of traditional
jazz and bluegrass. Maybelle may have learned this style from Les-
lie Riddles, a black friend of A. P.'s and a supplier of some of his
songs.

Hillbilly music was an unstable solution which required the catalyst
of Monroe's imagination to stablize; but in these bands to whom the
Monroe boys listened on record we see elements of instrumental technique, aesthetic posture, rhythm, and even the moral position Monroe
would adopt for his music. Given the importance of phonograph records
to their own development and in popular music generally, both during
the 1920s and now, it is curious that when Victor records first approached the Monroe Brothers with an aggressive telegram—"We
won't take no for an answer"—they ignored the offer.[34] A telephone
call and a persistant businessman ultimately persuaded them; but the
fact remains that the prospect of a phonograph recording, for which
musicians today will sell their first molars, did not much interest them.
They may have recognized what we have already noted—that a recording "used up" a song and in effect drew it out of a musician's
available repertoire. There was little money, moreover, in phonograph
records—at least for the musician. Often a hillbilly musician received
only a small flat fee for the privilege of being recorded and at most
could expect a royalty of only two cents a record. By comparison to
radio, phonographs and records were expensive and inconvenient;
while radio sales increased fourteen times between 1922 and 1929,
record sales declined between 1927 and 1932 to one-fortieth of what
they had been in 1922.[35] Furthermore the good radio sets sounded
better than the best phonographs, and recording technology had not
yet advanced to the point at which a record could be regarded as a
means of preserving what might otherwise be lost—though this is
precisely what it has done. It is probable that the Monroe Brothers
saw phonograph recordings as something less useful and certainly less
profitable than radio programs and personal appearances, and only a
little less ephemeral, somewhat as we now regard the portable cassette.

Between 1936 and 1938 the Monroe Brothers recorded sixty songs for Victor, in six sessions, all in Charlotte, North Carolina. Their songs show something of the same eclecticism characteristic of the rest of hillbilly music, but at the same time it is obvious that the principle of selection we have alluded to is at work. By far the great proportion of the songs were traditional songs of Appalachian or black origin, which later folklorists have acknowledged as such; many made specific reference to the places, scenes, occupations, and legendary characters of the southern mountains—the sheriff with his pack of hounds, the spikedriver and roustabout, the mountain railroad, the moonshine still, the cotton mill and coal mine, and the rabbit hunt:

> There's a rabbit in the log and I ain't got my dog.
> How will I get him? I know—
> I'll get me a briar and twist it in his hair,
> And that's how I'll get him; I know.

Approximately half of the Monroe Brothers' recorded songs were gospel standards, such as the "Old Cross Roads," "What Would You Give in Exchange," and "He Will Set Your Fields on Fire"; the few sentimental or popular songs they included, such as "In My Dear Old Southern Home" and "Just a Song of Old Kentucky," contributed through a central image or idea to the powerfully traditional and Appalachian emphasis which bluegrass music inherited. Many of the Monroe Brothers' songs have become bluegrass evergreens, and there are few bluegrass musicians who do not know all of them: "My Long Journey Home," "Nine Pound Hammer," "New River Train," "On the Banks of the Ohio," "Darling Corey," "Roll in My Sweet Baby's Arms," "Katy Cline," "Roll on Buddy," "Weeping Willow Tree," "All the Good Times Are Past and Gone," "Feast Here Tonight," and "Foggy Mountain Top."[36]

If the music of the Carter Family is a geological record of southern culture, the Monroes' music is a *vision* of it—one which partakes significantly of the documentary and regionalist mood which had overtaken American culture during the Great Depression, when, as Alfred Kazin wrote, America was "hungry for news of itself."[37] While the Monroes travelled and recorded, a vast documentary, descriptive, and journalistic scouring of American land and life was in progress including, among hundreds of other anthologies, collections, portfolios and paintings, the major folksong collections of the Lomaxes, the Federal Writers' Project on the forty-eight states, Agee and Evans' *Let Us Now Praise Famous Men,* and the federal *Index of American Design,*

an illustrated catalogue of American folk art. From the Monroe Brothers' records a kind of stylized picture of the Appalachian region
emerges—not a picture which a social or labor historian would comfortably accept, but a romantic one, the musical equivalent of, say, a
painting by Thomas Hart Benton, who drew heavily in his work upon
mountain lore and folksong: his paintings "I Got a Gal on Sourwood
Mountain," "Engineer's Dream," "Little Brown Jug," "Prodigal Son,"
"Ten Pound Hammer," and especially his last work, "The Origins of
Country Music," are visual statements of several themes belonging to
traditional and hillbilly songs, such as the mountain fiddler and square
dance, the train wreck, the return to a ruined cottage home, the moonshine still, the conflict of man and machine. Like another popular hillbilly duet, the Blue Sky Boys, who delivered old mountain breakdowns
and blues alike—"Cindy" to "The Midnight Special"—with the uniform
and diffident sweetness of comic opera, the Monroe Brothers *simplified*
Appalachian music. Through a consistent, homogeneous style fired by
heightened pitch and tempo, and a repertoire carefully culled of songs
not conspicuously archaic, southern, and folk or folklike, the Monroe
Brothers sought to sharpen the image of country music, to identify it
more closely with the southern mountain tradition—a "tradition" which
stood out more plainly in the new urban perspective, and in a more
pure and unified form than it had ever been in fact. Such an effort,
which may have originated in their advertising function, could not
succeed unless the musicians retained the power to limit and control
their repertoire and protected the freshness of their style—which is
perhaps why throughout his career Bill Monroe has only very conservatively recorded his music, at infrequent intervals, while vigorously
pursuing a schedule of personal appearances.

And, like the other commercial, technological, and high art of the
thirties—one thinks, again, not only of Thomas Hart Benton, but of
the automobile and of Art Deco architecture—the Monroe Brothers'
music was aerodynamic: efficient, fast-moving, and frictionless, perfectly integrated mechanically, with the archaic textures polished down
to a gleaming reflective surface which returned an image of mountain
music shaped to the contours of the age. With their pomaded hair,
their white hats, suits, and shoes, posed for a photograph like a couple
of gangsters beside a new streamlined automobile—Charlie with his
foot propped casually on the running board—the boys themselves presented an audacious and brilliant impression, full of the cool ruthless-
ness of the new youth spawned by the jazz age and thrust headlong
into the Depression.

For all its dynamism and glamour, though, the Monroe Brothers' music was not free of impurities. Though Bill's mandolin flowed smoothly, it had a rough edge and was driven by a scarcely restrained ferocity; in his voice, when you listened a certain way, there was an unmistakable sob. Moreover the very devices through which they and other hillbilly musicians chiefly addressed their audiences, the radio and phonograph, inevitably threw a kind of dust over the brightest and most lucid music. The human ear draws hundreds of inferences from the nature of the energy that presses upon it, measuring the distance of the sound from itself, the physical character of the sound-producing source, and the quality of the medium through which the sound has passed. By their incapacity to recover the subtler lights of the audial spectrum, the old recording and transmitting devices, like the cross-country phone call of today, seemed to shut the speaking or singing voice up into a suitcase. This is particularly true of the duets, whose technique was so finely adjusted to the medium. Anyone who will compare the old recordings, or reissues of them, to contemporary musicians playing in the same style (the records of the Blue Sky Boys, who recorded in the sixties what they had first recorded in the thirties are especially instructive) will feel the difference at once: the new recordings, though often quaint, are flat and irresolute, shallow and ultimately tedious: a few cuts will do you. But the old recordings, like the voice of a sweetheart, wife, or mother to whom the long-distance connection does not quite connect you, seem somehow just out of reach, melancholy, dreamlike, set in the acoustic half-light of another time and place whose veiled image rises to consciousness under the promptings of an old song.

Chapter 3

Folk Music in Overdrive
The Musical Moment

Bluegrass music echoes blues and ragtime, jazz and swing, and of course old-time mountain and hillbilly music. Depending upon one's point of view, bluegrass music will seem to withdraw elusively into one of its component parts, while the other parts assume a supportive or secondary role. Bluegrass, it has been insisted, is "white blues," or "country jazz," or perhaps "the intimate, personal music of a single man, Bill Monroe."[1] For many Appalacian people long familiar both with bluegrass and the hillbilly string bands which preceded it, bluegrass is simply an up-to-date and refined form of the old mountain dance band, particularly those North Carolina bands such as Al Hopkins' Buckle Busters or Mainer's Mountaineers, who made much of their instruments and of the traditional instrumental breakdowns. If we say "white blues," we are thinking largely of subject matter; if we say "country jazz," we are thinking largely of execution; if we say "Bill Monroe's music," we are merely repeating what the term *bluegrass* was intended originally to mean. But if bluegrass resolves itself chiefly into its instruments, what are we to say of the crucial element of bluegrass singing, which does not take precisely the same form in any other kind of music? And if the bluegrass instrumental style is somehow up-to-date and refined, in what sense is it so?

Bluegrass music is never more itself than when we hear it against the backdrop of, or in contrast to, other kinds of folk and popular music. Not only does it exist in the same dimension as, say, jazz or rock, but it seems to draw much of its very substance from the contrasts which are implicit in it. A bluegrass fiddle break, for instance, will typically include technical and stylistic elements belonging to jazz or even classical music; often a bluegrass banjo break will interpolate melodic ideas from ragtime, blues, and, more recently, rock. Bluegrass seems to be as much *about* music as it *is* a music, in the same way as Jelly Roll Morton's "Maple Leaf Rag" is "about" Scott Joplin's "Maple Leaf Rag" and not merely an interpretation of it.[2] Morton's piece analyzes, criticizes, and finally supercedes Joplin's, supplanting it with what is manifestly the next stage in the evolutionary sequence to which both ragtime and New Orleans jazz belong. Those who can recall their first exposure to bluegrass music will perhaps remember a similar sense of revelation—the sudden and unanticipated, yet perfectly fitting and intelligible, transformation of one kind of music into another. Never has bluegrass been more fresh than at that first approach; never has it seemed to communicate so much information about itself all at once. The birth of jazz in New Orleans is obscure to us, though perhaps we can infer from the various complex circumstances in that city, including the several black traditions such as blues and improvised hymn singing, the black marching bands, the cakewalk and ragtime piano which converged there, what its parturition must have been like. The birth of bluegrass, however, takes place in full view, on the stage of the Grand Ole Opry and on phonograph records, and although there are several steps in the process, the decisive and concluding step— which, as we'll see, was rhythmic, just as in jazz—is clearly audible.

Twenty years ago Alan Lomax called bluegrass music "folk music in overdrive,"[3] lighting upon a metaphor perfectly suited to the spirit in which Monroe, who once compared playing to putting a motor together, approaches his music. Lomax's brief essay in *Esquire* magazine, which initiated the intellectual discussion of bluegrass music, is worth quoting at length. "Out of the torrent of folk music that is the backbone of the record business today," he wrote in 1959, "the freshest sound comes from the so-called bluegrass band—a sort of mountain Dixieland combo in which the five-string banjo, America's only indigenous folk instrument, carries the lead like a hot clarinet." Taking up the jazz analogy, he goes on:

> The mandolin plays bursts reminiscent of jazz trumpet choruses; a heavily bowed fiddle supplies trombone-like hoedown solos; while a framed guitar and slapped bass make up the rhythm section. Everything goes at top volume, with harmonized choruses behind a lead singer who hollers in the high, lonesome style beloved in the American backwoods. The result is folkmusic in overdrive with a silvery, rippling, pinging sound; the State Department should note that for virtuosity, fire

and speed our best Bluegrass bands can match any Slavic folk orchestra.

Lomax's brief dispatch from Greenwich Village, written to sophisticated readers at a time when the tiny, politically-inspired folksong revival of the fifties was swiftly growing into a national fad, was designed to secure a place for bluegrass music in the new movement by testifying to its authenticity, while defeating the prejudices against hillbilly music inevitable in the minds of a generation still digging Gerry Mulligan, Thelonius Monk, and Dave Brubeck. "While the aging voices along Tin Pan Alley grow every day more querulous," he wrote, "and jazzmen wander through the harmonic jungles of Schoenberg and Stravinsky, grass-roots guitar and banjo-pickers are playing on the heartstrings of America." Lomax spoke with impeccable authority and with memorable succinctness and imagination. "Entirely on its own," he assured his readers, bluegrass was "turning back to the great heritage of older tunes that our ancestors brought into the mountains before the American Revolution":

> A century of isolation in the lonesome hollows of the Appalachians
> gave them time to combine strains from Scottish and English
> folksongs and to produce a vigorous pioneer music of their own.
> The hot Negro square-dance fiddle went early up the creek-
> bed roads into the hills; then in the mid-nineteenth century came
> the five-string banjo; early in the twentieth century the guitar
> was absorbed into the developing tradition. By the time folksong
> collectors headed into the mountains looking for ancient ballads,
> they found a husky, hard-to-kill musical culture as well.
> Finally, railroads and highways snaked into the backwoods, and
> mountain folk moved out into urban, industrialized, shook-up
> America. . . .

Though its origins were in ancient folk traditions, bluegrass was nevertheless strikingly novel and as thoroughly professional as any modern music. "Bluegrass began in 1945," Lomax observed, when Bill Monroe recruited a "brilliantly orchestrated" hillbilly quintet which contrasted sharply with the "originally crude" hillbilly orchestras that developed, Lomax suggests, in response to the presence of radio microphones. Monroe led the group with a mandolin and "a countertenor voice that hits high notes with the impact of a Louis Armstrong trumpet," singing and playing the "old time mountain tunes" which in twenty years of professional music hillbilly musicians had largely abandoned. "By now," Lomax concluded, "there has grown up a generation of hillbilly

musicians who can play anything in any key," with a revolutionary
new music which is "the first clear-cut orchestral style to appear in
the British-American folk tradition in five hundred years."

Lomax's few phrases admirably summarize the background of bluegrass, which folklorists since have elaborated, documented, and refined
but have done little to alter fundamentally, while his comparison of
bluegrass to jazz is an acute musical insight which a more methodical
comparison between the two kinds will only confirm. There are other,
less obvious insights in the article, too: the broadcast microphone,
whose role Lomax alludes to, has indeed figured significantly in the
evolution of the hillbilly orchestra into bluegrass; the bluegrass band,
like the Slavic folk orchestra, seems in fact to embody something of
the national character, for this is how European and Japanese enthusiasts of bluegrass regard it; even Lomax's innocent but much criticized
error—the banjo is indigenous to Africa, while the origin of the fifth
string, once attributed to the nineteenth-century minstrel Joel Walker
Sweeney, is in dispute, but may very well be African, too—displays
his strong instinct for the aesthetics of culture.[4] While the banjo may
be African, it arouses powerful regional and historical associations
peculiar to America, as do many other of the African contributions to
American music; few would argue, I think, that the five-string banjo
is not in some sense an "American" instrument, with an indelibly American sound.

Lomax has been criticized, too, for his contention that bluegrass is
"the first clear-cut orchestral style to appear in the British-American
folk tradition in five hundred years"; but if this carefully qualified
remark overstates the case (I think it does not), it nevertheless initiated a passion for hyperbole in intellectual writing about the music
which elevated Monroe to the status of Caruso, and Earl Scruggs,
who, with Lester Flatt and the Foggy Mountain Boys, became the
best-known bluegrass musician of the folk revival, to that of Paganini.
By the middle sixties several national magazines and journals, including *Time*, the *Saturday Review*, *HiFi/Stereo Review*, *Sing Out!*, and
the *Journal of American Folklore*, as well as the liner notes of innumerable record albums, had made contributions to a discussion in
which Monroe's name, following Lomax's original declaration, was increasingly prominent. A central figure in the folkmusic revival, Ralph
Rinzler, wrote early in 1963:

> At this point it is an easy task to evaluate the contribution of
> Bill Monroe. It was the combination of musical traditions, both
> the Anglo-Scots and the Negro, meeting as they did in that

area of Kentucky, which enabled Monroe to blend these two
powerful strains in his own instrumental and vocal style. In his
choice of instrumental treatment and repertoire, it was
Monroe who set the trend to play traditional songs on traditional
instruments, and this he did at a time when the trend in
commercial country music among performers of his generation
was directly opposed to him.

   Monroe pioneered mandolin viruosity and forged the driving
rhythms and tempos characteristic of his music from the time
of his first recordings with Charlie in 1936. . . . Bill Monroe is
still the most dynamic and subtle singer in the field of
bluegrass music, exhibiting a vocal style which could only have
developed from a background of rich and varied musical styles.[5]

Yet, for Rinzler, Monroe's achievement was more than merely technical or synthetic; Monroe had been empowered by a "conviction as
profound as a religious belief": "But more important than his function
as an instrumentalist, vocalist, creator and preserver, Bill Monroe is
a spiritual force, in his ability to sing and play with the fire and inspiration characteristic of only a great musician that draws people to
him and to his music."

   Rinzler, like Lomax, spoke with authority. In his effort to correct
what he regarded as the revivalists' neglect of Monroe in favor of Earl
Scruggs, Rinzler had gathered the first biographical information on
Monroe, penetrating long-standing social barriers to do so, and in short
time had become his manager, personal friend, and even a member of
the Blue Grass Boys; Rinzler supervised, edited, and annotated all of
Monroe's record albums from "Bluegrass Instrumentals," released in
1965, to "Bill Monroe's Country Music Hall of Fame," released in
1971—nine albums in all, by which Monroe's music, early and late,
was newly represented to its widened national audience.[6]

   Rinzler's influence upon the folk revival—as musician, fieldworker,
collector, producer, businessman, director of the Newport Folk Foundation and most recently of the Folklife Division of the Smithsonian
and of the Smithsonian Folklife Festival—has been immense and illustrates in the same way as the career of the Lomaxes the critical
interdependence of learned, folk, and popular traditions in the life of
modern industrial and post-industrial culture. In his youth Rinzler
came under the tutelage of his uncle Samuel Joseph, a lawyer and
folksong enthusiast who had been a protegé of Harvard's English professor and folklorist, George Lyman Kittredge.[7] Ralph Rinzler's thorough acquaintance, through his uncle, with the Lomaxes' Library of

Congress field recordings awakened him, as it had the young Mike Seeger and others,[8] to the existence of a still surviving musical tradition in the Appalachian region, which later in his life he undertook to ferret out and bring to the attention of northern urban audiences, as Lomax had brought Huddie Ledbetter and Woody Guthrie. When in 1960, for example, Rinzler and discographer Eugene Earle located the early medicine-show and hillbilly performer Clarence Ashley in the mountains of North Carolina, Ashley had all but given up his banjo; Ashley's neighbor, a blind singer and instrumentalist whom Rinzler helped to bring to fame as a traditional musician and guitar wizard, Arthel "Doc" Watson, had abandoned traditional music for the hybrid electric "rockabilly" music by which he hoped to supplement his modest income as a radio repairman.[9] This awareness, too, helped Rinzler and Mike Seeger to observe in the middle 1950s the "integrated elements of varied secular and sacred folk music traditions and styles" in Monroe's music and to recognize him as "a cultural figure of signal importance in our time."[10] When Rinzler and Seeger first encountered Monroe at a country music park more than twenty years ago, Monroe's career was flagging under the massive popularity of rock-and-roll, which had crowded nearly every bluegrass musician except for Lester Flatt and Earl Scruggs out of the marketplace. Television had virtually destroyed the live radio programs which had sustained Monroe's popularity in rural areas and stimulated the sale of his records, while commercial country music, under the impetus of Chet Atkins and Eddy Arnold, was striving for a richly produced urban sound. Monroe's once flourishing road show, with its gospel quartet, comedian, buck dancer, old-time fiddler, pop-singer, and "girl singer"—in the forties he even carried a baseball team—had collapsed, and because Monroe was no longer able to keep his musicians on salary he was scarcely able to keep a particular band together for more than six months at a time.[11]

By introducing Monroe into the mainstream of the folkmusic revival, through university, nightclub, and folk festival appearances, articles and notes, and record albums such as *The High Lonesome Sound*,[12] which surveyed Monroe's career retrospectively, culling a set of recorded performances from which the total shape of Monroe's achievement could be adduced, Rinzler was able to rescue Monroe and to free him from the intense sense of rivalry with other bluegrass bands which had impeded his own growth. Most importantly, Rinzler helped to awaken Monroe to his own centrality in a culturally resonant popular movement which by the middle 1970s had generated scores of summer bluegrass festivals, dozens of new professional bands, and hundreds of amateur bluegrass musicians, as well as thousands of enthusiasts who formed a vast new market for record albums, instruments, song and instruction books, and periodicals. "Bluegrass music," one of its more passionate chroniclers wrote in 1971, "is perhaps one of the largest surviving funds of traditional knowledge in the country outside of Indian lore and religion itself."[13]

By far the most scrupulous and scholarly description of bluegrass music, however, is Mayne Smith's "An Introduction to Bluegrass," which appeared in the prestigious *Journal of American Folklore* in 1965.[14] Bluegrass, Smith writes, "is a style of concert hillbilly music performed by a highly integrated ensemble of voices and non-electrified stringed instruments, including a banjo played Scruggs-style." It is a white southerner's music, Smith writes, and appears to be a reaction against the movement of hillbilly music, and probably of southern culture as a whole, away from the traditions of rural Appalachia. Though bluegrass music comprises only a tiny segment of the hillbilly record market, and few bluegrass musicians can hope to derive their income from music alone, we find it on radio and television, in school auditoriums, at race tracks, often in the taverns and roadhouses of the South and lower Midwest, and in recent years at northern concert halls. However, its most typical, and in a sense most fitting, setting is the outdoor park bandstand which less than a generation ago might have been the site of a medicine show or revival meeting. Here families come of an afternoon with picnic suppers to renew their acquaintance with others like themselves, in an informal atmosphere replete with the shouts of children, raucous applause, and casual conversation.

The musicians, too, differ little from the hillbilly musicians of the past, Smith observes; and their ties to the hillbilly background of tent shows, radio appearances, and disc recordings are strong. Most do not read music but learn their music aurally from records, radio, and from each other; though they often imitate closely the recordings of well-known bands, conscious and unconscious improvisation is the norm in bluegrass. Indeed most bluegrass musicians are of Appalachian origin and remain in close contact with the traditions that informed the old hillbilly music. Bluegrass musicians, like the old hillbilly professionals, emphasize outstanding singing, religious songs, speedy tempos, and showmanlike "arrangements," and typically open their performances with one or two of their recently recorded songs. But their audience has come chiefly to hear their old favorites, and these comprise the bulk of each band's offerings; a performance by Bill Monroe may consist entirely of requests called to the stage by members of the audience. These songs, even when they are originally composed by the musicians themselves, remind us strongly of hillbilly music, for the bluegrass repertoire, like the hillbilly, is rooted in Anglo-American folk tradition and has borrowed many songs congenial to that tradition from nineteenth-century middle-class parlor or sentimental songs as well as from Negro traditions. Many are sorrowful love songs, or songs of nostalgia for a rural home and departed parents, while traditional ballads, usually of broadside origin, tell of violent death or of impending execution or imprisonment, misfortunes which inevitably arise from the passions of love. This world, the religious songs conclude, is a vale of tears, from which death offers us both a release and a reward.

Bluegrass singing, too, Smith goes on, betrays obvious ties to traditional psalm and shape-note singing, as well as to Negro gospel singing and blues. Harmonies consist simply of a "tenor" part erected a third above the melody, sometimes supplemented by a baritone a fifth below and a bass on the tonic pitch; in three- or four-part singing the voices are expected to fill in each note of the triad, though anticipations, passing tones, and ornamental slides often create dissonances that "dispel the predictable homophony" of school or church singing. Bluegrass singing voices are typically tense and as high pitched as possible, often moving into falsetto or headtones, while songs are delivered in a "loud and piercing fashion, not unlike shouting," ornamented with flatted pitches, rising attacks, falling releases, and grace notes. Often lead singers will syncopate their singing, assigning stresses in a way that conforms to the use of accent in normal speech.

After his performance, the bluegrass musician typically greets his audience, selling record albums, song folios, and souvenir programs, signing autographs, and posing for photographs. Altogether the bluegrass performance, in substance, style, and setting, has retained the wholesome, convivial, even the communal mood of the hillbilly shows of twenty, thirty, or even forty years ago, in which "friends and neighbors" gather to share pleasures based in a long cultural past. Yet unlike most hillbilly string band music, bluegrass music, with its prominent upbeat rhythm, its tight ensemble integration, and improvised solo parts, conspicuously displays the influence of an urban and popular music—jazz. In fact it is upon this solid musical foundation that traditional songs, styles, and instruments, as well as the small stringband format, can be reëstablished and preserved. Using the microphone as an integrating device by which solo parts can be amplified and discriminated, the bluegrass band, like the New Orleans jazz band, presents an impression of "multiple parts in continual interaction." Its five instruments—five-string banjo, mandolin, fiddle, steel-stringed Spanish guitar, sometimes a resonated Hawaiian guitar, all unelectrified and chosen for their volume and brilliance of tone—divide the music into three planes: a lead part carried by banjo, fiddle, mandolin, or voice, and very rarely the guitar; a "backing" part in which a lead instrument recedes to provide a contrasting or complimentary accompaniment to the leading melody; and a heavily-accented rhythmic and harmonic base supplied by the guitar and string bass, often supplemented by percussive upbeat "chunks" on banjo or mandolin. In the typical bluegrass number, in which a verse is followed by a chorus in harmony and then an instrumental break, each of the instruments cooperates to maintain, as consistently as possible, all three parts simultaneously, so that the instruments are constantly changing roles in response to one another—thus the band's "continual interaction."

Bluegrass music was first played, Smith notes, by Bill Monroe and the Blue Grass Boys in 1945, a development out of earlier string band styles whose crucial new element was Earl Scruggs's three-finger banjo, with its unusual speed, clarity, and flexibility. Nearly all of the prominent musicians in bluegrass have worked with Monroe for varying periods, and all acknowledge not only his tutorial role but his high standards which it is a bluegrass musician's business to maintain. "You always play it the best way you can," Smith writes, quoting Monroe. "Play it good and clean and play good melodies with it, and keep perfect time. It takes really good timing with bluegrass music, and it takes some good high voices to really deliver it right."

Smith's dispassionate and exhaustive description, which requires that he play musicologist, anthropologist, sociologist, folklorist, and, finally, enthusiast all at once, suggests the complexity of bluegrass as a social and cultural phenomenon. As the amassed details of his account proliferate, one wonders what guiding principle can explain how this mass of musical and cultural material had marshalled itself into a coherent *genre* which contains the laws of its own evolution and which has an astonishingly wide appeal: the French, the Germans, the Finns, and especially the Japanese have bluegrass music, not to mention the Australians, the Canadians, the English, and the Swedes. How, one must ask, did hillbilly music, that scarcely intelligible mass of heterogeneous influences, become a unitary and autonomous form, called by many a classical art, whose emergence seems to have both continued and forclosed the evolution of its own tradition?

As Mayne Smith's article suggests, bluegrass music was, at the outset, a way that southern whites, typically young men with some connection to the Appalachian region and to the musical traditions which belong to that region, played the traditional stringed instruments—fiddle, banjo, mandolin, guitar, and so on—cooperatively, either *as* instruments or in accompaniment to certain kinds of traditional, tradition-like, sentimental or religious songs sung in what might be described as an exaggerated recapitulation of traditional song style. Like ragtime or traditional jazz, bluegrass appeared to be a transient phenomenon, arising out of the fleeting convergence of a number of social, historical, and technological conditions, a phenomenon which would very likely have disappeared with the dissipation of those conditions, had it not acquired in the imagination of its presiding genius, Bill Monroe, an image explicit enough to supply a model to a generation of musicians who carried on with the music for a period of roughly fifteen years between 1945, when the "original" bluegrass band was formed, and the early 1960s, when bluegrass entered, quite irreversibly, the northern and urban folk music revival with its roots in learned, not folk, traditions. Before 1945, when Bill Monroe appeared on the Grand Ole Opry with fiddler Chubby Wise, banjo player Earl Scruggs, guitarist Lester Flatt, and bassist Howard "Cedric Rainwater" Watts, there was no bluegrass music as such; after 1945 there was a sudden explosion of it, spread throughout the South from Louisiana to Washington D.C., absorbing a multitude of regional influences in between, and north into the hillbilly enclaves of industrial cities, where through record outlets, taverns, radio, and the like it swiftly passed into the hands of northern musicians, also chiefly young men, who innocently regarded it as a kind of authentic and homegrown "folkmusic" without an appreciable commercial background. By 1953, Mike Seeger estimates, there were at least ten different bands on commercial records, while every southern town of at least 1,000 population supported at least one amateur bluegrass band.[15] All of this music sounded like, and in other ways imitated, the music which Monroe and his group played on the Opry between 1945 and 1948. Yet, since the bluegrass style seemed no more attributable to a single man than, say, the alphabet, many bluegrass musicians, particularly in the North, were either unconscious of or indifferent to Monroe's decisive role in it, while in the South many musicians, particularly those belonging to his generation, slavishly imitated Monroe, not only in music but in personal manners and dress, sometimes to the point of unwitting caricature. In Louisiana a Cajun-flavored bluegrass music appeared; in Virginia a band emerged with a primitively beautiful music strongly influenced by Southern Baptist religion and song; in Nashville a band as richly orchestrated, effortlessly professional, and confident as a supper club swing band emerged to dominate the industry; in Washington a technically innovative folk-revivalist band established a "progressive" line of development, and so on. By the sixties the bluegrass style had already been so variously interpreted that it seemed entirely independent of Bill

Monroe, whose own deeply conservative music appeared, by contrast, to be strangely eccentric or parochial and, to some, influenced by the folk revival to think of bluegrass as an elaborate accompaniment to the five-string banjo played Scruggs-style, actually offensive: Monroe's unrestrained and strident singing was not always precisely on pitch, while his stage show, with its sale of record albums, announcements of personal appearances to come, its formality and apparent self-congratulatory spirit, was still strongly redolent of the rural tent show. The cool professionalism of Flatt and Scruggs, the technical wizardry of banjoists Reno and Adcock, the sullen piety of the Stanley Brothers—all these, for revivalists especially, seemed both more securely contemporary and more authentic than the music of the hillbilly mandolin player whose band had started it all, and in true oedipal fashion the child seemed to have displaced the father.

It is now commonplace among bluegrass musicians and enthusiasts alike to affirm that Bill Monroe "invented" bluegrass. The commonplace remains provocative, however, simply because the notion that a music can be "invented," as a telephone or lightbulb can be invented, is itself provocative. We may regard bluegrass as a melding of preexistent parts, joining, say, the "form" of jazz to the "content" of hillbilly music; but the term *bluegrass*, as it is commonly used, embraces a variety of influences which one string band could not possibly have absorbed and which one musician could not possibly have organized or controlled without a radical simplification. It is not quite right, perhaps, to be tiresomely precise, to say that Monroe "invented" bluegrass; better to say he awakened it. Monroe contrived an ingenious, distinctive, and novel form of hillbilly music. But bluegrass is also the massive exploitation, first by southern and rural, then by northern and urban, musicians, of a body of musical resources which Monroe's music had retrieved from obsolescence by fortifying it against the fundamentally alien circumstances in which it found itself and empowering it to meet and even to alter those circumstances. Bluegrass was the method which Bill Monroe designed to play old-time music in the modern world; that method, with its own powers, tendencies, and limits, other musicians adopted, imitatively at first, but in time more liberally and originally.

We are speaking, then, of at least three related but distinguishable kinds of music: of Bill Monroe's music, which was one of many kinds of string band music to be heard on the Grand Ole Opry in the late forties and early fifties; of the music of his colleagues, peers, and outright imitators, now sometimes called "traditional" bluegrass; and of the so-called "progressive" bluegrass, which is the style at its most technical, stripped of nearly everything that attaches to it by association, and which, significantly, has curbed the once pervasive role of the Scruggs-style banjo, the instrument whose burden of association, acoustically and culturally, is perhaps the heaviest.

Bill Monroe's original bluegrass band—Flatt, Scruggs, Wise, and Rainwater—was nothing more or less than a hillbilly string band. With its traditional instruments and vocal styles, and its emphasis upon traditional or old-fashioned songs and tunes, it was, like many of the original hillbilly string bands, some of which still played on the Opry, demonstrably Appalachian in origin, and consequently appeared to recover certain archaic elements of a music which had been self-consciously old-fashioned even in the twenties. By 1945, when country music was dominated by Ernest Tubb, Bob Wills, Gene Autry, and Roy Acuff and characterized by a now conventional western motif, that Appalachian string music had become quite antique. That is not to say, however, that Monroe's music was in every respect archaic, which is often what we mean by "traditional." On the contrary, Monroe employed a number of novel devices by which the Appalachian and archaic character of his music could be emphasized. This practice was in itself quite "traditional", for it is in the nature of traditional music, like all traditional arts, to adapt elements from outside itself for its own purposes: black banjo and fiddle styles, Victorian parlor songs, the mandolin of the gilded age—all had found their way into traditional Appalachian and hillbilly music. Thus Monroe's music, in spite of its novelties, could be regarded as a form of traditional Appalachian music, specifically, its social or "assembly" form; but because that form had been reconstituted for the concert stage, it was necessarily a *representation* of traditional Appalachian music in its social or assembly form, since we do not have actual square dances or house parties on the stage or in the studio, though sometimes we may have had representations of them, as the Barn Dance did in their exhibition square dancers.

Of the several elements Monroe's music annexed to itself from other traditions, the most important was the basic African practice of uncoupling rhythm and meter to rejoin them by means of syncopation. Syncopation allowed each musician, through improvisation, to maintain his individual identity within an orchestral structure. Furthermore, his independence allowed him, through techniques such as antiphony and allusion, to interpret his own music—that is, to make reference to it as well as to play it and also to make reference, should the fancy take him, to other kinds of music, such as blues and jazz. Hence syncopation liberated individual musicianship; but it also allowed the collective effort of the band, no matter how variegated, to be heard as an integrated whole—"multiple parts in continuous interaction."

How did Monroe use this new integrating and representational power? From the outset of his tenure on the Opry, Monroe had called upon the various members of his band, in various configurations, to play and sing several different kinds of hillbilly music, including the sentimental or nostalgic song, the brokenhearted love song, the cowboy song, the gospel quartet, several Jimmie Rodgers' yodels which become Monroe's vocal showpieces, the blues song, the individual instrumental tour de force such as "Orange Blossom Special," and the ensemble instrumental breakdown. In the new integrated style, all of these strains could conceivably be detected within one song, with its succession of verse, chorus, and break played against a background of improvised instrumental accompaniment, while on the audial periphery the musicians could be heard to take occasional excursions into the wider precincts of country music, particularly ragtime and western swing, represented by banjo and fiddle respectively. Monroe's band, in other words, had completely assimilated hillbilly music into itself, as a jazz band can assimilate popular or even classical pieces into jazz by interpreting them in the jazz style while demonstrating a capacity for extension beyond itself. Clearly Monroe's band was not merely compelled by the tradition to which they belonged to play hillbilly music; they had deliberately *chosen* to play it.

Obviously a bluegrass band has special affinities for hillbilly music, just as a jazz band has affinities to its antecedents, blues and ragtime; when the jazz band choses to play a blues or rag, we feel we are in the presence of a coherent and continuous tradition. By comprehending the entire substance of hillbilly music in a single complex aural image with conspicuous ties to a traditional music in its assembly form, Monroe's band decommercialized hillbilly music or, to put it another way, seemed to "authenticate" or "traditionalize" hillbilly music. *Seemed* to, that is. The important point is that Monroe's synthesis was imaginative and, like all works of imagination, invites imaginative participation. To hear Monroe's music one must attend to several independent lines at once, as one does when listening to jazz; one must "hear" the breakdown fiddle *as* breakdown fiddle roaming in the background; hear the gospel hymn somehow lodged in the harmonized chorus of the nostalgic song, the balladeer's cry in a tenor harmony, or the blues singer's holler in the lead; even hear the blackface minstrel and medicine show in the ringing of a banjo break. There is little doubt that Monroe's audiences, especially those of Appalachian descent, did hear these echoes, for the bluegrass style is designed to bring them out.

With the gradual extinction of hillbilly music during the 1940s and the emergence of a commercial country-western music out of it, Monroe's music appeared increasingly to be the "original and authentic" country music, all the more so because Monroe himself vigorously enforced in his music social and moral values belonging to rural tradition. Monroe's music became, like Thomas Hart Benton's painting, an imaginative representation of the origins of country music.

Bluegrass music began to be, and has largely continued to be, a formal reënactment of Bill Monroe's music, often with a scrupulosity suggestive of a ritual observance. As such it had a certain ceremonial quality, with various kinds of meaning. In the membership, arrangement, costume, instruments, and dynamic interrelationships of the bluegrass band in performance, instrumental and vocal techniques, and much of the repertoire, both original and traditional, bluegrass is fiction, making reference to a certain loosely coherent, imagined world located chiefly in the past; the music itself, of course, consists in the work of particular musicians *as* musicians: it is performance. It was hillbilly string band music, then, reauthenticated through style.

Hillbilly string band music, as we've seen, was already richly synoptic, essentially a social institution—the dance ensemble of the rural southern folk community—with a background of Irish, Scots-Irish, Afro-American, and various other influences. That background widened somewhat during the early period of commercial radio and recording to embrace certain popular influences such as jazz, with an accompanying emphasis upon the individual performer and a growing self-consciousness about a music usually regarded in the middle and upper strata of society, and increasingly so by the dissolving folk community, as something picturesque, quaint, comic, or grotesque—sentiments which have attached to traditional American music since the days of Dan Emmett's Virginia Minstrels before the Civil War. This accretion of influences could not become a true synthesis unless that accretive process were first arrested and conceived as a static whole with an unrealized pattern residing in it; inessential or irrelevant material would be rejected on the basis of a controlling idea and the pattern drawn out of the fabric through an intensification of its significant elements. All this Monroe did, on the basis of that self-consciousness just alluded to, which empowers the musician to reform his art from a position essentially beyond it, a position Monroe had been learning to occupy since his removal from Kentucky in 1929.

Among other things, bluegrass is simply an attempt to present a multi-faceted music over a single channel; and since old-time string band music, which is multi-channelled and social, cannot be presented over a single channel, it must be *re*presented over it. Its unity lies, of course, in orchestration. Any bluegrass musician—excluding guitarist-lead singers—will tell you that his music does not go well by itself. Each of the bluegrass instrumental styles is an adaptation of the instrument, both tonally and rhythmically, to the presence of and special contribution of the other instruments and is therefore a specialized function. This may have been the case in the early minstrel bands;[16] but it is not in old-time string bands, which are simply groups of musicians playing autonomous musical instruments, each of which will stand harmonically and rhythmically quite well on its own. In old-time string band music we hear many things going on at once; in bluegrass we hear only *one* thing, but it is a sound with many internal dimensions, each of which is kept carefully distinct. While old-time music, aurally at least, presents a multitudinous, two-dimensional surface, a kind of turbulence, bluegrass, both aurally and visually, presents a frame through which lines of force focused at any given moment by an instrument or voice in the foreground sweep into a three-dimensional background, shaping it into planes which other instruments can occupy.

This will become clearer, perhaps, if we consider the circumstances of the Grand Ole Opry in 1945, when bluegrass first emerged from Monroe's band, and compare them to the typical settings of old-time music. Old-time music, we recall, is social and domestic. I am thinking of the typical mountain string band, consisting of a banjo played claw-hammer style, a fiddle played in the syncopated, chordal or drone hoedown style, and perhaps a guitar or some percussion instrument. The immediate ancestor of this band is the medicine show or minstrel band, of which the aforementioned Virginia Minstrels are a good example: they played banjo, fiddle, tamborine, and bones.[17] Its ultimate ancestor, of course, is the folk music of plantation blacks, of which the minstrel show was a ludicrous but often authentic imitation. I am thinking, too, of simple domestic folk song, sung unaccompanied or with a banjo, fiddle, or dulcimer and later the mandolin and guitar, and of domestic instrumental music. Domestic folk music, obviously, is intimately attended by a few people; all its subtleties, its colors, textures, and accents, find an immediate and sympathetic response. Similarly, the typical setting of the folk string band was in the parlor of a house with the furniture removed, on school or church grounds, or perhaps in a swept barn or hall. The music was, to repeat, social and participatory, in which the lines between musician and audience were diffuse; one participated as a member of the community, either by actually playing or by singing, clapping, or dancing. It was not concert or "display" music, which we take passively; rather it was, and is, a kind of all-encompassing auditory environment into which one physically and emotionally incorporates oneself. For the musician, the atmosphere is relaxed, informal, and in effect domestic. He has the participation of his audience, but not, strictly speaking, the attention. He can play for himself and to the other musicians. His music might be exceedingly complex, anticipating the polyrhythm, though not the polyphony, of jazz. It could be heard from, and could inspire, a multitude of perspectives, emphases, and viewpoints, turning unpredictably upon the changing relationships among the musicians and between the musicians and members of their audience. In bluegrass these relationships are fluid, but orderly and conventionalized; significantly, a bluegrass band, when placed in the social circumstances of a square dance or house party, becomes a kind of old-time band.

Old-time music had to be radically reformed if it was to maintain its integrity on the Grand Ole Opry. In 1939, as we noted, the Opry had acquired network status and could be heard throughout the South. In 1941 it moved to the now-famous Ryman Auditorium, a converted tabernacle dedicated as a Confederate memorial and outfitted with church pews and a balcony. The hillbilly performer found himself on the stage of this theatre with an audience seated before him, more closely attentive than any social or even radio audience could be. Planted directly in front of him was the broadcast microphone, which would carry his music—the *sound* of his music—into parlors spread for hundreds of miles in every direction around him.

He would have been conscious, too, as we've suggested, that his particular kind of music was only one among many kinds of rural music which the show had garnered from several regions for broadcasting; beyond this he must have been aware of the fact that radio not only made of his music one kind among many related kinds, but made of the whole of country music a program to be presented alongside other programs of drama, news, and a hundred varieties of popular and classical music, all articulated by a single organ. George Hay, indeed, had named the "Grand Ole Opry" in ironic contrast to the program of Grand Opera which preceded it on the air.[18]

It is interesting to listen with this in mind to the tapes of some of Monroe's early performances with the original bluegrass band on the Opry in 1945 and 1946.[19] We hear first the urbane and resonant voice of our master of ceremonies, Mr. Hay, as gleamingly mercenary as an auto bumper, who introduces us with an apparently revived enthusi-

asm to our next act—his voice now rising to a pitch of excitment—
Bill Monroe and the Blue Grass Boys, with Earl Scruggs and his fancy
banjo! On at least one occasion Hay places Scruggs's name before
Monroe's, and in one instance drops Monroe's name altogether. What
follows is a wildly accelerated, almost violently high-pitched frenzy of
mountain music, one which while treading very close to the edge of
the bizarre displays an incredible virtuosity which audiences in those
days saw, and were plainly encouraged to see, as a prodigy. With
Monroe's voice blasting like an air-raid siren and Scruggs's banjo hurtling forward on ten thousand wheels, that band came at you like the
Normandy invasion. It is obvious that the rhetoric of this newly expanded and highly commercial radio program prompted its audience,
which had become a socially and geographically heterogeneous one, to
think of the show as a kind of musical circus, like the old blackface
minstrel shows, and of the musicians as acrobats or clowns.

Under these conditions, old-time music could not have survived *as*
music, and did *not* survive, except as Monroe's music or some variation
of it, with its intensity, virtuosity, its high resolution and density of
organization, its aural, visual, and moral three-dimensionality, and
above all, perhaps, its absolute seriousness, which defied the show's
comic conventions. It was a music played, in a sense, to three audiences
at once: to the southeastern rural audience who would have acknowledged it immediately as a native idiom; to the audience seated in the
auditorium, which, though chiefly rural, required devices of engage-
ment that the native audience would not; and finally to the radio audience, for whom the music must be made audially intelligible.

The significance of bluegrass can perhaps be understood with relation
to these three audiences. For its parochial native audience, bluegrass
symbolically preserved familiar traditions; for its wider audience it
represented its own tradition in an assertive way calculated to instruct
and to arouse appropriate associations, by releasing certain signifying
sounds and images; finally it articulated each of its elements in turn
with a definiteness that both displayed the powers of individual musicians and defined the auditory space three-dimensionally. Behind the
procenium of the concert stage, the band had to present itself to the
front; hence it had to solve the familiar dramatic problem of representing three-dimensional activity two-dimensionally. In the dark
spaces of the auditorium it had to, like an actor, project each note with
a force that the older instrumental and vocal styles could not muster.
And to transmit a complex music over a single channel provided by
the broadcast mike, it had to parcel the music into solo breaks supported by a backdrop of steady metrical pulsing and a carefully dis-

criminated instrumental response. This entire strategy, coupled with Monroe's defiance of the rube convention with a dignified white shirt and tie—he claims to have been the first on the Opry to wear a white shirt—and with the sheer animation, energy, and intense concentration the strategy demands, produced the original bluegrass.

Of course string music evolved in other ways as well, to meet new commercial conditions. Western swing, a creation of the thirties dominated by fiddler Bob Wills, enlarged the traditional fiddle dance band with more fiddles, steel guitars, and ultimately horns, striving to reiterate the popular big-band jazz of the period; though it combined elements of hillbilly, jugband, jazz, and even Mariachi music, its style was essentially orchestral and urban, having developed in the large public dance halls of the Southwest.[20] It was in the West, too, that electrical amplification was introduced by Texas musician Ernest Tubb and by Bob Dunn of Milton Brown and his Musical Brownies, who by attaching an amplifier to his steel guitar helped to introduce country music into the mainstream of American commerce and fundamentally altered its character.[21] Only Bill Monroe's music was essentially conservative or even reactionary, electing to revive an archaic music by changing its aesthetic status. As such it bore about the same relation to the past as the literary ballad to the ballad, or, for that matter, the minstrel show of the 1840s to actual plantation music. The literary ballad extracted the literary elements of the oral form, subjecting it to literary laws; the minstrel show extracted the comedic elements of black folk music, subjecting it to theatrical laws; bluegrass extracted, as I hope to show, the moral element of Appalachian music and subjected it to moral laws.

It seems that as soon as Bill left the Monroe Brothers he began to pursue the bluegrass idea, and that the idea had been, as the Monroe Brothers' music suggests, in the formative stages for years. With the establishment of a string band—he called them first the Kentuckians and then the Blue Grass Boys—he had already moved into the past, for string bands with explicitly regional connections had receded, in 1938, behind colossal figures such as Gene Autry and Roy Acuff, while the brother duets were becoming charmingly passé. Given Monroe's original interest in blues guitar and his admiration of Jimmie Rodgers, it is interesting that Monroe did not strike out for himself as a singing star, choosing instead to ally himself with a musical style which, if not yet quite obsolete, was certainly not the only alternative available to a musician of Monroe's calibre. Charlie had at first carried on in the Monroe Brothers' style, and even called his mandolin player "Bill," whether his name was Bill or not.[22] In time he developed a successful career as a solo singer in the prevailing mode, setting his reedy voice, at different times and in different combinations, in front of a mandolin, three or four acoustic and electric guitars, a pervasive and mellifluous fiddle, a bass, and sometimes a piano. Like Bill, he stressed traditional, gospel, and sentimental songs with a patina of age upon them, and he often picked up the tempo to a breakneck pace. His variety shows sometimes included solos on fiddle and clawhammer banjo, played by a girl singer. His voice was remarkably like Bill's, glowing ingratiatingly, though not, like Bill's later style, in flames; the breaks of his electric guitar and fiddle were usually congenial restatements of the melody, comfortably nestled in the jogging beat.

Bill Monroe moved in a similar direction, seeking to introduce this variety *within the band itself*. The short-bow hoedown fiddling of Art Wooten and, later, Tommy Magness broadened the background of Monroe's music, joining it securely to the backwoods; the addition of a fiddle to the basic mandolin-guitar duet which Monroe preserved could hardly be called daring, however. On the other flank Monroe had hired—odd to think of it now—one John Miller, a *jug player* who also played spoons and bones, and performed in blackface.[23] Miller linked Monroe's band directly to the early rural black tradition and to its white counterfeit, the minstrel show, whose music was the first commercial white adaptation of black music, and whose incursions into the southern mountains in the nineteenth century figured importantly in the establishment of "the old southern sound." The tie was perhaps too explicit, however, since in a matter of months Monroe dropped Miller in favor of Amos Garin's string bass. In spite of Miller's fleeting appearance, we must not forget him: he is one of the most graphic signs we have of the way Monroe conceived his music, and of the meanings which reside in bluegrass at a deeper level.

Less than a year after his break with Charlie, Monroe auditioned, in October 1939, for George Hay, who remarked to Bill that if he ever left the Opry it would be because he had fired himself. Apparently Hay thought Monroe's music was ideal for the program: not only was it plainly rural and southeastern in character, it was tight; Monroe had rigorously rehearsed the band before the audition.[24]

The Opry had been on the air only about ten years at this point and was dominated by two of the most memorable personalities in the history of country music, Roy Acuff and Uncle Dave Macon, the "Dixie Dewdrop." Uncle Dave was a vaudeville and medicine show entertainer born in 1870 in Warren County, Tennessee, and raised in Nashville, where his parents ran a boardinghouse that catered to theatrical people.[25] He brought to the Opry an encyclopedic range of folk material he had learned before the turn of the century not only from vaudeville entertainers but from railroaders, miners, and riverboatmen both black and white. He brought, too, a panoply of banjo styles which contemporary folk banjoists are still struggling to absorb. Bill Malone describes him as the "gay country gentleman" of the nineties, outfitted in a double-breasted waistcoat, wing collar, scarlet four-in-hand, and a black felt hat—altogether a figure who could easily have inspired the lovable old charlatan who became the Wizard of Oz in Dorothy's dream. With his uninterrupted patter of song, story, satire, anecdote, laughter, and joke, seasoned with wry social and political commentary, Uncle Dave was the living original of a character who years earlier, in the twilight of minstrelsy, had receded into the stereotypes of popular art, a folk savant through whom the rural imagination touched the wide teeming world beyond itself.

Acuff, whose career parallels Monroe's in many significant ways, was an original of another sort who, like Monroe, exploited the new radio medium as it had not been before and made a deliberate return to traditional music during a time when country music was becoming entangled in the popular imagination with the Hollywood cowboy. If Monroe's music was to bring to mind the Saturday night play parties of the backwoods, Acuff's evoked the Sunday morning meeting at the church. His singing was openly overwrought, sometimes actually bringing him to tears, and his repertoire favored tragic love and gospel songs, or moral fables such as "Wreck on the Highway," which issues the old warning against drink or, in this case, against drinking and driving. His voice, too—like Monroe's and like many mountain singers'—had, even when he was a young man, the ineffable quality of *age:* a certain angularity of tone, a quaver hidden in the recesses of pitch, a bite-like articulation that is produced somehow by a certain set of the jaw and attitude of the throat. Acuff sounded old. He styled himself as a fiddler—the fiddle being, in spite of Acuff's considerable ability, essentially a stage prop for him—stepping out from the hillbilly band which accompanied him to testify in song. His band, like Monroe's, rejected electric instruments in favor of fiddle, string bass, rhythm guitar, a banjo played clawhammer style, and a Hawaiian or "Dobro" guitar, and wore stereotyped rural costumes such as overalls or calico shirts and dungarees. In contrast to the exclusively male bluegrass group, Acuff's band regularly included a woman—a fact which some listeners found morally objectionable until the lady in question, banjo player Rachel Veach, was understood to be the "sister" of Dobro player Pete Kirby, "Bashful Brother Oswald." Though mandolin, accordion, harmonica, and piano were occasionally featured, no one instrument in Acuff's band ever found its way into the foreground as brilliantly or as decisively as in Monroe's music. Only the Dobro gained a continuous authority there, anticipating with its wailing, elastic tones—bluegrass musicians call it the "hound dog" guitar—the electric pedal-steel guitar that is now the signature of country-western music.

Altogether Acuff's music clearly displays, in a time of intense national crisis and swift social change, a species of withdrawal: "When Roy Acuff raised his voice in his mournful, mountain style," writes Malone, "he seemed to suggest all the verities for which Americans were fighting: home, Mother, and God." Even the Japanese, always astute observers of the American scene, recognized Acuff's importance when in battle on Okinawa they cried "To hell with Roy Acuff!"[26] With his long, lean face and protruding ears, the son of a Baptist minister, a boy raised on a tenant farm in the Smokies whose career in baseball, begun auspiciously at a Yankee training camp, had been cut short by a serious sunstroke, Acuff was an American original, one who, like Macon, was sinking into the past. His was an image which might still occasionally be seen, however, usually with a toothpick or chaw, on the pitcher's mound, winding up for a fastball, or, at a revival meeting, pounding a tightly clutched black book up on the pulpit. Acuff's famous "Wabash Cannonball" celebrated a mystical train that carried the hobo to a paradise of liberty and plenty, while his "Great Speckled Bird," the song which he introduced on the Opry—or as he would prefer it, the song which introduced him[27]—was an ecstatic vision of the evangelist imagination, and acquired the status of a hymn in the holiness churches of the South.

How was Monroe to enter this atmosphere of folk pageantry? In Macon and Acuff, a hillbilly minstrel and a pious knight, the Opry had figures born out of the two principal realities of southern rural life: isolation and strict morality. Like the medicine show doctor, the rounder, or any itinerant character, Uncle Dave embodied a multitude of influences from the exotic world outside—the minstrel stage and the southern city, the plantation, the chain gang, the riverboat—which through uncomplicated wisdom and humor he translated into an acceptable and intelligible southern rural idiom; young Acuff had the wholesome sentimentality and innocence that life on the farm was supposed to inculcate.

Listening to the Opry, however, one was compelled to acknowledge the obsolescence of southern rural images and values in order to take pleasure in theatrical and musical characterizations of them, however intended. The Opry required a characterization of rural music which might have the intrinsic interest of a living art, and the novelty of a popular one. Western swing, well established on the Opry in Pee Wee King—author of "Tennesse Waltz"—and his Golden West Cowboys, who joined in 1937, and in Paul Howard and the Arkansas Cotton Pickers,[28] was "modern" and a reliable sign that country musicians, if not country music, could enter the mainstream of popular music; but western swing, redolent of the large, smoke-filled dance hall, cheek-to-cheek dancing, and lipstick, face makeup, and beer, was built on a moral foundation radically opposed to southeastern rural morality, in a rural society which was, in effect, an urban society under agricultural conditions. Indeed both King and Howard had left the Opry by 1949, replaced by a new kind of country singer in Ernest Tubb, who joined in 1943, and Hank Williams, who joined in 1949. The genius of these men was that they grafted the country blues tradition in which they had been nurtured to the western motif, with all its associations, creating a complex expression of the struggle of rural conscience with modern urban life, effectively symbolized by the confusion and anonymity of the honky-tonk saloon. Williams's characteristically hillbilly voice, as pinched and nasal as Charlie Poole's, became in the new honky-tonk song a vessel overflowing the sorrow and strife; Tubb's more relaxed, avuncular style, obstinantly but ingratiatingly off-pitch, communicated something of the cowboy's clumsy honesty and charm. Yet this, too, was a kind of capitulation: though the honky-tonk singer was certainly contemporary and pertinent, in him the message of obsolescence, not only of a music but of attitudes, values, a way of life, and even of one's own self, was still more sweeping and insistent.

During his first few years on the Opry, Monroe and his band were noted for their absolute exclusion of nonsense and frivolity. Since rube and blackface comedy were a regular feature of Opry stage and travelling shows, and later of Monroe's own tent shows, the earnestness of the band must have been all the more striking by contrast. They presented their music in a thoroughly businesslike fashion, without extraneous comment or comic banter; the banjo, with its minstrel and medicine-show connotations, was absent. Wearing white shirts and neckties, jodphers, riding boots, and dark, narrow-brimmed Stetsons, the traditional costume of the Kentucky planter,[29] the band presented an image suggestive of the southern sheriff or federal ranger: "We wore riding pants and hats back in them days, and I suppose they thought we were the law," Monroe reports, recalling his efforts to find lodgings "in the roughest parts of town" for Deford Bailey, the black Opry mouth harp player; "nobody would ever bother us."[30] This manifestation of force, with its associated reserve, was an assertion of a high level of discipline and organization, and of the musician's radically revised attitude towards himself and his music. The band clearly regarded their presentation as a kind of mission, with heroic overtones, that did not require the implied apology of self-deprecation, self-parody, piety, moralism, theatrical emotional extravagance, electrical amplification, ostentation, a fourteen-piece band, or any daring incursions into formerly forbidden subject matter. As bluegrass music itself would later be, it was an effort to assert the band's cultural identity without bringing down upon it the immense burden of association, chiefly satiric, which that identity had acquired on the Opry and in hillbilly music generally.

Monroe's music during this period, which we know through recordings made for Victor in 1940 and 1941, much more closely resembles the earlier string bands such as Mainer's Mountaineers than it does the bluegrass music still five years ahead.[31] But there are certain eccentric new elements, especially in rhythm. What emerges most unexpectedly from these recordings, given the strong Appalachian character of the Monroe Brothers' music, is the extent of the blues influence upon Monroe, and a rhythmic phraseology very Latin in character—one almost senses the need of castanets and maracas—probably prompted by the popularity of Western swing.

The mountain blues, a style popularized by Jimmie Rodgers, was also practiced by many other hillbilly musicians, such as Frank Hutchison, Dick Justice, Clarence Greene, Daddy John Love of the aforementioned Mainer's Mountaineers, and, in Monroe's own band, guitar player Clyde Moody.[32] Like its black original, the mountain blues was a three-line stanza sung in a twelve-bar structure which allowed the musician, at the conclusion of each vocal phrase, at least one bar or more of instrumental or vocal improvisation: Rodgers introduced his "blue yodel" into this interval. Typically vocal phrasing, following the accents of speech, was set rhythmically in opposition to the beat, which was sometimes merely implied or understood rather than actually played on guitar, so that in a sense both guitar *and* voice could be said to have been playing against the beat. In "delta" blues, the Mississippi tradition represented by great primitive singers Robert Johnson, Charlie Patton, and Son House, the interplay between guitar and voice, owing to the almost complete reliance upon this conceptualized or conventionalized beat, was especially fluid, plastic, and, one might say, organic, since it was virtually free of mechanically repetitive elements. Often noted with a glass or metal slide on the left hand as well as with the fingertips, while being plucked, strummed, or percussively vamped with the right hand, the guitar could readily produce the sliding tones, flatted notes, and rich colors characteristic of the blues—effects which collectively made of the guitar, as many writers have noted, a second voice: in this way the solitary blues singer made a tiny society of himself, as required by the social character of African music. Frequently the guitar would echo the phrasing and intonation of the singer, or answer them, with instrumental cries, moans, wails of grief, or, on the other side of the emotional spectrum, bursts of laughter or exclamations of assent.

Of this extremely demanding technique, the white blues preserves many elements. Frank Hutchison, one of the earliest hillbilly musicians to record with a steel guitar, both sings and plays above the beat; but in general the white musician is distinguished from the black by his heavier reliance upon the instrument for a statement of the underlying meter. Dick Justice, for example, plays his "Brown Skin Blues" against a repeated ♫♫♩ (bumpa dede, bumpa dee); Clarence Greene's insinuating "Johnson City Blues" moves in a cycle of three phrases, one in each chord: ♩♫♩ ♫ (bump teede, bump t'dee), ♩ ♫♫♫♩ (bump dede dede dede dede dum), and ♩ ♫♩ ♫♫ (bump dede bum tee d'de). The basic unit of these phrases, it seems, is the eighth note, which the musician likes to group in twos and threes; though his accent may often fall on the offbeat, once the rhythmic pattern emerges from the repeated sequence, it tends to retain a steady duple time with a strong accent on the first beat of the measure, which is usually played by the thumb on one of the guitar's bass strings.

Of the white blues singers, however, the best known and most important, not only with respect to his influence upon Bill Monroe but to country music generally, is Mississippi-born Jimmie Rodgers. Like the country singers of today, Rodgers calls or croons out each line, adopting the nasal and at times impersonal tone of the mountain balladeer; set against his recitative is a heavily accented guitar phrase played with thumb and finger consisting of a weighted bass note followed by a stiff downward brush (boom chick, boom chick). With the emphatic opening syllables of the vocal phrase falling on or slightly after the bass note, and the guitar offbeat chord thrusting itself up into the lyric at predictable intervals, Rodgers brought into hillbilly music the easy swing of jazz. His work was firmly embedded in the popular music of the twenties and thirties—a fact which has helped to determine the ambivalent character of country music, which looks to the past and to the present at once. Rodgers recorded frequently with small jazz combos, which on one occasion included Louis Armstrong, and with Hawaiian bands, a craze of the twenties, whose falsetto tra-

dition influenced his own "blue yodel" far more than the Alpine yodel
to which it has been mistakenly compared.

On Monroe's Victor recordings, the rhythm is carried by the string
bass and by the guitar, vigorously and percussively strummed in largely closed-chord patterns, following the "sock rhythm" guitar of western
swing; these dense bursts of sound in rhythmically faceted phrases
penetrate the music nearly as effectively as a snare drum might, but
with considerable sacrifice of harmonic background. In "Dog House
Blues," for example, the eighth-note pattern is phrased in two
ways, as ♩ ♫♫♩ (bump teede teede dum) and as ♩ ♩ ♫♫ (bump
bump dede dede); the fiddle, imitating Monroe's voice, alternates by
"singing" the verse. Clyde Moody's "Six White Horses" and Rodgers's
"Blue Yodel No. 7," which Monroe sings, are both typical mountain blues, and each uses the familiar locomotive rhythmic phrase:
♪ ♫♫ ♫♫ (bump a-teede dedede). Significantly, though, these
phrasings are abandoned in Monroe's two mandolin pieces, "Tennessee
Blues" and "Honky Tonk Swing," in favor of a simple two-beat:
♩ ♩ (dumdee dumdee dumdee). Both of these are string boogies; in
any case, Monroe's mandolin, which plays what would be a boogie-
woogie pianist's right hand, requires the steady and continuous double
pulse of the guitar, or what would be the pianist's left.

Of the Victor recordings the most complex rhythmically is Monroe's
"Muleskinner Blues," a version of Jimmie Rodgers's "Blue Yodel
No. 8" with which Monroe made his debut on the Opry and which
continues to be one of Monroe's best-known songs. "Charlie and I had
a country beat, I suppose," Bill says of this piece, "but the beat in my
music—bluegrass music—started when I ran across 'Muleskinner
Blues'. . . . We don't do it the way Jimmie Rodgers sung it. It's speed-
ed up, and we moved it up to fit the fiddle [that is, moved it up in
pitch] and we have that straight time with it, driving time."[33] The
Victor "Muleskinner" does indeed move; but it rolls, not drives. While
its differences from Rodgers's blues version are pronounced, especially
in tempo, one does not feel suddenly in the presence of a new music.
As far as I know it is the only recording in existence of Monroe playing
guitar; he claimed that no other guitarist could play the rhythm he felt
appropriate for this song.[34] Of all the Victor cuts, "Muleskinner Blues"
is the one which one could most comfortably score in 4/4, rather than
in the more breathless 2/4 of the other up-tempo pieces, which may
be a consequence of Monroe's Latinate rhythmic phrasings, which he
delivers in an energetic, excited, almost irritable way. I can hear at
least five variations on the basic eight-unit phrase, as follows:

♩ ♫♫♫	bump dede dede teede
♫♫♫♫	bumpa dede dede dede
♩ ♫♫♫	bump d'de d'de d'de
♪ ♫♫♫	bump a-teede dedede
♩ ♫♫♫	bump a-dee a-dee a-dede

What Monroe heard, I'll venture to say, and what he was attempting to produce, was a layered polyrhythm, with accentual strata constantly shifting against one another, such as we normally hear in traditional jazz. But this requires, I think, the cooperation of several instruments, as well as a continuous, unaccented meter either wholly conceptual or expressed by a percussion instrument capable of many sharp articulations which further subdivide the basic pulse—a purpose for which mandolin and guitar are ill-suited, though drums or the aforementioned castanets or maracas are ideal. Monroe was perhaps foiled in his effort, too, by the persistent rhythmic pattern introduced by his fiddler, with its very strong accent on the third beat of the measure, or, if we are thinking of it in 2/4 time, on the downbeat: ♫♩ ♩ ♫ (bumpa de *tee* dede). This phrase, with its accent reaffirming the pattern of emphasis Monroe is attempting to dissolve through various syncopations, is disconcerting and generates, I think, considerable uneasiness—a rhythmic problem which bluegrass very effectively solves through the "driving time" to which Bill refers. In the Victor recordings we do not hear the emphatic offbeat or "backbeat" of bluegrass, except on occasion when Monroe concludes his mandolin breaks; he uses it as a rhythmic pathway by which to return to the band, and occasionally as a device for restoring a wandering tempo, but in an instant he has dissolved again into the steady double pulse.

This is not to say that the Victor sessions do not anticipate bluegrass: they do. Ralph Rinzler notes that in them Monroe has already established the eclectic pattern of his repertoire, cutting across the subjects which usually distinguished one kind of music, and one mode of address, from another.[35] There are five or perhaps six kinds of hillbilly music here, which taken together reflect the various segments of the Opry audience and embrace the kinds of music presented on the show as a whole. "Katy Hill" is a traditional hoedown fiddle tune, and "Orange Blossom Special" is a fiddler's tour de force popularized by Arthur Smith; "Cryin' Holy unto the Lord" is of course a gospel song, while "No Letter in the Mail" and "I Wonder if You Feel the Way I Do" are contemporary sentimental or "heart" songs in a typically hillbilly mode. The scope of these selections, including the aforementioned blues and the traditional dirge "In the Pines,"[36] suggests that Monroe's style, if not yet the integrated bluegrass style, was nevertheless sufficiently capacious to allow the ready adaptation of various materials otherwise irreconcilable: what would the effect have been, for instance, for a gospel quartet to liven up the mood set by some earnest recollection of sin, death, or suffering children with a riotous fiddle breakdown? Or for a giddy fiddle band to attempt to solemnize the proceedings with some ethereal hymn? Bill Monroe and the Blue Grass Boys undertook these juxtapositions with impunity, though in other respects they were not at first so vividly distinguishable from the other hillbilly string bands of the period, acknowledging the past, fairly readily absorbing influences from current popular practices, calling upon whatever internal resources they may have had, and as far as possible offering what their audiences expected and wanted; bluegrass music itself emerged as these expectations were met in the form of a unified musical idea.

The germ of that idea is perhaps to be found in the Victor "Katy Hill," played by Tommy Magness. "Katy Hill," Bill recalls, "had more in it when we recorded than it had ever had before. Those old-time fiddlers didn't have nobody to shove them along. Now Tommy Magness . . . it was right down his alley to get somebody behind him with that, because with that kind of little bow that he worked he could move you right along."[37] Magness plays the tune in the old-time shuffling style, in which the quick-moving bow couches the melody in a repetitive rhythmic phrase, producing roughly one note with every stroke. But Monroe and the Boys are driving Magness forward at a fantastic speed, far beyond what any dancers could accommodate. Quite remarkably, Magness keeps up his shuffle, with its strong offbeat, especially on the coarse part of the tune; on the fine part he may at times slip an extra note or two under the bow. Behind him the voices of the other band members are calling out encouragement: "Aw, play it!" or "Play it, son!" Monroe's falsetto laughter echoes in the background, as do the familiar calls of the square dance: "Swing your partner" and "Promenade!" It is no dance tune, of course, but, like the Skillet Lickers' "Soldier's Joy," a *representation* of one; beyond that, however, it is in a sense a representation of the fiddler himself who is being put forward and tested to the limit. It is as if Monroe intends this recording of "Katy Hill" to stand for all time as an example of a Georgia fiddle tune.

During World War II Monroe did not record, but had enormous success as a performer. Before setting out in 1941 on a tent show which included the Opry's blackface comedians Jamup and Honey, Monroe hired a banjo player and comedian named Dave Akeman, or "Stringbean," who also performed from time to time in blackface with a portly comedian named Bijou. Stringbean, playing the banjo in clawhammer style, restored the band's original link to the minstrel tradition, or what Monroe calls the "old-time years-ago flavor."[38] He took on an accordion player, too, in the person of Mrs. Howdy Forrester, his fiddler's wife; though he ultimately dropped that instrument, he had good authority for including it in the fact that his mother had played accordion. At one point the band included a harmonica player as well. During this period between late 1941 and early 1945, the band was a rather typical hillbilly orchestra—five stringed instruments and an accordion accompanying a personality whose reputation for playing and singing was thrusting him increasingly into the foreground; during this period, too, Monroe began to distinguish himself through costume from his band members, first with a darker hat, or a lighter shirt and hat, or a sportjacket. The sound of this band is richer and fuller than that of the earlier Blue Grass Boys, but at the same time more homogeneous, more uniform, without either the rough textures of the old dance bands or the intricate design, the fire, or the brilliance of bluegrass. The fiddle, in the fluid swing style characteristic of the period in country music, led the way, while Monroe in his mandolin playing restored some of the effortless falling or spilling movement characteristic of his days with Charlie, as if he were always slightly ahead of the beat, or in flight from it. In this band the individual instrument was virtually eclipsed, and though instrumental solos emerged from the orchestral background as a matter of regular practice, these were not intended as displays of virtuosity, nor did they entirely draw the instrument out of its orchestral setting through rhythmic or melodic improvisation. The musical foreground was instead reserved primarily for Monroe's lead singing. It was with this sort of accompaniment that Monroe recorded his first hit songs, "Kentucky Waltz" and "Footprints in the Snow," which, as Neil Rosenberg points out, were typical of most of the era's hillbilly hits.[39] Indeed they closely resemble the kind of music which *Charlie* Monroe was playing with his Kentucky Pardners, and, if Monroe's recordings can be taken as a guide, there is no other point in his career at which his voice so much resembles his brother's. Can the popularity of these two recordings be at least partly attributed to the likenesses, as well as the differences, between the two brothers, whose successful career together must still have been alive in the memories of the hillbilly audience? In any case, it was with "Footprints in the Snow" and "Kentucky Waltz" that Monroe attracted the large audiences to whom the original bluegrass band—Monroe, Wise, Flatt, Scruggs, Rainwater on bass, a band assembled only months after the commercial release of the two songs—would play.

How does it happen that this string orchestra and star singer, so like the country groups of the period, moving inexorably towards a more commercial style and away from the traditional past, became in a matter of months the champions of a restored traditional music and the type of an entirely new genre? The "foreground" into which Monroe had thrust himself, shared by Acuff, Autry, Eddy Arnold, Red Foley, and others, was swiftly taking on the character of a retailer's convention, soon to become a vulgar and glamorous hillbilly Hollywood, dominated by stars, promoters, and personalities, all exploiting the new urban, commercial, and popular market which the social upheavals of war had engendered around country music. This new concentration of merchandizing activity, its penetration of its widened audience extended by a quick succession of technological innovations—the long-play record, high-fidelity, the 45 rpm single, magnetic recording tape, and, of course, television—was a historical vacuum into which the entire musical heritage of the southern white would soon rush and in time be swallowed up by its own commercialism, just as twenty years before hill music and the blues had swept into the new regional and ethnic markets created by radio and phonograph and been dissolved by the Great Depression.

I do not say that Monroe felt entirely at home in this new environment; in fact I'm certain he did not. To many who recall the period he often seemed sullen, curt, or merely indifferent, a fact which perhaps suggests the price he paid in personal isolation for his keen competitiveness and which he himself acknowledges: "I would talk short to alot of people. . . . I had all my life ahead of me then, you see."[40] No doubt he felt more at home on the road, among rural folk, with his own Blue Grass Boys, his gospel quartet, blackface comedian, buck dancer, and girl singer, old-time fiddler, twenty-six men, seven trucks, and a circus tent. Nevertheless Monroe was solidly established in the popular imagination as the Opry's leading exponent, as "The Grand Ole Opry Song" puts it, of "them old Kentucky blues." The Opry, in other words, had fixed his image and secured his livlihood, and it was consequently *within* those limits that his career must develop. It could not drift uptown, to the honky-tonks, taverns, and eventually even the nightclubs there; and it could not stay the same: "If I had got up there and sang everything solos with a little fiddle music behind me or a guitar," Monroe recalls, ". . . it would have got awful old."[41]

It remained to cultivate his richest resource—his own music, which lay fallow in the hillbilly orchestra, not yet a bluegrass band, which stood behind him. His band had receded, indeed, into a visual and aural background, rural, regional, and parochial, with a poignant archaism still lingering in its sound and image. Who could look at dear old Stringbean, bandy-legged and lantern-jawed, who handled his banjo as if it were a fishing pole, or at corn-fed Chubby Wise, or at demure Sally Ann Forrester wearing a rose in her raven hair, or at Lester Flatt, who always looked as if he had just been to the barber for his first haircut, and not feel convinced that Monroe had somehow put together the most authentic country band imaginable? This band had become, practically and morally, his musical instrument, and had thereby acquired a voice: I do not mean a singing voice merely, but a channel through which a variety of archaic sounds, sharpened for the purpose, could be communicated individually from the musical promentory upon which Monroe stood. A social music, that is, now flowed through a channel that individualized and personalized it, dissolving the old synthesis and demanding a new one which would draw the newly awakened voices into an ordered interplay with a single voice, at any given moment, leading the way. This new synthesis, when it resolved itself, filled the gap which had opened between Monroe and his band with a new music whose subject matter was "the old southern sound" itself. Monroe had emerged, and moreover could be *seen* and *heard* to have emerged, from a humble and rustic world into the limelight, a triumph as gratifying to the imagination as that of the ploughboy who wins fame on the baseball diamond; and he had stepped forward as a *representative* of that world. *Through* him the old music, and the sense of life of which it was the auditory impression, flowed out of the hills and out of the past into the present.

A resynthesis of the old southern sound required a wide, unbroken, closely-woven band of tones, drawn through the teeth of a finely divided meter, which might carry several bright threads of improvisation into the orchestral design without tangling or occluding them. This conception, in part rhythmic, in part acoustic, was of course the warp and woof of hot jazz, which perhaps suggests why, at this juncture, Monroe added to his band two musicians whose experience had taken them into swing and jazz on the one side and ragtime on the other— Chubby Wise and Earl Scruggs. Wise had been playing in a western swing band; Scrugg's three-finger technique issued from the western Carolinas, where it had evolved from the ragtime style popularized years earlier by vaudevillians such as Vess Ossman and Fred Van Eps; thus though it was a bit old-fashioned in itself, it was the most intricate and sophisticated banjo technique extant, outside of the "classical" or parlor style, which had become esoteric. In fact Monroe had attempted to import hot jazz directly into his band as the swing bands had done, through a *tenor* banjo player, one Jim Andrews, the man whom Scruggs replaced and probably the most forgotten man in country music;[42] but in spite of the resemblances between the tenor banjo technique and Monroe's own mandolin style, the tenor's crusty, congested sound brought only something of the rough texture of urban jazz into the band, while leaving the weave itself behind. How, then, to impart an idea fundamentally African, and in jazz replete with urbanity, to southern white rural musicians? How, indeed, to do with strings what jazzmen did readily with drums, horns, and a piano, especially when Monroe's most exhaustive efforts on guitar and mandolin seemed to have shown the impossibility of doing so?

The answer was to touch Afro-American music, black music, at an earlier point in its evolution than that which it had reached in the twentieth century, at a point when it, too, was a rural, even a frontier music. To touch it, in fact, just where old-time music, through the minstrel show, had touched it: on the plantation, where, among plantation slaves, the "old southern sound" had been born. Not surprisingly, the old southern sound was locked in that most original of plantation instruments, the five-string banjo.

Chapter 4

Banjo
African Rhythms and
the Bluegrass Beat

The instrument proper to them," wrote Thomas Jefferson of the plantation Negroes of Virginia in 1781, "is the Banjar, which they brought hither from Africa, and which is the original of the guitar, its chords"—he means strings—"being precisely the four lower chords of the guitar."[1] Jefferson's note, which suggests that he had observed very closely the playing of the banjo or had even handled one himself, thus symbolically grafting black culture forever to the destiny of the American republic, simply repeats the testimony of a wide variety of letters, journals, memoirs, and the like which report banjos among black slaves throughout the slave-holding provinces of the New World from the late seventeenth century onwards. Though it went by several names—banza, banjar, banjaw, banjah, and so on, even, happily, "merrywang"—it was usually a hollowed calabash or gourd, later the hoop of a cheesebox, stretched over with hide or skin and fitted with a long fretless neck and strings of vine, gut, silk, or wire. This instrument appeared in Martinique in 1678, in Jamica in 1689, in Barbados in 1708, and by the mid-eighteenth century had become a familiar property of plantation life in Maryland and Virginia. E. P. Christy, banjo player and leader of one of the most famous minstrel troupes, heard the banjo in New Orleans' Congo Square in the late 1820s; by the 1840s the banjo had entered the circus and the minstrel show and with the spread of those traditions became a favorite instrument North and South, ultimately to be offered in shops, gleaming with the pride of industrial manufacture, to young ladies and gentlemen who might amuse themselves with intricate renderings of

"Darling Nellie Gray" or the "Moonlight Sonata" in a refined, guitar-like plucking style. It required about 300 years, then, to transform the banjo into America's "only indigenous folk instrument"; but the instrument which an English slave trader, and later an English physician, found in Sierra Leone in the eighteenth century and which an adventurer named Jobson found on the "river Gambra" in West Africa in 1621, the fretless African folk banjo, is still to be found, still in essentially its original form, in the mountains of Virginia and the Carolinas and at university folk festivals played by young afficianados who have constructed them from mail-order kits.

It made a "wild pleasing melancholy sound," a poet wrote of the banjo in 1763. "A sentimental and melancholy music," averred a French bishop in 1810. According to a touring European pianist, Henri Herz, the notes of the banjo were "solemn, resonant and harmonious." But how were these notes, this "sad and plantive melody from another hemisphere," produced? Some reports say the banjoist "beat" on the strings; others say he plucked them with his fingers like guitar strings; still another claims to have seen the banjoist "strum as on a Moorish mandolin." But a Negro folksong, cited by the Rev. Jonathan Boucher, a philologist and loyalist who returned to England from Virginia in 1775, very nearly pictures the style for us: "Negro Sambo play fine banjer/Make his fingers go like handsaw."[2] The image is cloudy and indefinite; but anyone who has seen the mountain frailing or clawhammer style will detect it in the song's metaphor, which, seen in this light, becomes, like all good metaphors, amazingly precise. The clawhammer style, as Robert Winans has impressively argued,[3] entered mountain music during the middle of the nineteenth century through that epoch's most widespread and popular mode of entertainment, the minstrel show—a grotesque and lovely wildflower which had bloomed in the sociocultural hinterland between the races which has since proved so fertile and been so intensively cultivated. A fuller discussion of minstrelsy must wait until our concluding chapter; let us merely note in passing that through the minstrel show, and very likely through more direct forms of transmission as well, mountaineers adopted from the plantation an African instrument and a way of playing it fundamentally African in conception.

"Listening to the Negro banjo players," Henri Herz wrote in 1866, "I have pondered the mysterious law of rhythm which seems to be a universal law. . . . In obeying the need to put rhythm in their music the blacks act by some sort of instinct."[4] What is this "mysterious law" and in what sense does the banjo—on the plantation, in minstrelsy, in mountain music, or in bluegrass—obey it?

Whether it is a gopher hide stretched over a biscuit tin or a two-thousand dollar, machine-made beauty of curley maple, bellmetal bronze, and gold plate, the banjo is visibly a drum: a drum with strings. As such it perfectly embodies the most elementary law of Afro-American music, which is its speech-like coordination of rhythm and melody. As the various names applied to it reveal—rapping, beating, frailing, clawhammer—the minstrel or mountain style of banjo playing is highly percussive, laminating rhythmic and melodic phrases together in repeated motives. In the clawhammer style the banjoist, using the force of his wrist and sometimes of his forearm, brings the back of his fingernail down upon the string, snapping it and striking the banjo head more or less forcefully at the terminus of its arc; this action encapsulates the note in a hard percussive shell which dissolves with the decay of the tone. "Sound the note on the first string by letting the fingernail slide off," wrote minstrel Phillip Rice in 1858, "then sound the thumb string immediately after with the thumb."[5] The banjoist's fingers are crooked, quite as if he were grasping a tiny invisible handsaw and attempting to divide some diamond hard substance with it; because the style produces discrete notes, but with a motion that appears to pass the hand over all the strings in a stroke, it could easily have been interpreted by an observer either as plucking or strumming. In fact it is both. Half the beauty of this style—and in the often delicate hands of mountain banjoists it is indeed "solemn, resonant and harmonious"—consists in the bright, sudden flight of pure tone out of a furze of percussive sounds. Percussive effects, anthropologists Alan Merriam and Richard Waterman have agreed, are the "deep, basic, organizational principle underlying African music."[6] But the "mysterious law" which Henri Herz observed at work in the black banjo players of Charleston over a century ago reflects still more fundamental principles of which an interest in percussion is but one expression. Black music, wrote an ex-slave named Robert Anderson, "is largely a process of rhythm."[7] But as Herz's remark suggests, it is the musician, not the music, that is rhythmical, and it is the musician's activity which either establishes or fails to establish through rhythm that structure of time, the "meter," with relation to which we perceive the order of the music. Meter is a pattern. Rhythm is a force—the force of the musician's action registered upon us in the form of an involuntary nervous response whose repetition the musician teaches us to anticipate, opening a channel in us through which time created and shaped by the musician may flow.

In European music meter is usually understood to be a regular distribution of accents. But accents originate in the musician; it is the musician who by means of accent establishes the regular alternation of strong and weak beats we call the "meter." Just as in geometry a point must be represented by a dot and the distance between two points by a line, meter as such cannot be explicitly present in the music except as it is indicated by rhythm. In European music, it appears, rhythm has been absorbed into meter; or perhaps it would be more accurate to say that meter has been absorbed into rhythm. Either way, the musician strives to distribute rhythmic accents as the meter requires, building through rhythm a wide avenue of expectation on a foundation of measured time. It is just this precise synchronization of the rhythmic accent to the meter, which the musician trains for years to accomplish, that makes possible the complex architectonic structures of sound which are the great marvel of European music, the "esthetic stasis" of which Joyce's Stephen Dedalus speaks, one "called forth, prolonged and at last dissolved by . . . the rhythm of beauty."[8]

Because it is rhythm which reveals the meter to us, there would be no "measure" in the music itself without some form of rhythmic accent—only an unbroken and continuous succession of intervals of time, a "tempo." Thus the measure is at bottom a *rhythmical*, not a metrical, feature, though musical notation has conferred metrical status upon it. Let us abandon the measure, then, and the musical score altogether, and, like a good jazz drummer, use rhythmic accents to suggest several groupings of notes or "rhythms" at once, bringing them into a contrasting relation to one another and building our music upon tempo alone. For the ear can do what the eye reading a score cannot—that is, attend to a number of rhythms at once. Let us, in other words, give the measure and all the rhythmic variation of which it admits to the musician, who will dispose of it as he will upon the stream of time, leaving the tempo to be inferred from, or even discovered in, the variety of contrasting and interlocking rhythms. The capacity to make this inference is what Richard Alan Waterman calls the "metronome sense," and from it all the rhythmic characteristics of African music follow almost inevitably.[9]

The typical African ensemble, with its solo cantor and chorus, its handclappers and gong or bellringers, its three or four drummers, is capable of at least eight, and often as many as eleven, simultaneous rhythms which move across one another in a myriad and multilevelled retrograde motion which to the Western ear sounds like syncopation of an almost supernatural order. It is as if the bar—and remember that the bar is now in the hands of the musician—is continually shifting; rhythmic waves arise in ghostly multiplicity out of the primary wave, retreating and advancing in sinuous occilations and weaving in amongst one another. Yet as A. M. Jones and others have pointed out, African music is not "syncopated," not at least from the musician's point of view, for no *one* rhythm has metrical status;[10] the *effect* of syncopation, however, arises naturally from the crossing of rhythmic lines, since the pattern voiced by one drum or gong, and the "measure" it evokes to the imagination, will seem in an instant to have been effaced by the accents of another, and that by another, in a cycle of vanishing and recurring sequential patterns which utterly defies the conventions of musical notation. "Any attempt to write African music in the European manner," writes Jones, "with bar lines running right down the score and applying to all the contributing instruments simultaneously, is bound to lead to confusion. It gives the impression that all but one of the contributors is highly syncopated, and the multitude of tied notes and off-accents makes the mind reel."[11]

But what is to prevent this confusion in the audial sphere? As Father Jones notes, it is just the opposition of rhythmic lines which wins the independence of rhythm by setting the bar in motion against the metronomic background; this contrary or retrograde motion is familiar in Afro-American as well as African music. But rhythm is compelling: how is the musician, having taken rhythm into his own hands, to hear the rhythm playing next to him, which he must in order to construct his opposing pattern, and at the same time remain independent of it?

Let us shift our perspective a bit and regard "percussiveness" from the melodic side and say, not that African music is "percussive," for this betrays our habit of identifying music with melody, but that African rhythms, of which the music is largely fashioned, are melodic. More precisely, let us say, keeping in mind the banjo's ringing, that the African musician manages the flow of time through rhythms carried out in regularly recurrent pitches or by a repeated regular variation in pitch. Imagine playing melodies on a drum capable of changes in pitch, as in fact all African drums are, and you will have the idea. "When Africans beat drums," writes Father Jones, "they play *tunes* on their drums."[12] Or think of the West African xylophone or slit gong, which marry rhythmic and melodic movement in tones produced by striking. One need not travel so far, of course. There is scarcely a melody instrument in Afro-American music, whether banjo, fiddle, guitar, piano, or horn, that is not played to some degree percussively, a rhythm not terraced by a pattern of notes, or a melody whose own rhythms do not stand out boldly against the rhythmic background of the music as a whole.

Whether he is playing a drum or a xylophone, a banjo or a piano, the African musician and his Afro-American counterpart attack the note with precision and force, so that we can know exactly where in time he has placed it. But the attack is absorbed at once into a tone— a tone which dissolves immediately, like that of the drum, or one which lingers. In the first instance the percussive note fully communicates its impact and sharply enunciates its place in time; for this reason "percussiveness" and rhythm, percussion instruments and rhythm are virtually indistinguishable from one another. In the second instance, depending upon the durability of the tone, the rhythmic accent fades into the harmonic sphere and may even dissolve in it altogether. But in both instances the rhythmic pattern is wed to a sequence of pitches whose repetition establishes a *melodic* image of the rhythm, independent of other rhythms as melody is independent of any other melody— by virtue of its particular pitches and their particular sequence. Thus each rhythm has its own melodic setting, which secures its independence, protects the independence of other rhythms by curbing the power of its accents to influence them, and provides the basis for their interaction in the harmonic sphere.

No abstract numerical formula, conceptually fixed for the musician, accompanies the African's execution of his art.[13] He conceives his rhythms aurally—as particular sounds or even as utterances—and generates these sounds to the fullest extent of the ear's capacity to perceive them, both with respect to the number of rhythms which can occupy audial space without congestion and with respect to the minute intervals of time necessary to integrate them.[14] Thus the technique of improvisation, so inseparably a part of Afro-American music in all its forms, is the inevitable corollary of those aural laws which deliver rhythm and through it the passage of time itself to the musician. Aural conditions in fact abolish the composer as such; we have only the performer, improvising in a structure established by the playing of his fellows out of materials belonging to the tradition in which all are working.

Though demonstrably related in principle, African and Afro-American music do not resemble one another in any obvious way. The music of the African drum ensemble seems to proliferate, blossoming out of itself in shifting patterns of percussion; Afro-American music, in North America at least, is more linear; it seems to roll or drive, in an atmosphere of rhythmic tension sometimes transfigured by a unique rhythmic bouyancy called "swing." The great proportion of African-inspired American music in its folk forms—the banjo-fiddle breakdown, the blues, ragtime and boogie-woogie, early jazz, and bluegrass—retains the duple and triple meters of the British, French, and other European musics such as the march whose conventions the African musician in America adopted, or was forced to adopt. We hear these meters, arrayed in African fashion upon a regular variation in pitch, in the clawhammer banjo, in the hoedown fiddler's bowing pattern, in the blues and ragtime pianist's bass figures, in the extended rhythmic lines of the early jazz band, with its rhythm section compounded of drums, banjo, and piano, and in the pulse of the rhythm guitar in bluegrass or rock-and-roll. It is true that not all these forms fashion melodies on the European model—blues certainly does not—but in general Afro-American music carries out rhythmic effects far more thoroughly in the harmonic sphere than does the African, though both are allied to regular variations in pitch. In North America drums have been suppressed since slavery days in favor of melody instruments, as they have not, for instance, in Latin America, where African drum music still flourishes. One wonders, indeed, if the general absence of drums in country music does not somehow ultimately go back to the slave owner's fear of the African talking drum and its power to inspire insurrection. This emphasis upon melody instruments, in any case, accounts for the urgent and inexorable forward motion of the mountain breakdown, of blues, jazz, bluegrass, and kindred forms. For just as rhythm, in the African drum ensemble, follows a melodic path, so melody, in the Afro-American milieu of fleetingly but perceptibly sustained tones, takes on the force of rhythm and imparts its qualities to that force. Thus the ubiquitous "walking" bass fiddle, the boogie bass figure that sounds like twenty tons of locomotive bearing down on you, the galloping jazz rideout that a gang of bank robbers could escape on, the bluegrass breakdown that could power the Indy 500. Rhythmic tension, too, increases markedly in the harmonic sphere, for strictly percussive rhythms, like star systems, are largely empty space, the percussions marking only *points* in time; when opposed they can pass through one another without trepidation. But tones are full of time, and in a medium of tones opposed rhythms generate a kind of rhythmic incandescence.

Can African rhythmic laws be said to obtain in a music which retains the European meters, particularly duple time? Like his African counterpart, the Afro-American musician delights in rhythmic opposition. In Afro-American music the European meter is given *independent* aural expression as an unaccented beat, almost always in the bass and almost always in conjunction with a melodic phrase or line, sometimes, but not always, punctuated by a regular accent. This becomes the fundamental rhythmic wave against which the musician directs his own rhythmic forces, which may include pitch and tone color as well as accent and percussion. Any repeated anticipation or delay of the expected beat, then, will establish a rival succession of beats, while a misplaced accent will seem either to shift the measure towards an adjacent beat or to suggest another rhythm altogether, even while the imagination retains an impression of the fundamental rhythm. To be effective, of course, the misplaced accent must be heard: thus though it may occur in the bass, as it does in blues piano, it more often occurs in some percussion instrument or an instrument played percussively, or else above the bass in a succession of chords or a melody line; and it is here, too, in the melody line, that anticipations or delays of the beat, regular or irregular, stand out most vividly against the fundamental rhythm and hence work to best effect.[15]

Because the fundamental rhythm is always present, though not always assertively put forward, the Afro-American musician perhaps can be said to "syncopate" the rhythm; but it is not, as the term implies, a rhythmic deviation or irregularity. It is a continuous, unremitting, sometimes remorseless rhythmic opposition (Stravinsky found it amusing) whose effect is rhythmic tension growing in direct proportion to the degree and intensity of that opposition—a tension which can be resolved only in the mysterious transfiguration of swing. Thus the African and the Afro-American practices, though essentially the same, produce markedly different effects. Because we identify the music—the song, the tune, the "melody"—with the prevailing fundamental rhythm, to oppose that rhythm is in some sense to oppose the music; and the character of that opposition largely determines the character of the music. The jazz musician, for instance, both plays the beat and, as Langston Hughes puts it, plays *with* the beat, in relative immunity to its accents; with the evolution of jazz he has won an ever more complete independence from it, learning in time to subdue and finally eliminate accents from the fundamental rhythm and, in free jazz, to banish the fundamental rhythm altogether, playing in layers of tempo alone.[16] Piano ragtime, one of the precursors of jazz, legislates a kind of treaty with the beat, integrating a melody based on eighth notes into a rhythm based on quarter notes and thus "syncopating" it with an agreeable regularity which can easily become mechanical and in fact did become literally mechanical in the player piano. But in the mountain breakdown, in blues, bluegrass, rhythm-and-blues, indeed in all the folk forms of Afro-American music, the fundamental rhythm meets with persistent, systematic, and unyielding opposition, joined with the musician in sportive play, or in a kind of eager rivalry, or at times in mortal combat.

Since the fundamental rhythm has, as we've seen, two components, an underlying metronomic beat and a "pulse," or accentual grouping of beats, it will require two kinds of opposition working together to "cross" the fundamental rhythm: a misplaced or off-accent and what is called syncopation by subdivision or "divisive meter," which splits the beat into two or three parts. These two kinds of syncopation recall John Work's remark that "in all authentic American Negro music, the rhythms may be divided roughly into two classes—rhythm based on the swinging of the head and body and rhythms based on the patting of hands and feet."[17] Here are the two characteristic rhythmic motions of Afro-American music: a reciprocal or back-and-forth motion and a continuous rolling, flowing, or driving—that is to say, "rock" and "roll," whose interdependency reflects the conjunction of pulse and beat in the fundamental rhythm and is the heart of swing.

Perhaps the most familiar form of off-accent in Afro-American music is the tendency to emphasize the normally "weak" beats in 4/4 time, beats two and four; the jazz drummer calls these accents "bombs." When this emphasis is stronger than the normally "strong" beat, it seems to throw the measure back upon itself, to the preceding adjacent beat; hence the term *backbeat*. The action seems to throw off the restraints of the fundamental rhythm, only to have them converge again at the next beat—like Bartholomew and his ten thousand hats. Consequently with each thrust the musician seems to emerge anew from the music, describing a progressive forward motion, a *push* whose force depends upon the aggressiveness and intensity of the accent relative to the downbeat. The rhythm seems to be shifting constantly in a direction contrary to the flow of the music, an image and its drifting after-image, from whose opposition a kind of swing—a rocking or swaying between adjacent beats—can potentially emerge. Though we have but one meter, the rhythm has in effect been crossed by an image of itself removed from it by the interval of one beat.

We seldom hear a strong backbeat without some accompanying form of divisive rhythm whose object is to attack the fundamental rhythm where it hurts—under the beat itself. A subdivided rhythm, in a jazz drummer's surging rolls for example, seems to undermine the beat with a spreading tide of percussion whose unbroken and undulating surface, swelling with the myriad occilations of divided beats, the metronomic equivalent of backbeat rock, seems to lift the fundamental rhythm off its foundations in a state of suspension or bouyancy. While the backbeat sets the rhythmic accent in motion against its metronomic base, the subdivided rhythm dissolves the base itself, setting rhythmic accents afloat on a more uniform and continuous rhythmic plane which develops below the level of rhythmic accent. Thus the fundamental rhythm loses its metrical status, becoming merely a convention around and against which the musician is free to play. A music which requires the complete autonomy of the soloist, such as modern jazz, usually calls upon some form of subdivided rhythm, the most extreme form perhaps being John Coltrane's "sheets of sound," while a music which favors powerful rhythmic tension such as rock—the name is precise— will rely upon the heavy backbeat that locks the musician in perpetual struggle with the fundamental rhythm.

A moment's thought will reveal that these two kinds of syncopation, "rock" and "roll," are at heart the same: both place a beat or accent *between* adjacent beats or accents of the fundamental rhythm; both are thus cross rhythms directed against the interlocking levels, metronomic and accentual, of the European metrical structure. Where the European meter prevails in rhythm, then—and outside of modern jazz it prevails in virtually all Afro-American music—it is their *conjunction* that completes the bifurcation of rhythm and meter, bringing a rich and gratifying sense of rhythmic completion.

The bluegrass banjo roll, pioneered by Earl Scruggs, is a subdivided rhythm that by dissolving the metronomic footing of the music completes the uncoupling of rhythm and meter. Monroe's string band, with its hoedown fiddle, clawhammer banjo, jazz guitar, and hillbilly mandolin, was already congested with accents and with the rhythms those accents redundantly enforced; with its unbroken and continuous stream of notes sharply voiced in bright, acid tones, the banjo roll broke up this congestion, bringing about a kind of rhythmic division of labor in which several strata of rhythm were distributed among the instruments—metronomic line to the bass, pulse to the guitar, offbeat to the mandolin or banjo vamp, subdivided rhythm to the banjo roll—while fiddle, mandolin, and banjo alternately carried improvised melodic lines rhythmically as flexible as any jazz horn player's. This is not to say that the banjo player does not call upon rhythmic accents; if he did not his music would seem little more than the mechanical ratta-tat-tat of a machine gun. But he always does so in a matrix which is consistently and thoroughly subdivided, from which the *idea* of the subdivided rhythm is never absent, and which has, by virtue of its African-inspired amalgamation to melodic movement, an unusual power to impart the idea to other musicians. Like the bones of the minstrel band, whose precision, Hans Nathan writes, "lent articulation to the ensemble," the banjo's flowing, sinuous, twisting ribbon of notes fills the entire length and breadth of the music, outlining its rhythmic infrastructure, sharpening and brightening its image, running within the music like a stream of water, now in a broad torrent, now in intricate rivulets below ground.[18]

What is the Scruggs style? The precise pattern differs from one banjo player to another; but basically the Scruggs style consists of a chain of eighth notes in 4/4 time played by the thumb, index, and middle fingers in a series of variable three-finger sequences or "rolls" which naturally group the notes into threes or, in some versions of the style, into two groups of three and one of two.[19] What is significant, of course, is the unstinting use of three fingers, one note assigned to each, in a continual mutual interplay. This provides for an unhesitating and often astonishingly rapid delivery of notes, since each finger has a full beat to recover itself for the next strike, and, since the bar always occurs in the middle of a roll, ties measures together in an unbroken train. At its most elementary level, then, the Scruggs style is a series of ascending and descending arpeggios, usually in the harmonic triad, dancing in a glow of dissonances arising from the unchanging tone of the fifth string and from the timbre of the banjo itself. Rhythmically, the arpeggio, which has been eliminated from the newer "Keith," or chromatic, banjo style, is important: it is the arpeggio which gives the bluegrass banjo its drive, using melodic figures to maintain the independence of two rhythmic lines, one duple and the other triple, continually sliding against one another. Advanced variations of the style exploit the mobility of the thumb, which, Scruggs writes in his own teaching manual, "is most capable of bringing out the stronger melody notes"[20] and which by substituting itself for the index finger at appropriate points can sustain the roll and the melody at once. Altogether it is a rangy, treasonous, brilliant sound, and a sound full of the South.

What, finally, can be the connection between a North Carolina three-finger banjo style and African or Afro-American music, especially when the three-finger style is apparently derived from guitar or "parlor" techniques and grew up among white musicians who until this century had had little contact, as far as we know, with blacks?

Studies in African music show that the African builds his rhythms out of eighth notes grouped in twos and threes; the independence of one rhythm from another is thus secured on the strength of a simple numerical principle, that of odd and even. "To beat 3 against 2," writes Father Jones, "is to them no different from beating on the first beat of each bar."

> We have to grasp the fact that if from childhood you are brought up to regard beating 3 against 2 as being just as normal as beating in synchrony, then you develop a two-dimensional attitude to rhythm which we in the West do not share. This bi-

podal conception is so much a part of the African's nature
that he can with ease not only play a broken pattern in duple
time, containing notes and rests of various values against a
similarly broken pattern in the time-relation of 3 against 2, but
he can also do this when the bar-lines of his short triplets are
staggered permanently with the duple bars, and, still further,
he has no need to regard these short triplets as triple at all,
and can perfectly well play a duple pattern at the speed of the
individual notes of these short triplets.[21]

This ingenious African practice survives here as a basic rhythmic
figure, ♫ ♩ ♫ , heard in whole or part throughout the Americas,
particularly in the Caribbean.[22] In North American black music it has
become *the* characteristic form of syncopation—groups of three in duple meter—whose lineage extends from the minstrel banjo through
the cakewalk to piano ragtime. It is richly represented in blues
rhythms, old-time fiddle, and jazz solo work, where French jazz critic
Andre Hodeir finds in the "ternary division of the beat" the basis of
the swing phrase;[23] it is the basic syncopation of boogie-woogie, and
it appears with perfect simplicity in Earl Scruggs's bluegrass banjo
roll.

From a strictly mechanical viewpoint, Earl Scruggs's three-finger
bluegrass banjo style does resemble the classical or "parlor" style of
banjo picking and quite possibly developed out of it, mechanically. The
style had a continuing currency in Scruggs's native North Carolina.
But the classical arpeggiated or "guitar" style plucked or pulled the
strings with the *flesh* of the fingertips, in an effort to subdue the banjo's
characteristic twang. As Frederick Bacon, the banjo manufacturer,
teacher, and champion put it in 1904: "Strings should be picked with
tips of fingers, and never get under strings far enough to lift them
up—giving the disagreeable snapping tone. *Avoid picking the strings
with the nails.*"[24] Like the highly percussive ragtime banjo style of
Fred Van Eps and the ragtime-influenced style of Charlie Poole, both
of whom plucked the strings with their fingernails, the Scruggs style
overthrows Bacon's dictum with wild abandon, using metal finger picks
shaped like tiny spoons which pull the string and snap it back, allowing
it to slide off the curved surface of the pick just as in the clawhammer
style it slides off the fingernail; in fact the finger pick is actually an
artificial fingernail affixed to the pads of the finger, in effect rotating
the fingertip a half turn. Thus the banjo player gains the guitarist's
dexterity and precision, while retaining the minstrel's sliding nail,
whence comes that unique projectile-like note, one which fixes upon

its own center from a ragged margin of off-frequencies and blazes through it, trailing the parched dust of grazed rock. Indeed some bluegrass banjo pickers dig more earnestly for the old clawhammer sound by filing or bending their picks, burying the note more deeply in the soil of friction and stress, so that its bursting through is proportionately more hairy and wild—that "disagreeable" quality in which all the character and all the beauty of the old banjo tone resides.

The bluegrass and clawhammer styles resemble one another, too, in the regular chiming of the thumb string: "We'll dance all night, an' all de day," goes an old Virginia plantation song, "an make de banjo chime."[25] Or, as the minstrel songs tirelessly repeat, "You could hear dem banjos ringing." A persistant tradition attributes the banjo's thumb or "fifth" string to the minstrel Joel Walker Sweeney. Its unchanging "drone" note has been compared to the drone of the Scottish pipes, suggesting a Scots-Irish influence in the mountain banjo and a plausible analogy to the frequent use of drones inherited from Ulster fiddlers who came to Appalachia near the end of the eighteenth century. But there is every reason to suppose that the thumb string, like the banjo itself, originated on the plantation, if not in Africa. It matters little that the early banjos had four, not five, strings; what is important is that the top string is affixed to a tuning peg halfway up the neck and takes the downward sweep of the thumb at the conclusion of the frailing stroke. At least one representation of the plantation banjo, a late eighteenth-century painting called "The Old Plantation," shows us a thumb string of this kind.[26] Whatever its origin, the thumb string is in any event not a drone string, because it does not drone. It chimes, as the songs say, or tolls, or peals, or rings like a bell. This chiming is far more African than European in character, for across Africa, writes Father Jones, some sort of ringing instrument, whether bell, gong, or axe blades clinked together, provides a rhythmic background to music, dance, and song.[27] In both the clawhammer and the Scruggs styles we hear it twice every measure, every fourth note in the clawhammer style, just on the tail of the offbeat, and in Scruggs' basic three-finger roll every third—usually, in actual practice, on the rise of the first beat and the fall of the second. These successive pairs of chiming notes, passing like the double wheels of a line of freightcars over a gap in the rail, have a steadying or sobering effect on the music; they seem to stand apart from it, spreading tidings of joy or sorrow from some distant sphere of activity.

In all likelihood, though, it is ragtime which most directly links the Scruggs style banjo to the Afro-American tradition. There is, to begin with, a close connection between ragtime and the banjo historically.

Ragtime, writes Gilbert Chase, evolved out of the late nineteenth century "coon" songs, which were themselves excrescences of the later minstrel tradition in which blacks, by the 1870s and 1880s, were significantly involved, often as banjo virtuosos.[28] The first ragtime *piano* piece, "New Coon in Town," by one J. S. Putnam, published in 1883, was subtitled a "Banjo Imitation."[29] This suggests that banjo ragtime preceded the now more familiar piano ragtime with which the music is usually associated. Since during the same period, however, the "guitar" or three-finger banjo style, promulgated by white performers and teachers, had almost entirely eclipsed the older clawhammer style on the minstrel stage,[30] being better adapted to popular melodies, it is likely that ragtime was a late contribution of black performers, many of whom were emancipated slaves, to the minstrel banjo, just as the clawhammer style had been an early one. It was simply the playing of the old plantation cakewalking song on the banjo in a three-finger style: the cakewalking song, for anyone who has heard it, is virtually indistinguishable from the rag and shares rhythmic figures with minstrel tunes as early as Dan Emmett's "Old Zip Coon" and "Old Dan Tucker."

Probably, then, ragtime entered the Appalachian tradition, just as the clawhammer banjo style had a generation earlier, through the minstrel show and the banjo, not through the piano, the piano-roll, and sheet music, which is the route by which it entered the national consciousness some twenty years later. Once established in Appalachia, country or string ragtime became an autonomous popular style annexed to the older string band music—"Ragtime Annie" is a familiar example—and, as is well known, was richly represented in the region where Earl Scruggs grew up.[31] Most of the three-finger banjo pickers so numerous there in the early decades of this century played not only pure banjo rags but adaptations of the style to hillbilly and mountain songs; we need only mention Poole, whose own music is so obviously indebted to ragtime and whose idol, Fred Van Eps, was the foremost exponent in vaudeville of the banjo rag. Van Eps's three-finger arpeggios could easily have become the bluegrass banjo roll, the ragtime banjoist's practice of grouping his eighth notes in twos and threes giving way to a continuous stream of eighth notes in a series of three-finger arpeggios. But hang all that: *Scruggs himself* is an expert in ragtime banjo, whose traces can be heard in most of the Scruggs-style licks which have now become standard bluegrass formulae.[32]

Ragtime, not surprisingly, is built up out of eighth notes; the simplest form of its basic rhythmic phrase is 𝅘𝅥𝅮𝅘𝅥𝅮𝅘𝅥𝅮𝅘𝅥 𝅘𝅥𝅮𝅘𝅥𝅮𝅘𝅥𝅮𝅘𝅥   or

♪♩♫♫ ; Gunther Schuller cites a handful of variants, all of which appear in Scott Joplin's *Maple Leaf Rag*.³³ Joplin's father, incidentally, played fiddle and banjo. This phrase is remarkably like Charlie Poole's characteristic motive, which can be heard quite plainly in his "White House Blues" and "Don't Let Your Deal Go Down": ♪♩♫♫ . These songs have a distinctly bluegrass flavor and entered the bluegrass repertoire directly from Poole's recordings. This same phrase, moreover, frequently reasserts itself in many bluegrass fiddle breaks. But the Scruggs roll, with its groups of three and one of two, is *identical* to the basic ragtime phrase Joplin employed, played in double time.

By splitting the beat in two, the Scruggs roll transforms the stiff and mechanical 2/4 measure of hillbilly music into the more spacious and flexible 4/4 measure typical of bluegrass, opening the way for Monroe to express his black-inspired preference for the offbeat. This was in fact precisely the contribution of Jelly Roll Morton's right hand "manipulations" to his music, and in this respect the emergence of bluegrass out of Bill Monroe's string band is strikingly parallel to the emergence of jazz out of ragtime. By more fully exploiting the opportunities of the break, without which, Morton said, there would be no jazz, and by devices such as double time, Morton introduces, in Schuller's words, a "smoother, more swinging syncopation," loosening the original "square" feeling of ragtime in favor of a more liberal and more elaborate play of improvisation; as Morton himself put it, he "changed the color from red to blue."³⁴

In bluegrass we can hear this subtle but critical change quite plainly on record. Monroe's first recordings with Flatt, Scruggs, Wise, and Rainwater on September 16, 1946—the band had been together about eight months—are in most respects bluegrass music, especially "Toy Heart" and "Blue Yodel No. 4," a Jimmie Rodgers song. But rhythmically they are not quite bluegrass. Monroe is hastening the band along in a dapper 2/4 measure which with its alternating strong and weak beats generates the characteristic dance hall bounce of western swing; Wise's swing fiddling contributes mightily to the impression that Monroe's group at this juncture was a hillbilly *swing* band modified by certain novel elements such as Monroe's lucid tenor voice, his darting mandolin harmony lines, and of course Scruggs's uptown three-finger banjo style. But in 2/4 time Scruggs is noticeably rushed and cannot set forth his full complement of eight notes per measure without allowing short chains of melodically peripheral notes to fall, dynamically, by the wayside. We hear not a continous roll but a series of swiftly fading bursts of notes marked by dynamically shallow intervals and audible pauses: Scruggs is phrasing his breaks syllabically, as if he were singing.

There is an important new element, however, which is Lester Flatt's guitar. Unlike the percussive closed chording of Monroe's earlier guitarists, who were essentially swing musicians, Flatt's open chords and stout bass runs contribute both a richer harmonic atmosphere and, in conjunction with Rainwater's bass, a much sharper image of the *pulse*. Even more significantly, Flatt's bass-and-brush picking style provides for a strong expression of the offbeat and, with its alternating bass notes, produces two pairs of beats, the second being a slightly weakened echo of the first; the style seems, in other words, to call for a four-beat measure. It is worth repeating now that though the origins of this style are obscure, its lineage reaches back through Maybelle Carter, Jimmie Rodgers, and Rily Puckett to black guitarists. Very likely it is a late nineteenth-century black guitar riff developed at about the time that the guitar took over from the banjo in black folk culture. Technically it resembles the clawhammer banjo style, especially as Lester and Maybelle played it, with a brushing finger and not a flat pick; but more significantly, it exactly reiterates the clawhammer style rhythmically: a melody note followed by an offbeat brush with a trailing note attached to it by picking up on the first string—the guitar equivalent of the banjo's ringing thumb string. Both of Flatt's parents had played clawhammer banjo. But as Neil Rosenberg points out, Monroe's breakneck tempos often forced Flatt to abandon the brush and set forth the pulse in downbeat bass notes alone.[35] It is significant, then, that the first recorded bluegrass song should have been played at *medium* tempo: parking-lot pickers take note.

"Will You Be Loving Another Man," regarded by most bluegrass afficionados as the first full-blown bluegrass song on record, was the first of four numbers recorded the following day, September 17, the others being gospel songs and a conventional hillbilly heart song in waltz time, "How Will I Explain about You?" Here the hounds of syncopation—an emphatic backbeat and a driving, unflagging banjo roll—have been let loose, flushing the rhythm out of the meter and opening a wide antiphonal frontier behind the lead where Monroe's parallel harmony lines become, by a kind of rhythmic refraction, improvised countermelodies playing around the beat and welling up between lead phrases in patterns built on the call-and-response plan of Afro-American music. The rhythm no longer bounces but floats, like a jazz rhythm, while the musicians drive it forward, like jazz musicians cooperating to *fill in all the spaces* with licks and runs contrived to sustain a balanced structure of opposing rhythms. A true 4/4 measure, articulated by Rainwater's walking bass, has been established at a gentler lilting tempo; though the pace is still swift, it has become more deliberate, and the temporal space in which it moves far grander and more abundant. Once the pursued, the musicians are now the pursuers, and the music is suddenly deeper, richer, more complex and powerful. This rhythm became the blueprint for the classic bluegrass recordings made by the same band one year later, in October 1947: "I'm Going Back to Old Kentucky," "It's Mighty Dark to Travel," "Little Cabin Home on the Hill," "When You are Lonely," "I'm Travelling On and On," "Bluegrass Breakdown," which anticipates Scruggs's famous "Foggy Mountain Breakdown," "Molly and Tenbrooks," the first song recorded by another band in the bluegrass style, and "My Rose of Old Kentucky," simply one of the high-water marks of American music.

Other banjo players of course had perfected a three-finger roll. But none of them had been able to liberate the roll so completely from the pulse; none had been able to divide rhythm and meter so decisively. Why? Bill Monroe, Scruggs recalls, "had a solid beat that could support anything you wanted to pick."[36] This can only mean, I think, given everything we've said about rhythm under aural conditions, that Bill Monroe has the African's "metronome sense" upon which a "solid beat" depends. That Monroe does think with the beat rather than the pulse is suggested not only by his love of the offbeat but by his notion of the mandolin as a "timekeeper"—that is, a metronome. It ought to be obvious, too, from those rhythmic experiments he undertook in the "Muleskinner Blues" of 1940. It is not so much the various rhythmic phrases themselves as their wide variation, which suggests a keen and durable sense of tempo. A repetitive rhythmic motive, or even two or three of them, does not of course necessarily imply a metronomic sense: one can simply learn a number of phrases and use them interchangeably. This we discovered in our brief discussion of mountain blues in the last chapter, where we noted that while the mountain blues guitarist may use a number of rhythmic phrases, he does not freely manipulate them against an underlying regular rhythm in the fully improvisatory way characteristic of his black counterpart. "Muleskinner Blues" very strongly suggests that Monroe does. But nowhere is Monroe's phenomenally acute sense of rhythm more strikingly revealed than in his mandolin tremolo. For many mandolin players the tremolo is really nothing more than a sort of palsied and irritable attack on the string designed to produce a sustained tone. For Monroe, however, the tremolo or "tremble" is an occasion for changing rhythmic currency into a coinage of eighth or sixteenth notes, an operation he performs

in his mandolin breaks with a calculator-like accuracy and which may
very well have laid the groundwork for the banjo's poised integration
of continuous and discontinuous patterns. Though Monroe's mandolin
style has mellowed with age, each note of his tremolo on his most
recent recordings remains as discrete and whole as a raindrop.

The rhythmic "division of labor" in bluegrass has multiplied geo-
metrically the hillbilly musician's powers of control, coordination, and
expression. By use of the backbeat, for instance, he can interpret,
manipulate, or reconstitute various rhythmic relations. If it is very
strongly accented, for example, it will seem to resist the flow of the
music and restrain the tempo, perhaps bringing back a musician who
is getting ahead of himself or gathering up a too widely divergent
improvisatory flight; a lighter accent will seem to open up the music,
expose it to the air, inviting a dispersal of improvisatory lines and
perhaps a quickening of tempo. Or, if it is subdivided between phrases,
yielding the rhythm briefly to the pulse, it may seem to relieve tension
and restore order, to reestablish continuity, or to disentangle several
rhythmic strands. This is certainly the effect of the subdivided mandolin phrases which Monroe introduces between instrumental break
and verse, or verse and chorus—wherever a shift in the relation among
band members poses a kind of rhythmic crisis which only the authoritative pronouncements of the backbeat can resolve.

Because bluegrass is more strictly bound by song structure than
jazz, it must retain a strong impression of the fundamental rhythm.
That is why the banjo roll is desirable in bluegrass: without it the
rhythm would break up into two large opposing forces, the pulse and
the backbeat, whose insistent face-off dissolves swing and generates
the powerful tensions typical, say, of blues and rock-and-roll. In fact
many bluegrass bands, under the spell of rock, incline towards this
arrangement. If the banjo is *too* prominent, constantly dinning the roll
into our ears, then the music becomes a tedious musical doggerel; but
with judicious modulation the roll seems to pacify the music, or rather,
to pacify us. Rhythmically, as we've seen, it completes the music,
refining a beat which would normally provoke us to dance into a more
sublime and malleable substance.

Bluegrass rhythms, moreover, lend dimensionality to the medium
in which the music moves, depth to surface, background to foreground,
locating the musicians in its musical landscape. A lead instrument, for
instance, emerges from the ensemble body not merely by submitting
to the sway of the pulse but by thrusting it forward assertively, measure by measure, until all traces of the backbeat are thrown off. Similarly a background instrument, whether spinning countermelodies or

simply playing the backbeat, can withdraw more deeply into the music by intensifying its upbeat accents. Both lead and background instruments can linger in, wander about, or cross the rhythmically unincorporated tract between pulse and beat, where we hear the play of improvisation—the cry of the fiddle, the banjo's claptrap and doubletalk, the mandolin's muttered prophesies and riddles. Concluding his break, a lead instrumentalist may attach a lick of six or eight notes which commute him directly into the background, or he may take the opportunity afforded him by this critical juncture to escape the rhythm with a wild scattering of notes or shatter it with a note or two dropped into a vulnerable interval. Sometimes such unruly tours may suddenly explode in the midst of a lead break, or heavy off-accents from deep within the music may well up in it, creating oblique, blues-like rhythmic angles. In accompanying instruments, off-accents will place the musician in opposition to the lead, where he can repeat, refute, paraphrase, or interpret its declarations; lighter accents will place him in the open terrain between rhythmic boundaries, where he may wander far afield along meandering trails of melodic elaboration.

Synthesized from a variety of sources, bluegrass rhythms are deeply dyed with social and moral implication. The backbeat, for instance, is distinctly Afro-American, and bands which favor it, throwing off the pulse with an easy lilt in an atmosphere of relaxed improvisation, have a hip or swinging quality reminiscent of cabaret jazz. Depending upon its regularity, concentration, and the richness of its subdivisions, the backbeat may lope like ragtime, drive like boogie-woogie, hammer passionately like the blues, or even sweep in gorgeous circles like dancers to the Latin strains of a supper-club swing band.

The pulse, on the other hand, retains an impression of the march, or, in 3/4 time, of the waltz. The pulse can carry bluegrass almost anywhere, of course: to country-western song, English ballad, gospel hymn, or mountain folksong. But in Appalachian music the pulse has acquired a very strong emphasis upon the first beat of the measure. Since there is scarcely a mountain string band which does not to some degree favor this accent, it may reflect the square dance and the musician's effort to establish a rhythm for the dancers which echoes in the pounding of their feet; even Monroe will break into a fiddler's shuffle on his mandolin and call out, "Now can't you see them dancers!"— suggesting what, for him, is still the basis of Appalachian string-band music.[37]

An accent upon the first beat of the measure is of course only the aural form of the bar; an emphasis upon it, I suspect, is likely to be particularly strong in any music that is normally aural in practice—as much southern music, sacred and secular, has been. In any case blue-grass not only preserves these emphases but magnifies them, recalling, perhaps, the exhilaration of the dance or the joy and fervor of church singing; they bestow upon the singer a hortatory energy and upon the music generally a surging quality which, if not unique to bluegrass, is certainly one of its distinguishing marks, an almost conventional prac-tice which the bluegrass musician, if he does not do it instinctively, must take care to learn.

Rhythmic tension may at times break out into open conflict, as fiddle and banjo lock horns or a bandleader uses his mandolin or guitar rhythms like a hickory stick or riding crop. A banjo player, especially, seems to require strict discipline: strafed by a backbeat if he is ahead of the tempo, spurred by the pulse if he is behind it, buried by fiddle or mandolin syncopations if he is too obtrusive or hypnotised by his own. Rhythms can be played sensitively, deliberately—even, I sup-pose, competitively—or they can be played mechanically, compulsive-ly, or violently. A solid backbeat can generate a mood of heightened awareness and anticipation or a keenly erotic restlessness; but at racing tempos it may become merely giddy or nervous, and at slow, insin-uating tempos, ponderous, menacing, or even sinister—a display of power for its own sake. The pulse, too, may be too aggressive, and the first beat of the measure or vocal line attacked a bit too greedily. A lively pulse may be stately, like a march, or gay, like a dance; but an angry, arrogant, or even hateful one easily becomes slovenly; it is out looking for trouble, and swaggers. In bands which exaggerate the pulse this way, the sociocultural compass of bluegrass points away from Appalachia towards the deep South, where bluegrass, most un-fortunately but in a sense inevitably, has come to be associated in recent years with white supremacy and the Ku Klux Klan—in total ignorance, certainly, of the colossal debt bluegrass owes to black music. There is just a hint of meanness in it, as if the first beat of the measure were intended not merely to convince you of your sins or to carry you to some imaginary dance floor, but, like a cattleprod, actually to hurt you.

Syncopation is no mere technical device of anticipation or delay, but a particular disposition of rhythmic forces. It is an art—that half-physical, half-imaginative coordination, spontaneity, humor, and grace arising immediately from the nerves, instinctive and yet replete with intelligence, an art very like that of the ice-hockey or ball player, demanding an electronically precise sense of timing, unflagging readi-ness, and cool detachment at the same time, with the important difference that the musician's actions have not only beauty but meaning. "Everybody was playing what he wanted to play," wrote Eddie Condon, recalling his first encounter with King Oliver's jazz band, "and it was all mixed together as if someone had planned it with micrometer calipers . . . notes I had never heard were peeling off the edges and dropping through the middle . . . the music poured into us like daylight down a dark hole."[38]

Syncopation is an art by which rhythmic tension is created, complicated, brought to a crisis, and finally resolved—not consecutively, but simultaneously—in an equilibrium of musical energy called *swing*. If syncopation divides rhythm and meter, swing brings them back together again: not as in the European tradition, at the foot of the music, through synchronization, but in the head, through what Gunther Schuller patriotically calls the "democratization of rhythmic values"— a "perfect equality of dynamics" among rhythmic forces which preserves the "full sonority of notes" as well as the powerfully explicit or "propulsive" quality characteristic of music doing service in rhythm and melody at once.[39] At the point of perfect equilibrium, off-accents arouse waves in the rhythmic medium, but without turbulence; quickenings of the pulse expand and contract the melodic stream but do not arrest its flow. Thus "rock" and "roll," the two kinds of syncopation arising from the fundamental rhythm, one discontinuous, the other continuous, merge in an eerie, oscillating stillness for which *swing* is a wonderfully accurate term. In effect the completion of our kinesthetic response to rhythm has been strategically deferred, channelled upward along lines of unrelieved rhythmic tension until it can occur simultaneously with our apprehension of the musical idea. Thus one can never know exactly whether swing is a nervous phenomenon or a musical one: we seem to have accepted the music bodily into ourselves at the same moment that the perfect repose of contemplation has fallen over it. As Hodeir puts it, "the feeling of relaxation does not follow a feeling of tension but is present at the same moment."[40] When a jazz or a bluegrass band swings—and bluegrass *does* swing—the very music seems to withdraw behind successive waves of sheer disembodied force which emanate from a region of silence beyond music.

With its two kinds of syncopation balanced against one another, the bluegrass banjo, like the old-time fiddle, embodies in microcosm the mysteries of swing, particularly in relation to tempo. For the rate at which the banjo delivers notes, in the tempos typical of bluegrass— at about eleven notes per second—challenges the capacity of the ear to distinguish intervals of time as such: the tones tend to merge.[41] Consequently a perfect equilibrium between rock and roll in the banjo demands that the banjo player approach, without actually violating, the line at which discrete tones become to the ear a continuous sound without gradations, at which point it is not a "rhythm" at all. At slower tempos this presents little difficulty, since even in the midst of strong accents the ear will readily interpret a sequence of notes of equal quantity as a continuous line, however modified dynamically. But at very fast tempos—and bluegrass is full of them—the rhythmical interval in effect disappears, and rhythmic integration with it; the banjo roll becomes little more than a strident blast, scattering the rhythm in a sort of syncopated panic which is the fate of many an over-eager, Saturday-night bluegrass jam session. In certain frenetically accelerated bluegrass instrumentals we might as well not have the banjo at all, for the duple rhythm asserts itself apart from syncopations of it, generating neither bouyancy nor drive but a cloying hesitation, as if the rolling wheel had a flat place in it.

It is a crisply articulated syncopation and a vivid metronomic sense that puts to rest the craving after tempo that arises in syncopated music out of the urgencies of rhythmic tension; accelerated tempo, indeed, can be seen as a kind of shortcut to the "democratization" of rhythmic values, through the most egalitarian method of all, their obliteration. This is simply to say that the banjo player must have, or have available to him through an accompanying musician, a very fine sense of rhythm; it is particularly important that he hear or inwardly feel the fundamental rhythm, since his technique does not incorporate it. He must know not only where precisely to place the note, but *how* to place it so that its vitality is not sacrificed to its accuracy. He must have a note as sharp as a drum's, and yet one which will resonate in the harmonic sphere where the catalysis of swing takes place. Thus the minstrel's sliding fingernail and the bluegrass banjo picker's finger pick: for the banjo tone—I am borrowing Schuller's discussion of the bass pizzacato in jazz—

> has precisely the acoustical "attack and decay" pattern that provides the essence of swing. If we picture the production of a pizzacato in graphic terms as ⊏◥ or ⊏◣ we see that it contains a sharp rise in tone, a nearly immediate impact that is a prerequisite of precise rhythm and swing. The decay's relation to swing is more complex. A plucked note cannot be sustained at the level of its attack; there is bound to be a more or less rapid decay in the volume of sound. . . . In order to fulfill one of the conditions of jazz inflection and jazz swing— namely the full sustaining of pitches (or at least the illusion

thereof)—he must perforce create the *illusion* of sustaining the notes. The natural, gradual decay pattern of a plucked note helps him to do this, for it *fades* into silence. . . . It therefore creates the illusion, particularly in long durations, of sustaining through what in fact may be silence. . . .[42]

That's why de banjo rings: because the banjo that rings is the banjo that swings. In fact *all* the bluegrass instruments—guitar, mandolin, bass, even the fiddle in its way—are played to ring: a fact which when we reflect upon it begins to yield up some of the meaning of bluegrass music.

Tapping the springs of human vitality itself, African "syncopation" transformed the hillbilly string band into a dynamic social organism, bursting with attractions and rivalries whose very intensity brings musical ferment towards the point of "perfect equilibrium" that calls down the strange hush of swing and reveals a profound and inviolable human unanimity. The mechanical quality of the old hillbilly string band is gone; in its place is a supple and even glamorous instrument whose power now far exceeds what is necessary for it merely to perform its function, and hence becomes a challenge to the musician who, if he can control it, can make of it a medium of expression. The Model "T" has become the Olds 88: "folk music in overdrive."

I believe it is fair to say that the Scruggs-style banjo was the first instrumental style unique to bluegrass. It is a kind of microcosm of the music. As a technique it is relatively simple, readily summarized in handbooks and readily abused by thousands of parking-lot banjoists; as an art it is enormously capacious; in its own internal relationships it reflects the whole rhythmic interaction of the bluegrass ensemble, and in this, perhaps, resides its integrating power. With its versatility, brilliance, and drive, the Scruggs-style banjo awakened a rebounding echo of influences among the bluegrass instruments which has helped to galvanize the style and to build a fund of instrumental formulae within it. Because the Scruggs-style banjo is specific to Monroe's music and its immediate family, it carries bluegrass with it, sometimes quite inappropriately, wherever it goes—into movie scores, television commercials, and pizza parlors. Yet for the same reason the bluegrass banjo could not evolve with the music without modification of Scruggs's original technique. It was the gradual fortification of the banjo roll, or the idea of it, in bluegrass that made possible the development of the melodic or Keith-style banjo—Keith played with Monroe in the early sixties—and beyond that, the complex string-jazz idiom bluegrass has recently become.

Standing motionless as a dream, smiling with a kind of radiant mastery upon his work, his right hand fondly pressed to the banjo's bright white face and all his attention concentrated there, Earl Scruggs tamed the wildness that is still in the banjo; but he did not domesticate it. His dense, pure, golden tones, streaming out from under his fingers like bees from the seams of a violated nest, pollinate the heart with ideas of a past known, perhaps, only as a certain sense of life of which the banjo's astringent tone is the world's only auditory image. Its ancient ancestors, the West African *halam* and *bania*, are still found in Senegal and Gambia; but the American grandparents of the bluegrass banjo belong to scenes lodged deeply in the first frontier, among the blackface clowns and gat-toothed rubes who still dance about in its prismatic glow. The Scruggs style alchemizes the banjo back to its irreducible original elements—back as far, I think, as the 1830s or thereabouts, when black tamborine players, accompanying a fiddle, played an intricate rhythm with their fingers they called the "rattlesnake note." Longstreet recalls it in his *Georgia Scenes* and Charles Dickens in his *American Notes*. For the banjo is only a tamborine with an education, a rattler with bells on his tail.

Chapter 5

Ancient Tones
The Roots of Southern Song

The deacon of a tiny country church, a raw-boned man wrapped in a tight black suit, with a head of wooly, storm-colored hair, has just risen out of the group of men who sit behind the altar in order to line out the concluding song of this morning's service, a psalm; he begins to sing even before the last periods of the preacher's sermon have died away. Out comes a shrill, declamatory call, answered almost instantly by a swelling pentatonic chant that gathers in the air like pilgrims from many far-flung cities convening upon a holy place, ascends in harmonious steps to a kind of gale that seems filled with the laughter of young women, and gradually descends until it meets a reiterated cry from the deacon. As the song develops, deacon and congregation encroach upon one another ever more deeply, until the surf-like alternation of their voices, each washing over the other, locks them together in the rhythm of a spiritual embrace.

We might be among the African Methodists of Alabama or in Kentucky, among the Old Regular Baptists. By itself the sound is exotic and timeless, like the voices of children in a schoolyard. Even a bluegrass gospel song comes to mind: Flatt and Scruggs's "Cabin on the Hill." In fact, though, we are in the Irish Sea, on the greatest of the Hebrides, the thorny Isle of Lewis, where lives a lean race of Scots Presbyterians whose intensely introspective and strict Calvinism, and whose tradition-bound way of life, is as close as anything in Britain to the religion and culture of the original Scots-Irish who began to settle in America early in the eighteenth century.

If the "high, lonesome sound" of bluegrass music has British roots, they are probably here, in a tradition part Gaelic, part medieval and ecclesiastical, whose primitive vigor was reawakened in America by the touch of Afro-American song, with which it shared an uncompromising adherence to the aural laws of harmony and melody.

Birdsong notwithstanding, only man can make a tone, and it is the singer, not the song, that moves from one tone to the next. Tones sung successively describe to the imagination a movement among a number of fixed relative positions in musical space; this illusion is the working principle of melody. The number of these positions, or tones, may be many or few, but since tones are always sequential and though several different sequences may be available to the singer, the sequence itself is always fixed: else it would not provide a field of movement but be itself in motion. Whether sounded successively or simultaneously, every tone has a particular relationship to every other, with a particular sensory and emotional impact, so that any melody, or any harmony, evokes a mood unique to it, and a unique configuration of stasis and movement.

Nature has given us a series of tones whose harmonic relationships are said to be acoustically "pure"—that is, whose frequencies can be expressed as whole-number ratios. These intervals are the fifth (3/2), the fourth (4/3), the major third (5/4), the minor third (6/5), and of course the octave (2/1), which embraces the rest. To hear these on the piano, play, respectively, middle C and G above it, C and F above middle C, C and E, C and E-flat, and C with the C above it. The ear recognizes these whole-number ratios, feeling them to be somehow complete or in repose, a repose in which most melodies begin, from which they depart, and in which they end. The manner in which the tonal realm is divided between the principle intervals is largely a matter of culture. Our modern system of equal temperament divides the octave into twelve semitones an equal distance apart; but to the Bengali musician our scale sounds as if it has gaps in it. Western folk music, on the other hand, generally divides the octave more simply, into five or seven tones, emphasizing the acoustically pure intervals and permitting to the thirds, the sixth, and the seventh a limited flexibility which depends upon their immediate harmonic or melodic environment.[1] Hence these intervals in folk song, especially when measured against the tempered scale, may appear to be uncertain or ambiguous, torn between the third and fifth harmonically; but the folksinger, whose ear has been tuned by God and not by the local piano tuner, has found in that ambiguity an instrument of exceedingly subtle expressive power.

The overall tonality of a particular melody, what might be called

its perspective or point of view, is determined by the intrinsic relationships among the fixed sequence of tones from which the musician
chooses. Our own major and minor scales, which are theoretical sequences based on pitch, illustrate the principle: each has a particular
hue or attitude arising from the disposition of its semitones, or half
steps, with relation to the "final," or what we would call the tonic or
keynote. If in our music we typically call upon seven potential tones,
our diatonic scale, it follows that there are seven distinct ascending
sequences, each with its own character, which can be formed from
these tones, each one placing the two available half steps in a different
position relative to the final.

Sit down at the piano and play, on the white keys, six successive
ascending sequences of adjacent tones; begin on C to hear the major
scale, and then on D, E, F, G and, to hear the natural minor, on A.
These sequences are an ancient system of tonal organization called the
modes.[2] They are neither major nor minor but seem to shift bewitch-
ingly between a major and a minor tonality as the melody formed from
the sequence passes at different points over the boundary between
whole and half steps; the points in the sequence at which these boundaries occur determine the *ethos* or "feeling" of the mode. Though with
the introduction of chromatic intervals in the late middle ages the
modes passed out of art music, they had been the basis of it for two
thousand years—described, systematized, explored, and elaborated
first by the Greeks and then by the medieval Church, which not only
drew upon folk tradition in studying the modes but reintroduced its
modal music into folk tradition. Plato thought the Greek Lydian mode,
our major scale, weak and lascivious, suitable only for nuptial songs
and young girls' choruses, and warned against it in the *Republic*. Of
course he banned poetry from the Republic, too—so we know where
he stood. The Greek Dorian, our E to E′ sequence, was more manly,
he thought, and he stressed its educational value. The Greek Phrygian
mode, which the Church renamed the Dorian, our D to D′ sequence,
a mode richly represented in Western folk song, was widely used in
the Greek cult of Dionysus, being ecstatic and enthusiastic—which
may suggest, perhaps, its durability among the folk, be they Phrygian
or Kentuckian.

The Church defined the mode as a pentachord, five tones within the
interval of a fifth, tied by the fifth to an "adjunct tetrachord," four
tones within the interval of a fourth. Play the sequence from D to D′
on the white keys, and you hear the Church Dorian; play our major
scale, and you hear the Ionian; play the sequence from G to G′, and

you hear the Mixolydian. I cite these three—the Ionian, Dorian, and Mixolydian—because they are the modes which most frequently occur in our folk music; they are, in fact, closely related tonal realms, with many features in common.

The Church recognized, too, that the character of a mode was affected not only by its particular sequence of tones but by the orientation of the melody to the final. Melodies which moved primarily *above* the final had a different mood than those which dipped below it, as if the final were a boundary between the outward life and the inward, the world above ground and below it. Above the final, melodies are confident and open; below it they are pensive or melancholy. Thus the Church distinguished a secondary class of modes, the "plagal" modes, in which the tetrachord was added below the pentachord, instead of above, as in the "authentic" modes, and assigned the prefix *hypo-*, which means "grave," to each of them. Thus, for instance, the Hypomixolydian mode is identical to the Dorian except that its final is the fourth, not the first, tone of the sequence.

The evolution of European folk song in the Middle Ages certainly owes much to the Church, in which plainsong, or litergical song, achieved a very high level of development; plainsong, in turn, had owed much to the folk, as ancient testimony shows, as early as the second century.[3] At any rate our folk melodies, sacred and secular, especially those in Appalachian and Afro-American music, are virtually all modal in organization and ethos, with the important difference that the folksinger often employs only six, or five, of the seven available tones. These are the so-called "gapped" scales, which confine melodic movement to a restricted set of tones, corners in musical space; unlike a fully developed diatonic or chromatic tune, which seems rounded and flexible, the gapped melody darts along rigid straight lines from point to point, describing what amounts to tartan-like geometric design. The gapped scale is an expression of the aural imagination and its love of consonance. In fact it is simply a set of consonant intervals—a major triad, say—whose rule is continually brought home to us by a melody which steps among intervals by means of two or three intermediate adjacent tones, building and rebuilding a stable underlying harmonic structure. Like an Irish step dancer, the melody moves in place. What pleases us, as is often the case in folk or primitive music, is a form of repetition, for in effect a single chord is sounding over and over again.

Our wistful "Poor Wayfaring Stranger" is in the Dorian mode, from which it takes its emotional coloring, its sense of simplicity and peace arising from the fact that it is pentatonic, excluding the second and sixth degrees; the haunting murder ballad "Pretty Polly" works with the same tones but dips to the fourth below the tonic. The wild "June Apple," a fiddle breakdown, is in the Mixolydian mode, with its fascinating whole step between its seventh and eighth degrees—a "flat" seventh, from the viewpoint of the major scale—and the strange sinking sensation that comes when we hear it. The plagal form of this mode, the Hypomixolydian, has the interesting property that its final divides a major from a minor key—major above it, minor below. This is the boundary which the widely known fiddle tune "Red Haired Boy," with its strong Celtic feeling, crosses with a kind of perverse delight, answering every flight into the major with a sullen retreat to the minor. A rich vein of the mountain sound lies in the Mixolydian. "Darlin' Corey," that gemstone of the tradition, is a pentatonic version of it; bluegrass standards such as "Little Maggie," "Love Please Come Home," Monroe's "Bluegrass Breakdown," and a host of others less well known, all turn upon the Mixolydian's dying fall from the final into the dreary realm that lies about its seventh tone.

Every musical tone carries its harmonic affinities in the form of overtones, while sequences of tones always suggest that harmonic effect which would obtain were they to be sounded simultaneously. The tunes and songs which come to us from British folk tradition evolved largely outside the milieu of harmony, which is a relatively late development in European music; but in America, first on the fiddle and banjo, but principally on the guitar, they have acquired a chordal dress. Guitarists in the old-time bands of the twenties such as Riley Puckett were not always entirely certain, when accompanying a fiddle tune, what chord went where. But bluegrass guitarists have discovered that a modal tune, with its alternating major and minor, can be accompanied by a major chord with its relative minor, or with a tonic chord, a major chord a whole step below it, and a dominant. Other progressions are possible, some quite sophisticated and beautiful. By these techniques the guitarist negotiates the shifting terrain of the mode, stirring its ancient roots to fresh life.

Our most common gapped scale by far is a pentatonic based upon the major scale, which exludes the fourth and the seventh. The important feature of this scale, which like other gapped scales is built upon a major triad whose root is the final of the mode, is its exclusion of the fourth, which it may be said to abhor. Though the fourth is a principle interval, its harmonics are bitterly dissonant with those of the major tonic chord; since the gapped scale demands a stable harmonic matrix, it is the fourth, in the major pentatonic, that must go;

to sound it is to shift a melody's harmonic weight, establishing a diatonic sound whose interest lies in such shifts. The major pentatonic loves the sweet third and the resonant fifth.

This major pentatonic has been called the "African" pentatonic because it is so richly represented in Afro-American music, particularly in the spirituals, such as "Swing Low Sweet Chariot" and "Nobody Knows the Trouble I've Seen." Of the published Negro spirituals in the major scale, better than a third are pentatonic, and a greater number banish the fourth. In all cases it is certain that tune transcriptions cannot do justice to the tonal complexities of Afro-American singing. Henry Edward Krehbiel, one of the first writers to argue that Afro-American music retained many African elements, noted that the Dahoman harp, which he heard at the World's Columbian Exposition in Chicago in 1893, was tuned to the "African" pentatonic. Of this scale he says: "The temptation is strong to look upon the pentatonic scale as the oldest, as it is certainly the most widespread and the most serviceable of intervallic systems. It is the scale in which melody may be said to be naturally innate. Play it at random on the black keys of the pianoforte, and so you keep symmetry of period and rhythm in mind you cannot help producing an agreeable melody; and it will be pentatonic." Krehbiel notes, however, that the scale is strongly characteristic of another body of music in America, "the one body of specifically national song with which the slave of the United States could by any possibility have become familiar—the Scottish, with its characteristic pentatonic scale and rhythmical snap."[4]

If in the old South, with its pervasive Irish and Scots-Irish settlement, there occurred on the folk level an energetic interchange and fusion of black and white song, it is perhaps because between the two traditions there were strong musical affinities, reinforced by a social system that discriminated against both groups. The African love of cross-rhythm found a home, albeit a narrow one, in off-beat accentuation, which was in the gait of Scots song and was a favorite device of Irish fiddlers; African gapped scales and modalities found an echo in those of the Gaelic tradition; folksingers from both parts of the world delighted, in different ways and in different degrees, in high pitches, a declamatory style, vocal tension and ornament, and improvisation. All these traits reflected the aural universe in which both traditions had grown up and, it seems, reinforced one another, giving rise to a regional folk music whose strange and wonderful trenchancy attracted the attention of popular entertainers such as blackface minstrels whose imitations and caricatures not only threw those traits into still higher relief but introduced them into popular consciousness and ultimately into popular song.

Consider, for example, how much the Afro-American "blue tonality," as Marshall Stearns calls it, has in common with the ancient modes of our British folk music.[5] We hear the blue tonality in the third and seventh degrees of the scale, which the blues singer, like the spiritual singer who preceded him and the many mountain, country, and jazz singers who have followed him, sings "flat," producing a tone somewhere between major and minor and beckoning the major scale away from its wholesome and happy way of life. The blues guitarist, as is well known, will typically sharp or "bend" the minor third toward the major, and both the fourth and the sixth towards the semitone above it; for him these pitches are not fixed but elastic. But in the context of the major scale, we can hear a kind of blues "mode," consisting simply of a major scale with a flat third and a flat seventh added, the fourth and the seventh omitted; when we are singing the blues, these are the tones with which we work.[6] Now the Mixolydian mode shares the blues' flatted seventh, and when mountain or bluegrass musicians work in the Mixolydian, as in "Little Maggie," they frequently add a flat third, tinting with blues the Celtic twilight of the Mixolydian. The blues' mode, moreover, like the major pentatonic, omits the fourth; one has merely to add the flatted third and seventh to it to make the blues, which is precisely what the bluegrass musician does when, following Bill Monroe's example, he works in a pentatonic tune such as "Uncle Pen." Finally, the blues' flatted third and seventh virtually repeat the shape of the Dorian mode: between the two modes there is but *one semitone's* difference: flat the Dorian's fourth, and you have the blues mode. In fact this is one of the tricks of mountain banjo tuning. What is called "mountain minor" banjo tuning, ᵍDGCD, gives us the tonic, fourth, and fifth in G, carrying us into the Dorian mode, where the fourth, which clashes harmonically with both third and seventh, drives them both down a semitone. Most bluegrass banjo players play Ralph Stanley's "Clinch Mountain Backstep" in this tuning; many a lonesome Kentucky fiddle tune, such as "Lost John," lives here too. By fretting the third string to produce an A, we can play in the Dorian mode in D, its modal quality emphasized by the C or seventh, sounding out a whole tone below the octave. Now if we tune the fifth string down a half step, to F-sharp, we introduce a major third, whose continuous chiming against the fourth creates a wierd modality banjo players call the "graveyard" tuning, whose blue tones they intensify by irresistably bending the F towards the F-sharp, like a blues guitar

player. Against this tuning mountain coal miner and banjoist Doc
Boggs, who learned many of his songs from race records, used to sing
a haunting lament, probably descended from an Irish come-all-ye, that
he called "Country Blues."[7]

George Pullen Jackson argues convincingly that the ambiguity of
the third and seventh tones is one feature that distinguishes folk from
art tonality, noting that the folksinger typically chooses the "neutral
third"—somewhere between major and minor, never as sharp as the
tempered third and often nearly as flat as the minor: "I am convinced
it is the feel for the neutral third which induces our blues and swing
piano players, when playing, let us say in the C-major or C-minor, to
strike both E-flat and E-natural at the same time or in very quick
succession. The neutrals . . . are of the essence of folk tonality."[8]

"Folk tonality," certainly; but it is the black musician who taught
us to explore the tensions lurking in these intervals. The white singer,
as Jackson notes, may sing "off key" relative to the tempered scale;
but it usually the black singer who will create dramatic effects by
carefully tightening the minor interval towards the major, or relaxing
the major towards the minor. He can do so because, as we've seen,
these intervals are naturally elastic, and out of that elasticity may be
created harmonic stresses which seem to weight or intensify melodic
movement. Thus these stresses have an emotional value, for melodic
movement, again, is the musician's movement: watch B. B. King's face
when he bends a note high up the neck of his guitar and throttles it
until it tells the truth. The psychological core of the entire phenomenon,
I suspect, is the aforementioned abhorrence of the fourth. Even in
diatonic realm the blues guitarist or singer almost invariably will sharp
the fourth to relieve its friction against the third, a semitone distant.
Probably the same impulse is at work in the major seventh, which
approaches so closely to the octave. "The folksinger does not like big
intervals," writes Dr. Jackson; but he does not like semitones either.
The folk melody suggests a stable underlying harmony rooted in the
acoustically pure intervals, particularly the third and the fifth, and
often seems to be constructed in such a way that its principal tones
are in an acoustically pure relationship to one another.

"What songs," asked Anton Dvorák in 1895, "belong to the American
and appeal more strikingly to him than any others?"

> What melody would stop him on the street if he were in a
> strange land, and make the home feeling well up in him, no
> matter how hardened he might be, or how wretchedly the tune
> were played? Their number to be sure, seems to be limited.

> The most potent, as well as the most beautiful among them,
> according to my estimation, are certain of the so-called plantation
> melodies and slave songs, all of which are distinguished by
> unusual and subtle harmonies, the thing which I have found in
> no other songs but those of Scotland and Ireland.[9]

An independent American song tradition emerged in the nineteenth
century based on British forebears but influenced by the oral-formulaic
methods of Afro-American singers. The black influence appears, Alan
Lomax points out, in shortened phrases, a more careful matching of
pitch with speech sounds, and, of course, in syncopation.[10] Think of
"Liza Jane" or "Shortnin' Bread," which everyone has sung in school.
Simplified repetitive phrases, recurrent melodorhythmic figures, formulaic refrains, and gapped scales—all these reflect the aural and social
character of Afro-American folk tradition and obtain in both vocal and
instrumental music. Such are the changes which Protestant hymnody
underwent during the Great Revival, producing the distinctly American spiritual song or "spiritual," which though shared by black and
white clearly displays the African musical genius. John F. Watson, in
his *Methodist Error; or, Friendly Christian Advice to Those Methodists in Extravagant Religious Emotions and Bodily Exercises* com-
plained in 1819:

> Here ought to be considered, too, a most exceptional error,
> which has the tolerance at least of the rulers of our camp
> meetings. In the *blacks'* quarter, the coloured people get
> together, and sing for hours together, short scraps of disjointed
> affirmations, pledges, or prayers, lengthened out with long
> repetition *choruses*. These are all sung in the merry chorus-
> manner of the southern harvest field, or husking-frolic method,
> of the slave blacks. . . .
> . . . the example has already visibly affected the religious
> manner of some whites. From this cause, I have known in some
> camp meetings, from fifty to sixty people croud [sic] into one
> tent, after the public devotions had closed, and there continue
> the whole night, singing tune after tune . . . scarce one of
> which were in our hymnbooks.[11]

Black influence was not confined to the church, camp meeting, and
plantation frolic. Hans Nathan notes that in the minstrel shows of the
1840s a new strain began to sound—one which spoke in uniquely American accents. Here was a lively syncopation, steady duple rhythms, a

sporadic use of modal features and a blues-like tonality, a marked
frequency of recurring tones, an habitual use of small intervals favoring
the recurrence of two or three adjacent tones, and a "relentless repetition of brief motives."[12] The minstrel had caught the "primitive"
quality which the African had awakened in our folk music—particularly
the African practice of annealing rhythms to melodies: tunes on drums.
It was that impulse especially which altered the phrasing of "The Jolly
Miller," an Irish tune, and "Miss McLeod's Reel," a Scots one, to
transform them into "Zip Coon" and "Jump Jim Crow"—a pattern
which I suspect lies in the geneology of many of our traditional fiddle
tunes. Generally speaking, a reel becomes a breakdown when the
rhythm accent shifts from the third to the second and fourth beats.
Dan Emmett's "Old Dan Tucker" had all the features of which Nathan
speaks, coupled to a witty lyric which, as a nineteenth-century admirer
wrote, offered "a series of vivid pictures, disconnected in themselves,
varying as rapidly as the changes in a kaliedoscope, and yet presenting
to us the character of the hero, as a most artistic whole"[13]—precisely
the poetic form of oral-formulaic song and a characteristic of all Afro-
American folksong.

Emmett's "I Wish I Was in Dixie's Land," which had strong echoes
both of an old German hymn and of an English music hall song he used
to sing in his youth,[14] had a happy Scots snap and an exhilarating
melodic scope; but it caught something too of the folk tonality emerging
in the South. Except as a brief passing tone which seems to betray a
trace of Yankee sympathy, the fourth is absent from "Dixie," while
the tones of the major pentatonic, the third, fifth, sixth, and the tonic
itself are thrust into the foreground by a combination of rhythmic
emphasis and repetition, lingering before us in the chorus in the wistfully prolonged notes which ask us to "look away" to Dixie's land.
Stephen Foster, too, in "Oh Susanna" and "Suwanee River," composed
the verse in a strict major pentatonic, witholding the subdominant
chord until the chorus, which itself returns to the pentatonic after four
bars. In both the fourth makes only a cameo appearance. This is the
harmonic strategy, too, of Dvorák's *New World Symphony* theme,
"Goin' Home." These buxom melodies, pervaded by the healthy consonance of two closely linked major triads, are interestingly in contrast
to the clever "Yankee Doodle," a product of the English music hall,
or the pious Shaker hymn "Simple Gifts," both of which trip narrowly
along successive whole steps, rarely venturing beyond the fifth above
or the fourth below the tonic. The northern melody makes many fine
tonal distinctions in rapid succession, amusing and perhaps fascinating

us, keeping us intellectually alert, while the southern melody spellbinds us with repetitions we do not recognize as such; like the passionate and glorious tunes of the warlike Scottish clans, it is meant to inspire. The northern song thinks, even calculates; the southern song dreams.

Between the pentatonic scale favored by the minstrels and that of the Negro spirituals, which entered popular consciousness later in the century through the efforts of the Fisk Jubilee Singers and their counterparts, there is, however, one important difference: the minstrel songs, generally speaking, favor the authentic major mode, the spirituals the plagal. That is, the minstrel songs develop principally above the final, returning to it in cadences, while the spirituals dip well below it, to the fifth below or deeper, with a rising cadence to the final. From this arises what Y. S. Nathanson called in 1855 "the perfect and continual lightness, spirit, and good humor" of the minstrel song and the emotional density and moral weight of the spiritual.[15]

Where does bluegrass music belong in this picture? Many bluegrass songs, which may originate in folk or popular music, are simply and straightforwardly diatonic. But the overwhelming preference by far in bluegrass is for the pentatonic song, one which, like "Old Susanna" or "Suwanee River," shifts to the subdominant in the chorus. Song after song in bluegrass displays this pattern, but with one significant difference: the bluegrass song tends towards the plagal, not the authentic mode. The bluegrass song, in other words, is a kind of *minstrel song spiritualized*.

"Swing Low Sweet Chariot," Bill Monroe has often said, is one of his favorite songs; often he uses it, with audience participation, to close his shows. Its imprint is strong in his music: compare it to "On and On" or "Highway of Sorrow." Almost without exception Monroe's originally composed songs are pentatonic in the verse, moving into the subdominant in the first strain of the chorus, returning to the pentatonic in the concluding strain. "Kentucky Waltz," a popular composition of his pre-bluegrass period, is an outstanding exception; and I think it is fair to say that it is melodically anomalous in the bluegrass repertoire, with an urbane quality the music as a whole does not share. Bluegrass apparently cannot tolerate the pure authentic mode, with its "perfect and continual lightness" and the rest; tunes such as "Uncle Pen" in the authentic mode will be generously salted with blue tonalities. It is the absence of the fourth, again, that is significant. Monroe's antipathy for it may perhaps be illustrated by the difference between "My Rose of Old Kentucky," a traditional melody, and his "My Little Georgia Rose," which was "written off" the older song.

Monroe has simply removed the fourth tone from "My Rose of Old Kentucky," and substituted a return to the fifth below the tonic, making "My Little Georgia Rose" a perfect minstrel spiritual.

With a few interesting exceptions, traditional and original songs associated with Monroe show a similar tendency. His early and popular "Footprints in the Snow," a nineteenth-century sentimental song, omits the fourth but moves, for a bluegrass song, along unusually wide steps: its melody reaches all the way to the third above the octave and in the chorus drops a full octave in a jump. "Molly and Tenbrooks," on the other hand, is uncharacteristically narrow in range for a bluegrass song, reaching only to the sixth and never dipping below the tonic, with a fourth that ties the end of the first line to the beginning of the second; it began as a black song in the 1870s, with an Anglo-Irish street ballad lying in its more distant past.[16] Monroe's gospel songs, such as "Walking in Jerusalem" or "Lord Protect my Soul," besides echoing the black gospel tradition in style and substance, are also pentatonic, but demand wider vocal leaps than the secular songs, generating a melodic vigor which translates as religious enthusiasm. Monroe's instrumental pieces, too, such as "Gold Rush" or "Scotland," favor the pentatonic, the Mixolydian, or the ordinary minor. His unforgettable "Jerusalem Ridge" alternates between the plagal and authentic versions of a minor mode in four discrete parts, creating a structure of doubly reflected melodies, in which plagal strains echo the authentic.

"If you listen to my work," Monroe reminds us, "you see that there's blues in it."[17] We have already seen how much the blue tonality has in common with the modes of Irish and Scots folk song. The blues chord progression, with its two departures from home, the first tentative and reflective, the second thorough and conclusive, appears in bluegrass not only in traditional blues songs but in many traditional and original songs of other kinds. This points to the fact that the blues shares with a large family of American folk songs, represented by "Skip to My Lou" and "On Top of Old Smokey," a harmonic system descended from the "waits" songs of Elizabethan towns.[18] What is interesting about the blues chord progression, though, is that its shifts underline changes in the singer's *poetic* perspective; the blues line undergoes a transformation of meaning as its harmonic setting changes, the harmonic resolution of the third line being a resolution of thought as well as feeling finds expression in a discovered metaphor:

See that freight train, comin' around the bend; (tonic)
See that freight train, comin' around the bend: (subdominant)

Ain't had no lovin', since the Lord knows when.
(dominant)   (tonic)

This coordination of harmonic and poetic progression points to the fact that blues song, though it may call upon every tone in the major scale, is not genuinely diatonic—not like "Yankee Doodle." Actually it is a tripartite image of the blues mode reflected in the three major triads, to which the blues singer has reconciled the primitive verbal energy that lies in the contours of the mode. Something similar might be said about a minstrel song like "Suwanee River" or "Dixie" where melodies, as Hans Nathan notes, lend to the words "the naturalness of colloquial speech."

Generally speaking our country music, and bluegrass in particular, has been far more influenced by the blues *singer* than by the blues song. The blues singer obeys laws arising from the close conjunction of song and speech in West Africa, and these laws affect his music, even with its strong British strain, in vocal style, melodic shape, and rhythm. The affinity of blues song for speech is apparent for example, from the blues singer's tendency to maneuver within a small melodic compass—this may recall the minstrels' "small intervals favoring the recurrence of two or three adjacent tones"—that sometimes resolves into a humming or moaning vocal drone; blues songs, as anyone who has tried to sing blues in the shower knows, are not "melodious." Moreover the folk blues usually follows the downward slope of a declarative sentence, yielding a characteristic falling cadence in the melodic line which we hear all the way from "Shortnin' Bread" to Joe Turner's "Shake, Rattle and Roll." A. M. Jones heard this "downward drift" in West Africa, and Hans Nathan notes its emergence in the minstrel songs of the 1840s.[19] Within these limits, the blues singer is at liberty to produce his own melody melismatically, especially in the more primitive unaccompanied styles hardly distinguishable from their African ancestors.[20] Often his variations are so rich that scarce any "melody" in the familiar sense can be detected at all.

If the blues singer has reconciled modal music to major chords, he has also accommodated speech rhythms to musical rhythm. Since he cannot entirely ignore the musical rhythm, nor scatter his syllables over the melodic line in the relaxed and elastic manner of the lyric song or unaccompanied ballad, instead he makes a terrific compromise, one entirely consistent with the "process of rhythm" which his music is: he compresses words into rhythmically negotiable phrases or motives separated by mute intervals which he yields to his guitar or piano; the words are virtually stolen from the music. He must manage the

rhythm by means of speech, delaying, anticipating, or firing the beat
with strong speech accents, subdividing it with tough, dense syllabi-
fication, or with a precise melismatic tour, creating rhythmic phrases
out of the linguistic moment:

> Woke . . . UPthis mornin'I . . . lookedaround for m'SHOES
> You knowIhad themmeanold . . . OLD WALKin' blues. . . .

This disrupts natural phrasing radically—in blues, phrasing is everything—but saves, and even intensifies, the natural shape, integrity,
and *pace* of speech *within* the phrase. The words of the song are
rhythmically magnetized, delivered with far greater energy than either ordinary speech or lyric song, in sentences wierdly fragmented
by what becomes, dramatically, the force of emotional intensity or
struggle.

These traits are not peculiar to the blues of course; they are the
family traits of black singing, religious singing especially, and have
been carried into every quarter of our folk life chiefly by the singing
church, and thence into country music and bluegrass. But bluegrass
singing, even more than its hillbilly and country cousins, seems to have
drunk deeply from the black well. Like blues singing, bluegrass singing
is undeviatingly rhythmical—a rigorous, clattering, indignant delivery
which seems to favor groups of three or four syllables tied to a strong
accent but which in any case leaves no syllable of the lyric rhythmically
untouched. It retains its animated "talking" quality even at its breakneck tempos and in songs that do not necessarily have the blues' easy-
going "downward drift" or any appreciable parallel between speech
contours and musical pitch; so energized may the syllables of the bluegrass song become, in fact, that they may not always be intelligible
as words at all. But the sheer effort required to sing in this style
imparts a passion and a drive to the singing that is simply unparalleled
in country music.

The bluegrass song is characterized, moreover, by a marked preference for the top note of a melody, and the bluegrass repertoire as a
whole by melodies which offer a prominent tone in the upper registers.
The bluegrass singer's impulse is to concentrate vocal force upon the
highest available note in a phrase and through long duration to give
it full and exhaustive expression, often at the very outset of the melodic
phrase. This is "hollering," and it is of course strong in black tradition,
from primitive field hollers to shouters like Leadbelly or Howling Wolf.
Bluegrass singers call it the "high, lonesome sound," and nearly all of
Monroe's best-known songs—"Muleskinner Blues," "Blue Moon of
Kentucky," "Used to Be," "On and On," to name a few, not to mention

certain classic bluegrass tours de force such as Ralph Stanley's "Little Maggie"—open with a vocal blast one, two, even three measures long. The "downward drift" of black song, with its accompanying quality of declamation, like a line of epic verse, is very vivid in these songs. *All* bluegrass songs approximate the quality with energetic leaping accents, always coupled with a forceful shouting or barking attack on the high note, which is almost always extended into a kind of call when it occurs at the end of a phrase. This "shouting" style belongs to the folk church, and Monroe says he learned it from a singing-school master, one Granville Morris.[21] Bluegrass singer Peter Rowan compares this phrase—one which hastily dispenses with a few brief syllables, in order to attain the long, satisying cry: "Sweetheart of miiiiiiine . . . "[22]—to fiddle phrasing, where it does indeed regularly occur. Even when a particular melody does not offer a leaping ascent, its *effect* is created by a forceful attack. Some originally composed bluegrass songs such as Doug Kershaw's "Sally Jo," which Monroe has recorded, seem to have no justification beyond the fact that they provide the singer with a note he can bust his tonsils on, which may be justification enough. Always we feel the prolonged high note as a kind of victory, an escape from the brackish currents of the lower register where the voice must feel its way. The note becomes the focus of melodic expectation; some songs, by lingering sullenly in the deeps, seem to delay the expected outcry, increasing dramatic tension; others may build *up* in a chorus to the note which introduces the verse and restores the downward sloping pattern. Monroe's "Dark as the Night," for example, does the first, his "Used to Be" the second.

Cecil Sharp noted years ago that the English folksinger liked to sing at the highest possible pitch; his informants, he says, would sometimes apologize to him for not singing high enough.[23] Josiah Combs, another early collector of mountain music, noted the "wierd effect" produced when his informant would "pitch the air an octave too high"—a practice which occurred principally among women singing Primitive Baptist hymns.[24] Jean Ritchie recalls that Roscoe Holcomb, sometimes cited as a folk original of the bluegrass "high, lonesome sound," would sometimes pitch his songs so high that after ten or fifteen minutes his voice would give out.[25] To discover an origin in history for the exceedingly high-pitched singing found in eastern Kentucky probably is impossible. But the fact that it seems primarily to be associated with Primitive Baptist hymns suggests that it may have been, at some time in the past, the practice of religious people who had taken literally the Biblical language surrounding song, such as Isaiah's "lift up thy voice like a trumpet" (58:1). It has indeed the same strange, anomalous quality as

the other relics of religious noncomformity based on Biblical literalism
we find in the region, such as foot-washing, speaking in tongues, snake-
handling, and baptism by immersion.

   High-pitched singing is not, in any case, limited to mountain singers.
"Every voice was in its highest key," wrote an observer of an Afro-
American festival in early nineteenth-century Hartford.[26] "Their voices
seem oftener tenor than any other quality," wrote Fanny Kemble in
her *Journal of a Residence on a Georgia Plantation,* recalling the song
of some Negro boatmen she heard in the 1830s.[27] We hear high-pitched,
pellucid singing in the country blues singers, too—in Robert Johnson,
Blind Willie McTell, and Blind Lemon Jefferson, for instance, and a
bit later in Kokomo Arnold, whose "Rocky Road Blues" Monroe himself
recorded in 1945, at almost twice Arnold's tempo. It is not high pitch
by itself that marks bluegrass singing, in any case, but the bold vault
to the high note, and the wild declamatory cry wrought out of it. Can
this style possibly have an ancestor in the Old World?

   Mountain singing, Alan Lomax observes, is more "British" than
anything which may be found in Great Britain.[28] There is scarcely a
feature of Appalachian singing, with the notable exception of bluegrass'
intense rhythmicality, which does not have a relative across the water.[29] There is a declamatory song style, for example, in the Irish
"come-all-ye," though it is not necessarily associated with high pitch.
The mountain balladeer's highly decorated "oriental" voice, with its
tense throat and nasal, "womanish" tone, its regular momentary slip
into falsetto at line ends—Texas Gladden, Sarah Ogan Gunning, Al-
meda Riddle all sing this way—smacks strongly of the Gaelic ballads
of southern Ireland. Uncle Dave Macon's manly "punch" on the first
beat of the measure will be heard in the public-house bawdy song of
a Dorset shepherd. And between the singing styles of Virginia's Horton
Barker and English folksingers such as Bill Squires or Joseph Taylor
there is no detectable difference save that of speech accent, as Peter
Kennedy demonstrated to me with a remarkable juxtaposition of tape
recordings; both display a foursquare rhythmic regularity, a stout,
virile, and straightforward delivery, a very sparing use of vocal decoration, and smart, crisp enunciation. To hear them one cannot but
conclude, as Cecil Sharp did, that "the mountain singers sing in very
much the same way as English folksingers—in the same straightforward, direct manner, without any conscious effort at expression, and
with the even tone and clarity of enunciation with which all folksong
collectors are familiar. Perhaps, however, they sing rather more freely
and with somewhat less restraint than the English peasant. . . .They
have one vocal peculiarity, however," Sharp remarks, "which I have

never noticed amongst English folksingers, namely, the habit of dwelling arbitrarily upon certain notes of the melody, generally the weaker accents. This practice, which is almost universal, by disguising the rhythm and breaking up the monotonous regularity of the phrases, produces an effect of improvisation and freedom from rule which is very pleasing."[30]

Unrestraint and freedom from rule—perhaps Sharp regarded these as expressions of the American temperament, as they may well have been. But another Englishman, one G. B. Chambers, noted the vocal "peculiarity" too, as he sat with a group of American soldiers from a mountain battalion, stationed in the English West Country during World War II. Chambers was a folk-song enthusiast, but unlike Sharp, he was also a churchman, and to him the "vocal peculiarity" was an unmistakable survival in American folk tradition of a very ancient relic indeed—the long, drawn out country call or *jubilus* which at a very early period the medieval Church had annexed from folk tradition to its own vocal music. "On one occasion," Chambers writes, "when the enthusiasm rose, the surge or jubilation burst forth, and I heard what I most wanted to hear, the long drawn out notes on the vowel sounds."[31]

The earliest allusions to the *jubilus*—a Latin word which means a "joyful call" or "country cry"—occur with reference to the oldest form of Christian worship, the psalm-song, adopted from Jewish ritual in Jerusalem at the dawn of the Christian era. "We name the call of the peasant and agricultural worker a 'jubilus,'" wrote St. Hilary in the fourth century, commenting on Psalm 65, *Jubilate Deo*, "when, in solitary places, either answering or calling, the jubilation of the voice is heard through the emphasis of a long drawn out and expressive rendering."[32] St. Cyril of Alexandria, commenting on Psalm 94, *Venite*, said: "A jubilation is a call of triumph sent forth to a wounded foe and conquered enemy—come therefore and sing a jubilation to our Savior and Redeemer."[33]

Psalmody has an exceedingly complex history spanning many centuries; in the Catholic church it evolved into a rich and elaborate cultivated tradition we know as Gregorian chant, in which the final *a* in the word "Allelulia" traditionally receives a long drawn out vocalization: the *jubilus*. An antiphonal style of psalmody, sung by alternate choirs, emerged at the same period; here the *jubilus* was a melismatic chant retained either for the concluding vowel of a phrase in the recitation or, in the response, a melismatic tour upon *any* unaccented vowel.[34] The *jubilus* had two forms, then—on outcry or call, and a chant or surge—and it was traditionally linked to psalmody.

There is ample precedent in liturgical song, then, for our "vocal peculiarity," the "long drawn out notes on the vowel sounds." Yet how can this medieval and Catholic tradition have emigrated to Protestant America? In folklore, I suspect, which has sustained the life of many a fine ancient expression of the human heart. For the traditional manner of psalmody clung tenaciously to the psalm-song, by whose agency it rode out the Reformation, the psalm becoming the principal song-fare of the Protestant church in Britian and America during the sixteenth and seventeenth centuries.[35] Indeed the psalm-song, connected as it was to the early Church and to the Old Testament, must have had a special savor for the Protestant imagination; hymn writers in Britain and America diligently undertook to gather folk tunes for adaptation to psalm texts. Despite many objections to cathedral singing and to the psalm-song itself by radical dissenters in England, the psalm, unlike the composed hymn, was understood to be the word of God and by the seventeenth century had almost the status of the popular ballad: "Psalms were sung at the Lord Mayor's feasts. . . . soldiers sang them on the march or beside camp-fires; ploughmen and carters whistled or sang them at their tasks; and pilgrims sought a new continent in which to gain liberty to sing only the Psalms. Far from being the songs of the sour faced, they were sung by ladies and their lovers."[36] "But one Puritan among them," reports a Clown in *The Winter's Tale*, "and he sings psalms to hornepipes."

Nowhere was this practice of fitting folk airs to psalm texts more fecund, though, than in the upland South, where the Baptist and Methodist churches, the seats of our folk religion, were concentrated. Both churches had left New England in numbers after the Revolution; two-thirds of all Baptists were in the South by the end of the eighteenth century, and many thousands left for Kentucky; there were over thirty thousand there by 1809. Four-fifths of all Methodists, too, were concentrated in the region by 1800.[37] These were the religions, moreover, which proselytized most actively among Negroes, who not only swelled the ranks of white congregations but established Baptist and Methodist churches of their own. "Our congregation consists of five hundred souls and upwards," Methodist Bishop Francis Asbury noted in his journal in 1793, "three hundred being black."[38]

The life of psalmody is in its aurality and in the freedom for improvisation which allows for melismatic turns upon the melody; not surprisingly, then, it was in the black church, among people whose music is everywhere characterized by improvisation, antiphony, and the like that psalmody found willing and able adherents. "The Negroes . . . have an ear for Musik," wrote Samuel Davies, a New Light

Presbyterian who introduced psalmody to blacks in Virginia in the mid-eighteenth century, "and a kind of extatic delight in Psalmody."[39] Missionaries among blacks consistently noted their preference for psalm-singing and for Isaac Watts's *The Psalms of David, Imitated in the Language of the New Testament and Apply'd to the Christian State and Worship*, a songbook published by the English physician and minister in 1717. "I can hardly express the pleasure it affords me," Davies wrote, "to turn to that part of the gallery where they sit, and see so many of them with their Psalm or Hymn books . . . and then all breaking out in a torrent of sacred harmony, enough to bear away the whole congregation to heaven."[40]

We hear the psalm-song in the black folk church of today under the name of the "long meter" hymn, the "Dr. Watts," or, as George Pullen Jackson calls it, the "surge song," which is an elaborately melismatic, glacially slow-paced improvisation upon a simple basic melody, perhaps a familiar folk hymn such as "Amazing Grace," lined out tunefully at a "fair speaking pace" and ending on a held note that glides into the response:

> The deacon then starts singing, and by the time he has sung
> through the elaborately ornamented first syllable the whole
> congregation has joined in the second syllable with a volume
> of florid sound which ebbs and flows slowly, powerfully, and at
> times majestically in successive surges until the lined-out
> words have been sung. Without pause the deacon sing-songs
> the next couplet, and the second half of the four-line tune is
> sung in the same manner. . . . the singing surges on with so
> many graces and strings of graces . . . that all words, syllables
> even, lose their identity and evade recognition. It becomes
> vaguely evident that each complicated tone surge or tone
> constellation accompanies a single syllable of the text.[41]

Psalmody in white tradition did not fare so well, as the gradual ascendancy of the hymnbook rendered its aural and collective methods superfluous, fixing the melody and banishing the improvised melismatic turns which are the essence of the tradition in its ancient form. In New England, the "endlessly droned out" and "quaveringly sung" psalm-song died out early on, to be replaced by the formal hymn; the psalm suffered a similar fate in most of the upland South, where by the mid-nineteenth century the shape-note hymnal had become the foundation of religious song, though of course many of the formal hymns sung in that tradition had psalm texts.

It was only in the remote areas of Appalachia, where even in the presence of hymnals and songbooks aural methods of worship still prevailed, that the rudimentary structure of ancient psalmody persisted. In the Old Regular Baptist and other folk churches of Appalachia hymns are still "lined out;" the deacon chants one or two lines, usually dropping by two or three steps from a fifth to its tonic, with which he gently calls the congregation to himself; they gather closely together in the tonality he has given them, ascending and descending the simple altar of the melody in an imperfect unison, which at its point of highest intensity glows with an unmistakably blue radiance. The procedure is a deeply gratifying simple formality, like baptism; it does not have the luxuriance of surge song, the mystery of Gregorian chant, or the wild beauty of its counterpart in the Isle of Lewis. But the *jubilus* in its two forms, as "a long drawn out note on the vowel sounds" and as the melisma by which the singer may shape it, can still be heard awash on the tide of voices. If you doubt it, listen to the preacher's hymn, which he will sing to introduce himself and his sermon. It will come out in one of the old Church modes, the Dorian maybe; it will be earnest and deliberate, a meditation, as if he expected to call up the spirits of the dead with it and was preparing himself to meet them. And with the sweet outcries he makes of the long notes, his voice falling from them in troubled melismas which seem to place a weight of conviction upon some inexplicable grief, he sounds for all the world like Carter Stanley, or Larry Sparks, or even George Jones—or shall I say, they sound like him?

In its two forms the *jubilus* has come down the ages to us to be reforged in the nineteenth-century religious fervor which alloyed the African way with a song to our British song legacy, sending the shout and the surge of church singing into secular song. For the vocal ornaments in our country music are not the curious devices of Gaelic ballad which, like the illumined letter of a Celtic manuscript, add intrigue and immediacy to an incorruptible and impersonal design; the Gaelic singer dresses his song, which preceded him in the world and will endure long after he is gone, with a decorative tracery that is as intricate and fragile as the song is hard and unyielding. This style will be heard in the southern mountains, especially among women singers, by the hearth and in the nursery. But the eloquent, harrowing, insistent melismatic singing of our country singers has far more in common with Afro-American song and the tradition of melismatic variation which comes from Africa. These vocal ornaments, writes opera singer James Morris, do not "sit easily or gracefully on the musical phrase, but agitate the line, keeping it rough and strong. . . . The vocal line in the country song frequently seems to be thrust forward from note to note. . . . The musical gestures are deliberately and intrinsically muscular rather than soft and graceful. No artificial refinement of the speech pattern occurs as it does with many popular or classical singers."[42] When the country singer, like the spiritual shouter or the blues moaner, embarks upon a melismatic tour he is not decorating but composing—improvising, as we say; each turn is a probe into melodic darkness, an exploration of the psychic gaps that lie between the notes of southern song. These variations are not incidental to the song but are a part of its meaning, as gestures of the head and hands are part of the meaning of words. Thus the country singer, black or white, takes the song to himself, investing it with the potency of the spiritual moment.

One of the intriguing facts of American folk life is that it preserves various customs which long ago vanished in the Old World. The way the backwoods fiddler cradles the instrument in the crook of his arm, for instance—that's a relic of Baroque art music, and we see it in medieval woodcuts, too. So with the surge song, which is probably as close as we will hear to what was sung in the Protestant churches at the dawn of the modern era. Is the "high, lonesome sound," the sound of the bluegrass singer soaring with voice unbound in the polar regions of song, an American folk descendant of the ancient *jubilus?* I don't know. But it is tempting to think so. For the high, lonesome sound, like the *jubilus*, springs from the very heart of the folk imagination, as timeless and powerful as the "long, loud, musical shout" of the slave which Frederick Law Olmstead heard in South Carolina in 1853, "rising, and falling, and breaking into falsetto . . . ringing through the woods in the clear frosty night air, like a bugle-call."[43]

Afro-American influences have worked consistently over time in several quarters of southern folk life, imparting to its various forms of musical expression something of an African character. The African influence may perhaps be said to have awakened in our European musical legacy certain latent features such as the gapped scale, rhythmic complexity, a close alliance between song and speech, which we associate the world over with primitive music, with the incredible consequence that an American regional music, in a number of popular forms, has in effect become the "folk music" of the Western world. Though many of the historical channels, sacred and secular, through which these influences flowed have been lost, obscured, or forgotten, it is certain that the musical intercourse between black and white began the moment the African set foot on this continent and that the unique sound of American music has to an unacknowledged degree been shaped by his presence. Mountain music, long supposed to have evolved in isolation from an original Elizabethan deposit, seems at some early time to have taken an especially potent draught; J. P. Nestor's haunting and enigmatic "Train on the Island," for example, with its rolling terrain of strange, stark calls, its distinctly falling melodic contour, its monochord harmonic background, its deep blue tonality, its broken, chimerical lyrics, sounds to me like something once heard from afar, across some dark and compelling human frontier, and only imperfectly recalled—the "sad and plaintive melody from another hemisphere" described 150 years ago by a traveler to Louisiana.[44]

Deeply conservative by nature and protected by isolated circumstances from sweeping or cataclysmic change, Appalachian music displays an ontogeny of black influences that represents stages in the life of mountain culture, from early Piedmont emigrations, to the visits of minstrel shows on the riverboats, to the incursion of the railroads and, finally, of radio and phonograph. That is why bluegrass music, a deliberate attempt to epitomize the "old southern sound," can have done so with Appalachian music as a background and why the "old southern sound," when we listen closely to its representation in bluegrass, is to an astonishing extent an Afro-American sound. Modern black influences upon bluegrass—blues and early jazz especially, precisely because they have preserved the enduring traits of black tradition—work paradoxically to reawaken the original genius of Appalachian music which popular commercial influences in this century had begun to dispel.

We cannot leave the matter of Afro-American influence, then, without pausing briefly to consider what the nature of that influence has been at bottom, and to do so will require that we say a bit about African music itself.

Let us recall that Western music, with its written language, its technological sophistication, and its theoretical development, especially in the realm of harmony, is, as the world's music goes, a bit of an anomaly. No other music in the world has secured such a nearly absolute, mathematics-like independence of other forms of expression. Though all music is set apart from the rest of the audible universe by the same natural laws that set ours apart, the laws of rhythm and harmony, the world's classical and folk traditions outside the West retain their ancient mimetic alliances to ritual and drama, poetry and dance, reflecting the expressive nuances of human gesture, movement, and particularly of human sound—that is, of voice and speech.

This is nowhere more true than in West Africa, where music, song, and speech are virtually indistinguishable from one another. Father Jones's study among others reveals to us that African melodies and rhythms follow speech tones and speech rhythms very closely, departing only in predictable ways dictated by the grammatical requirements of the language; consequently the art of song consists in the variation upon and ornamentation of a basic melody constructed on the intonation and rhythm of the words. Such an alliance may seem peculiar to us but it helps to know that the African languages are themselves highly "musical"—languages in which variations of pitch may have a grammatical or a lexical function, where rhythmic patterns may have rhetorical significance, and where the better part of the substantive vocabulary is idiophonic.[45] The miraculous phenomenon of the Yoruba or Ashanti talking drum, then, has as its backdrop the aural acuity of African society itself, in which music is really an extension of speech and its functions. "The principal and essential traits of African music," writes Jean Baptiste Obama, "its melodic, harmonic, and rhythmic characteristics, are all linked to the making of the essentially 'speaking' instrument."[46]

We have already seen what these "essential traits" are. Because the ear can attend to many different things at once, African music is polyrhythmic: in actual African performance, however, "polyrhythm" is really a species of conversation, a sort of musical symposium, in which a number of independent speech lines, all "spoken" by means of a drum, a gong, a xylophone, or similar instrument, are woven together at once. The same thing happens, of course, in African social conversation, which to the Western ear may be quite nerve-wracking, with a number of people talking simultaneously, often at the top of their lungs; to do this intelligibly, to communicate effectively with several people at once and at the same time to be communicated to, requires a language differently constituted than our own, a more "musical" language, full of the inflection, repetition, and redundancy characteristic of aural languages. Thus African music is improvisatory, but not in any mysterious sense; it is improvisatory the way speech is "improvisatory," which is to say it is only the exercise of a natural expressive capacity which calls upon a multitude of formulaic and conventional expressions, a "language" which in the case of most West African music is the native language itself, given *musical* character by the cultivation of melodic and rhythmic characteristics already quite well developed in themselves. Finally it goes virtually without saying that an aural music such as the African, given its particular virtues and powers so different from those of Western music, given the radically different culture from which it springs, is likely to have a different role in the life of African society than Western music has in the life of Western society. To describe fully what these uses may be is beyond the scope of this discussion, but we can say at least that African music is, as the anthropologists say, "functional": it unfolds on behalf of some adjunct activity such as ritual or work from which it is not formally distinguished, and in this capacity has the power to draw the community together in a coordinated collective effort. Like African speech, African music is performance, not text; the musician imparts through sound a sense of the occasion. Its virtue, broadly speaking, is to bring something hidden, inaccessible, or covert to light—to draw something in the heart or mind, something in the past, something in nature or in God, into the collective presence. This may be the praise of a chieftain which humility would quell, the insult which shame would forestall, the gathering tedium of an essential task, the ancestor or spirit concealed in nature or in time, even the joy or grief that cannot be contained. Think for a moment of our own blues singers and remember that African music is a form of privileged speech, speech protected by music as our own innermost thoughts and feelings are protected by silence—silent thought being one human contrivance which in aural cultures is as rare as the letters and books which elsewhere encourage it. "Woe to the man in Africa who cannot stand perpetual uproar!" wrote Mary Kingsley, who visited West Africa in the 1890s; " . . . even when you are sitting alone on the forest you will hear a man or woman coming down the narrow bush path chattering away with such energy and expression that you can hardly believe your eyes when you learn from him that he has no companion."[47]

The question for us, then: what happens to Western music when the African musician plays it? However "universal" our music as a "language" may be, Western music does not speak—not like the talking drum, which does literally *talk*. Western music is mute, and that is just its virtue—that it is not tied to speech, or to bird song, or to anything else in nature but the physical properties of sound. It is, theoretically at least, an autonomous system of pure tones, true notes, regular rhythms, and independent pitches in fixed relationships determined by the capacity of the human ear to appreciate consonance and tolerate dissonance. Consequently we should expect the Western system of music to suffer under the African influence, as to the European-trained ear it has suffered: tones grow hair, go blind, or explode; notes bend, break, weaken, collapse, or leave home; melodies compulsively juggle handfuls of notes or fling them wildly away;

rhythms spill over in syncopations. Nor is it only our musical syntax that suffers: horns growl, hiss, cough, and squeak; banjos snarl, snap, and bite; fiddles cry and wail; singing voices shout, holler, call, moan, and weep, fill with gravel, smoke, or weeds, cower in the nasal cavities or in one corner of the mouth or sink luxuriously into some lower region of the anatomy, and sometimes even slip into mere speech or something worse, like nonsense syllables.

This isn't "suffering"—not really. The words which in poetry grow molten in the heat of metaphor, or mysteriously deepen in the under-tow of rhythm, or dissolve in solutions of sound and sense are suffering too; for the poet, language itself is dumb. These effects, musical and poetical, are the signs of a tension between the artist and his medium, of the stress he has placed upon it in order to wring out those transient vapors of meaning which cannot exist apart from their particular em-bodiment in language and sound, the ineffable dimension that is "lost in translation." The medium, as we say, is *hot* and sheds its excess energy in meaning.

What we call jazz is Western music played by ear, for the ear, by musicians who are accustomed to thinking of music as spontaneous playing and singing. The very early jazz bands of New Orleans, where European music of all kinds was everywhere to be heard, may illustrate the point: called "fake bands" locally, they played the ordinary score-based music of the marching band and beer-garden orchestra *by ear*, releasing it from the enchantment of the musical score and opening it to all those aural influences—musical, dramatic, and poetic—which have virtually reversed the direction of Western musical tradition. What has happened, simply, is that the role played by speech in African music has in jazz been supplanted by Western melodies, especially popular ones which lent themselves to aural performance, because the Afro-American musician could not transplant to America the entire linguistic and social order with which his native African music was bound up—as in fact it was transplanted, in cult form, to parts of the Caribbean. For the Afro-American musician, this has all been immea-surably liberating: in a sense African music, for all its subtlety and complexity, especially rhythmic complexity, was tied to speech and limited by it. If the aural genius of the African musician has been set free in America, it is precisely because he was forced to adopt the autonomous system of music which he could revitalize by means of the very same aural powers which, in the age of Bach and Mozart, had originally given rise to it. What Bach and Mozart could do with im-punity—improvise by ear—the black musician would do again, work-ing not in the harmonic language of European tradition but with his own mimetic imagination—a process which inevitably took him *back to speech.*

Preaching, talking, testifying, telling, confessing—in the minds of its performers and audiences alike, jazz, blues, and the many related species of Afro-American music have always been understood to be a special kind of speech, a *virtual* speech. It is possible, indeed, that early jazz men "talked" to one another in a language the white could not understand. Jazz writers, by their constant recourse to such terms as *phrase, paraphrase, statement, allusion, cliché,* and so on, have implicitly acknowledged that Afro-American music is a language in more than a figurative sense. "The notes will work the same as the words," Bill Monroe has observed; "they'll tell you lots of things, if you want to put yourself in there and be just thinking like the music goes."[48] It is not only that jazz instruments often mimic the voice or that Earl Scruggs, "the boy that makes the banjo talk," can make his banjo call for its Mama and ask quite plainly for a drink of water. Because the Afro-American musician uses rhythm as we do in speech, to shape his meaning, his music seems to mimic the many *movements* of speech, its dynamic form, and beyond that seems to reflect in its structure of licks, runs, riffs, and breaks the phrases, clauses, sentences, and longer threads from which discourse is woven. Nowhere is the impression more powerful than in blues singing, which is actually a kind of musicalized speech. "You pattern the words to rise and fall in a way similar to the way you would speak them," says blues singer Al Wilson, "and construct the words not just any way but so that they flow naturally with the flow of the melody."[49]

A similar and equally remarkable development as the evolution of jazz took place on the folk level, where the African musician found many musical traditions, also aural in character, congenial to him: the pentatonism of Scots song, lively traditional dances, the antiphonal psalmody of the Church. In southern fields, on the levees, in Baptist and Methodist churches, at the camp meetings, the African sang white songs and formal hymns, as Lomax puts it, "to pieces," forming the formulaic vocabulary of a new Afro-American aural tradition which has given us the spirituals and the blues, and has permanently altered the phraseology and rhythm of American music, infusing it with new mimetic powers and establishing in it that coordination of rhythm and melody ("the Africans play *tunes* on their drums") which is speech-derived, gives to music the grip of speech upon our attention, and above all taps in the musician the natural and spontaneous language-uttering power from which musical improvisation arises. Finally, the Afro-American musician has communicated to us something of his culture's sense of the place of music in life and society. We have felt its power to bind communities together, to give voice to our innermost feelings, to renew the sense of life, and even to lend its emotional hues to the whole of our experience. In America, Afro-American music has restored to us something of music's ancient vatic force.

But the great triumph, as the world well knows, has been in rhythm. Free to use rhythm expressively, the solo instrumentalist can almost literally speak to us with his music, communicating with his audience through the subtle impact of rhythm, speaking, it seems, sometimes so personally and intimately that we seem more to overhear than to hear him, as if his meaning were something we could carry away with us and even somehow repeat to other ears, like a secret. The singer, too: he can use words as poets use them, setting the rhythms of speech, and all the natural signs that are in the voice, against an underlying regular rhythm, engendering rhythmic densities and discontinuities which, as W. B. Yeats wrote, "prolong the moment of contemplation."[50] This intensification of attention, and the apparent deepening of meaning which attends it, is one of the most powerful and familiar effects of the blues, for instance, in which a line such as "Come back, baby, baby please don't go," so innocent or even fatuous outside its musical setting, takes on *in* its musical setting the dramatic impact of a Keatsean ode. "The colored people get to singing right from the heart," Monroe observes; "they get to living that song . . ."[51]

The bifurcation of rhythm and meter, the strange mitosis by which a piece of music is stripped of its accents and left in a metrical form to which accents may return in the neurological fingerprint of the musician himself, has had profound consequences for music and for society, as in each generation some new strain of black or black-inspired music sweeps the culture and awakens it to its own obscure discontents. Early jazz, with its thick and explosive collective improvisation fuelled by the sounds of barrelhouse, brothel, and bandwagon, was a tribal bonfire in which all the sordid piety and vulgar sentimentality of bourgeoise popular culture went up in smoke, and the history of jazz has been the search for an ever more original idiom by the individual voices forged in that heat. Bluegrass, too: though its origins were in the mountain community and its dance band, it spoke at once in the individual voices awakened by Monroe and integrated by the syncopations of Scruggs's banjo; today at its most sophisticated it is as carefully worked out as a mass transit timetable.

But its acoustics, unlike those of jazz, belonged to the past and infused the music with a quality of the past from which technical sophistication has not yet absolved it. Out of the sparsely settled regions in the heart of the bluegrass band, almost, it seems, out of the past itself, the voice of fiddle, banjo, or mandolin welled up to call the music back to the South. That voice, like the steady moan which rises out of the black church congregation to lead it towards unity in song, came from the depths of American music, from the point at which imagination focuses its many influences, each one sounding the timbre of an epoch, a human culture, a way of life, and makes them one.

Chapter 6

Upstairs, Downstairs, Out in the Kitchen
The Tradition

Vaughn and Lawrence Eller, the Eller Brothers, are two musicians of Bill Monroe's generation from Hiawassee, Georgia, in the Blue Ridge. In the summer of 1980 they appeared with guitar and banjo at the National Folk Festival to play, in a rough, home-built, bluegrass style, Bill Monroe's "On and On." It was just an old song, they said, and they couldn't remember who wrote it or where it had come from. In utter defiance of copyright laws, "On and On" had "entered tradition"—at the ripe old age of about twenty-seven. Bluegrass was and is *the* music of the Appalachian people. It attracted, and still attracts, hundreds of young men, and a few women, from the region—a cultural area that includes parts of Washington and Baltimore, as well as Dayton, Cincinnati, Columbus, Detroit, and Chicago—who otherwise would have taken up country-western, rockabilly, or rock-and-roll, or who would never have become musicians at all, and in so doing renewed the lease of many old songs and the many old influences that accompany them, which would otherwise have expired. It inspired professionals to contribute in unique and original ways to what must have seemed at first to be only a continuation of a familiar native tradition: "We called it mountain music then," says an Osborne Brothers' song. In short order these contributions of song, style, and technique, captured and disseminated by radio and phonograph, became a body of conventionalized material upon which the amateur musician could draw and proved consistent and durable enough to become eventually a distinct kind of "traditional" music: traditional, that is, in practice, the long spans of time normally associated with

tradition having been violently foreshortened by radio and phonograph. Yet, while remaining essentially Appalachian, the bluegrass
style was elastic enough to attract musicians and musical influences
far removed from Appalachia; the widening of those influences, combined with the evolution of a community of participants whose means
of exchanging information have become ever more sophisticated, has
engendered a kind of string-band renaissance in which bluegrass bands
emerge with old-time bands, western swing revival bands, jug bands,
skiffle bands, Irish caeli bands and bands that elude classification from
the tidal pools of folk and country music, moved by impulses ranging
from self-conscious and scrupulous archaism to space-age experimen-
talism: listen to what Sam Bush, on the electric fiddle, has done with
the old fiddle tune "Lee Highway Blues." Bluegrass itself, like jazz,
now has "traditional" and "progressive" strains.

Neil Rosenberg has shown us how, under the impact of the emerging
"hit-star" system in country music, Bill Monroe's work inspired immediate imitation and with it an intense professional rivalry.[1] He takes
us to the moment at which, as he puts it, the bluegrass "sound" became
a "style," through Ralph and Carter Stanley's recording of "Molly and
Tenbrooks," released in September 1948—one year *before* the release
of Monroe's own version, but in all respects an attempt to reproduce
Monroe's performance. The lead singing, for instance, was given to
Pee Wee Lambert, the band's mandolinist, who since his early teens
had been a Monroe admirer and imitator—imitation that included posture, dress, and facial expression. It is odd, perhaps, that Lambert
did not take a mandolin break in the song, but Monroe had not taken
one either; he regarded "Molly and Tenbrooks" as a "banjo song" and
used it as a showcase for Scruggs. Ralph Stanley backed Lambert with
his new banjo roll, built upon his earlier double-thumbing style but
obviously inspired by Earl Scruggs. Both Stanley and Scruggs had
played on radio station WCYB in Bristol, Virginia, and both trace the
lineage of their styles to the same man, Snuffy Jenkins of North Carolina.

The Stanley Brothers had learned the song from one of Monroe's
live performances. Rosenberg notes that while the recording industry
generally lay fallow during the years of World War II, the sale of
hillbilly records grew phenomenally, owing to the migrations of southern whites to northern cities and to the popularity of hillbilly music in
the armed forces. While before the war hillbilly music had been largely
the province of the local radio station with its staff of musicians, after
the war it became a commodity to be purveyed by phonograph record
and hence a property managed and manipulated by the recording com-

pany, the booking agent, and the disc jockey. Monroe's stardom, Rosenberg reminds us, was firmly established after the war by the release of his "Kentucky Waltz" and "Footprints in the Snow"—songs which had been recorded in 1945, before the formation of the "original" bluegrass band and which, as we've seen, were not markedly different from other hillbilly hits of the period. It was the "original" band, however— Flatt, Scruggs, Wise, and Rainwater—that accompanied him on his extensive tours throughout the South for which his records had prepared the way. Rosenberg notes that southern audiences were exposed to the original bluegrass style, then, through personal appearances, Opry radio broadcasts, and finally through recordings made in 1946 and 1947, for four years or more.

When Flatt and Scruggs left Monroe and formed their own bluegrass band in 1948, the same year in which the mountain duo Ralph and Carter Stanley took up Monroe's style, the evolution of bluegrass as a genre began. It is now commonplace to observe that in a few years the field of bluegrass music was populated by musicians who had begun with Monroe—Flatt and Scruggs, Jimmy Martin, Don Reno, Mac Wiseman, Sonny Osborne—whose work in their own bands collectively became the mine from which "traditional" bluegrass has been quarried. "The earliest period of bluegrass history," Rosenberg writes, "has been constantly repeated, as musicians decide, like Flatt and Scruggs, to start their own groups . . . most of the major bluegrass bands have some members who have played with Monroe." He notes that this early transmission of style and material from one band to another aroused a sense of rivalry in the musicians, especially in Monroe himself; "but more than rivalry is involved, for the turnover in band personnel has led to constant recombination of musicians in a limited number of bands. With this exchange of personnel comes an exchange of repertory and musical techniques which constitutes a kind of oral tradition within the style."[2]

What kind of oral tradition, or as I prefer to call it, "aural" tradition? Really, it is an amazing phenomenon, this convergence of individual enterprise, folk tradition, commercial expedience, audial technology, and social cohesion. Mike Seeger reports that by the mid-1950s nearly every town of any consequence in the Southeast harbored at least one bluegrass band.[3] Many of these enjoyed some small commercial exposure; some achieved a modest but durable professional success; most eventually dissolved. The history of bluegrass will record a few of their names—the Church Brothers, the Bray Brothers, Red Allen and the Kentuckians, Earl Taylor and the Stoney Mountain Boys, the Lilly Brothers, the Lonesome Pine Fiddlers, the Stoneman Family, Bill

Clifton, Hylo Brown, Buzz Busby, Vern and Ray, Bob Baker and the
Pike County Boys, the Mountain Ramblers, Mac Martin and the Dixie
Travelers, Bill Box and the Dixie Drifters, Bill Britten—the list runs
into hundreds, and in the 1980s continues to grow out of the same
impulse, and largely out of the same social and regional connections,
as it did in 1950.

With the folk revival of the 1960s, bluegrass, for obvious reasons
attractive to folk revivalists, took on a following in the North, among
the educated middle class; the formation of northern and urban bluegrass bands introduced new influences into the music, first from the
folk revival itself and later from the rock music which overtook popular
culture in the late 1960s and 1970s. The musical and social spectrum
of bluegrass has continually widened, so that we find conservatory-
trained violinists and bassists, say, in bluegrass bands, as well as
farmers and working men who play only for recreation; sometimes we
find them in the *same* band. Bluegrass bands will perform in three-
piece suits for the Folk Song Society of Princeton University or at
Lincoln Center, or in the smoke and din of a local bar, or at summertime
"boogies" in a park or campground, over a weekend which promises
at least one good dogfight, perhaps a drunken brawl or two, and, with
luck, a shooting.

But departures from the original bluegrass styles began very early
in the music. A Missouri band adorned its repertoire of mountain songs
with flashy instrumental arrangements and a slick vocal delivery reminiscent of popular folk groups such as the Kingston Trio. A band from
New England included contra-dance tunes and sea chanteys in its
repertoire, while a band from Oklahoma borrowed heavily from western swing and cowboy songs. One young duo performed only the recorded repertoire of the early Stanley Brothers, with uncanny accuracy
to their source; many confined themselves piously to gospel songs.
Some groups performed various kinds of popular music accompanied
by bluegrass instruments or imported a bluegrass banjo or fiddle into
what was otherwise a country-western or rock band in order to give
a backwoods or mountain flavor to a particular song. One group from
Louisville, in all respects a rock-hard bluegrass band, under the influence of its sultry-voiced female lead singer who was attracting all the
attention, began to favor her cabaret blues and early jazz; another,
with an Irish fiddler, drifted towards Ireland; another unpacked a
hammer dulcimer, and with it a string of obscure jigs, reels, hornpipes,
and waltzes whose florid melodies nearly smothered the bluegrass
style. With the addition of new instruments—harmonica, piano, pedal
steel, drums, even a saxophone or clarinet—the borders of bluegrass

became unstable; yet there seemed no other class to which these bands could belong. Finally a few old-time string bands, with roots in the folk revival, took up some of the original and neglected recorded bluegrass, which in the lapse of years had acquired a distinctly "old-time" quality, and in so doing became, as their bluegrass repertoire grew, *de facto* bluegrass bands.

The kinds of bluegrass differ principally in their aims. There is a kind of bluegrass music played, for example, by professional musicians in the recording studio—committing their music to recording tape and thence through a phonograph record to a commercial market and a degree of permanence: in a consciousness of which the musician prepares his music. His music is, in a sense, "cooked up," so let's call this kind of bluegrass "kitchen" bluegrass. Kitchen bluegrass is undertaken in a milieu of recording—inspired and informed by it, harboring ambitions shaped by the expectation, hope, or fantasy of it; kitchen bluegrass excludes, however, recordings of live performances, which form another category.

When, on the other hand, amateur musicians play together at a summertime bluegrass picnic or festival, or on the neighbor's back porch on a Saturday afternoon, simply to recreate themselves and to indulge their interest in bluegrass, with little thought to the originality, permanence, or perfection of their music, they play, let's say, "back-porch" bluegrass. Back-porch bluegrass, like kitchen bluegrass, has the recorded music of professionals as its background; but unlike kitchen bluegrass it is conventional, conservative, even formulaic in character. From the practical standpoint it is a genuinely spontaneous, collective, and participatory music, a "traditional" music, which the bluegrass festival has done much to enrich and consolidate.

Closely related to back-porch bluegrass, because of its amateur status, and yet fundamentally different from it, is what we might call "parlor" bluegrass, recalling the "profitable, instructive, and amusing" parlor music, to quote an old Sears catalogue, of the Gilded Age. This is the music that comes out of instruction books. Sometimes garnered from phonograph records and sometimes originally composed, parlor bluegrass commits music to writing, either in tabulature, which is a kind of schematic representation of the neck of a fretted instrument, or in actual musical notation, for the purpose of selling it to the novice. Parlor music may move easily from the parlor to the back porch or the kitchen, or, if mother insists, to the barn; but as long as a consciousness of the tabulature or transcription figures into it, it retains the decorous and exacting attitude of the parlor.

Affecting and affected by these kinds of bluegrass is of course the live performance, whose form depends largely upon the nature of the audience and the occasion, which, as we've seen, may be the concert hall, the tavern, the outdoor bandstand, or even the television studio. It is out there where everyone can see and hear it, so let's put it on the front porch. Bluegrass grew up in a concert setting, and it is in concert that the bluegrass musician and the bluegrass band are most fully realized; it is in concert, too, that the music and the musician must ultimately be proved. For though bluegrass, like jazz, is the cooperative activity of living musicians, it is also, like jazz, an exhibition of that activity: thus whether he learned his music in the kitchen, the parlor, the back porch, or the barn, the musician must finally try himself on the front porch, under the pressure of others' attention and on the swell of the moment.

What closet, bedroom, basement, or bathroom bluegrass may be, I leave to the reader's imagination. I once heard a first-rate version of "Dixie Breakdown" by a banjo player who was standing in a bathtub; you can't beat a bathroom for acoustics. But let us climb to the attic, where Aunt Maude's collection of old 78s is gathering dust. By "attic" bluegrass I mean a learned, even academic, bluegrass, one which partakes, to whatever degree, of the spirit of scholarship, of antiquarianism perhaps, of revivalism. All bluegrass imbibes this spirit somewhat, even Bill Monroe's original bluegrass, which sought to epitomize the "old southern sound." Yet bluegrass and "old-time" music are now estranged, sometimes with considerable mutual rancor; not infrequently old-time musicians express abhorrence of bluegrass and close the gates of their festivals to bluegrass musicians, who must consequently get in by stealth. But this is a family squabble. The impulse which moves the folklorist-musician to reproduce with painstaking exactitude the recorded performances of traditional and hillbilly musicians fifty years old and the impulse which fired Monroe's original bluegrass are at root the same: only their methods differ.

The old-time band typically ferrets out recorded material from the past which they either revive in their own way or imitate closely; this includes traditional and hillbilly music, as well as many obscure, quaint, or merely eccentric pieces of music. The earliest bluegrass recordings, too, have in time taken on an antique quality, and from our elongated temporal perspective display that continuity with Appalachian tradition which was plain to the Applachian musician himself at the very outset. Thus several old-time bands such as the Red Clay Ramblers or the Hotmud Family have introduced into their repertory, beside the usual fiddle tunes, Carter Family songs, early jazz and string rags, bluegrass songs recorded twenty or twenty-five years ago, in the 1950s, by the first generation of bluegrass musicians, adopting some early version of the bluegrass style to do so and thus acknowledging the affinities among Appalachian traditional music, hillbilly, and bluegrass music and advancing the boundary of "old-time" music a whole generation. Attic bluegrass simply retrieves from a phonograph record a song or tune no longer performed by the band which first recorded it, often one with some archaic, idiosyncratic, or nostalgic quality: the outdated morality of the Stanley Brothers' "She's More to be Pitied than Scolded," the wistful harmonies of the Lonesome Pine Fiddlers' "Windy Mountain," or that same band's curious relic of the fifties, "No Curb Service:"

> Don't blink your lights,
> Don't blow your horn.
> I hate the day that you were born.
> There's no curb service anymore.

Attic bluegrass has the exacting attitude of parlor bluegrass but not the exactness itself; it has the professionalism, but not the originality, of kitchen bluegrass, except in its choice of material; it has the authenticity, but not the spontaneity, of back-porch bluegrass, being in effect a learned and self-conscious execution of the same material, which the back-porch musician, in aural fashion, "dissolves, diffuses, dissipates," as Coleridge puts it, "in order to recreate."

Back-porch pickers who have never played together can meet in the parking lot at a bluegrass festival and in a matter of moments make a bluegrass music as well planned and coordinated as a professional burglary. Back-porch bluegrass stands upon a body of recorded music, largely the legacy of the first professional bluegrass musicians, consisting of songs, instrumental tunes, runs, phrases, and licks, as well as a set of standardized chord progressions, modes, and of course instrumental techniques which taken together form the back-porch "tradition" and which every back-porch musician knows at least in part. This body of music is "traditional" in several senses. First, it has undergone a process of selection by the bluegrass community: not *every* recorded song or tune enters the corpus permanently; it must have something which touches the heart. A particular summer may bring its fashionable song, but many disappear, especially if they are over-performed: this has been the fate of "Orange Blossom Special," for instance, and "Fox on the Run." This body of music does not constitute, as it does to a degree in parlor bluegrass, a series of fixed "texts" to be reproduced more-or-less faithfully, though the discographer or folklorist might regard it as such. The back-porch picker regards it as a continuous field of discrete and separate elements which, when once adapted through practice to his personal use, can be used interchangeably with any other element. It is a resource—not, like a musical score, a plan. Back-porch bluegrass, then, is formulaic and allows for the extemporaneous cooperative performance—the "simultaneous composition and performance"—which Albert Lord and Milman Parry in their study of Balkan epic-singers showed us is the essence of an aural tradition. Musicians with a great variety of these elements at their disposal are quite obviously best prepared to participate; but one need not have a great variety of chords, runs, licks, and so on at one's fingertips *in order* to participate. At the same time the tradition admits and encourages a certain degree of inventiveness and originality, but the kitchen musician may find himself left behind on the back porch, just as the back-porch musician may sound merely hackneyed and dull among kitchen musicians. If, however, an invented element exceeds in complexity what can plausibly enter the tradition aurally, it belongs not on the back porch but, perhaps, in the kitchen or even the parlor, and though the musician who comes to a back-porch session with a fistful of hot licks or convuluted chord progressions may be admired or envied for his technical achievement, it is evident at the same time that he wishes to declare his independence of the tradition, which most back-porch musicians will readily grant him.

Simply by calling it "traditional," bluegrass musicians seem to have located back-porch bluegrass in the past, assigning its origin to the great original musicians now vanished or in the twilight of their careers and suggesting, albeit covertly, its obsolescence, for in this sense "traditional" is a kind of euphemism.

All music generates, in a sense, an "aural" tradition. But in bluegrass even thoroughgoing professionalism, as the cases of "On and On" and "Molly and Tenbrooks" illustrate, has not secured the rights of proprietorship which prevail in popular music generally. Bill Monroe left Columbia records when they signed on the Stanley Brothers, because he felt they had trespassed upon his proprietary right to the music he had created. But why did the Stanleys trespass, if it *was* trespassing, so readily, and why have all other bluegrass musicians, back-porch, front-porch, even in the parlor, done the same with impunity?

Consider, by analogy, the possible benefits to music or to literature were the rights of proprietorship, and the laws which enforce them, to be abolished: the musician could draw from the repository of composed music discrete independent elements—themes, motifs, figures, and the like—to modify and recombine them as new music, composing, perhaps, Beethoven's "Tenth" symphony, or finishing the Unfinished Symphony. Or the writer could annex to his own work the characters, plots, settings, even the words of other writers, fabricating new works in which, perhaps, Tess's letter might not slip under the carpet, or the man from Porlock be detained. This was in fact the case in music at the time of Mozart, and in literature at the time of Shakespeare; it is the rule of the aural universe, in which all is suspended in an aesthetically neutral space. It prevails in modern jazz—though not, alas, in modern literature, where in spite of T. S. Eliot's brave insurrection plagarism is still a crime. The appetite for originality and the sense of proprietorship, feelings connected to our individualist culture in much the same way that sexual roles are connected to it, prohibit access to the immense communal resources of art and thrust the artist into a vacuum where the accomplishments of others can help him only as "influences."

In a traditional culture, and in other kinds of communities such as the family in which beliefs, values, ideas, attitudes, habits, practices, and experiences are conscientiously preserved and shared, in which the individual, perhaps, has neither the opportunity, the necessity, nor the means to formulate his own private and independent sense of life, the artist expresses, in a sense, the imagination of the community as a whole, *its* sense of life: a condition to which the modern individualist artist can only aspire. Thus the individual in a traditional community can compose out of traditional materials, say, a ballad, which at the conclusion of its first performance has acquired already the impersonal or anonymous quality of traditional song; or, conversely, the community—the congregation of the black holiness church, for example—can compose communally a song which though it may only be performed once, on the occasion for which it was created, has the personal intensity and the structural integrity of deliberate individual art.

Bluegrass music, we noted several thousand words back, seemed to "reauthenticate" or "traditionalize" hillbilly music; it was a representation of traditional Appalachian music in its social or assembly form. Consequently, though it was an original and individual creation, it aroused a powerful response in a people whose allegiance and sentiments were still largely directed toward the region and the community from which social change had separated them, a people who were still essentially the dispersed "folk" of a folk culture. Back-porch bluegrass, whether in a Dayton suburb, at a bluegrass festival in Michigan or Indiana, or in Appalachia itself, is a kind of reunion of this community based upon that widespread response and upon the power of radio and phonograph to engender it among people otherwise isolated from one another economically, geographically, even socially. That a "reunion" takes place at all depends upon the accessibility of the music to the people who recognize themselves in it, for the musical order is underwritten by a social and economic one; that accessibility depends in turn upon a uniform willingness to relax the principles which would tie particular musical inventions exclusively to their inventors. Anyone who has played back-porch bluegrass with Tennesseans or Kentuckians, or has been to a bluegrass festival, recognizes at once that the mainspring of the occasion is a tribal sympathy of which the love of bluegrass music is only one manifestation, bringing people into a temporary but intense association both musical and social. Bluegrass music is a representation; by imitating that representation, back-porch pickers make it real.

In societies which rely upon oral communication for the retention of vital cultural information, the so-called "oral" cultures which can preserve the products of imagination and experience—all that goes by the name of tradition—for the most part only in memory, the convention and formula are likely to dominate art, for conventions and formulae reflect the social dimension of art; they are ways of securing its context and of preserving the fleeting word or tone. As its name implies, an artistic convention is a formal device whose function artists and audiences have agreed upon; in jazz and bluegrass, the solo break is a convention, as is the blues chord progression. A formula is the irreducible element of the special language belonging to and circumscribing an art. "Old Kentucky" and "Sunny Tennessee" are familiar formulae of popular song; Lester Flatt's endlessly copied "G-run" is only one of a host of brief melodic figures out of which bluegrass musicians, banjo pickers especially, "solve the problems of improvisation, innovation, and even of routine performance," writes Thomas Adler, "in a manner that seems to be closely analogous to the use of oral formulae."[4] The names of these figures—"turn-arounds," "potatoes," "tags" and so on—suggest that like oral formulae each has a specific function and thus regularly appears in the same contexts; most have an original on record and most have spawned new formulae through variation. Through bluegrass, then, the back-porch picker can summon the same spirits of human solidarity that reign among Harlan County miners and southern white autoworkers in Detroit, both of whom incorporate back-porch bluegrass into their union life. The formulaic and conventional character of back-porch bluegrass invites participation, and it is participation in one form or another which rewards the individual, admitting him into the community in a way that embodies its transpersonal nature in deep personal experience.

Back-porch bluegrass, then, is an aural tradition built largely upon a technological, not a social, foundation—phonograph records and the broadcasting of phonograph records—but one which can generate new social and personal realities which replenish or replace those that have lapsed or decayed or in fact never existed. It would seem that because the phonograph record preserves the performance an aural tradition, which presumably demands the absence of documentation, cannot coalesce around it. But about recordings of all kinds there is one salient fact: we can slow them down, speed them up, alter, adjust, repeat, and study them, but we cannot stop them. The recording retains far more information than the musical score in a far less accessible form. It remains auditory, not visual, and consequently challenges the retentive and discriminatory powers of the ear, inviting the analysis by theme and phrase favored by the aural imagination and fixed by it as convention and formulae. The phonograph record is the audible dimension of a particular past performance, which though repeatable is as fleeting and indefinite the hundredth time as it was the first. As such it cannot actually be "read," but only imitated: imitation being, as Aristotle reminds us, a representation of its apparent, not its actual, form. Though our impression of a performance may be better secured through repetition, it remains an impression, however coarse or fine. The musician striving to imitate a performance, out of allegiance and dedication to the original, will call upon its identifying signs in his own performance, upon the musical inventions and habits of a Bill Monroe or Earl Scruggs, and thereby transform them into common property. For when he plays them, they seem to belong to him, just as the wisdom of a proverb seems to belong to us when we repeat it.

Thus an aural tradition is free to develop even in the context of stiff professional rivalry; the impersonality and anonymity we usually associate with aural tradition can flourish side-by-side with fierce identification of the musician with his music. For what the phonograph record communicates that the musical score does not is the *impact* of a performance, which, whether it becomes a model for imitation or not, attaches as surely to the performer as the score attaches to the composer. The knot is sometimes so tight that other recordings of the same song, *even by the same musician*, may have an air of fraudulence. But the recording is tied to the performer *as* performer; thus by virtue of an exceptional performance a musician may wrest a piece out of the composer's hands: Bill Monroe composed neither "Muleskinner Blues" nor "Good-bye Old Pal," yet they are consistently identified with him by bluegrass musicians and fans. All performances, in other words, are in a sense original. The classic bluegrass recordings seem to present some single feature—a chord change, an instrumental break, a vocal tour de force, a lyric—upon which new performances can be based without eclipsing the original, but rather calling attention to it. We can add as many variations to Scruggs's "Foggy Mountain Breakdown" as we like; but it is the guitar's E-major chord, which Lester Flatt introduced, set against the banjo's E-minor that confers the mark of authenticity, perhaps because it establishes a link with the original recording. We can add or subtract verses to Monroe's "Molly and Tenbrooks" or even alter their sequence; but, like the Stanley Brothers, we shall probably follow Monroe in singing the song as high as we can, in B or better, and in featuring the banjo. Few performers will abandon the flatted note which Monroe introduced into the tenor part of his "Can't You Hear Me Callin'" or the shuffling fiddle break which Red Taylor used on "Uncle Pen." Each of these devices reveals the musician's sense of his song, his awareness of its particular alignment of style and subject matter. Flatt's E-major, for example, frames Scruggs's minor like wildflowers arranged in a vase; the bright, excited cry and high-stepping banjo of "Molly and Tenbrooks" brings fair weather and big money to the story of a famous horserace; the flatted note in "Can't You Hear Me Callin'" rends with despair the fabric of the harmony; Taylor's shuffle conjures up the sound of Uncle Pen's fiddle and with it a Saturday-night hoedown in the hills.

Yet, at the same time as the phonograph record or radio performance ties performance to performer, so does it hide the face of the performer. A radio personality or "recording artist," as he is called in the industry, is free to make a representation of himself in music which, whatever its relation to reality, eventually returns to him as a live performer and personality, and, in the sight of his audience, may transform him from an actuality into what is in effect a dramatic character, a *persona*. In theater, however, we are always conscious of the fiction: here the illusion does not vanish; it informs artist and audience alike, ultimately perhaps to replace in the musician the personality which, say, his mother would recognize. The eclipse of the performer by the recorded performance, in other words, not only establishes the condition of fiction but permits its exploitation to a degree impossible in the traditional arts. Like the author, who writes himself into existence, the "recording artist" literally sings himself into existence.

Traditional music in folk communities is in any case never as purely auditory as the message transmitted by radio and phonograph. Folklore and language involve a complex participation in the family and community on many planes of experience; in aural tradition one inherits not only language and song but the entire moral universe of which they are a part. In very sophisticated aural traditions such as that which Lord and Parry studied in the Balkans, contact between the tradition bearer and his apprentice is prolonged, intimate, and intense; the bearer himself occupies a sharply defined social station and plays a specific role in his community. Like the African *griot*, he may belong to a caste whose insularity the community takes care to maintain. In Africa, in Afro-America, and in Appalachia, too, musical training, formal and informal, begins in childhood, inseparable from all the other influences that figure into growth and development; it is as true in Kentucky as in Vienna that the best musician is one whose talent found encouragement in childhood; fiddlers, for example, tend to run in families. Thus at fiddlers' conventions and bluegrass festivals family bands, child bands, and contests for young fiddlers and banjo players are a regular feature, sending the roots of back-porch bluegrass deeper into traditional culture. One can, or course, "study" a phonograph record, and many back-porch pickers do. But the most dedicated often leave their record collections and cassette tapes behind and follow the revered musician to wherever he is to be found: five minutes under his tutelage will impart what hours of poring over his recordings will not—the *how*, as well as the *what* of his music.

The radio or record, then, reflects only the audial facet of a many-faceted tradition; but in reflecting it, it frees it. The aspiring musician can find access to the music even outside its cultural milieu; he can embrace it, an honest and innocent impression of the human spirit, without embracing as well the debris that follows in the wake of all human traditions: prejudice, superstition, ignorance, and error. And the music, freed from the sometimes dazzling processes of performance, presents itself to the ear *as* itself, an aural effect for which the musician, by a kind of musical detective work, must contrive a physical and mechanical cause, discovering techniques of his own as he goes. By a strange uncoupling, a social event has retired, like a memory, to inward experience, where the imagination must reach into the darkness surrounding the disembodied music to reveal the human forces that created it. I wonder if the grass-fire-like spread of the bluegrass style, or, for that matter, of parallel forms like jazz and rock-and-roll, is not at least partly due to the eclipse of the performer by record or broadcast. Just as a poem or novel establishes in us an idea of the author we ourselves have constructed, so does the radio or record communicate an idea of the musician, his moral and physical attributes, we must infer from musical sounds. When the performer, as a public figure, can fill the shoes of the fictional being he has created in sound, as Elvis Presley did, his appeal may be immense. Bill Monroe in time has learned to present himself as the idealized figure his music makes him, and, I believe, has personally matured in response to that ideal. In the hearts of those in distant places—mountain cabin and college dormitory alike—who heard him on radio or phonograph, he must have appeared a splendid and powerful figure. Red Allen recalls: "I heard Bill Monroe when I was nine or ten years old, back in Pigeon Roost, Kentucky, over in the hollow. We had a battery radio. My grandma had one of those crank-up talk machines. I used to lay in a little cot of a night, and Charlie and Bill would sing "What Would You Give in Exchange for Your Soul." I would lay there on my stomach and think, "Boy, if I could meet that man."[5]

Chapter 7

Workin' Music
Bluegrass and Jazz

When the musician composes on his instrument, without benefit of a score whose symbols he may manipulate as a writer manipulates written words, we say he improvises. What he plays and the way he plays it are inseparable from him, as speech is inseparable from the speaker. As a sound, the improvisation is transient and irrecoverable; but as music it can be repeated, as words can be repeated, in ever changing musical contexts both by its creator and by his imitators—the music, again supplying the occasion for improvisation, not the improvisation itself. Thus, like speech, improvisation can be carefully planned in practice and carried out in performance, or it can occur *ab ovo* in performance, extemporaneously, perhaps to be deployed again in succeeding performances in the same and in different contexts.

Extemporaneity implies spontaneity, and spontaneity implies originality; yet extemporaneous improvisation is rarely as original as that which has been labored over. For the extemporaneous musician, like the extemporaneous speaker, tends to rely upon convention and formulae to carry him through the crisis, while the more deliberate musician may in the midst of his labors unexpectedly deliver himself of an idea as spontaneous and original as the stinging rejoinder that flashes in the heat of an argument. Originality, in any case, isn't everything. What the musician plays may show his mind; but the way he plays shows him; and for this purpose a highly conventionalized music, whose content is more or less fixed, may serve better than an original one, for it isolates the musician's sensibility and facilitates the comparison of one musician with another. All other factors being the same, we distinguish one musician from another only on the basis of the subtle and inimitable qualities: the particular way he produces and shapes a tone, his particular feeling for rhythm, his special interpretation of a song or tune. In a sense the music as such may be said to have disappeared. What we have heard a hundred times before we can scarcely hear anew; but we cannot but notice the *way* it is played, just *because* we have heard it a hundred times before.

What, indeed, is the status of the musical idea in jazz or bluegrass improvisation? It is far more the fruit of intelligence in action, a kind of readiness, than intelligence in contemplation, the reflective inquiry into form that belongs to the composer. In fact the musical "idea" may begin with the idle or even unconscious play of the fingers upon the instrument as they modify or elaborate upon mechanical patterns already laid down, yielding out of motor activity alone new and essentially unpredictable music directed and censored at any given instant by the ear. Thus the musician's readiness may extend not only to what he hears around him but to *his own activity*, for he cannot be entirely certain what he is going to play next.

Extemporaneity, or course, has a special fascination, for the music seems to visit the musician from some locale beyond him—from the "unconscious," or, as Coltrane would have it, from God. Extemporaneity brings immediacy and life, and the musician most interested in his capacity to perform—and this has been consistently true of the black musician—will favor it at the expense, perhaps, of the originality, the magnitude, and the permanance of his art. For it is the "tradition"—the availability of the formulae and the embrace of performing conventions—that promotes extemporaneity and is promoted by it; the musician expert within a tradition may find himself completely at a loss outside of it.

If extemporaneous improvisation *outside* a tradition is to be something more than a string of accidents—and musicologists have shown that the great extemporaneous solos of men like Ellington, Parker, Coltrane, and Coleman are fully realized formal constructions—the musician must have grasped a particular tradition thoroughly, so that he may know where its boundary is and when he has stepped over it; beyond that he must know his instrument and its possibilities—this includes, of course, the human voice—so that his vision of music, however instinctive or theoretical, may find expression in it. He must know piano, as well as ragtime piano, as Morton did; he must know sax, as well as rhythm-and-blues sax, as Charlie Parker did; he must know banjo, fiddle, guitar, or mandolin, as well as the bluegrass style, as many young bluegrass musicians are now striving to do. Through him one musical tradition may thus be fertilized by another and ultimately evolve into a new original music, for all improvisation, whether extemporaneous or not, whether mindlessly routine or keenly resourceful, appropriates prior musical ideas, aptitudes, and habits as well as unexpected and spontaneous elements in a bewilderingly complex synthetic process which, like speech, is action and construction at once.

Whether traditional or original, extemporaneous improvisation is an immediate response to a specific situation, as a ballplayer's action is a response to the bounce of the ball; and, like the bounce of a ball, that situation may itself be swiftly and unpredictably changing. For the solitary musician, the musical situation may simply be the equation formed from his mood, the resources of his mind, and his technical range; or, in the ensemble context, it may include such fixities as melody and tempo, or a harmonic progression. But the musical situation may also include the changing and unpredictable improvisations of *other musicians*, to which the musician's own improvisations must be an immediate response. Thus improvised music may be a kind of spontaneous individual creation, like figure skating; or it may be an individual performance in an ensemble context, like baseball; or it may be an extemporaneous competition, a "cutting contest," analogous to some adversary sport such as boxing; or it may be a cooperative collective performance, like the offensive drive of a basketball team, in which every player's action is the spontaneous and immediate issue of every other player's action.

All the evidence suggests that early New Orleans jazz, in its original, if not always in its recorded form, was this last kind of music—a cooperative collective action psychosocially equivalent to the African drum ensemble and historically linked to improvised baptism or burial singing and the "long meter" hymn. Collective improvisation took the form of contending voices in which extemporaneous lead passages, usually composed from short-winded "swing" phrases suggested by a familiar melody—one of the enduring traits of black folk music—awaken fusillades of response in the other instruments, which very nearly smother the lead; he must thrust himself contentiously into the excited throng, which at every moment is both dissolving to let him pass and condensing anew around him. Every musician in the front line of the early jazz band was *aware of what every other musician was doing*, and his music grew out of that awareness. We look back wonderingly at Louis Armstrong's improvised accompaniment to Bessie Smith's "St. Louis Blues," but let us remember Armstrong's licks were responses to Bessie's deeply expressive calls, and informed by them. An attentive listening will reveal, I think, that her every inflection, the plasticity of her phrase and supple dynamics, all found their way into

Armstrong's inventions, which both reflect and reconstitute them. For among Armstrong's many virtues was a phenomenal capacity to *imitate* sounds—to imitate instruments with his voice and to imitate the voice with his instrument.

That this music, in which every musical utterance was a response by one musician to another, every idea the fruit born instantly out of a seed planted by another, should be "extemporaneous" perhaps goes without saying. The acute audial sensitivity of the musicians to one another drew them into a close-knit society with physiological roots, in which an organically unified music, "all mixed together as if someone had planned it with micrometer calipers," might be created.[1] This was a daring and sophisticated aural tradition, a back-porch music whose rich repertoire of formulaic materials ultimately became the clichés of popular music. For with strains of several musical traditions, folk and popular, converging and merging in it, the early jazz band occupied the center of the ever expanding musical universe upon which it drew, evoking, ordering, transforming, and being transformed by it.

Collective improvisation was a mode of human interaction with its origins in Afro-American folk life. Its manifestation in early jazz was short-lived, though we have a substantial body of recordings which testify to its existence. As soon as the black musicians of New Orleans and Chicago came to be admired and emulated as soloists, typically by young, first generation European-Americans such as Biederbecke who could feel keenly the countercultural force of jazz, the early responsive density of the music began to dissolve in favor of the solo tour de force. That a great tradition of soloists, stretching from Louis Armstrong to Ornette Coleman, should have emerged from an Afro-American tradition with African antecedents is perhaps surprising, since these traditions are prevasively social; yet at the same time the autonomous individual voice is, as we have seen, the thread from which these musics, even in their most elaborate social forms, are woven.

With the rise of the soloist and the swift transformation of the jazz performance into a succession of solo breaks, improvisation came to seem not so much a mode of exchange and interplay as a mode of composition, with all that composition in our culture implies—originality in particular. The hot lick, escaping out of the boil of jazz rhythms through melodic gaps and fissures, had been virtually a reflex; reinterpreted as the musician's effort to declare himself and his independence, it became the first step in his flight from the conventional languages which music of all kinds compels him to speak. The difference is subtle but crucial: the sporting mood of early jazz, the spirit of irony, play, and put-on, deepened gradually into an ethic of intense personal striving and ultimately of revolution, musical, social, political, and cultural—jazz was hip.

Louis Armstrong's agile "paraphrases," to use André Hodeir's suggestive term, had prepared the way for a complete break with the melodic line, which Charlie Parker's delirious improvisations, beginning as parodistic inversions of melody and ending as new and independent melodies, accomplished. This was the point at which a way of playing music, the jazz style, became an independent art in the Western sense, *jazzmusik*. For it represented a fundamental departure from both African and Afro-American folk practice, in which a prior melody, whether musical or linguistic, provided the musician or singer with his occasion. Parker found himself in the European harmonic landscape, whose terrain he explored with linear improvisations based upon chord progressions. Miles Davis and John Coltrane abandoned chords for a more ancient kind of musical organization—the mode— thus blazing trails into the remoter districts of the harmonic universe. As the familiar landmarks of rhythm and tonality fell behind him, the jazz musician drifted in a rarefied medium shaped only by sound and tempo. Consequently a new kind of ensemble relationship ensued, paradoxically very like the original African drum ensemble or the early jazz band, demanding that the musician break the spell of introspection and attend closely to his fellows, seeking ways to cooperate rather than to diverge in a medium virtually free of binding conventions. This was the organizing principle of Ornette Coleman's *Free Jazz*, the album which gave its name to the movement, in which extended solos are born erratically out of the collective improvisations of two opposed quartets, like flames from a kind of musical friction. Modern jazz musicians, searching for modes of organization which the freedom of their music both permits and demands, have opened themselves to the influences of Indian, Arabic, Caribbean, European, and, of course, West African music; and yet, among black musicians at least, speech itself remains the primordial creative force. John Coltrane is said to have written his "Alabama" from the rhythms of a funeral oration Martin Luther King delivered for five girls killed in the bombing of a Birmingham church in 1963—not from the speech itself, but from a *printed text* of it. Few jazz musicians, though, speak more intimately than Miles Davis, in whose breathy notes, emerging from and disappearing into nowhere, the declamatory blast of the trumpet has become the jargon of lovers in each other's arms.

Jazz was a folk art which has become high art, one in which composition of every kind has played an increasingly prominent role. It is quite common, now, for the jazz musician both to compose and to play from a musical score. At its center, and especially, I suspect, among black musicians, jazz is still largely an aural tradition; but it is an aural tradition which feeds a literature, and thus one which must constantly reform itself in order to live. Even supermarket musak thrives on the genius of Duke Ellington or Fletcher Henderson.

Bluegrass, though, remains as yet largely a style linked mimetically to its own roots, just as early minstrelsy was linked to plantation music, and hence seems internally to resist the evolution along strictly musical lines that jazz has followed. This is not to say, of course, that jazz has not profoundly affected bluegrass music and musicians, or that a new acoustic string music, unlike anything heard before in our music, has not begun to grow on the edges of bluegrass, among musicians such as fiddler Vassar Clements, as in progressive bands such as the Country Gazette, the New Grass Revival, or the David Grisman Quintet, which styles itself after the Quintet du Hot Club de France. Since the early days of bluegrass, as Lomax observed, bluegrass has not only adopted the ground rules of jazz, and absorbed its experimentalist spirit, but actually echoed the music itself. In Chubby Wise's fiddle, Bill Monroe's mandolin, and Earl Scruggs's banjo one can detect the imprint of Johnny Dodds, King Oliver, and Mr. Jelly Roll; one wonders if Armstrong's trumpet does not figure somewhere in the genealogy of the bluegrass singing style, as Lomax has suggested. Bluegrass fiddlers very early took the influence not only of country-jazz fiddlers such as Clayton McMichen and Arthur Smith—Monroe cites McMichen as a major influence—but of Joe Venuti and Stephan Grappelly, opening avenues of influence which have brought swing and rhythm-and-blues into bluegrass instrumental breaks. Kenny Baker cites Benny Goodman and Tommy Dorsey among his influences. And, as the fiddle breaks of Baker or his young protegé Blaine Sprouse often reveal, jazz has no monopoly on "sheets of sound." Bluegrass, then, is bound up with jazz; but *all* serious American music is bound up with jazz. More to the point, perhaps, is that the deposits of jazz in bluegrass have already entered our musical vocabulary and acquired a glow of connotation that colors the bluegrass sound. In the voluptuous glow of Storyville, the hillbilly heart song may cast an ironic shadow, while the rustic mountain breakdown, sizzling with the nervous riffs of atomic-age bohemians and black pariahs, may burn with forbidden thought.

It is simply one of the mysteries of human communication that in aural cultures such as the African a level of synchrony operates which to the European or Europeanized American is imperceptibly profound, and thus becomes a source of considerable misery and misunderstanding between cultures and between people, especially when we are entirely at the mercy of communications made to us which we do not understand or to which we have an irrational response. A quick anticipation of actions and reactions, a close attention to and understanding of minimal cues and other subtleties of communication are essential to the success of improvised ensemble music such as jazz and bluegrass. Many of the recordings of the parent bluegrass bands, such as Monroe's, as well as the Stanley Brothers, Lester Flatt and Earl Scruggs, Jimmy Martin and the Sunny Mountain Boys, Don Reno, Red Smiley and the Tennessee Cut-Ups, and a handful of others less well known, seem to display something of the deep organic unity of the audially bonded jazz ensemble. We hear in the King recordings of the Stanley Brothers, for example, or in Monroe's Columbia recordings, or in the early Mercury recordings of Flatt and Scruggs, a solid mass of integrated sound, sharply discriminated and richly developed in every dimension, rhythmically alive and, perhaps most importantly, interresponsive in every vocal and instrumental part. This was the original bluegrass sound, which contemporary bands of every stamp are very hard put to achieve.

Much of this unity, of course, had a cultural, social, regional, or even familial basis, and if it has been a unity difficult to recover it is because many of these forces have weakened or dissolved. Since the death of his brother Carter, Ralph Stanley, who once emphasized to me the importance of hiring musicians from the same region or even the same district as oneself, has taken on a series of lead singers—Larry Sparks, Roy Lee Centers, Keith Whitley—whose voices capture the specific mood of Carter's voice without actually imitating it; "Now Roy Lee," Ralph says, "he sounded *exactly* like Carter. I couldn't tell them apart."[2] Moreover these singers achieved a vocal blend with Ralph uncanny in its precision—of phrasing, of dynamics, of timbre—and yet apparently spontaneous and natural rather than rote. "We never rehearse," says Keith Whitley; "I just try to follow Ralph."[3]

The Stanley Brothers, the Osborne Brothers, the Lilly Brothers, the Goins Brothers, the Bray Brothers, the Church Brothers, Jim and Jesse McReynolds, the Lewis Family, the McLain Family, the Marshall Family—the persistance of blood ties in bluegrass illustrates its continuity with rural life, with long-standing rural traditions, and, of course, with hillbilly music. It suggests, too, what the psychosocial origins of the musical organization of bluegrass may be. If the bluegrass band is not actually a family, it is one symbolically. It is patriarchal and masculine, a band of father and sons acting in defense of, on behalf of, and even sometimes in spite of the home, where, of course, woman resides. Symbolically, the bluegrass band is usually absent from home: an embassy of men sent from one household to another to defend a sister's honor, or a kind of junta, established to declare the rule of law in lawless territory, or only dad and the boys out all night on a coon-hunt. All of these familial forms, of course, smack of the frontier. The father, or father figure, whose personality dominates the group, as Monroe's does, may be absent, in which case an elder brother or brothers may rule; or, interestingly, brothers may become fathers, as is the case in the McReynolds brothers' band, in which Jesse McReynold's son has become a regular member. Or father may establish and nurture the band, as Red Allen has done, and then leave it to its own devices: the Allen Brothers have become one of the best of the young, progressive bluegrass bands, literally and figuratively a second generation in a music which often does not sharply distinguish the literal and figurative. Or there will be no figure in authority present at all, in which case the boys cannot but seize the opportunity for horseplay and buffoonery. Herein resides the charm of many a bluegrass band such as the Country Gentlemen, whose on-stage antics, as unthinkable in Monroe's band as in a color guard, might even include a comic impersonation of the old guy. A woman may be present on the periphery, as a bass player perhaps, in which case she is symbolically or actually a mistress or moll; or mother and daughters may join under the men at the center of the band—an increasingly popular arrangement in bluegrass—in which case we have entered the domestic atmosphere, where decent traditional values are likely to prevail. Not surprisingly, many of the so-called "family" bands play only gospel music, for where they are it is always Sunday morning.

Things differ in what they have in common. Both the bluegrass and the jazz band are held in an aural synthesis originating in some form of close human association; between them is the natural magnetism of forces which occupy opposite poles. For the jazz band is not a family, actually or symbolically, but a kind of confederacy or faction, a fellowship formed out of rage, honor, and youth on the edge of a people surrounded by an oppressive ruling order against which the band is pledged to unremitting harassment and, when possible, direct aggression: no capitulation, negotiation, or compromise for them. They are a kind of raiding party, and their music a kind of brigandage, rending the fabric of white music and spiriting it away in rags from which to sew their own gorgeous banner. The traditional jazz band, bursting at the seams, hurtling collectively toward a critical mass which seemed to foredoom the complete disintegration of itself—this was the essence of jazz, a plunge for freedom, a gamble, for freedom can only be won *from* the oppressor by incursions into his dominion. The old jazz band did, in fact, disintegrate, sending out agents of improvisational espionage into the sanctuaries of European music first to embrace, and then to weaken, and finally to destroy such structures as rhythm and tonality, for in jazz to win freedom is necessarily to break constraints. It is guerilla warfare, and even in the wildest free jazz, where it seems the country has been won and the oppressor vanquished, the jazzman plays with one foot upon a fallen Goliath.

The commotion of the old jazz band, in which forces intersect one another to generate heat at the core of their intersection, has become in bluegrass, again, a structure of "multiple parts in continual interaction," in which forces potentially at odds have been integrated and coordinated. This is the order of families, of institutions, of establishments, of machines; the bluegrass musician is outwardly the maker and preserver of such forms. As Monroe himself says, bluegrass is like "putting a motor together."[4]

Why, then, is bluegrass comparable to jazz at all, if the bluegrass musician chose at the onset a restrained, conservative course, and placed the melody and rhythm in the foreground? Because within the establishment, within the institution, within the family, there is restlessness, craving, and discontent, as within the machine there is friction and heat and wear. The jazzman demands, and wins, his freedom; the bluegrass musician desires only to desire it—not actually to overthrow the established order of rhythm and melody. If he cannot actually win his freedom, he can wish for and dream about it, and this is the office of the wandering backup line, not thrusting itself hard upon the lead but drifting centrifugally, in bluegrass music's boundless internal fourth dimension, toward the frontier of the music, carrying the imagination into distant parts. Though clearly jazz-derived, this technique arouses an emotion simply unique in American music, a longing which it seems could only have grown up in the vastness of our continent, with its undying promise of unsettled territory beyond the farthest hill.

As we noted in our chapter on rhythm, the specialization of rhythmic functions in bluegrass vastly increases its efficiency, so that its power far exceeds what is necessary for it merely to perform its function, which after all an old nurse in a rocking chair could accomplish as well—or better, as some would have it. "Changin' over to bluegrass," says Curley Lambert, echoing Lomax's automotive metaphor, "was like going from a Model T to a steam engine. . . ."[5] Monroe explains: "It's exciting, you know, a lot of people thinks you work against each other, and in one sense of the word you probably do, because if the

fiddler's playing a number and then the banjo comes in and he sells
his chorus good, the fiddler knows he's up against it—he's going to
have to get to work. And the mandolin, he follows to do his part as
good as the banjo or better. . . ."[6]

We have seen that there is rivalry in jazz; but, like its verbal counterparts in such black street games as the Dozens, it is fundamentally
playful in character. With several lines of improvisation bearing down
upon him, the jazzman has a fertile and animated medium in which to
work, one which presents him at every moment with a new puzzle to
solve, a new knot to untie. Or if the front line has dispersed, as in
most modern "cool" jazz, he has plenty of elbowroom in which to maneuver. But the bluegrass lead singer or soloist, with improvised lines
packing their bags behind his back and a relatively strict regime before
him, is more alone; like the ballplayer at bat, he acts for the band,
which depends upon *him* to create the occasion. They in turn invest
him with that rhythmically generated, impersonal strength which to
master requires vigorous and consistent effort. "Bluegrass is a workin'
music," Lambert continues. "It's *work* to play bluegrass."[7]

The bluegrass musician belongs to a family in which the approval of
others must be consistently sought and won. Both in and out of the
bluegrass ensemble there is competitiveness, more earnest and intense
than the rivalries of jazzmen, which tends to isolate the musician:

> . . . you can see a feller that's coming up alongside of you over
> there that's playing a good banjo, playing a good fiddle, or
> mandolin, and you know he's gonna come up on and pass you if
> you don't stay in the collar . . . all the way through, bluegrass
> is competition with each man trying to play the best he can, be
> on his toes. You'll find it in every group. You'll find it in one
> group and another group following him. It works that way.
> They'll still be friends, but they'll work hard to be better
> than the other.[8]

"Bill loved to work," Don Reno recalls of Monroe. "Nobody could work
him down."[9]

For all these reasons, bluegrass music is often extemporaneous in
the backup part, but almost never extemporaneous in the lead. Though
the door between back porch and kitchen always stands open, with
traffic moving in both directions, it requires only a few repetitions to
transform an extemporaneous and participatory music into a self-conscious and highly individual art. Most bluegrass bands, professional
and semiprofessional, the sort of group which performs regularly at
the local nightspot and which may record for a small independent

record label, are at root back-porch bluegrass bands, and thoroughly proficient at it, individually and collectively. But when such a band has been working together for a period, playing a relatively stable repertoire, the element of chance diminishes, and what had been, perhaps, extemporaneous becomes fixed and predictable; the musician begins to seek variety, novelty, originality, complexity. He spends more time in the kitchen with his instrument, working out the breaks, and perhaps the backup lines as well, he will use in songs and tunes the group has determined to make its own.

Bluegrass musicians are conservative: they often choose to build the familiar dwelling, calling attention to its workmanship rather than to its design, even when they are perfectly capable of original designs of their own; thus kitchen bluegrass, even at its most polished, is often a perfected form of back-porch bluegrass. It happens that musicians with some cultural tie to Appalachia tend to conserve the traditional and conventional character of back-porch bluegrass, along with its idealism and moral intensity, while musicians in New York and Los Angeles interest themselves in technical virtuosity, originality, and often contemporaneity. Because kitchen bluegrass is built principally upon the contributions of individual musicians, who sometimes queue up for their breaks like commuters at a bus stop, it may suffer as an ensemble form. Piecing together his breaks and his collection of riffs, runs, turn-arounds, tags, potatoes, and other backup devices in solitude, the musician acquires the habit of independence and may come to think of the performance simply as a series of opportunities to exhibit his work. Exhaustive rehearsal, or a demanding bandleader, may bring the band together, though both may at the same time drive away the elusive and delicate life of the music; no amount of virtuosity, complexity, or originality can salvage a bluegrass band whose members aren't really listening to one another.

At its leading edge, where it is characterized by sophisticated orchestration, inventive and elaborate ensemble arrangements, more complex harmonies and chord progressions, and even by extended solo parts, kitchen bluegrass is a progressive form, touching both studio rock and jazz. Bluegrass has of course always been technical and progressive in a sense; Monroe and Scruggs, among others, were innovators of the first order, whose example has encouraged mandolinists, banjo pickers, fiddlers, and, more recently, guitar players to explore more boldly the technical range of their instruments and the potentials of their music, which they must do as the folk and hillbilly background of the original bluegrass comes gradually to be replaced by bluegrass itself, and an independent music emerges.

We cannot catalogue the name of every musician who has left an indelible impression, but we ought to cite a few of the principal innovators. Don Reno, who replaced Earl Scruggs in Monroe's band in 1948, spliced three-finger rolls together with plectrum-like melodic phrases reminiscent of ragtime banjo; in time he acquired a reputation as a banjo virtuoso which rivalled Scruggs's. The folk revival late in the 1950s brought banjoist Eddie Adcock, whose athletic backup licks, influenced by fiddle and pedal steel guitar and executed in a Travis-like guitar-picking style, were imitated by every banjoist of the period. Excluding Scruggs himself, however, no banjo player has exerted more influence than Bill Keith. By abandoning the roll and stopping the strings in various combinations chiefly above the fifth fret, he was able to build melodies *among* the strings, with the right hand, rather than *along* them, with the left; this gave to the banjo a melodic mobility comparable to the fiddle or even the piano, and it was in fact with two traditional tunes, "Devil's Dream" and "Sailor's Hornpipe," that Keith first won a reputation. Bill Monroe, who is said to have introduced Keith's style as "the new bluegrass banjo," admires the young musician deeply and openly:

> Brad Keith, he understands music. He's a good listener and he's a good man to listen to. He's done a lot of good for music and especially for bluegrass. At a time when I needed a boost, I think that Brad gave it to me. I think it just came in when I needed it. Before he came along no banjo player could play those old fiddle numbers right. You have to play like Brad could play or you would be faking your way through a number. It's learned a lot of banjo players what to do and how to do it to where they can come along and fill that bill today.[10]

Since the early sixties, when Keith played in Monroe's band, banjo players have amalgamated his style with the Scruggs style, yielding a virile hybrid which combines rhythmic drive with melodic flexibility, applying Scruggs's rolls to Keith's left-hand combinations. Keith was a kitchen musician *par excellence*, though his "kitchen" was an Amherst College dormitory room.

Monroe himself has dominated the mandolin since the forties, but others have made a mark as well. Jesse McReynolds developed a cross-picking style which reflected Scruggs's three-finger roll, creating a sustained ringing tone not heard before on the instrument. A specifically bluegrass style for both mandolin and banjo has grown up in the music; fiddle and guitar and the resonated Hawaiian guitar, or "Dobro," have annexed the bluegrass style to other influences. "Mr. Bill Monroe taught me to play bluegrass,"[11] says Chubby Wise, though the great bluegrass fiddlers—Wise, Benny Martin, Kenny Baker—owe their immediate ancestry to western swing and its presiding genius, fiddler Bob Wills, whose style clearly anticipates the bluegrass style.

Bluegrass fiddle has continued to develop along these lines, leaving behind the shuffling and open-string chordal drones of old time fiddling, as well as the standard keys of D, G, and A, in favor of brilliant, singing, concert tones, and light, swift, multitudinous notes. But the sophistication of bluegrass fiddle has not entirely polished out either the rougher textures or the sweet tunefulness of old-time fiddle. The late Paul Warren, for over twenty years a member of Flatt and Scruggs's Foggy Mountain Boys, made a stout, vigorous music out of double stops and the saw strokes of a Virginia hoedown fiddler, while Curley Ray Cline, for many years associated with Ralph Stanley, answers Stanley's melancholy sound with long, brooding, inquiring tones and wistful descending blue cadences. Many have thought that Scotty Stoneman, who died in 1973, was the best bluegrass fiddler that ever lived: his techniques were those of a Georgia fiddler, but he wrought them to a pitch of excitement and intensity in which one might detect dark overtones of torment and despair.

The Hawaiian guitar, which had been introduced into hillbilly music by Jimmie Rodgers and was later popularized by Pete Kirby of Roy Acuff's band, earned a place in bluegrass primarily through the efforts of Josh Graves, of the Foggy Mountain Boys. Graves, too, was impressed by Scruggs's banjo roll and adapted it to his guitar, which, like a banjo, was tuned to an open chord; often in the instrumentals of the Foggy Mountain Boys the banjo and dobro sounded like two sides of the same instrument, the one snapping and biting, the other howling and baying—bluegrass musicians call the dobro the "hound dog" guitar. Contemporary dobroists Mike Auldridge and Jerry Douglas have enriched the instrument with the techniques of its electric cousin the pedal steel, yet the dobro remains—in spite of its mournful, nocturnal, and deeply southern sound—somewhat redundant in bluegrass: like Nashville's pedal steel, it performs an acoustic function closely akin to the fiddle's.

Though there have been many fine lead guitarists in bluegrass—Earl Scruggs and Don Reno, both also banjo players, and George Shuffler among them—the guitar did not emerge decisively as a lead instrument until guitarists came to use the flat pick as a rock or jazz guitarist might use it, with a rock or jazz guitarist's understanding of the guitar neck. The great Doc Watson, a rockabilly musician with an exceedingly rich background of traditional mountain music swept up into the folk revival of the sixties, dazzled his young audiences—and many fledgling guitarists—with fiddle tunes transformed into flat-picking tours de force and mountain songs accompanied by breathtaking ascending and descending runs which dissolved the old familiar chords into cubist refractions of themselves. While conservative lead singer-guitarists such as Larry Sparks preserve the old rural style of flat picking based principally on the bass strings, as Scruggs and Reno played, most bluegrass guitar breaks are compounded now of various uptown styles, though as far as I know no bluegrass guitarist has yet ventured far enough up the neck to require a cutaway, even though several acoustic guitar manufacturers are eager to supply him with one.

Bluegrass is crowded with expert young musicians who are advancing its frontiers on every side. To discuss them all, of course, is impossible, though we might mention a few of their names for the record. On the banjo, then, Doug Dillard, Vic Jordan, Alan Munde, Tony Trishka, John Hickman, John Hartford, and Bob Black; on the fiddle, Byron Berline, Blaine Sprouse, Richard Greene, and the incredible Mark O'Connor; on the guitar, Norman Blake, Dan Crary, and Tony Rice; on the mandolin, Sam Bush, David Grisman, Doyle Lawson, and Ricky Skaggs, who has introduced his bluegrass singing style into commercial country music with immense popular success. Other men whose careers began earlier, such as Vassar Clements and Bobby Hicks on the fiddle, Bobby Osborne and Frank Wakefield on the mandolin, the late Clarence White on guitar, Sonny Osborne and J. D. Crowe on the banjo, have already won lasting reputations and fostered bluegrass substyles around them. Most of the musicians I've mentioned—and my list is really only a superficial one—were born south of the Ohio River, and nearly half of them have actually played with Bill Monroe, whose band after thirty-five years is still a school for bluegrass.

Influence, innovation, and experiment have at last yielded a kind of music which afficionados are pleased to call "newgrass," after a band formed around Louisville mandolinist Sam Bush called the New Grass Revival, which included, at the outset, Courtney Johnson on banjo, Curtis Burch on guitar, and John Cowan, who did most of the lead singing, on electric bass. Except for Burch, who was born in Savannah, all the musicians are western Kentuckians, and, with the exception of Cowan, all have backgrounds in country music and bluegrass, which they encountered early in life, citing Bill Monroe, Flatt and Scruggs, fiddler Tommy Jackson, mandolinist Red Rector, the Stanley Brothers, Jim and Jesse, banjoist Bobby Thompson, and dobroist Shot Jackson among their early influences.[12] Cowan's electric bass, on the other hand, symbolizes the impact upon bluegrass of the rock revolution of the sixties; many bluegrass bands, traditional and progressive, have adopted it. As for his own influences, Cowan remarks, "I was in love with the Beatles."[13]

With its long strings of complicated and subtle chord progressions, its lush and ethereal vocal harmonies, its gradual linear evolution, its consistent use of bridges, vamps, and other structural devices such as modulation, a plastic, programmatic use of rhythm, and a thorough-going orchestration, the music of the New Grass Revival is unquestionably original, self-conscious, and commercial, though it resonates with the rural and traditional textures belonging to the bluegrass instruments, whose various voices stand out in sharp relief. One thinks not only of the Beatles, of course, but of rock groups of the sixties such as Crosby, Stills and Nash or The Grateful Dead, whose use of acoustic instruments revealed their origins in the folk revival. Astonishingly, scarcely a traditional lick is to be heard in the entire recorded opus of the band; they have divided the instrumental break among two or three instruments and integrated it into an orchestral pattern which does not permit to any one instrument, except in specifically instrumental pieces, the prominence accorded alternately to the soloists in bluegrass. From the band's recordings, one has the overwhelming impression of effortlessness, and an integration of vocal and instrumental parts that is almost chilling in its perfection: kitchen bluegrass, one supposes, *cordon bleu.*

What becomes of the New Grass Revival in performance? The stone-steady bluegrass musician, bound like Gulliver by ten thousand tiny ligatures, has won his liberty with a wild revolt whose success still leaves him in ecstasy. With an array of vocal mikes before them, and contact mikes affixed to the faces of the instruments, the New Grass Revival is free to do what for 200 years, until Elvis Presley's one-man insurrection, was permitted only to blacks and to minstrels in blackface: to give the whole body to music—and with the body, the self. With his mandolin tucked under his arm like the Sunday *Times*, Bush is jiving, grooving, and trucking over the stage, music following him like children dancing after a piper; Cowan, his head bobbing violently as if he were trying to fling it away, or thrown back in a mighty shout, is bouncing up and down or pacing urgently back and forth, long bass lines rolling from him like the grave exhortations of a Methodist sermon. In this exalted and uninhibited atmosphere, bluegrass undergoes a revealing metamorphosis. In Cowan's lungs, Monroe's "A Good Woman's Love," an outcry torn with conflicting emotions, comes out with holy joy, scarcely distinguishable musically from a black gospel hymn as Mahalia Jackson or Sister Rosetta Tharpe might sing it, while the old fiddle-contest piece "Lee Highway Blues" becomes in Bush's hands an exhaustive anatomy of the tune's acoustics, with all its innards—overtones, harmonics, reverberations, echoes, and interferences—exposed in the scan of Bush's electric pickup. In the New Grass Revival as in most of our rock and soul music, the lid is off, and what was contained is contained no longer.

If the jazz band is a kind of confederacy, and the bluegrass band a family, then the New Grass Revival, and all the young bands which have followed their example, is a kind of cult, formed to call up again out of bluegrass that vital unanimity whose spell temporarily elevates a spontaneous creative power out of a body of fixed and premeditated matter. "So much of it's not planned," Courtney Johnson says, "especially the jams . . . anybody can play anything they want to and it seems like everybody else is right there." "The way we improvise," Cowan adds,

> is kind of like being a blind person. You have all these places in your house that you know where they are all the time. You can get up and walk around for as long as you want and they'll still be there when you get back. So, we have all these rhythm patterns and chord changes that we know when they're coming, so we know we have so much time to improvise or do whatever we're doing and then get back to that. We just take basic things and improvise on them without changing the foundation totally.[14]

The musical extemporizer, like a blind man, must supply an invisible reality out of the other senses; he must construct imaginatively a musical architecture on the strength of aural cues whose sequences eventually establish in him a pattern whose repetition he can anticipate unconsciously. With the pattern established, the sequence itself can be abandoned, and new sequences created in its place: behold, the music begins to drift out of the kitchen, through the screen door, and is set free somewhere in the extemporaneous universe out back. Even Miles Davis, recalling his early gigs with Charlie Parker which sent the lead musicians onto three or four divergent paths of rhythm, could feel amazed that "eventually it came around as Bird had planned and we were together again."[15]

The success of this kind of improvisation, as Cowan's analogy implies, demands that the familiar places will all "still be there when you get back"—which in ensemble music is a feat not only of memory but, as we have already noted, of acute intersensitivity. "Everyone is conscious of the timing," Burch relates, "who is soloing, rather than wandering off on their own."[16] Though the music of the New Grass Revival differs substantially from that of the original bluegrass bands, its aims, as Bush expresses them, clearly reflect Monroe's original ideals: "The four of us will try to make this wall of sound at all times, which you can do and you don't have to have ten million watts. You learn where somebody's going to punch it taking a break and now we all punch it together. To us that's just the logical way to do it, the way to make four pieces fit together really well."[17]

The lesson here is that kitchen bluegrass must be served up piping hot. A complex musical idea challenges the musician in performance as it does not in its construction, and to execute it successfully calls upon certain moral as well as technical resources. Kitchen bluegrass is often more dramatic in performance than on record simply because the musician must ride the crest of the music. Too thorough a technical mastery, too exhaustive rehearsal and repetition, or insufficiently demanding music will erode this quality, which the musician must renew with ever more abstruse and arbitrary experiments. In traditional music extemporaneity, which can untie this knot, may mean nothing more than singing and playing with intensity, imagination, and conviction, and I am perfectly content to leave the matter there. But we must acknowledge the musician's technical interests, and the important place of innovation and experiment in *any* art. Kitchen bluegrass in performance—but we're on the front porch now—may be exactly what it was in the recording studio; but, as the New Grass Revival demonstrates, it may be something else altogether. The heart of improvisatory music, it seems to me, lies in this short excursion from the kitchen to the front porch, where the dynamic nature of music itself releases the fixed idea from the musician's grasp, so that he must pursue it again.

In performance, the musician's personal repertoire of materials, traditional and original, has exactly the same status psychologically as the body of formulaic materials which the back-porch musician calls upon. It is, if you will, an internal and personal "aural tradition," which, like the rhetorician's "commonplaces," can supply the materials of extemporaneous performances that in any given piece may range widely over the field of music outside the piece, and even outside the tradition to which the piece belongs. Just as the jazz musician may touch upon five different popular melodies—everything from "Tea for Two" to "The Battle Hymn of the Republic"—before he comes home again, so can the bluegrass musician look back to a Kentucky fiddle tune, or a

British ballad, or alongside him to a rock-and-roll guitar lick, or even ahead of him, as does Peter Wernick, who plays his banjo through a phase shifter, or as Sam Bush has done, to the intergalactic mode of a synthesizer. Thus though an improvisatory music must have the back porch, the kitchen, or even the parlor or attic to which to retire, it is only on the front porch, in performance, that the musician can test his mettle in the one situation which is a reliable measure of his musicianship, and in which the music *itself* can grow and change. Here the musician is brought to an inspired state that opens him to unanticipated and novel creations; here the music is allusive, reaching into and reflecting its own musical environment, ultimately to change it as it changes; here the music is whole, taking the vital form of the human community within it.

I know I am not alone in thinking that Bill Monroe's recorded music, fine as it is, does not live up to the music he plays on stage, in the presence of an approving and enthusiastic audience. *All* bluegrass musicians are aware of the salutary effect the approval of an audience has upon their work, and many will introduce their shows with an announcement to that effect. Readers who have never seen Bill Monroe in person must simply take our word for it: the real Bill Monroe cannot be heard on record. The fantastic power, the brilliance and vitality, the inventiveness and flexibility, the sheer energy which, among other things, compelled this long-winded book: these belong to the Bill Monroe whose career has been one of performances—in school auditoriums, in tent shows, on the Grand Ole Opry, and on the road.

In the future, bluegrass is certain to develop, as it has in the past, in the kitchen and even, perhaps, in the study, among composition books. I once heard fiddler Tex Logan lead some fellow musicians through nine different variations upon Monroe's "Roanoke," which he had scored and was carrying about in his fiddle case; solo parts have already been written for banjo and mandolin with symphony orchestra. I have heard hot backstage jam sessions, too, in which instrumental magicians like Vassar Clements or Norman Blake carry bluegrass far into the labyrinths of modern jazz. Where in the house to place this music, which is extemporaneous, collective, and original, I don't know. It might go in the parlor, like good conversation, but probably it doesn't belong in the house at all. It is a subterranean, after-hours music, transpiring in unexpected places where pirates lurk with tape machines and jugs of moonshine. Perhaps we should put it below stairs, in the basement.

These various kinds of music are never as distinct in practice, of course, as we've pretended. There's often a good deal of originality on the back porch, and a lot of spontaneity in the kitchen. The kitchen musician is an artificer and, depending upon his gifts, will aim to transport and inspire his audiences, to fascinate them with complexity, or simply to impress them with virtuosity. The back-porch musician has formulated a bluegrass style out of allegiance to Monroe's original, taking pleasure in his participation with others in the ritual: and these are powerful.

That the original has remained strong, that it has ripened and borne fruit to become the genuinely classical form it first promised to be, is apparent on Bill Monroe's recent instrumental album, *Master of Bluegrass*. Here a series of mandolin reels and waltzes, all structurally related and melding into one another, kaleidoscopically, capture the precise quality of Monroe's musical imagination and affirm his place as an O'Caralin of our traditional music. The lively "Go Hither to Go Yonder" and "Old Dangerfield" might have come, at some early time, from County Clare or Galway; and yet they stand as squarely in our tradition as "Dusty Miller" or "Bill Cheatum," and might have as easily been jigs of Ohio River boatmen. "Lady of the Blue Ridge," in a dreamy waltz time, echoes a ballad Monroe recorded nearly thirty years ago, "You'll Find Her Name Written There," turning the wistful circles of an old dame around the memory of lost love. The album closes with a solemn and haunting meditation upon a very old melody whose roots are in an English ballad but which we know as "The House of the Rising Sun." With an exotic dissonance tuned into the high strings, Monroe seems to be bidding farewell to us—he calls the tune "My Last Days on Earth"—and ends it with four slow knells of mandolin harmonics. And, for the first time in his career, he plays alone.

Chapter 8

Old Time Music
Parlor Books, the Phonograph, and Folk Revivalism

The human heart is time-entangled, music time-infused. To snare what flies, to recover what is lost—these music can do, though music itself can never be arrested or recovered. To have it we must play it, for it lives where we live, in Time.

A folk musician, who has been Time's companion and collaborator, will feel a certain distress when he hears a musician or a band playing music too complex for him to learn in the familiar way, by ear. This distress arises from the simple recognition that the music is no longer inclusive but exclusive—that it has passed into the hands of specialists who have enforced the right of proprietorship over their compositions, and who may even have fabricated their music for that reason alone. Simple music can be great, and terribly demanding; complex music may or may not be great, and may exist for no·purpose but to be complex. At a certain distance from back-porch bluegrass, kitchen bluegrass may become not a folk tradition but an esoteric one around which a sort of priesthood may form, which can in turn interpose itself between the music and those who aspire to it, maintaining its power by that old device—literacy—which it can exercise even at elementary levels where the ear would serve far better than the eye. Pardon the biased and, under the circumstances, blatantly hypocritical metaphor. At a Christmas party recently a well-known and well-respected folk-lorist assured me that there is nothing even remotely resembling an oral tradition in bluegrass, that his son, an aspiring banjo picker, sits himself down (in the parlor, I wonder?) with a book which he studies until he can reproduce note for note the piece printed there in tabulature. Sure enough, folks, that ain't oral tradition. That is parlor bluegrass, a written tradition based partly upon tabulature and partly upon conventional notation, which requires of the musician what no back-porch picker ever bothered with—that he know how to read music in some form.

I remember the first time I tried to read tabulature. I think it was Pete Seeger's honest little book, *How to Play the 5-String Banjo*. After fifteen or twenty minutes of poring over a formidible-looking lick, I realized that I had been playing it for a couple of years, and really couldn't remember where I'd learned it. The racks of music shops are laden now with instruction books and anthologies designed to introduce the banjo, mandolin, fiddle, or whatever to the beginner through tabulature or notation, as well as with books directed to the more advanced musician, offering him inventions of particular musicians which he can learn to play *exactly* as they were invented or, in many cases, recorded; it is the very exactitude and fixity of the tabulature or notation which confers upon it the special authority that compels the musician to repeat another musician's version of, say, "Blackberry Blossom," rather than to create his own, and which places the bluegrass musician in roughly the same relation to the composer as the classical musician—though in bluegrass the "composer" is often, it happens, anonymous, forgotten, or simply ignored, once the music leaves the parlor.

Parlor books are of several kinds. Some treat their subject only on the most elementary and superficial level, what in fact anyone with a small talent might exhaust in an hour's time; most supplement this basic information with photographs and drawings of old-time and bluegrass musicians, antique instruments, picturesque hill-country scenes and the like which add to the charm of a book that very shortly will prove musically ephemeral. Yet the tug of such a book upon the heart can be acute: it is almost as if the act of purchase will bring us into possession of something which money cannot buy; we are in the same strange anxiety that comes over us when at a flea market or antique show we encounter some relic from our childhood, a kitchen implement or toy, beckoning from a clutter of obscure things freshly lapsed into the past. Many books supplement the text with useful sound sheets, cassette tapes, or long-playing records, while a few, such as Marion Thede's *The Fiddle Book*, are collections of songs and tunes gathered in the field by professional musicologists or folklorists and transcribed, in the grand tradition of Child, Kittredge, Sharp, and Lomax. Interestingly, some are collections of transcriptions made from phonograph records of early and even contemporary musicians upon whose work most of bluegrass is built. Kenny Kosek's and Stacy Phillips's *Bluegrass Fiddle Styles*, for example, which surveys the field of fiddlers from G. B. Grayson and Arthur Smith to living and breathing Kenny Baker, captures in notation the licks which still ring in the ears of traditional musicians who heard them first on radio and record, and which probably cannot be learned except in an approximate way through notation: for the transcribers, after all, began by listening, just as the musicians did; moreover it was, again, as much the way that music was played as what was played that first recommended them to the attention. What, for instance, can be the value of a transcription of Tommy Magness's "Katy Hill," when the tune is traditional, and Magness's version of it, by virtue of its fantastic tempo, less note-oriented than most? Finally there are books offered by well-known musicians, such as Scruggs's *Earl Scruggs and the 5-String Banjo*, their associates, or by out-and-out pirates, often by mail order, of original compositions; these appear, too, in some of the many magazines and newsletters addressed to old-time, folk, and bluegrass enthusiasts. Someone benefits, of course, from these efforts, which are not usually protected by copyright; and it is not inevitably the musician, but the transcriber.

In this respect the parlor books function as if they were simply a written component of a still vital aural tradition, like the sixteenth-century rhetorician's commonplace book, the broadside ballad, or O'Neill's *Dance Music of Ireland*. As long as music transcribed in the parlor books, traditional or original, may reenter tradition, subject to traditional interpretation, variation, and change, this seems plausible and even desirable. But the fixity and apparent permanence of notation, like that of print, tends to enforce a kind of fixity upon the music, simply because its continuous existence appears to win reality away from that which is ephemeral—that is, which seems to exist only when it is being performed. And out of that apparent priority springs inevitably the authentic or authoritative version, the craving to possess it, and the acrimonious quarrels over it, which I have heard young fiddlers pursue as spitefully as withered and disappointed philologists: "You didn't play that right. Here's the way to play it. . . ." "No, he doesn't play it that way, he plays it this way. . . ." "That isn't how it goes. It goes like this." Moreover the explicitness of tabulature or notation—precise, abstract, and irrecoverable as numbers—tends to relieve the learner of any responsibility for or stake in the composition as such, which consequently falls into the hands of—who else?—the composer. It is the *notation itself* which creates composers as such, and confers the right of proprietorship.

The popularity of parlor books reflects, of course, the popularity of bluegrass. That popularity in turn erodes the ethnic, regional, and cultural foundations of the music, while perhaps forming a new sort of foundation—a commercial one—under it. For the parlor book, far more decisively than the phonograph record, reduces the music to a commodity. When we buy a phonograph record we buy not the music but the *sound* of it, and incidentally pay the musician and the recording company for their services. While the recording widens aural access to one of the musician's performances, it leaves the music itself untouched, as secure in its cultural context as we remain in ours—far more secure, indeed, than the folklorist and his informant, or the concert performer and his audience. Yet the sound of music is rich with information; though we must generate for ourselves from a phonograph record what knowledge we have of the music—aural, technical, emotional, cultural—this is an act of imagination by which we graft its sound to the living tree of our own experience. But no recording can guarantee to the buyer any knowledge of the music, and certainly not the capacity to play it, any more than a copy of *Crime and Punishment* can guarantee to the reader the knowledge required to write it, though he may feel he has acquired it with the purchase price and conspicuously display the volume on the subway back to his flat. Thus the phonograph record cannot seize and absorb the music in the way of tabulature or notation, which *store* the music in an inventory of written signs just as a secretary stores an oral dictation in shorthand.

Through notation we seem to gain access to the music itself, precisely because the notation strips the music of everything that would separate us from it—everything, that is, by virtue of which it *is* music and not simply a series of mechanical operations. But this, of course, is an illusion; the trained musician knows this, as does anyone who has compared the real fiddle tune, which often seems merely stupid in notation, to a transcription of it. Whatever music may be, it has yet to emerge from the pages of a book. We must know what the music *sounds* like and, beyond that, what its sound means, which only the sound can communicate. And, as we can learn French far more readily in France than in French class—this, at least, has been my experience—we can best enter an aural musical tradition aurally.

Bluegrass, it happens, is one of the few forms of American music in which sheetmusic has not played a central role; hillbilly music and bluegrass passed directly from an ethnically grounded aural tradition into a technologically grounded one. Even the blues, whose aural stream survived its diversion into the commercial field, achieved its standard twelve-bar structure largely through the agency of popular composers, of whom W. C. Handy is the best remembered. At present notation figures significantly only in the prehistory of bluegrass—in church hymnals and in nineteenth-century popular song.

But notation itself is not at issue. At issue is its commercial exploitation. Like other articles of trade in a mass society, the parlor book dissolves the association of provider, provision, and provided-for; by silencing the music it absolutely eradicates the human circumstances in which it has its meaning. Can jazz have been disseminated through parlor books? Indeed the lavish use of photographs, which in a folio of Mozart's works, say, would be merely impertinent, seems almost essential to the parlor book, as an attempt to restore the human environment without which the contents of the book are likely to seem oddly meagre or impoverished. For the musician who has learned by ear, the contents of the parlor book may appear merely superfluous, in the sense that braille is superfluous for readers with normal vision. One *might* use braille for readers with normal vision, of course, if the aim were to reserve the message for some and withold it from others; and this is precisely the aim of the parlor book publisher, who would bottle the April morning. Thus the traditional musician can quite legitimately feel that a book has stolen a song or tune from him, even if strictly speaking it has never been his. He has perceived, correctly, that a human resource has been converted into private property by a kind of musical Enclosure Act; not only has his own tradition been given away, or sold rather, but the many parts of it inaccessible to him as an individual have been opened to those on the outside, with the appalling consequence that a venerated fiddler from the North Carolina hills, invited to a college folk festival in the midwest, may find among his hosts one young upstart who has learned more fiddle tunes in a year than he could have learned in twenty. "Where d'ja learn that 'un?" he may ask—in an aural tradition, the fundamental question, one which speaks to the time, the place, the occasion, and the human communication which sustained the life of the song and fleetingly exposed, like the spark across a gap, its unbodied psychic energy. Indeed the question is important enough that the musician will often introduce his song with the answer to it, as if to legitimize his authority to play it. "I'm going to play for you this time," announces Rily Puckett on a record, "a little piece which an old darkey I heard play, coming down Decatur Street the other day, called 'His Good Gal Done Throwed Him Down,'"[1] presenting the tune, somewhat disingenuously, as if it were an anecdote touching upon Negro life in Atlanta. Tommy Jarrell, on the other hand, fixes each fiddle tune to a moment in his own past, and always to a particular person:

> Right here's a little tune that my Daddy learned from old man Houston Galyen up at Low Gap, North Caroliner—I guess before I was born. And he called it the "Drunken Hiccoughs." Well they play a tune out yonder around Nashville, Tennessee, they call "Rye Whiskey." And alot of folks in this country calls it "Jack of Diamonds." Daddy said that old man Houston said the right name for it was the "Drunken Hiccoughs"— so here she comes.[2]

And the tune reminds him of the occasion on which he learned it:

> Here's a tune I heard my wife's uncle Logan Lowe play. We danced over at his house one night just about all night and laid down and slept a little bit, and he got up the next mornin' and he got the fiddle . . . and he says, "I'm a-gonna play old General Washington's tune for you this mornin'" . . . and he called it "Bonyparte's Retreat."

The music carries him to the middle of the last century:

> Here's a little tune I learned from old man Pitt McKinney; he was an old Confederate veteran. I met him on the road—I'd started to a dance when I was about fifteen or sixteen years old and I had my fiddle under my arm. He says, "Son, let me see your fiddle!" He took it and tuned it like this . . . that was the first time I ever heard the fiddle tuned that way [standard tuning!]. And he played that tune over, and I said, "How 'bout playin' it again, Mr. McKinney?" And he played it again for me. And I learned that tune right there.

In an aural tradition, the moment and the manner of a song's trans-mission ties it to the web of the musician's experience, investing it for him with a particular association and meaning, and supplying his au-dience with a moral and imaginative setting in which to listen to it. "Neighbors," appeals bluegrass bandleader Bob Baker tenderly, "Neighbors, I'd like to say that this is 'bout one of the oldest songs I can possibly remember; it was taught to me a long time ago by my mother, when I was just a little small boy. I hope you enjoy some of the words to it, the title of the song is 'Little Willie.'"[3] The traditional musician's body of songs is consequently a vital whole pieced together like a patchwork quilt out of many discrete shreds—Nancy's gown, Harold's necktie, the old kitchen curtains—each of which has the power

to awaken a memory and keep it fresh. Thus quilting for her, fiddling
for him, is a kind of soul stewardship, by which they maintain the
order, health, and wholeness of their psychic lives. That lonesome tune
the fiddler played on the afternoon his sweetheart went away, though
it did little to assuage the grief of her going, could at least concentrate
and give form to it, intensifying the feeling of life at a moment when
it seemed the forces of life would dissipate; thus playing it today, years
later, recalls her to the pattern of his life, which he can see now in the
larger scheme of things; for the music absorbs, objectifies, and in a
sense redeems his experience, as any real art will do.

Plainly this is not the status of the tune for the book learner, at
least not at first. The music for him is no tradition or creed, however
he may protest that it is, but a vogue or fashion or, heaven help us,
a trend, one in which he has no necessary stake beyond the fact that
in some inexplicable way it seems to complement western wear, window vans, and Billy Beer, as "Wall Street Week" is quick to point out.[4]
For like other trends it generates a tiny class of enterpreneurs who
stand to benefit from the marketing of it (bluegrass musicians never
get rich, though parlor-book authors often do[5]) as well as a hermetic
fraternity of technical experts who comprise a loosely structured commercial establishment. Phonograph records can be fashionable too, of
course; but here the audial burden of a human communication remains,
and few will listen to a record which has not touched them. Moreover
the history of phonograph records in, say, the black South of the
twenties, or among the middle-class young in our own time, demonstrates that a record can be a center around which social groups,
however primitive or transient, may revive or grow anew.

But an alert and impartial friend has reminded me that from the
silent score the joy of fresh discoveries, and even a thoroughgoing
recreation of the music, may arise; a score, too, can be read with
imagination after all. Even Yeats's fiddler of Dooney bought a book of
tunes at the Sligo Fair. A tune learned from a book may of course
ultimately enter the musician's wider experience, gathering association
and a mantle of connotation there. Finally, I suppose, it is better that
a music otherwise inaccessible should be accessible in written form.
Bluegrass music is not everywhere accessible even now, either live or
on record, even in Appalachia, for it has always suffered from competition with more commercial and more popular music. In fact there
is plenty to challenge the transcriber in bluegrass, and much to interest
the serious composer. Its handful of modes, its three or four chords,
its matched pairs of rhythm and syncopation are a richly composted

and ancient garden, which the musical imagination has had much time to cultivate and create.

It has not been the parlor book, after all, by which the bluegrass gospel has spread, but by that other parlor toy, the phonograph. By storing sound in a sound-induced form of "writing"—the grooves scored in the surface of a cylinder or disc—the recording device takes the acoustic impression of, say, a musical performance; "phonographer" was the nineteenth-century name for stenographer. The phonograph releases the sound from storage by generating it from the vibrations of a stylus moving through the grooves. This uncoupling of the sound of the performance, or rather the impression of it, from the performance itself has two curious effects upon the music: first, it thrusts the musical performance, which normally is always present, into the past; for no matter how current or popular, the phonograph record is always an impression of a past performance, though the sound it produces occurs of course in the present. Though it appears to "play," as the computer appears to "think," in fact it merely recapitulates mechanically the physical issue of a human action which is not in itself mechanical. Second, it *replaces* the musical performance with its own acoustic impression, a kind of echo, which unlike the performance can be indefinitely repeated, as the impression is lodged in a technological component which can be mass produced, distributed, sold, played and replayed as readily as a windup toy. The technology, in other words, divides music in half, so that the two halves, like Aristophanes's two sexes, are ever seeking their reunion with one another.

There are several ways, then, to exploit audial technology. It can document acoustically a human event in which it otherwise has no part. Or it can document a human event undertaken especially on its behalf: the musician may perform for the recording device, which technologically supplies the place of an audience. Or he can perform *by means* of the device, using its special powers, of which recording itself is the first, literally to create sound. He can choose *what* to record, setting it apart from the rest of the audible universe for special attention, and *how* to record it, using the sounds of the performance as the raw materials of a technological art which in the modern recording studio has been incalculably ramified. In these cases, the recording itself is the performance.

Except in the metaphorical sense that it may be the composer's "performance," a musical score is not a performance. The score mediates between the composer and the performer, retaining the composition, an imaginative work, in abstract form, while documenting it in the concrete form of written symbols. This is in contrast to the phonograph record, which mediates between the performance and the sound of the performance. Being doubly time-bound it cannot have the abstract force of the score, as we have seen; it is just for this reason that an aural tradition can arise from a body of recordings.

But what happens when recording enters an already existing aural tradition? The two may at first live side by side, the one to sing, the other to scribe down, each in its separate and independent sphere. But because the new technology is without a content of its own it will feed upon the aural tradition, ultimately to exhaust and perhaps to consummate it in some encyclopedic display in which the total order of the tradition manifests itself as in aural performance it never could; a new art based on the technology itself, as the novel is based upon the printed book, succeeds the aural tradition. But for a brief historical moment, the moment of the transition, as the aural tradition begins to spill into the vast, empty reservoir of the new technology but before the artist has discovered its specific properties, he will call upon the old methods, the methods of aural composition, to create in the new medium. This was the character of the literary renaissance of the sixteenth century, as eloquence passed into literature; the literary colossi of our culture—Homer, Dante, Shakespeare, Joyce—stand astride the straits joining aural and written traditions. Under these conditions the recording, like the score, may be said to mediate between the composer and the performer; for in an aural tradition the composition and the performance are the same. Moreover the recording represents the composition in an unrealized state, for the composition in aural tradition must be a performance, not a recording. Finally the composition can be aurally inferred from the recording—that is, the recording can be "read"—because it remains aural in form and thus lends itself to aural reduplication.

The dawn of a technology, it seems, always prefigures its day. The movie lens, for example, has always been a bit of a voyeur: that is its nature, for it permits us to see the world as it were through a keyhole. The earliest "motion pictures," Edward Muybridge's "Animal Locomotion" series (Muybridge is the fellow who proved with a photograph that a galloping horse has all four hooves off the ground at once), presented a baseball player, a cricketeer, boxers, wrestlers, fencers, and a tumbler, all naked, as well as over 240 pictures of naked women, including a mother and daughter, a fan dancer, and two women bathing one another.[6] If this was a trick of voyeurism, the early phonograph was a trick of ventriloquism, or so Edison's early skeptics supposed, for he had made a machine *speak*. "The machine inquired as to our health," wrote the editor of *Scientific American* in 1877, "asked how we liked the phonograph, informed us that *it* was very well, and bid us a cordial good night."[7] But the phonograph does not "throw" the voice; it catches it. Edison saw the documentary power of his new device while it was still on the drawing board. "There is no doubt," he wrote with characteristic bravado, "that I shall be able to store up and reproduce automatically at any future time the human voice perfectly."[8] The voices of Henry Stanley, Teddy Roosevelt, William Jennings Bryan, and William Howard Taft all found their way to Edison's cylinders, as did those of William Gladstone, Robert Browning, P. T. Barnum, and Florence Nightingale. But the cylinders could not do justice to the human voice; and, as its history has shown, the real metièr of the phonograph is not orders of words, which print had already commandeered, but orders of sounds—music.

The first musical recording was made in Edison's laboratory about ten years after the first experiments with the phonograph. It was "Mary Had A Little Lamb"—traditional enough, I suppose—played by Margaret Atwood, the wife of Edison's assistant, George Atwood, in 1887.[9] By early in the nineties Edison was mass-producing cylinders—as many as 200 a day. Among the most popular in this early series was a line of "darky" songs and skits. Edison had met a black man on the ferry from New York whose whistling impressed him; he recorded the man as "The Whistling Coon," becoming, perhaps, the first folk-song collector to use the technology. Another of these titles, "Row at a Negro Ball," opened with a banjo and fiddle and ended with the drawing of razors, the sound of pistol shots, and the arrival of the police. Most serious musicians eschewed the new device—Hans von Bulow is said to have fainted when he heard a false note in a Chopin mazurka he had recorded[10]—but in fact Edison's colleague H. de Coursey Hamilton, traveling in Europe, managed to record the Handel Festival at the Crystal Palace and Edward Strauss playing "The Blue Danube" at Vienna. In any case the documentary power even of the relatively crude early technology was not lost upon folk-song collectors. Frank C. Brown's collection of North Carolina folk songs and John Lomax's cowboy songs were both recorded on cylinder within the first fifteen years of this century; still earlier is a cylinder collection of Afro-American folk song made around the turn of the century by the Hampton Institute and only recently discovered there, in 1976—the earliest known recordings of black folk music in the country.[11]

The attempts of early recording engineers to accommodate musical performances to the deficiencies of the technology represent the very first stage of its development into a medium of art. Tubas and trombones, for instance, which at close range could break the delicate recording membranes, were placed well in the background, while strings, especially at a low pitch, often could not be recorded at all and so were replaced by woodwinds and brasses. In order to create the illusion of dynamics, singers might move back and forth, but at first it was necessary to sing close to the mike at full voice in order to be recorded at all. The recording device, then, had begun to influence the recorded matter, generating in effect a new species of music, *recordable* music, which because it occurs only on record oddly anticipates the studio art of the present day.

Electrical recording widened the acoustic range of the device from 2,000 to 5,000 cycles, securing a firmer union between performer and recording, and by increments the technology of sound recording became a medium of art in its own right. We now have, of course, "recording artists," who exploit the resources of the studio to compose in sound itself. Music in the studio, then, has become the acoustic raw material of an electronic art, the art of making records: while sophisticated studio bands such as Steely Dan create musical pieces which cannot exist as such except on record, bluegrass and old-time bands, using all the resources of the mixing board and other devices, reconstitute the sound of their performances as independent acoustic creations which reflect complex agreements among musicians, producers, engineers, and promoters. Now that modern computer-based equipment can record and reproduce sounds far more subtle than the human ear can detect, with virtually no extraneous noise, it appears that recorded music, as "present" to the ear as is technically and organically possible, actually enhances the audial perception of music; like other arts in their achieved forms, it is consciousness-expanding. At the same time it encourages us to identify music ever more strictly with sound, just as the score encourages us to identify it with notes, at the expense, in both cases, of its ancient alliance to poetry, drama, and dance.

The lesson here is that a record-keeping medium such as writing, photography, or sound recording is a medium of art only insofar as its inherent resources are exploited.[12] We must compose *in* writing, *in* film, *in* records; otherwise we have merely documented arts executed in other media. Carried into the presence of summit meetings, ship launchings, and treaty signings, the movie camera was an instrument of immense documentary force; but the cinema did not become an independent art until the cinematographer learned to manipulate the medium itself—to move the camera about, to compose the visual image as a painter might, to edit and splice the film, and so on. Between documentation and creation there is no fixed and definite boundary, but a gradual absorption of subject matter into medium through which the two are formally united in a particular way. If for instance we wished to imitate a photograph or sound recording of Edison's time, we would have to adopt not only some old-fashioned subject matter— a naked baseball player, perhaps, with a handlebar mustache, or "I'll Take You Home Again, Kathleen," with piano accompaniment—but Edison's technology as well. To do otherwise would destroy the illusion. This suggests that it is the formal unity of subject matter and medium which generates and sustains artistic illusion, since the medium, while seeming in its characteristic way to refer to the world, is in fact no longer simply the record of something other than itself, shaping itself to the contours of its subject, but an active agent, enforcing its form upon the subject matter, lending its authority to it, charging it with its own substance. It is the medium, itself a part of the phenomenal world, that compels us to participate in its activity, to build characters and actions out of sequences of words or images, and that channels feeling through the flow of musical sound. It is just this imaginative participation which empowers us to read a novel, view a movie, or listen to a musical performance, since it allows us in effect to transcend imaginatively the merely technical dimension of the medium, regarding it as the agent of experiences which, though illusory, belong to the order of our experience as a whole.

The improvisatory intensity of hot jazz issued during the twenties in a body of striking performances, many of which were repeated in, or were deliberately created in, the recording studio, in a full consciousness of two complementary facts—the transience of the extemporaneous jazz performance and the power of the recording machine to capture it. Improvisation had made an artist of the musician in the fullest sense, compelling him to find a means of preserving his work, and his audiences to study it, as we study the work of any poet or painter.

An extremely fertile alliance developed as a result among the jazz musician, the disc, and the discographer: jazz and discography, indeed, seem to have grown up together.[13] Some early jazz musicians such as Buddy Bolden and Freddie Keppard shunned the studio because they feared other jazzmen would steal their work;[14] others, particularly Louis Armstrong and his "Hot" bands, the Five and Seven, could scarcely resist the impulse to get into the studio. Here was an overflowing well of music which had to be tapped at once; often the greatest jazz performances, such as Armstrong's "West End Blues," as well as certain combinations of musicians, occurred *only* in the studio. These discs, of course, became the basis of "dixieland" jazz, in which young white bands such as the Austin High Gang and Biederbecke's Wolverines studied the recordings of the jazz masters they had heard in South Side clubs and imitated them note-for-note, "reading" the discs like scores.

Dixieland of course repeats a familiar cycle: like the minstrels who made field trips to plantation cabins, "bringing along a jug of whiskey to make things merrier," like the white hillbilly singers of the fifties who tuned in on black rhythm-and-blues radio stations, the dixieland bands were simply carrying a music from one audience to another, making certain modifications along the way. But the availability of discs had closed the gap between the music and its imitators. Both blackface minstrels and dixieland musicians claimed authenticity; but whereas the minstrels kept a safe distance between themselves and their models through parody, the dixieland musicians, young men absorbed in the sounds of jazz as in a new philosophy, emulated the black style and, as in the case of Mezz Mezzrow, endeavored even to take on the black personality.

The jazz musician had used the studio to alter fundamentally the form of his music, from action to artifact, recognizing that only an audial technology could capture and preserve improvised music as such, in which every idea is the momentary fusion of musician and music. Like the modern studio musician, his aim was to create artifacts of sound out of improvisation—a kind of audial action painting; the dixieland musician, by an act of imagination, could hope to transform the music back again, from artifact to action, and thereby perhaps plant in his heart the power of action which he so admired. Anyone who has heard a jazz trumpet or trombone, however—as Carmichael and Biederbecke, who had stood within a few feet of the blast of King Oliver's horn, had heard—knows that 5,000 cycles, or for that matter 20,000, cannot reproduce the whole incredible reality of a jazz ensemble performance, which is visual and dramatic as well as auditory. No: though the musician's purpose was to capture and objectify what in reality could occur only once, the disc could only cast a shadow of jazz music. On the disc, that is, was accomplished art in an unrealized state—that conjunction of aural tradition and recording technology which we have said can only occur in the moment of transition between the aural and technical phases of an art. It remained only for musicians listening to the discs to "read" what had been recorded. The music itself, as the subject matter of studio art, had been released from time; but it lay in an auditory sleep from which the dixieland musician could lift it *only by playing the music himself*. This is precisely what we do when we perform a musical score: we remove the technical agent—that is, the written symbols themselves—and replace them with living tones.

The jazz disc of the twenties, in a word, was a fiction, formed like coal from the transmutation of living matter to release its energy again in another world. The old jazzmen are gone, and the entire way of life from which their music sprang vanished away; we have only their recordings to remember them, from which we must imagine the entire character of the music. But *how* are we to imagine it, having never heard it in fact, as Carmichael and Biederbecke heard it? Would this not be a bit like reading a novel about forgotten, lost, or dimly remembered places and people, which we must flesh out from our own experience, in effect creating from the mingling of past and present an altogether new strain? Would not the old story have first touched us, indeed, precisely because it had fallen upon the fertile ground in some wild and neglected corner of our capacity for experience?

"Like the city dwellers who doted on 'Moonlight Bay,' 'Sweet Adeline,' and other songs of their youth," writes Doug Green,

> a sizeable number of farmers across the nation looked back fondly on the pleasant days of barn dances and apple peelings. . . . As rural people began to acquire Victrolas and radios, it wasn't long before canny record industry executives and radio men sensed a growing market for "old-time" tunes of a rustic nature. Subsequently they sent their field representatives into the mountains to scour out musicians who could still play and sing like their fathers did in barn dance days. Of course, musicians aspiring to professionalism being what they are, there was often an attempt on the part of would-be recording artists to perform their own rendition of a hit of the day. . . . But such efforts were nearly always rejected: it was the old standard, the old fiddle tune, the sentimental ballad of the 1890s that was wanted, not the modern song.[15]

"Folksong revival" literature, largely influenced by a turn-of-the-century folk-song revival in England, had already prepared American audiences for native material, as folklorist Archie Green reminds us in *Only a Miner;* this literature included Negro spirituals, plantation and cabin songs collected from slaves, the songs of the Fisk University Jubilee Singers, the Sargeant–Kittridge abridgment of the Child ballads, and John Lomax's *Cowboy Songs*, which was endorsed by Teddy Roosevelt. Early recordings, too, which as Archie Green points out included a "potpourri of rural dances, minstrel routines, monologist bits, laughing songs, spirituals, and country fiddling, as well as concert arrangements of traditional ballads," reflected many of the same influences.[16]

But the hillbilly idiom itself, with which we are chiefly concerned, began when a record dealer named Polk Brockman, visiting Times Square in June 1923, happened to see a *newsreel* of a Virginia fiddlers' convention at the Palace Theater.[17] The documentary powers of one medium, apparently, had alerted him to the documentary powers of the other; and, interestingly, both were in about the same stage of technical development, both, like the early printing press, avid for material to fill their spreading estates. Brockman called Ralph Peer— whose name shall stand for record-company advance men who performed the same work, including Art Satherly, Frank Walker, Don Law, John Hammond, and others—the production manager of the Okeh Record Company in New York to Atlanta to attempt a few preliminary recordings. The recordings made in this pioneer expedition were, for the most part, rather predictably conventional: a collegiate dance band, a theater pianist, the Morehouse College Quartet, a violinist, and two jazz bands. But among them were three traditional artists—blues singers Fannie Goosby and Lucille Bogan, and Fiddlin' John Carson, a local folk fiddler who when he was not working in the textile mills or as a tradesman painter was entertaining at political rallies, club meetings, on the trolley cars and streetcorners of Atlanta. Carson's "The Little Old Log Cabin in the Lane" and "The Old Hen Cackled and the Rooster's Going to Crow" sold 500 copies almost as soon as the pressings arrived in Atlanta, where Carson's reputation was already well established on the folk level. Within a year, Green writes, the Okeh catalogue offered "a full sampling of folk material in straightforward style: sacred, secular, ballads, lyrics, vocal solos, instrumental combinations."[18] Peer had created hillbilly music, and in a few years Paramount, Columbia, Victor, Brunswick, and other record labels were presenting folk material to rural audiences in the same way as the radio barn dance had begun to do. "We call them Songs from Dixie," a Brunswick flyer announces:

> They are recordings of songs and tunes that were born in the hills of Kentucky, the railroad towns of West Virginia. . . . most of these songs have been carried down from generation to generation by word of mouth and are closer to what may be called American Folk Music than anything in the United States.
>   They are recorded not by imitators, but by people who have been born and raised in the sections of the country where

they are popular, and the obvious sincerity of their efforts will make them interesting to everyone. Many of the numbers recorded have been heard by all of us at some time or other in our lives and their simplicity offers a pleasant change from the elaborate syncopations of the present day dance orchestra.[19]

"Many of the best-loved American melodies," an Edison catalogue concurs, "sung and played as you like them best—in the good, old-fashioned manner."[20]

Authenticity, sincerity, simplicity, universality, traditionality, regionality, historicity—who could fail, in a culture in which these qualities seem always to be slipping away, to put his money down? It isn't simply that the recordings of "old-time" music have become old, then; the junk shops of America are laden with old discs to which age has conferred no value whatever. The hillbilly recordings, made both in the field and in studios in Atlanta, New York, Chicago, and elsewhere, first acoustically and then, after 1925, electrically, roughly until the descent of the Great Depression, were *already old-fashioned* when they were recorded. Even the musicians themselves were conscious of obsolescence; while A. P. Carter sought out songs from aged and isolated people in the various places he visited, and Charlie Poole admired and emulated Fred Van Eps, Rudee Valley, and Al Jolsen, Clayton McMichen was chafing under his own popularity with the Skillet Lickers, believing quite rightly that his fellow musicians were twenty years behind him. As Archie Green and others have pointed out, many of the musicians, such as Al Hopkins and the Hillbillies, or the Opry's Dr. Humphrey Bate, were themselves revivalists.

To make art with record-keeping media, one must realize what most of us do at income-tax time: that nothing binds the record to reality but the whim of the keeper. A record, as we've seen, can document; but it can also create, wantonly asserting the existence of what we can neither affirm nor deny, as the words of the novelist bring us white whales and wild-eyed sea captains. The eclipse of the performance by the recording, whose effects upon the public personality we have already noted, made it possible not only to document musical performances in an obsolescent tradition but, by virtue of the mimetic power of music, actually to *retrieve* from the past what historically speaking had already slipped into it—in other words, to generate an illusion. "The music of the banjo," a Columbia catalogue informs us, "has a fascination peculiarly its own. There is a barbaric vigor to its ringing tone and a drumlike rhythm which carries us away from the staid music room of our home out under the stars over Southern levees where groups of dark-faced negroes, with shining teeth and eyes, sing plantation melodies to the strumming strings. . . ."[21] By ferreting out musicians who, in the history of culture, belonged to the past, Peer exploited the *first principle* of recording technology, which is that it divides the sound from that which has produced the sound: the recorded performance itself, as we've already noted, is *always* in the past. Expanding that gap until it became historical in scope, Peer sought to *bring back the past acoustically*. This was *cosmic* ventriloquism, catching a voice from the past. "These rollicking melodies," the Okeh catalogue promises, "will quicken the memory of the tunes of yesterday."[22]

It scarcely matters that the record executives' motives were entreprenurial rather than learned, though there is little doubt that popular forms of learned conceptions figured into them; the consequences were propitious. Banjos and fiddles went into the closet or under the bed when word came up the holler that "Professor" Sharp was on his way;[23] but when Peer advertised for old-time musicians in the Atlanta *Constitution*, the entire musical legacy of the nineteenth-century South flowed out of the hills into the recording machine. The very root of the phenomenon, as Doug Green's remarks suggest, was the availability of the medium itself; it was, again, a young technology searching for its own use and finding it first in oral traditions which it would ultimately supplant. Much of the old-time music favored in the early commercial period was appropriate to the social niche into which the phonograph had fallen; matter and medium joined in the small domestic society which each generated around itself. It is possible indeed that the phonograph itself had awakened a nostalgia for what it had replaced.

Insofar as they exploited their new medium, Peer and the other advance men were artists; and when we contemplate reality, past or present, through the refracting lens of the artist's mind, we see an *image*—no matter how "real" its original may have been. "Old-time music" is an image, as much so as the Forest of Arden, whose authenticity is a catharsis, aesthetic in form, of the expectations established in us by our culture's reflections on itself. When Peer and the rest first sought it out, old-time music was the relic of a generation which swift industrialization, mechanization, migration, and war had virtually buried. The withdrawal of history on the vast tide of the Great Depression and World War II exposed American life to a blaze of modernization which bleached out its color and obliterated the epoch of the old-time recordings. But the discs themselves survived. Reclaiming them relights the lamp of an era which not only has become history to us—that is, a kind of fiction—but which was vividly fictional even to itself—young, rich, fantastic, immoral—the Jazz Age. Among the gleaming and elastic figures of this period we can detect Peer, Satherly, Walker, and the rest, presiding over recording sessions in makeshift hotel-room studios—amused, no doubt, at their own situation, that they should hope to profit from the efforts of a bunch of cloverkickers in whom it would never have occurred to them to be interested had it not been for the historical frontier at which they found themselves, gazing back at the past whose abandonment they could perhaps take a moment to regret. Yet through the wilderness which divides America from itself, Peer's recordings found a path.

The music, of course, was the work of musicians. But the records were the work of men who, like the picture faddists of the eighteenth century who carried their Claude glasses into the countryside to compose "landscapes," framing the natural scene and varnishing it with tinted glass, had transformed actuality into illusion—time-laden and culture-charged musical images set apart from the formless present to awaken in us unprecedented dreams. Charlie Poole and A. P. Carter and Jimmie Rodgers even were flesh and blood; yet the record companies, in a sense, created them.

Well, it has been a long climb, but we've finally made it to the attic and to Aunt Maude's collection of old-time discs. There's even some bluegrass up here, some old Mercury, King, and Starday albums; Dad got them when he was working in Cincinnati, after the war. It's a gold mine up here for the old-time band, which can garner material from the old-time discs, and for the bluegrass band, which can not only do the old songs in the bluegrass style but bring back some of the original bluegrass in its original form. Our contemporary "old-time" music, much of our "traditional" bluegrass, carried on by a number of young string bands and small record labels and almost exclusively based upon discs, and even to some extent the original bluegrass itself, is the imaginative completion of the act of retrieval which Peer and the rest undertook. No such compulsion accompanies merely documentary recordings such as the Hampton cylinders, for these are complete as documents, and in a state of repose; but the hillbilly record remains in a potential state, the program of an unrealized imaginative effort—unrealized because the music has not, in fact, been retrieved. It has only been recorded, and hence remains in the past. To make it present, then, we must play it ourselves.

If music is the audible form of the impression that life makes upon the heart, then a thoroughgoing revival, authentic in content and style, will send echoes into life itself, influencing its form. The revivalist's nostalgia is not for the music alone, but for the whole way of life it

represents to him. Between folk revivalism and social or political discontent there has always been an uneasy alliance; even Cecil Sharp's
discreet piano arrangements could strike a note of revolution into the
hearts of principled young ladies. The theatrical setting and costume
of the radio barn dance, the outdoor bluegrass festival, the loose association which has developed among folk festivals, craft fairs, and
historical restoration—all suggest the power of the music to generate
its own context. The potentially subversive power of old-time and
bluegrass music cannot always be reined in by devices of theater;
introduced into the stream of contemporary life, these musics can
waken the eternal restlessness and apocalyptic vague hopes of a spirit
morally amazed, just as vividly as postwar French philosophy or grass-
roots evangelism. Old-time music, in its contemporary form, is a way
of life. That is why the "folk-revival," an intermittent tide of influence
flowing to us from the European romantic movement along both
learned and popular channels, and the related "rock revolution," which
in many respects is a folk revival too, of black folk music by whites,
may have immense social and cultural impact, as a huge segment of
the society lives in an association with a phonograph or tape deck as
close and constant as the Methodist with his Bible.

With its retrieval of ancient texts, its voracious appetite for new
texts of ancient origin, its attempts to purify and systematize the
ancient languages, its emerging sense of history, even the evolution
of a new genre based upon the ancient ones, the entire phenomenon
of old-time music, which from this perspective includes bluegrass and
is included by the postwar folk revival, resembles a kind of phono-
graphic renaissance. The old-time musician is a kind of discophile,
husbanding the ancient texts and copying them in his performances.
This is an imaginative, creative labor, for as we have seen the phonograph record is addressed to the senses and not, like the score, to
the intellect. Bluegrass differs from old-time music only in its methods,
really; rather than copying particular texts, it attempts to retrieve the
entire tradition in a single unitary image, a representation. We have
already seen the important role which phonograph records played in
Monroe's own development, consolidating, widening, and enriching the
traditions in which he was personally rooted. His early professional
career, in turn, formally educated him, providing the scope and detachment, the overview, of the folklorist, while early professional success empowered him to organize and unify that knowledge, to master
his experience and to distill it to a symbolically pure form.

In purifying the style Monroe provided many mountain musicians
with a way of recovering their own music. For them, bluegrass was

among other things a way of playing old songs, and this is just what it became during the urban folk song revival of the 1960s. As the audience for the original bands spread to northern cities (Earl Taylor and the Stoney Mountain Boys appeared in New York at an Alan Lomax concert, "Folksong '59," in 1959, the Osborne Brothers at Antioch College in 1960, the Stanley Brothers at the University of Chicago in 1961),[24] southern musicians, especially the most popular bands such as Flatt and Scruggs, were encouraged by the new market to draw more deeply from their own folk backgrounds, or even to explore that background anew, as revivalists were doing, through phonograph records and songbooks. It is well known that Ralph Rinzler, seeking out the medicine show performer Clarence Ashley whom Columbia had recorded in the twenties, in the North Carolina hills, "discovered" Doc Watson; less well known is the fact that Doc was at the time a confirmed rockabilly guitarist and was persuaded only with the utmost difficulty, and at the very last moment, to return to the old music. Henceforth Doc garnered his professional repertoire not only from his own background, which like that of many of his friends and neighbors included the original hillbilly discs, but from contemporary sources as well, including record albums, songbooks, and living performers such as John Hurt, who had also been rediscovered by folk revivalists. Under the impetus of the folk revival, then, Appalachian tradition was dramatically replenished. Jim Stanton, founder of the pioneer bluegrass record label Rich-R-Tone, recalls: "I used to book Lester and Earl into tiny little schoolhouses propped up on sticks in the coal fields, and really it was the best bookings I could get them and then years later after we lost track of each other, I'm sitting home watching TV and they're on the UCLA campus. Thirty thousand people raving, and I can't believe it. . . ."[25]

The history of old-time music in this country is a story of a gradual widening of access, as musicians who imitated the original hillbilly recordings were themselves imitated by their audiences, who eventually found their way back to the original recordings, to reissues of them, or even to the surviving old-time musicians themselves. In this way the recorded archives of hillbilly music, as well as the efforts of many otherwise isolated bluegrass bands such as the Lilly Brothers which had themselves been discovered by northern revivalists, recorded on esoteric labels, and brought to university folk festivals, entered an aural tradition which though far from universal is national in scope and securely built on a foundation of phonograph records. Social, historical, cultural, and even geographical gaps had formed a kind of psychological Jordan at whose banks the legacy of the past massed together at once; and only a disc could transport the music to the other side.

I think many will agree with me if I suggest that the original body of hillbilly recordings is surrounded by a kind of gravitational field which draws certain rare musical recordings made before it, and certain recorded music after it, into itself. The classic bluegrass recordings—Monroe and Martin on Decca, the Stanleys on King, Flatt and Scruggs on Mercury, many lesser-known bands now defunct such as the Lonesome Pine Fiddlers—are separated from the original hillbilly discs by twenty years or more; yet with the passage of time the gap between them seems almost to have closed. Listen again to Monroe's "On the Old Kentucky Shore," the Stanleys' "Man of Constant Sorrow," the Lonesome Pine Fiddlers' "Windy Mountain," or to certain modally flavored instrumentals such as Monroe's "Bluegrass Breakdown," the Stanleys' "Clinch Mountain Backstep," or the Lonesome Pine Fiddlers' "Pretty Little Indian." These recordings have a compelling and sometimes bewildering temporal ambiguity which arises, I think, from the paradoxical conjunction of a fundamentally archaic music with a new technology, for technology is in a sense always "new," its state at any given period embodying and even signifying the present. In contrast to the recorded professional bluegrass of our day, which stereo thrusts into our presence with all the brilliance and immediacy of a kitchen fire, all twenty-seven strings sparking out like dying light bulbs, "high fidelity," an innovation of the fifties, has very nearly, but not quite, delivered the music into our presence. It remains separated from us, rather hurtfully out of reach, not so much because an acoustic barrier stands between us and it but because even high fidelity organizes auditory space more narrowly than human perception; and the nature of the music, as well as the nature of the medium, which places a space of time between performance and recording, prompts us to interpret the distance temporally. Because the music is not entirely "present," then, it is past. It is almost as if we were to discover musical recordings of, say, minstrel music, made before sound recording had been invented. Moreover bluegrass in its formative period was still principally a live concert music, aural in form and improvisatory, if not completely extemporaneous, in method. Though it was certainly made in the studio, it had not been made *for* the studio; if these recordings have any one feature in common it is that they all sound like the *radio broadcasts* of the period. Finally of course there is the substance and the style of the music itself, which is not only rich with archaic elements but deliberately calculated to symbolize and evoke "the old southern sound." Thus its merest recession in time, which eclipses the particular cir-

cumstances of its creation and breaks its links to history, causes it to
be swallowed up in the past, as in its native element. Peer found the
past in the north Georgia hills; but if authenticity is a catharsis of
expectations, then Bill Monroe's bluegrass was authenticity itself.

Thus it was that the first and most important of the postwar revivalist string bands, the New Lost City Ramblers, included some of the
original bluegrass, such as Monroe's "Little Girl and the Dreadful
Snake" and the Stanleys' "Little Glass of Wine," in a repertoire which
consisted largely of painstaking imitations of original old-time recordings. This band—Mike Seeger, John Cohen, Tom Paley, and later
Tracy Schwarz—warrants a book of its own; with a background rich
in folklore this band pioneered the revival of old-time string-band music
and continued its dissemination for nearly twenty years without a rival,
not only playing and recording the music themselves but bringing many
of the still-living mountain musicians, Doc Boggs and Tommy Jarrell
among them, to the attention of an ever expanding northern audience.
Like Monroe's their work has a scholarly quality; but, like Monroe,
the Ramblers were performers too, and if they were at times too
scrupulous or too slavish in their interpretations of the old-time discs,
we must remember that it was out of many of the same allegiances
that drove Monroe. It is no accident that Seeger, along with his friend,
Ralph Rinzler, took an interest in Monroe, in whom they saw the living
continuation of the tradition they were seeking to call up from the
past—and *did* call up. Bluegrass, as we've seen, pursued its own
course, while during the seventies the revival of old-time music has
gained strength, and is a far more liberal kind of music than that
promulgated by the New Lost City Ramblers—less scrupulously im-
itative, less confined to a particular body of material, and highly original in its own right within a wide spectrum of once archaic, now
current, styles.

Yet its subject matter remains essentially the phonograph record,
and its medium as well. Many new record labels have grown up to
accommodate the exploitation of the record as a medium not only of
performance but of transmission. A recent recording of Tommy Jarrell
on County, for instance, a label which features both reissues and original recordings of old-time and bluegrass music, offers the narrative
of the fiddler as well as his music, as he tells us in each case how to
tune the fiddle: he is playing for us but also teaching us. The participatory or communal aspect of old-time music is strong. In the early
seventies the Fuzzy Mountain String Band of Chapel Hill, a group of
young amateurs who abandoned academic and professional careers in
order to pursue their music, issued two albums of fiddle tunes which

had been collected in the field by the band members themselves from traditional fiddlers in the region; these records provided in liner notes the source and tuning of each number, and were clearly designed not principally to earn a reputation for the musicians but to disseminate the material. That this effort was successful is evident from the huge numbers of young fiddlers who trace at least some part of their repertoire to one of these albums, and from the prominence of the band's informants, especially Jarrell, Franklin George, and Henry Reed. Many new string bands have followed the Fuzzy Mountain String Band's example, so that the body of available material grows constantly with the collective efforts of individual musicians and their recordings. Some of the old-time bands such as the prestigious Highwoods, now disbanded, confine themselves to the fiddle tunes and dance music of Appalachia; others are broader in outlook, dipping into sources which include Irish traditional music, early jazz and blues, bluegrass, thirties western swing, forties country-western, even fifties rock-and-roll. The principle operating here, it seems, is that the music must be generically trenchant and securely tied by association to the period or the place from which it comes. One of the best of the thriving old-time groups, the Red Clay Ramblers, offers a repertoire ranging from the Carter Family and Jimmie Rodgers to the Inkspots; the breadth, intelligence, and energy of this group make them a kind of human radio tuned in on the past, through whom much lively, evocative, sweet, quaint, eccentric, and comical music, but above all interesting music, traditional and popular, urban and rural, flows into the present and becomes present. "We call it 'Old-Time,'" writes one young musician, "but it's current to us."[26]

An art may perhaps be said to have come of age when it can refer to itself. One of the most intriguing events in bluegrass was the issue in the early seventies by two teenaged Kentucky musicians, Ricky Skaggs and Keith Whitley, of an album of early Stanley Brothers' songs, imitated so perfectly as to be scarcely distinguishable from the originals, except that technologically they were better recordings. This was attic bluegrass in the purest sense. During the summer of 1971 Skaggs and Whitley performed in Ralph Stanley's band, so that the performance of this group became a kind of seánce, annealing the vocal sounds of three stages of the brothers' career into a single complex audial image: the ethereal harmonies of the young duet, the repining voice of the dead Carter Stanley, eerily lodged in the throat of his replacement, Roy Lee Centers, and finally the voice of the surviving brother, the cry of a vendor of sorrows.

Skaggs and Whitley have both gone on to pursue successful careers in country music. Whitley eventually joined Ralph as his lead singer, leaving behind him a number of moving and memorable recordings, particularly Carter's "I Just Think I'll Go Away," to which Keith lends his intense, agile, ornamented style; at present he sings in J. D. Crowe's progressive band, the New South. As a session musician, bandleader, and individual recording artist, Ricky Skaggs has become the leader of a new generation of bluegrass-inspired country musicians who still like to get their material by poking around in the attic. Skaggs's album *Waitin' For the Sun to Shine*, which has made an unprecedented success by sending every cut except for the title song well to the top of the country charts, included two bluegrass standards, Ralph Stanley's "If That's the Way You Feel" and Flatt and Scruggs's "Don't Get Above Your Raisin'," as well as a handful of country-western classics, among them Webb Pierce's "I Don't Care," Carl Butler's "Crying My Heart Out Over You," and Merle Travis's "So Round, So Firm, So Fully Packed"—tunes popular in the fifties, when Skaggs was in his infancy. In fact, Skaggs has been at it most of his life: he first appeared on stage with Bill Monroe at the age of six. "What do *you* want?" said the Father of Bluegrass Music, peering down at him. "I want to pick," squeaked the boy, lifting his mandolin, "I want to pick."

Chapter 9

The High, Lonesome Sound

Ritual, Icon, and Image

f a man listening to it will let it," Bill Monroe says, "bluegrass will transmit right into your heart."[1]

Music is the most mimetic of the arts; so Aristotle tells us. Mimesis is a power—that power by which the poet, narrating the speech of Priam to the proud Achilles, "imitates," in voice and gesture, the aged king, *impersonating* him and, for his audience, *becoming* the king before their eyes. It is the same power that father calls upon in his bedtime story to transform himself, briefly but terrifyingly, into the Big Bad Wolf. Mimesis is the power by which the artist generates illusion. Aristotle likens the pleasure we take in mimesis to the pleasure of learning, for "this," the artist teaches, is "that"—these pigments a woman's eyes, these words a year at sea, this stone the dead Christ. In the power to generate illusion, no art excels music; the very act of hearing is an act of imagination, every sound an unreality, an erosion of the sensorium which we seek to repair with material from the substantial world of touch and sight. Sound situates us in the midst of a world of diverse and unpredictable immediate activity, presences which because we cannot see or touch them bring with them fugitive and transient interpolations of sight and touch, indefinite images without objects which allay the primitive anxiety—"What's that?"—of what we cannot know. Our involuntary attention to it, which may take the form of excitement or alarm, and the deliberate act of listening by which we open ourselves to it, betray the spontaneous effort of imagination to complete the round of sense by assigning shape and substance to the shapeless and insubstantial.

Hearing registers force. The character of a particular sound is determined by the physical relationships of some wave-producing interior—the density of steel, the dryness of wood, the hollowness of the violin—relationships which may, in the human voice for example, arise from psychological or emotional factors. Consequently, as Walter Ong observes, sound exhibits interiority *as such*, "without the necessity of physical invasion" required by the other senses, to which interior space in its integrity is not accessible.[2] Thus we tap the coin, or run our thumb along the lip of a crystal goblet, to *hear* if it is genuine. Sound thus draws from the memory of all that we have seen or felt an inference about itself, "both what we half perceive and half create," by which we might experience it. By mimesis, sound means. *This* sound is revealed by imagination to be *that*—a leaky faucet, a carpet sweeper, a banjo string, a god who speaks in thunder.

Musical sounds, too, exhibit the physical relationships of some wave-producing interior: the human voice, or the musical instrument whose interior relationships are a human contrivance which human contrivance at any given moment can modify. That is to say, they are artificial, clearly marked off from the rest of the audible universe and independent of it. Thus for the same reason that we do not attempt to deliver the letter which Friar Lawrence could not, or to eat the apples which Cezanne has hospitably served with a paring knife and a napkin, so do we entertain the ineluctably complex stimuli of musical sounds without attempting to objectify them, attending instead to the sounds themselves. Unless the musician chooses to imitate some other sound— a bird's song, human laughter, cannon fire—musical sound will not lead us by any sensory inference to the objective world, for music can only make the sound of itself.

Yet musical sounds are sounds nevertheless, and imagination is not immune to them. That we know Friar Lawrence's letter, or for that matter Friar Lawrence himself, to be a fiction does not prevent us from hoping for its safe delivery; that Cezanne's apple is probably poisonous does little to curb our appetite for it. Musical sounds— consonance and dissonance, rhythm and tempo, harmony and melody, timbre and tone-color, articulation, intensity, modality and pitch—all give rise to effects of sensation and movement which are the immediate natural consequence of these sounds but which *are not peculiar to them.* By acknowledging that these effects are the same which might otherwise arise from contact with the objective world, which we can do precisely because music does not emanate from that world, we lay ourselves open to the power of music. Such kinesthetic phenomena as tension and the release of tension, conflict and the resolution of conflict become, imaginatively, the attitudes, emotions, and moods of which they are normally the organic background. "This" is "that."

In other words, music exhibits human interiority: consciousness itself. It works because consciousness is part of what can be experienced; we are capable of experiencing our own vital processes. Insofar as our own interiority may be regarded as an object, therefore, music as such *does* lead to an "objective" world and thus, like the other arts, engenders an object in the mind when there is nothing objectively present to the mind but the activity of the medium itself. We look at paint, we see apples; we read words and witness acts of love or murder; we hear musical sounds and feel our souls rise and fall to occasions which are not there. While the other arts offer objects, or representations of them, *to* consciousness, music arouses the sensation of consciousness, in all its vital activity; it stirs those parts of the physical body through which the gods, especially the gods of love and war, gain access to us.

Through long service in the human community, music, like language, acquires a connotative surface inseparable from its mimetic power. Whatever the musical instrument, style, or kind, it will carry its connotative message into the music, linking it for that culture to particular times and places. The great European composers have marshalled all these mimetic forces into a comprehensive and coherent impression of life. Unlike most popular music in which expediency, accident, vague intentions, and simple low motives play a large part, bluegrass, too, is a thoroughgoing auditory order, what musicians call a "sound," in which effects belonging to the system of music are impregnated with auditory features culturally, historically, socially, and psychologically significant, all proceeding from musicians whose actions and interactions figure as an important dramatic element in the meaning of the music as a whole.

The instruments of bluegrass—a good place to begin—quite obviously belong to the folk background of the music; banjo and fiddle are historically connected to a species of southern music which antedates the Civil War and in the popular imagination are emblematic of a historical era symbolized by the blackface minstrel. The mandolin, too, belongs to the more recent domestic background of hillbilly music, being more specifically connected to that music than either the banjo or the fiddle, and far narrower in its range of reference than the guitar, whose echoes reach in several directions at once, though principally to the cowboy and the West. Each makes its special contribution to the bluegrass sound: the bass a meter and a foundation tone; the guitar a chordal setting and a steady pulse; the fiddle intensity, continuity, and tensile strength; the mandolin texture, rhythm, and force; the banjo brilliance, plenitude, and drive.

The structure of bluegrass admits each of these instruments into the foreground, where they are played in a fashion that somehow captures the peculiar timbre of old-time music and the special character of the instruments themselves. We must have, for instance, the steady bass runs of the guitar, the characteristic snap or twang of the banjo strings, the mournful wail of the fiddle constantly before us. One has merely to hear the banjo's strings touched, or one double stop drawn out on the fiddle, to recognize the sense in which the meaning of bluegrass begins quite simply with what these instruments essentially are; it is the aim of the bluegrass style to set forth what the instument, or for that matter the man playing the instrument, essentially is, and to do so *by putting man and instrument to the test.*

"Separate your notes," counsels the Father of Bluegrass Music, "keep your timing right, and *let your tones come out.*"[3] In contrast to the dense, closed-chord "sock" of the swing guitarist, which seems to bottle up the instrument, or the agitated scratching of the tenor ban-joist, which seems to bind its feet, the bluegrass instrumental technique, with its love of the freely vibrating open string and the unchecked decay of its sound, is a rigorous assay of the instrument's capacity to resonate and project a tone. Every note must be resolutely set forth—snapped, plucked, or drawn out with vigor sufficient to exhibit the instrument's nature (its interiority) and to evoke all that attaches to it by association. Unlike the old-time fiddler's shuffle on the bow, which seems to *save* notes, counting and stacking them like coin, the long, drawn out strokes of the bluegrass fiddler seem designed to *empty* the fiddle of its sound, pouring it forth in a stream channelled into one note or strewn with notes brief and light enough to be carried away upon its surface. By these techniques the musician concentrates his strength and focuses his intention, displaying through the instrument the human forces that figure into the genesis of a tone. That is one important reason why the bluegrass musician insists upon acoustic instruments; the acoustic instrument receives and communicates *his* strength, *his* touch, his shaping hand, while the electrically amplified instrument places the musician in control of massive forces which, however supple and dynamic in themselves, belong not to him but to the power company, and which abolish the interiority of the instrument altogether.

Fine music has been composed for mandolin, banjo, and of course for guitar and violin. But the bluegrass sound erects an acoustic barrier between the musician and music itself, one which can and must be crossed but will not *readily* be done away with. Monroe's gritty mandolin playing, or the snarling banjo style of Rudy Lyle, or the smokey one of Sonny Osborne do not immediately suggest a place for these instruments in art music of the European-American tradition. It is likely that, certain Italian compositions notwithstanding, no formal techniques are available which will arouse in the mandolin the intensity and brilliance of the violin or the dignity of the cello; nor are further technical improvements likely to give to the banjo the warmth of the guitar or the ductility of a mechanically more sophisticated stringed instrument such as the harpsichord. My point is that in bluegrass the emotional impact of these instruments is the issue of the musician's struggle to advance ideas sufficiently complex to draw the instrument out of its background of associations, *but never at the expense of that background.* The bluegrass instrumental style strives to keep alive the identity of the instrument so that we may consistently measure the musician's performance with reference to it. What distinguishes the great bluegrass musician is his sense of limit, his ability to balance the musical idea against the auditory image. His improvisations will never eclipse the signifying elements of the style, nor will he permit style alone to overwhelm his musical idea. When his ideas do come out, they are more likely to cut radically into melody, rather than to weight it with ornamentation; if he does permit himself a flight of fancy, it will always proceed from conservative passages which plainly set forth the chord progression, the melody, and the style from which he plans briefly to depart. Above all he will keep his right hand strong: it is the soul of his music.

It appears, then, that the bluegrass instrumental style emphasizes the tension between the imagination of the musician and the available means of manifesting it—a tension which requires that he make the best possible use of limited resources and that he sustain in himself the strength, concentration, and endurance necessary to do so. One cannot but detect in it the imprint of the Celtic imagination, with its love of the hard life; its self-reliance, independence, and pride; its reverence for the invaluable resources of age and custom; and its fear of higher presences by whose whim we presevere or die. Repudiating doubt, indecision, weakness, self-indulgence, and waste, severely abridging the vocabulary of expression while demanding intensity, fullness, and power within that vocabulary, the bluegrass style reflects an ethic of strict economy such as that which arises under conditions of scarcity, for it is scarcity of natural, material, social, and cultural resources that gives the edge to rural life. Perhaps this is why Bill

Monroe and other bluegrass musicians have insisted that bluegrass is the only true "country" music: the idea is moral, not musicological. Between bluegrass and its Nashville cousin, the one restrained and severe, the other irrepressibly ostentatious and vulgar, there is apparently a yawning moral gulf; but it is only that the bluegrass musician has wholeheartedly, even willfully, embraced his lot, while the country-western musician has taken a kind of Saturday-night holiday from it. For no one knows better than he does that life on the farm is rarely, if ever, a picnic.

They say in the mountains that a fiddle sounds better with rattles inside it—from a rattlesnake. It's easy to miss the point of this old tale. The rattles don't affect the tone of the fiddle somehow, as we usually suppose. But to have gone out and got them—that testifies to the worthiness of the fiddler, and that is what we hear when he plays.

"I think you can watch people," Bill Monroe has observed, "any kind of work they do in the way of music, and tell pretty well in their life what they've gone through, if you watch it close enough."[4] Bluegrass music is an ordeal designed to challenge and, in challenging, to display the musician's intellectual, imaginative, and moral resources, and to provide a field for the development of those resources. It is a test of character. All serious music presents such a challenge; but it is one of the *purposes* of bluegrass to discriminate one man from another, to discover which man is the best, and to carry out that purpose in a medium which richly figures forth the substance of its discoveries. No doubt we admire the brilliant Itzhak Perlman, and may draw certain moral inferences about him on the basis of his musicianship; but *that* we make such inferences is incidental to his art, while to Monroe's it is central. I think it is fair to say that in bluegrass we listen *to* music, but *for* the man. Thus in bluegrass an unsophisticated or even a primitive musician can conceivably do better than an accomplished one. Until you grasp this, you cannot appreciate bluegrass music.

Nowhere in bluegrass is this ordeal undertaken more valiantly, nowhere is the musician's moral nature more powerfully revealed, than in his singing. Vocal tone is an open channel through which the human sensibility flows; every facet of vocal tone is the effect of one of a multitude of physical forces in the chest, throat, mouth, and head which centuries of evolution and culture have assigned to specific psychic states. Alan Lomax has argued with eloquence and conviction, and with a world-wide range of suggestive evidence at hand, that between folk-song style and culture there are certain persistent associations which seem to reflect the impact upon the psyche of the conditions of life.[5] Social and economic organization, political structure, technological development, domestic traditions and child-rearing practices—all figure somehow into vocal expression. Lomax has observed, for example, that agriculturally intensive societies tend to sing at higher pitches, while vocal restrictions in a general way seem to reflect the relative severity of the sexual code. Nasality, for instance, which as all parents of young children know is a form of complaint, is apparently most likely to occur in societies which require that children become independent very early in life but which at the same time fundamentally attenuate that independence by sanctifying marriage, placing a premium upon sexual purity and exacting rigorous penalties for premarital sexual play—among which, of course, is marriage itself. Anthropologically, at least, Lomax's evidence sheds light upon the apparent likenesses between the music of the Moslem Middle East and the Gaelic North which history cannot. Psychotherapists have at least partially borne out these findings by noting that "overcontrolled" behavior may show itself in pinched, narrow, and often irritatingly nasal vocal tones, though perhaps we do not need scientists to tell us that vocal tension and conflict, in song and in speech, arise from and communicate emotional tension and conflict.[6]

Our country music comes mainly from parts of the South where the conditions of life have favored the retention of values belonging to pioneer America. This was a world of nuclear families in widely dispersed settlements largely reliant upon the labor of one man who was in turn dependent upon the productive capacity of marginal or intransigent lands. Here the habit of independence arose far more from necessity than from enlightened philosophy; hardship quickly swallowed up youth and compelled the suppression of its impulses. As we've seen, the young boy or girl passed almost directly out of the infant gown into the work clothes of a man or woman, solidly grounded in the early affection of the family but incapable of the moral daring which is the special privilege of the bourgeoise child who comes up in a milieu of free imaginative play. The moral pall which in the rural imagination hangs over freedom from care, over song, dance, and drink, over love and all the joy it brings, has never entirely dissipated; what Lomax calls the "gulf fixed between pleasure and righteousness" has yet to close completely.[7] Its roots, in Scots Presbyterianism and English dissent, in Puritan and Calvinist philosophy, in social ostracism and economic marginality, are far too deep, and the conviction of sin upon which it feeds, to which human psychology has proved so hospitable, too important in the life and integrity of our culture. "The folklore of sin," writes Lomax, "put iron in the backbone of the pioneer, made him sober and hard-working, but left him with an inner sense of guilt and shame which no one in nineteenth-century America could really escape."[8]

Or has yet. Consider, for comparison's sake, the intensely emotional, and yet dour and undemonstrative, voice—the *reluctant* voice—of country-western singer George Jones, who was born into a fundamentalist working-class family near Beaumont, Texas, and grew up listening to the Opry's Roy Acuff and Bill Monroe.[9] Early in his career Jones affected the mica-thin nasality of the then flourishing Hank Williams, but in time found his own voice in a slightly lower register, creating a style now much imitated both by country-western and by bluegrass singers. For George Jones, song is a battle with that monster, Self, which stands between us and others; his is a voice beset at every level by the springs and snares of personality. He approaches his song manfully, with chest expanded and lungs full. But he cannot entirely let go; instead the force of his lungs is squeezed through a kind of knot formed behind his breastbone, like the first reflex before a cough. This is the way we might sound if we had just eaten too much, or were grossly overweight; if I am not mistaken it is the way a boy talks when he wants to sound like a man, driving his voice down into his chest because he cannot actually deepen it—perhaps because to "be a man" has in some sense been required of him since babyhood. When Jones's song rises to his mouth, having come from the heart in an almost physiological sense, it meets the barrier of his jaws, which he barely opens. Jones sings with the fixed grin of the ventriloquist, as if singing embarrasses him, thus imparting to his voice a dusky nasality and to his physical struggle itself an intense dramatic force. When at last his song escapes him—or, rather, when he succeeds in mastering all the forces which would hold it back—it is preternaturally animated by sudden dynamic changes, contractions and swellings of volume which seem to register astonishment or surprise, predicated with earnest descending melismas with which the singer seems to shake his head penitentially.

In decorativeness Jones's style owes much to traditional hymn singing; in voice it suggests a debt to rhythm-and-blues pianist-singers such as Peetie Wheatstraw or even Fats Domino. In both respects it is a true country style, leavened with an exclamatory energy and often delivered at a plodding, deliberate tempo which intensifies its mood of probity. The style seems to lend itself to the expression of the private, intimate, or inward life, of images which might otherwise appear only as obsessions or fantasies and which carry a weight of anxiety or even paranoia. One of Jones's best-known songs, "The Window Up Above," in which the singer witnesses his lover's betrayal of him from a second-story window, recalls a Kafka story or a Munch painting, and it has been recorded by Ralph Stanley and the Clinch Mountain Boys.

One way to overthrow the emotional barriers to song is simply to abandon the morality which gave birth to them. By setting the woody nasality of the hillbilly complaint and the sentimentality of the old-fashioned heart song against the accompaniment of contemporary jazz combos and Hawaiian bands, easy, black-inspired rhythms, and an open-voiced yodel, Jimmie Rodgers literally and figuratively thrust off the community which had nurtured him, embracing his unregenerate status with cheerful equanimity. His relaxation and sense of humor became, in the meantime, irresistably attractive to those who remained within that community. His tradition is carried on now by the great Merle Haggard, whose relaxed, debonaire, deep-throated voice, the voice of the cinema dreamboat, consolidates country music's moral revolution. In rougher singers such as Dave Dudley, purveyor of truck-driving songs, Haggard's implicit sexual invitation becomes a sexual boast, laden with heavy, drawling tones that seem to swagger and leer.

One might sanctify the voice, of course, with sacred songs. Gospel quartets—the sanction is a social one—are characterized by mellow basses at one end and reedy tenors at the other, in general dominated by a complacent bass and baritone sonority simply unheard of in other country music. This is the voice of the outward, not the inward, life, of social commonplaces and conventional values more suburban than rural. As secular song, which this music has become in the popular Oak Ridge Boys or the Statler Brothers, it skewers experience on the point of a pun, or salvages it in sentimental inventories of some harmless and benighted year like 1959; listening to it is like looking through a neighbor's high school yearbook.

But the bluegrass singer's style, like Jones's, is the audible record of the conflict between oneself and one's moral endowment, so that in both it is style, not subject, that bears the principal burden of meaning.

There are many ways of singing a bluegrass song; but it is clear that the rich, full, operatic voice, or the cabaret singer's mellow, ingratiating voice, or even Merle Haggard's lusty drawl have no more place in bluegrass than the saxophone. Rather the singer must sing through some impediment or difficulty—that acoustic barrier—by which the dramatic tension between himself and his resources of expression may be maintained. His aim is not to relieve or to escape vocal stress, but to excite it to such a pitch of activity and to concentrate it so intensely that its various physical causes, all morally imprinted, may unite in a new voice, a new-made vocal gem, his bluegrass voice. To this end bluegrass exploits the traditionally high registers of mountain and hillbilly music, which call upon the singer's maximal vocal force and direct it toward a definite object, the note itself. In other words, bluegrass has done with vocal technique just what it has done with instrumental technique—drawn out of the folk background certain signifying sounds from which to fashion its own style. Once the singer has acquired his bluegrass voice, which he does by the consistent application of force to song over a period of years, beginning most often in childhood, in a church choir perhaps, or, as Monroe did, alone in the fields, it will not depart from him; it is a physical effect, like the calcium deposits that gather at the site of a broken bone.

Bill Keith remembers that in riding from show to show Bill Monroe would attempt to sing the songs of the last performance a half-tone higher for the next.[10] This is not high singing for its own sake, but an effort to preserve the morally resonant tension between voice and song. Where that tension is lost, in singers for whom high notes pose no difficulty, though the broader mimetic effects of the style will remain in force, its *moral* dimension is lost. Were this not the case, bluegrass would be dominated by eunuchs, sopranos, or both. When Bobby Osborne sings "Ruby," a vocal tour de force in an unearthly D, he does it effortlessly, and may sound like a woman. When Earl Taylor sings it in the same key, the same twin banjos streaming behind him like a vapor trail, there is no mistaking his sex, or the tremendous effort he is putting forth; the strain introduces a fine, pumice-like abrasiveness into his voice. At the same time, to sing *above* one's range invites a damaging inference. "If you sing *too* high," Monroe says, "people'll say, 'now that man's used bad judgment.'"[11] This is not to say that high pitch is not important in itself—it is—but that we must understand it first as an object of striving, and as a precondition of certain vocal textures such as nasality essential to the bluegrass style. "That feller sings higher than me," Red Allen once said to me about another bluegrass singer, "but he says I *sound* higher than him." A singer's judgment consists in knowing at what point in his vocal range—a point that shifts from day to day, morning to evening—a song can be attacked to produce a certain emotional effect popularly called the "high, lonesome sound"; and if that should happen to be in B-flat, well then, let the fiddler figure out on the spot how to play today in B-flat what he played yesterday in C. For the "high, lonesome sound" occurs only at the apex of an arc which describes the line of equilibrium between vocal force and what might be called vocal flavor or value.

Not pitch, then, but force, of which high pitch is the handmaiden. Bluegrass singing, with all that force behind it, all of it strictly controlled, is at the very least venturesome; at most it is ardent, daring, angry, reckless, desperate, or wild. Certain habits must be put away, certain fears overcome, certain inhibitions relaxed. It seems sometimes almost as if the powerfully expansive sound might blow the singer's head apart, and often the expressions on his face as he sings suggest that its release is harrowing or painful, like exorcism. His delivery may be intensely personal, but it is never intimate or consultative. It is public and, as we have said, declamatory, thrown across some gulf of understanding or feeling, or set free into the empty spaces to discover what the boundaries of the living world may be.

In a sense the bluegrass singer is not singing at all—not in the way that gondoliers, yon solitary highland lasses, or bluebirds sing. He is driving life-force through the language-uttering organs of his body; under its concentrated energy the seasons of his voice pass more swiftly; it loses the quality which normally only the years can wear away, the quality of youth. Though it is never weak or infirm, bluegrass singing almost always somehow sounds old. No man of seventy could have lifted the roof of Ryman Auditorium with his voice, as Bill Monroe, in his thirties, did with his high, lonesome holler; yet around the sound of Monroe's voice at that period appears and disappears the image of a very old man. Ralph Stanley in his twenties sounded something like an eighty-year-old woman, but no elderly woman could have sung with the steady, delicate clarity of Ralph's "I Am a Man of Constant Sorrow." It is an illusion, but one which refines the moral identity of the singer and heals the sexual wound that lies open in youth. In bluegrass there is no conspicuous display of sexual motives, as there is in country-western singers of both sexes; yet the bluegrass singer is as virile and straight as a Douglas Fir.

And with youth, too, goes the legacy of youth, personality. The bluegrass singer has *broken out* of the snares of personality—broken out, that is to say, *of his own voice*, of which George Jones's is the type. At a forced high pitch—at the *right* pitch, one had better say—the voice is physiologically lifted out of the environment of constraints of psychological origin which work upon it in the chest. Other impediments spring up against it, of course—the tense vocal cords themselves, the nasal cavities, certain very narrow or very wide vowel sounds—but these can all be turned to good advantage, challenging the singer to overcome the merely strangulated tone of sexual hysteria, or the irritating whine of self-pity. Between these poles lies the vocal window through which the bluegrass singer can escape the gravitational field of Self. Bill Monroe, Ralph Stanley, Jimmy Martin, Jack Cooke, Ricky Skaggs, a spectacular new singer from Ohio named Dave

Evans—many have found it, but not all. A good bluegrass voice is made of the finest metal, carefully balanced and gracefully proportioned, heavy in the hand, with a gleaming surface and a razor-sharp edge.

The bluegrass singer's rhetorical style, too, suggests the communal or public character of the occasion, for he is always either testifying or preaching. Both styles are rooted in the Southern Baptist injunction to believe *from the heart*. The first of these is that sincere, repentant, sometimes pious or dispirited voice, sometimes called the "Baptist whine," often nasal or tearful—"Yes, folks, that's the way I lost myself in the darkness of sin"—of the Saturday-night tabernacle meeting, where we go to hear the narratives of souls who have been rescued from sin and degradation: conversion stories. This is the manner in which the late Carter Stanley sang, and all the bluegrass lead singers who have followed him. Its orientation, rhetorically, is toward the congregation; the testimony comes from the soul who has volunteered himself from out of its ranks and who speaks as one of them. Thus, though it is a public attitude, it is a style suited to more intimate circumstances often implied by the sacred or heart song.

The preaching style, on the other hand, comes from the pulpit, though pulpit may easily translate into crackerbarrel or barstool. With its intense conviction and unnerving directness of address, this style resembles pulpit oratory; but the same style can set out to raise hell, communicating some of the enthusiasm, as well as some of the desperation and meanness, of a night on the town. Though certainly not confined to gospel songs, the style is appropriately most intense in gospel music: Monroe sings "Walkin' to Jerusalem" as if the earth were about to swallow him up. To that intensity, of course, lyric is usually subordinate, as, indeed, it is in the church house, where the preacher's message is always and ever the same.

Monroe himself is best known for his calling or "hollering" style, airborne and suggestive of wide open spaces. Many of his recordings are intended simply to showcase this style, catapulting his voice into the upper atmosphere upon shimmering tracks of long double stops on fiddle or twin fiddles. This calling style implies the greatest distance, physical or emotional, between singer and auditor, and is thus appropriate both for a brokenhearted lover and a carefree or lonesome cowboy. But Monroe's voice is not always in flight. He has a weeping or complaining style, in which his voice sways and cracks with tears, a sorrowful voice such as he uses in "The Girl in the Blue Velvet Band" or "Letter from My Darling." He has too a pledging or vow-making style, which delivers a song earnestly and declaratively, as a groom might deliver his wedding vows. This style, which is "emotional" more by virtue of fullness than intensity of feeling—something seems to want to burst out of it—resembles the sentimental style of hillbilly singer Bradley Kincaid, the "Kentucky Mountain Boy," who once substituted for Monroe with the Blue Grass Boys on the Opry.[12] One of Monroe's most dramatic vocal techniques is his climb up from a pledging style in a middle register into a more forceful calling style at higher pitches; the effect—listen to "Dark as the Night" or "Body and Soul"— is of an unruly emotion trained, directed, and finally harnessed to carry the singer to freedom.

The chilling and sometimes eerie beauties of bluegrass harmony singing, too, are wrought out of high energies and powerful tensions. Bluegrass harmonies are not choral; bluegrass harmony seeks to oppose, not to join, voices, not to blend but to fuse them. Everywhere there is friction or stridency, a kind of electrostatically charged field that seems to surround the singers at the point of their closest contact. Jim McReynolds calls it a "clash," Mike Seeger a "tear or strain"; Peter Rowan claims that when singing with Monroe he could "physically press" his voice against his, that it seemed to offer solid resistance: "When you get those two notes vibrating together, there's often a strange overtone . . . almost a buzz rather than a note."[13]

Bluegrass is often noted for "close" harmonies, but this is misleading, because no attempt is made to achieve a tonal blend for its own sake. On the contrary, the extraordinary proximity of one voice to another achieved by parallel harmonic lines, duplicated phrasing, maximal volume, and the preponderance of high or "tenor" harmony serves to exacerbate the *dissonance* of vocal tones, a dissonance which a tenor singer may intensify by dropping a tone from his head to his mouth or throat, where it is more strident, or by flatting a note slightly toward an astringent interval. The approach of one voice to another at a high volume and pitch is like the approach of a knife blade to a grinding wheel; their actual meeting is an abrasion which seems to compel its own intensification. Its energy will either fuse voices as if by heat or fling them widely apart. In Monroe's "Travelin' Down this Lonesome Road," which he sings with Mac Wiseman, the highest note of the chorus occurs in the second line, "the wind and storm, a-raging high, and it's awful cold," sung in parallel thirds; here the effect is of a howling wind, a freezing blast, suggested, of course, by the lyrics and imitated onomatopoeically by the harmony. "Memories of You," by contrast, sung with Jimmy Martin, opens a windy, cavernous space, a kind of darkness in which the singers are lost to one another; the third with which the harmony opens drops out as the tenor springs to a tiny falsetto fifth; miles, it seems, stretch between them. A narrowing of the voice in the tenor generates a searing sensation as the highest note, like a struck match, brightens and burns out; the addition of a third or fourth part will introduce, so long as the high note is prominent, an element of mystery and foreboding suggestive of night, death, and the supernatural. Such harmonies characterized early Stanley Brothers' recordings such as "Lonesome River," in which the opening line of the chorus, "Oh the waters roll high, on the river at midnight," seems to have been sung by a band of ghosts. The high note is a focusing point below which the other parts are arranged pyramidally; often in bluegrass the tenor part becomes an independent melody heard over and above the melody itself. With a bass part absent, and the root note of the chord laminated to the others or else missing altogether, the harmony as a whole glows spectre-like above our heads.

The bluegrass harmony, then, is tightly contained, but in its stridency and power, in the relish with which it opposes fevered and raging voices, it is almost violent. Like the vocal style itself, harmony has rhetorical variations from which different dramatic effects may be adduced. In Monroe's trio "On and On," for instance, in which the tenor and baritone parts are given approximately equal weight and the high part is softened by an open-voiced delivery, the singers seem joined together in convivial fraternity, whose warmth mitigates the isolation of the wanderer who is the song's *persona*. The grief-stricken lament "Little Girl and the Dreadful Snake"—"Our daughter wandered far away, while she was out at play"—seems to be sung, in Martin's and Monroe's crossing thirds and fifths, by husband and wife, the bereaved couple. For sacred songs, as we've seen, Monroe redefines his band as the "Bluegrass Quartet"—a device more effective on radio, I suppose, than elsewhere. Here the galvanic bluegrass harmonies we've described are plentiful, but we have in addition contrapuntal arrangements which tend to distinguish the singers. The presence of a bass part at one end and a falsetto at the other, coupled with contrapuntal arrangements, suggests, I think, the sexually and generationally mixed community of the church; often the movement by one singer from one part to another, from natural to falsetto and even to bass, a technique which bluegrass shares with black gospel music, presents more voices than there are persons singing.

The bluegrass singer presents us with several dramatic situations belonging to old rural life in which emotion must be curbed and contained but in the end given vent *by* speech, if not *in* it. In bluegrass harmony we go a bit deeper; we hear not words, or speech even, but voice itself, which emerges as a mysterious adjunct overtone from the self-immolatory confrontation of voices. We hear, not voices, but *one* voice which has been revealed in its interior and exterior dimensions at once. The high tenor harmony seems an exteriorization of the unexpressed interior outcry of the lead voice; the tighter the phrasing, the more exact the pitch, the finer the dynamic balance between the two voices, the more thorough their fusion, the more entirely have they emptied themselves. The aims of bluegrass harmony singing and of bluegrass lead singing are really one aim. Both strive for that moment of consummate intensity at which conflict and pain, and the consciousness of them, have transcended themselves.

In human affairs the proper locale for the ordeal, the test of the man, is game or ritual; by means of it he proves himself to others and to himself. In human society the ordeal consolidates and affirms the values upon which that society depends, whether it is bravery in war or excellence in scholarship; but for the root of the ordeal we may look to the animal world itself, where biological evolution provides for the elevation of the strongest male to a position of sexual sovereignty. Primordially the ordeal is erotic, and it is erotic worthiness that is fundamentally at stake; as the old fabulists and romanciers knew, it is always the hand of a lady that the candidate wins by passing his tests successfully, for with her hand goes the future of the kingdom.

It should not surprise us that in surveying the world's folk music Alan Lomax discovered the primacy of sexual mores in folk song style. Music is essentially erotic. This is of course an ancient commonplace, supported not only by philosophy—Plato treats it in the *Symposium*—but, in our own day, by science. Ability in music, we learn from one psychoanalyst, seems to originate in the "infant-mother sensomotor relationship" and through hearing, "the chief sensory modality" of the earliest stages of our existence, which is developmentally related to holding and touch; in later life these become the foundation for the evolution of memory and the emergence of a moral sense—precisely those areas where music's affective power is greatest.[14] "All music," writes another, "represents the deeper sources of unconscious thinking." It has the peculiar power to induce "narcissistic and erotogenic pleasures," and is the only mental creation in which "libidinal processes can be found in pure culture."[15]

All the African-inspired forms of American popular music are "erotic" in a narrower and more familiar sense as well. African and Afro-American dance, as everybody knows, are freely and openly erotic, characterized by seductive or explicitly sexual movements; African culture itself, and African cosmology, are pervaded by the principle of sexual polarity. African-inspired rhythms, too, place the musician and his music opposite one another, like dancers; the strong backbeat which suggests sexual thrusting is only the grossest and most violent of the many subtler kinds of erotic interplay between musician and music occasioned by the musician's independence of the fundamental rhythm. He plays the music, but at the same time may caress and fondle it, love it and make love to it.

Between the musician and his instrument, too, joined together by physical sympathy, there may be erotic magnetism. Two large classes of instruments may be distinguished on the basis of the relation between their sound-making power and its human counterpart—those which modify or extend the human voice and those which mimic the body's entire sound-making apparatus. Horns and woodwinds shift the laryngeal vibration to the lips, drawing like the voice itself upon human breath and, in the case of the jazz horn, employing the lips and tongue to shape sounds, just as they do in speech; these instruments extend the voice and, *by* extension, the musician.

Stringed and percussion instruments, on the other hand, have respiratory and vocal structures of their own. The resonant body of the guitar or drum models the resonant human breast, and a vibrating string or membrane the voice; these instruments constitute independent organic presences which the action of the hands rouses to life. They do not extend but complete us; they are other beings whom we take in our embrace. In the release of a plucked string, which is the erogenous crux of a stringed instrument, even lies a physical mimicry of orgasm. This may suggest why European tradition has eroticized the guitar and violin with feminine shapes. It may suggest, too, why in this country at least rural music belongs principally to stringed instruments and not to horns. Horns assimilate themselves to speech, annunciation, to society; the horn is at base a giver of alarums and signals, an instrument in the coordination of social groups: think of the herald's trumpet, the hunter's horn. The horn is gregarious. The lute is egregious. It is at base a kind of effigy or doll, modelling not the outward and visible part of the human organism but the articulate and interior part; as such it assimilates itself to feelings, to stirrings in the heart and its sensory agents in the body. Like David's harp it is a companion to solitude, a bringer of health and relief, an accompaniment to love and bearer of its burdens.

The erotic may be expressed on a purely sexual level, as it is in much popular literature and song; or it may ascend to the spiritual level, as it does in Dante, or in Bach's B-minor Mass. But the vast expanse of human life lies between these two poles, between pure animal and pure spirit, in the kingdom ruled by the heart. Here Eros takes on as many forms as there are forms of human desire and loathing—in aspiration, fantasy, wish, yearning and hope, in dreams, anxieties, fears and nightmares—the whole environment of personality, conscious and unconscious, in which we live. And just as personality, and not either a sensual obliteration of it or a spiritual transcendence of it, is the central theme of most ordinary mental life, so is the extensive territory of folk and popular literature, and, in a covert way, much high literature and art, stretched between what we universally and instinctively reject and fear, and what we universally desire and idealize.

Northrop Frye, the great literary critic and scholar upon whose work the entire discussion here and in the next chapter is based, calls this world *romantic,* using the term in a familiar sense most of us can understand, however hard put we may be to define it. We know that a certain kind of inspiring and highly imaginative sexual love is connected to it, as are a certain kind of youthful self-centeredness and idealism, and perhaps a longing for adventure or some sort of superior life, however indistinct; and above all we know that while actual experience is seldom romantic, and can turn into a kind of monstrosity when we strive too successfully to make it so, life would be a pretty dreary business without romance, for on the other side lie irony, cynicism, and despair.

The narrative and symbolic expression of the romantic world is a family of related literary forms Frye calls "romance"—"the genuine form of the world that human life tries to imitate,"[16] whose character reflects the preoccupations of the heart, and whose structure the tensions of human ambivalence. Love, adventure, death, and the past, then, will be of special interest, bifurcating, like our own dream life, into wish fulfillment and nightmare, or what in romance becomes a world with idyllic and abhorrent or "night" phases and transfigurations; this world, moreover, will take on a distinctly vertical orientation, with its sky above and earth below macrocosmically reflecting the human body, with its "higher" and "lower" functions.

Romance places human life at a distance adequate to reveal what Wordsworth called "the primary laws of our nature," while remaining within the slightly liberalized boundaries of plausibility and morality that wish, desire, hope, and fear allow. Within these boundaries, for instance, supernatural, but not divine, intervention may occur; adultery and murder may be committed, but not without suffering and the ultimate operation of justice against the offender. The romantic may trespass against society, but it cannot transcend it.

To fix half-real, half-imaginary distance between itself and its audience, romance will typically choose some idealized natural setting— exotic, pastoral, antique, or, in our culture, simply historical or rustic. It may use a synthetic or antiquated language such as Scott's or Spenser's; or it may invent anomalous symbols to express familiar, usually sacred, ideas covertly, freeing them from an accumulated burden of interpretation and opening an immediate apprehension of their meaning. Coleridge's albatross, for instance, covertly expresses the Holy Ghost, whose conventional symbol is a white dove; the juniper tree of the Grimm fairytale is Christ's cross in disguise. Finally romance may interpose some mediating agent between us and its subject, representing it *as if* it had some mysterious, impersonal origin in an ancient, esoteric document or in folklore: Bronte's Nelly Dean is such an agent, as is the mysterious cabalist whose quaint marginalia are a mad accompaniment to *The Rime of the Ancient Mariner.* So, too, is Bill Monroe, who stands between us and Appalachian traditional music, and may be said to have reinvented that tradition. By these devices, ballad becomes literary ballad becomes *The Rime;* folk tale becomes fairytale becomes Madame de Beaumont's "Beauty and the Beast"; Scots-Irish dance tune becomes hillbilly showpiece becomes Bill Monroe's "Bluegrass Breakdown" or "Jerusalem Ridge."

With its studied evocation of the past, its emotional power, its synthetic language of vocal and instrumental technique, its traditional or tradition-like repertoire, its interest in the anomalous banjo and mandolin, the country fiddle by which it voices jazz sounds in a medium free of the moral associations of jazz, and in its mediation by presiding figures such as Monroe and his protegés, bluegrass music is a form of "sentimental" romance—what Frye calls "a later reconstruction of an earlier mode."[17] It awakened a new naive form, "traditional" bluegrass, through which the original Appalachian tradition has been extended.

"Bluegrass is essentially a style of instrumentation,"[18] writes Bill Malone, and this is so because through the instruments of bluegrass the musician gains access to an extremely diverse romantic world which he surveys from the fixed point of the historical moment from which the instruments as artifacts emerge. Access to the romantic world ought not to be too easy, of course; we must have a desert to cross, some brambles to penetrate, or a secret word to pronounce. It happens that the signature instruments of bluegrass—the authentic Gibson F-model mandolins and Mastertone banjos, the Martin Dreadnaught guitars—are extremely rare and hard to come by; of Lloyd Loar's signed mandolins only 170 were manufactured, though they seem to have proliferated like relics of the True Cross. Since most bluegrass musicians play copies of originals manufactured by different companies specifically for bluegrass, the authentic instruments are the more highly prized; serial numbers, dates of manufacture, and secrets of construction by which authentic instruments might be distinguished from copies are all a regular part of bluegrass folklore. Reprints of turn-of-the-century instrument catalogues and serial number chronologies may be purchased at music shops along with records and songbooks, while the bluegrass magazines carry features on instrument making, makers, history, and technology, as well as a lively trade in instruments in the classifieds. When the musician *has* secured the authentic instrument, he usually has a story to tell—of some delicate negotiation, a long journey, or a huge price tag.

All the bluegrass instruments except the fiddle were designed during the first third of this century for various kinds of popular orchestral music. The Loar mandolin, with its flat back, arched neck, and elevated bridge, was intended for the mandolin orchestra; the Gibson Mastertone banjo, with bellmetal bronze tone ring and hardwood resonator, was adapted from the tenor banjo developed for jazz bands; the Martin Dreadnaught guitar was built for use in the string sections of large orchestras. Why, it might be asked, given the folklike quality of bluegrass music, are not the bluegrass instruments the rustic, homemade, or antique kind favored by folk revivalists? The answer, first, is that bluegrass *is* an orchestral music and requires orchestral instruments: no mandolin can bark like the F-5, no banjo ring like the Mastertone, no guitar boom like a good old D-28. Second, the bluegrass instruments *are* antiques: they belong to recently lapsed epochs which provide a foothold upon the histories which reach back from them into the remoter past; for the generation in which they were current, these instruments had for the rural imagination the glamour that attaches to things urban, modern, and machine-made. Finally, as representations they must perforce be distinguishable from what they represent, and it is that energy, the mimetic energy, that carries the musician from a historically fixed point into the imaginary past.

The banjo, for instance, remains covertly an Afro-American instrument, retaining the comic quality it acquired in the minstrel show. To play the banjo is always in a sense to play the Fool, and even Earl Scruggs continues the tradition of banjo virtuosity which the black minstrel brought to the stage after the Civil War; "Look," George Hay's introductions of Scruggs's "fancy banjo" seemed to say, "look what the boy has done with *that!*" In America the banjo is by virtue of its Afro-American connections the essential folk instrument, the instrument which to play is always to make do, which we cannot ad-

vance into the precincts of polite music without somehow refining out
of existence its uncultivated twang. The bluegrass banjo technique, as
we've seen, does quite the opposite: it exaggerates the banjo-ness of
the banjo and arouses its whole sphere of associations to resonance.
Hence the banjo remains the anomalous instrument, one which country
music outside of bluegrass has largely abandoned, except when it wishes to color its productions with the bluegrass sound. For the root of
that anomalous quality we may look to the fact that the banjo is African,
not European, in origin and is consequently the only stringed instrument in the American tradition which has not been feminized. It is not
maidenly, like the violin, nor voluptuous, like the guitar, but, like a
tomboy sister or spinster aunt, full of gristle and sass.

Allied to the banjo historically is the fiddle, which in bluegrass resides on the margin of the band, a zone through which the musician
crosses from other kinds of music and emigrates out of bluegrass into
other styles. Significant as it is in bluegrass, it is an accompanying
instrument primarily, peripheral precisely because it is central in the
broader tradition of European music. The eclectic character of the
bluegrass fiddle style, drawing as it does upon both jazz and classical
techniques, and at the same time upon traditional southern sounds as
the shuffle, the double stop, and the drone, retains the name of traditional fiddle within a far broader musical vocabulary. The bluegrass
fiddler can make reference to a barn dance as well as to a nightclub;
but to what is he referring when he casts his eyes upwards and draws
out a long, moody, singing note with his bow—certainly not to the
concert hall?

At a festival held in his honor in 1965, Bill Monroe boasted that the
bluegrass fiddler had advanced the instrument, that he could play
anything that, well, anything that *Rubinoff* could play.[19] Rubinoff?
Who is Rubinoff? You may remember David Rubinoff from the "Chase
and Sanborn Hour" or "The Eddie Cantor Show," of thirties radio; he
used to open his program with "Fascination," and they called him "The
Voice of the Gems."[20] Earlier, in vaudeville, he had impressed his
audiences with ostentatious classical pieces adorned, as a Nashville
record review describes it, with pizzicati, wierd double stops, and a
"long drawn bowing effect."[21]

Because his techniques grew up principally outside of bluegrass, the
bluegrass fiddler is always a kind of guest in the bluegrass band, albeit
an honored one. He might be compared to the ordained minister who
attends a Quaker wedding: though he does not actually perform the
service, his presence is required to authenticate the union to the world
at large. As the other instruments speak from within the music, the

fiddle speaks from without; thus Bill Monroe, who as the Father of Bluegrass Music must play the mandolin, chooses as a tradition bearer to speak through his fiddler, whose music touches the boundaries of a wider universe.

To this universe, too, we must assign the guitar. By whatever route it entered our music—some have suggested the Spanish-American War—the guitar is now inextricably connected to all of our folk, rural, and rurally derived music, associated not only with country music but with such diverse figures as Gene Autry, Elvis Presley, Woody Guthrie, and even John Denver. It is the singing cowboy, though, who touches country music most closely. The gradual synthesis of the rural music of the Southeast with the image of the Old West—a complex process involving actual emigration from Appalachia to Texas and Oklahoma, the growth of a native Spanish-influenced southwestern music, and a long-standing popular tradition of literature and song idealizing the cowboy which culminated in the Hollywood "western" with its singing cowboy—has placed the country singer in the ingratiating glow of pastoral romance, from which he has wandered along the paths of his own tradition into the contradictions of that ideal with the facts of experience.

Traditionally the singing cowboy, like his chaste medieval counterpart the knight-errant of chivalric romance, was sexually innocent or even naive, preferring the company of other cowboys or even of cattle to that of women; above all, though, he desired his own company, seeking out some desolate place to sing, as an old cowboy song goes, a kie-yippie kie-yea—hence the guitar, auto-erotic effigy of himself. Being free from sexual passion, he is, like baseball players and bluegrass musicians, a "boy," and thus an image of perfect independence, for from manhood follows love and marriage, and with these paternity, responsibility, society—the very world into which country-western music thrusts the singing cowboy, burdening him with the realities of heartbreak and sending him to the honky-tonk, where he finds solace in the jukebox and a bottle of beer.

The singing cowboy reappears, subtly transformed, in the bluegrass guitarist-lead singer. The wildness, as well as the openness and ostentation, of the country-western singer has been subdued in him; his link to the west may be betrayed only by a string tie, a cowboy hat, perhaps even a pair of western boots, though otherwise he dresses conservatively, unless he wishes to identify himself with country-western music for commercial reasons. Even his guitar reveals his change: it is not the cowboy's gorgeously decorated and shapely instrument, but an austere Martin, nearly trapezoidal and as severely functional as a Shaker harvest table. He has been reintegrated into the human community, having exchanged his independence for his innocence.

Banjo, fiddle, and guitar are venerable instruments in our rural music. Not so the mandolin, which is *dated*, a kind of period piece, paradoxically the most "modern" instrument in the bluegrass band and the most old-fashioned, having already passed its prime in hillbilly music when Bill Monroe resurrected it for bluegrass.

American experience of the mandolin begins probably with a vogue of the 1890s, when it shared the parlor with zithers, mandolas, ukuleles, and other novelties designed to amuse the increasingly leisured middle class. By 1900 mandolin ensembles were touring the vaudeville circuit, and mandolin orchestras were forming in schools and colleges. The ornate, scroll-cornered mandolin now associated, through Monroe, with bluegrass belongs to this period and visibly expresses the tastes of the era. Orville Gibson, the furniture maker who founded the Gibson company, was apparently obsessed with ornament, particularly the scroll, which appears in a variety of forms upon his guitars, zithers, and mandolins—fully eight times on the zither—carved into tailpieces, bridges, pegheads, sound holes, and into the instrument body itself; most of Gibson's early handmade instruments also carried an occult star-and-crescent inlay, his hallmark. Gibson emphasized the importance of machines in precision manufacture, and offered his products in literature redolent with the florid prose of gilded-age advertising.[22]

The mandolin is a miniature lute and was probably contrived, says the *Harvard Dictionary of Music*, to fill out the scale of sixteenth-century lute ensembles. It entered our folk music through popular channels because it was in essence a fiddle with frets that could be plucked or picked like a guitar. Yet it has remained relatively free of specific associations; we know only in a vague way that it is, given its diminuitive scale, its toy-like tinkle, and elaborate decoration, something rather quaint, like a stereoscope or platform rocker, and at the same time something vaguely foreign, a kind of icon.

Icon: is it not strange, when all is said and done, that a hillbilly musician should win a place for himself in the highly commercial Country Music Hall of Fame by accompanying himself on the *mandolin?* We have had great guitar pickers and great fiddlers and a few great banjo pickers in country music, but how many *mandolin* pickers have we got? Now Jethro Burns, he's good too, but he's jazz, not country. How does it happen that the Father of Bluegrass Music, who is a pretty tough guitar picker himself and probably would have made a super fiddler, has clung to Lloyd Loar's little fantasy, ornate, outdated,

faintly morbid, which was in turn a part of mad Orville Gibson's—
himself an outlandish and rather fantastic man—larger pipe dream,
built entirely on the strangely suggestive notion that instruments, like
furniture, should be built of carved, not stressed, pieces?

The mandolin entered the mainstream of popular culture during the
first epoch of substantial immigration from eastern and southern Europe, a period of prosperity and vulgarity, when things exotic and
foreign dominated popular taste. Like other diversions peculiar to the
machine age, like Japanese fans, parakeets, and mah-jongg, the mandolin was only superficially exotic; covertly it embodies values belonging to the class which had embraced it, a class which in turn-of-the-
century America, like its British counterpart a generation earlier, was
busy vandalizing the world's culture to furnish the culturally empty
parlors and sitting rooms that industrial wealth had erected and
opened.

Machine made, scientifically engineered, elaborately feminized, Orville Gibson's mandolin is romantic, dimly connected in imagination
not to Confederate camps or mountain cabins, but to Catholic countries
and sunny climes, where love—love that withers in the stern, Protestant, industrious North—triumphs over duty, and where the lover
in his passion approximates the worshiper, elevating woman to the
status of virgin goddess, a Madonna. Its theme, echoed in a thousand
popular novels and films, is the ravishing of idealized virginity by
implacable virility, just as the implied theme of the Hawaiian guitar,
which entered popular culture at roughly the same moment as the
mandolin and for roughly the same reasons, is innocent promiscuity in
the primal garden of Polynesia. Both reflect the yearnings of sexuality
repressed by a strict identification of morality with sexual propriety:
ravished maiden and sensual savage alike remain fundamentally innocent. But, while the Hawaiian guitar remained principally in the
hands of professionals, the mandolin was an amateur's instrument, and
as such entered the precincts of middle-class life—parlor, glee club,
sorority—where what Ann Douglas has called "the feminization of
American culture" had its most decisive victories.[23]

What happens when these instruments move through popular channels such as the mail order catalogue into the rural South? Both mandolin and Hawaiian guitar were adopted by bluesmen, who as always
found ways to make them talk. The popular Hawaiian ensembles of
the twenties gave the Hawaiian guitar, along with the blue yodel, to
hillbilly music, where it became the table steel of country music and
the dobro in bluegrass. In mountain music, the mandolin found its
place at once: it went into the hands of the *youngest child* who wished

to participate in the family music but who could not manage the grown-up instruments. Even Bill Monroe, whose elder brothers demanded that he play with only four of the normal eight strings, took up the mandolin in this fashion.

The popularity which the mandolin enjoyed in the hillbilly music of the thirties arises in part, I suspect, from its association with children. Recall that the hillbilly duets of the thirties sang a music of childlike simplicity in which the toy-like tinkling of the mandolin perfectly complemented the naive but durable association of the rural South with purity, innocence, sweetness, and light—one of the many legacies of the minstrel show. The mandolin, moreover, was a token of that historical moment at which rural life had touched the urban, and was thus the appropriate instrument to carry back into that world on the commercial airwaves, for the same reason that the farm wife wears to the city the hat which she bought on her last visit there—never mind how many years ago.

What does it mean, then, to play this Victorian parlor instrument, which seems almost to wear skirts, in the hard-driving bluegrass style? I should like to make this point indirectly, by analogy, to give it the amplitude I think it deserves. One of the best female singers in country music, Dolly Parton, continues to use the tense, high-pitched, decorative style of her native east Tennessee; her voice is sweet, pure, and girlish—powerful, to be sure, but definitely *juvenile* in character. The juvenile theme is carried out not only by her very name, "Dolly," but by the outlandish coiffures, massive as the silver wigs of Empire high fashion but suggestive of the golden curls of innocent girls, that Dolly used to wear before her career took her into the popular field.[24] Yet Dolly Parton, as everybody knows, is not a child. She is a voluptuous and beautiful woman—"resplendent," Doug Green calls her—whose elaborately decorated and close-fitting gowns, their modest high necklines and long hems only sharpening the effect, set forth her abundant figure with the explicitness of a dress form. Dolly's sex appeal is enormous, but it is not that of the sylphs, waifs, and nymphs who lie about in the fashion magazines. It is the wasp-waisted, broad-bottomed, and buxom sexuality of the Victorian age, which regarded woman as the child eroticized.

It is perhaps an insight into the affinity between them that convinced the producers of the current Grand Ole Opry to bring Dolly Parton and Bill Monroe together for a performance of "Muleskinner Blues," which for a time became a regular feature of the program. Between them they present with almost allegorical precision an idealized vision of sexuality brought to the summit of its social expression. Jane Aus-

ten, with her dashing landed aristocrats, her intellectually independent
but shapely and ever-blooming bourgeoise heroines, would have recognized Dolly and Bill at once. Here is Bill—dignified, aloof, gazing
into the distance as he always does, splendidly handsome and venerable
as a Supreme Court justice, his awareness of the glamorous and ebul-
lient Dolly betrayed only by a grin—you can hardly see it—gathering
at the corner of his mouth. Music for Bill is nothing if not serious
business, but to resist this adorable girl-woman, who giggles as she
sings and actually makes fun of the old man to the audience, as if he
were a cigar-store Indian—this is a man made of, well, wood! On the
one hand, this tantalyzing beauty, animated but demure, implicitly
challenging, irresistible, and, of course, accessible only to wealth and
station; on the other, that intrepidity and pride, repressed desire,
perhaps the faintest hint of disdain: in this sexual tension, which Western society for its own purposes spent several hundred years conceiv-
ing, nurturing, and bringing to perfection and which in the last century
has, for better or worse, begun to rot, lay a civilizing energy which
the Old South probably thought it was going to war to preserve and
whose withdrawal has left a cultural vacuum that our sexual revolution
has so far not filled. Dolly and Bill are both heirs to a sexual culture
which has vanished almost everywhere but in the southern mountains.
To rekindle the old images emblematically, as both obviously do, on
the stage of the Opry, in whose pure phantasmagorical atmosphere
the old familiar flame burns dazzlingly bright, is at once an act of
unyielding moral integrity, personal transcendence, and cultural
sabotage.

   With his instrument in hand, then, the bluegrass musician enters a
diverse and colorful romantic world, and reconstitutes himself upon a
more universal plane. That is why he loves to be photographed, for
the album cover which testifies to his arrival, with his instrument; the
impulse is the same that has us snapping the shutter at the lip of the
Grand Canyon—to say we've been there. Usually the musician is not
actually playing his banjo, fiddle, guitar, or mandolin in the photograph, for that would only catch him in transit. Rather he has his hands
resting amicably upon it, as if it were the car that had just won the
Daytona 500 or the rifle that felled a seven-point buck, in the relaxed
attitude of one who has reached his destination. For the same reason
many bluegrass anthologies and reissues, intended either to revive
early material or to introduce the music as a genre to a new audience, offer to bring us, the buyer, into the romantic world by picturing
the instruments *alone* on the album cover—leaning against a rail
fence, or on a cabin porch, or on the fender of an old sedan, their

necks crossed like the rifles of a bivouaced army. It's as if the instruments could make the music all by themselves, or as if the musicians, transported to that other world, had decided not to return to this one.

Chapter 10

Bilin' Down Creation
The Landscape of Bluegrass

Like John Bunyan's *Pilgrim's Progress*, the landscape of bluegrass song contrasts an idyllic and an abhorrent world, one "above the level of ordinary experience, the other below it." The one, writes Northrop Frye, is associated with "happiness, security, and peace; the emphasis is often thrown on childhood or on an 'innocent' or pre-genital period of youth, and the images are those of spring and summer, flowers and sunshine. . . . The other is a world of exciting adventures, but adventures which involve separation, loneliness, humiliation, pain, and the threat of more pain."[1]

The idyllic world is the basis of the entire bluegrass gospel tradition, in which fond recollection of a childhood spent in a cabin home among rolling green hills, secure in the love of parents, brothers, sisters, and friends, provides an image of the heavenly world to which death will someday restore us. Occasionally the literal world of childhood and the figurative heaven are shockingly confused:

> I wandered again to my home in the mountains
> Where in youth's early dawn I was happy and free;
> I looked for my friends but I never could find them.
> I found they were all rank strangers to me.

Secular songs, too, are filled with images of this idyllic rural world, to which the singer either longs to return or expresses his intention to return—"I'm going back to North Carolina, where the mountaintops are blue"—and which he furnishes in his imagination with other objects of longing such as a young sweetheart, a grey-haired mother, or the land itself, with its protective valleys and lofty hills:

> How I'd like to be upon a windy mountain
> Where the treetops scrape the sky;
> There I'd forget all my worries and my troubles;
> I'd just let the wind blow them by.

For this world, which is the subject not only of songs but of album-cover photographs of isolated log cabins, rolling Kentucky horse farms, or autumnal woods, we cannot but feel the "persistant nostalgia" so characteristic of romance, and the elegaic sentiment which is one of its prevailing themes: one thinks of the concluding scene of *Wuthering Heights*, whose entire extravagant action comes to rest with "sleepers in the quiet earth." The bluegrass singer, too, in songs such as Monroe's "Memories of Mother and Dad," may stand pensively over a mossy grave, and in reflecting upon it and upon the past may permit the fears and doubts of ordinary experience to tarnish the idyllic vision. The concluding verse of Carter Stanley's "White Dove," one of the finest of bluegrass sacred songs, with its coordinate images of the Holy Ghost, childhood mountain home, and choirs of angels coupled with a hair-raising quartet harmony, asks:

> As the years roll by I often wonder
> Will we all be together someday?
> And each night as I wander through the graveyard
> Darkness finds me as I kneel to pray.

In Carter's song "The Fields Have Turned Brown" the singer-persona, far from home and recalling his parents' parting words—"We will be waiting for you here at home"—learns from a letter that they have been dead for years and that their fields have withered. Many of Monroe's songs, too, touch upon the tragic return to a formerly idyllic world blighted or decayed:

> I'm on my way back to the old home;
> The road winds going up the hill;
> But there's no light at the window
> That shined along the road where I lived.

Even in John Prine's popular "Paradise," a song about strip mining in western Kentucky which bluegrass singers instantly adopted as their own, the singer returns to find his childhood home carried off in railroad cars: "Mr. Peabody's coal train has hauled it away."

For the idyllic world is not, of course, the one we occupy. The same aspiring force that draws us out of the idyll, the Eden, that lies at the origin of consciousness—

> Take me back to the place where I first saw the light,
> To the sweet sunny South take me home;
> Where the mocking bird sings me to sleep every night—
> Oh why was I tempted to roam?

—carries us into experiences which blight our power to recover it, thrusting it inaccessibly into the past and confounding our images of it with our hopes for heaven. As "Paradise," "Sweet Sunny South," and a hundred other bluegrass songs reveal, the idyllic world is perfidious, a snare of stasis and illusion to which no real return, at least in this world, is possible:

> The path to our cottage they say has grown green
> And the place is quite lonely around;
> And I know that the smiles and the forms I have seen
> Now lie in the dark mossy ground.

Thus the bluegrass singer-persona is a hero whose wanderings have the character of a romantic quest—"On and on, I'll follow my darling"—which supplies the object of his existence:

> I have to follow you, my darling
> I can't sleep when the sun goes down;
> By your side is my destination;
> The road is clear and that's where I'm bound.

He is an exile, making reference in his songs to a vision of heaven on the one hand and of the idealized past on the other, visions whose interdependency closes the cosmic circle where memory, feeling, and the community of mutual experience meet. His principal theme is "the contrast of memory and experience";[2] the locale of his unending dream is "that long lonesome highway," and disappointed love, in which the sense of exile is most powerfully concentrated, is his constant preoccupation:

> Traveling down this lonesome road, oh how I hate to go;
> The wind and storm a-raging high and it's awful cold;
> My mind gets back to you, sweetheart, and I love you so!
> Why did you go and leave me here to travel this lonesome road?

In romance, Frye suggests, experience is a descent—often a literal one, as into an underworld or grave—into confusion or bondage, where identity is obliterated and action weighted or impeded. It is just such a descent that the bluegrass singer makes when he becomes the disconsolate rambler touring a nightscape of honky-tonk and tavern:

> I'm a walking from one bar to another;
> I don't know where I'm going or where I've been . . .

In this city of dreadful night, he is likely to encounter symbols of fate or chance, as in the gambler's dice or cards; or he may sing to us from a prison cell, where fate or chance has landed him:

> Now I'm down in prison, got a number for my name.
> The warden said as he locked the cell, boy, you've gambled
>   your last game . . .

A city street may be the setting in which the disoriented soul, whose symbol is often an orphaned child, confronts an earthly existence from which all light has withdrawn into the ineffable glory beyond, itself accessible only through death. The well-known Carter Family song, "Jimmy Brown the Newsboy," now secure in the bluegrass repertoire since it was recorded by Flatt and Scruggs, is the *locus classicus* of the theme:

> My mother often tells me, sir, there's nothing in the world to
>   lose;
> I'll find a place in heaven, sir, to sell the gospel news.

Bill Monroe's famous song "The Girl in the Blue Velvet Band," descended from an Irish traditional song, joins the themes of sexual betrayal, the city of dreadful night, and false imprisonment into a single narrative: the naive persona, out walking the streets of San Francisco at night—"the hour was just about nine"—meets a girl whose blue velvet hairband seems to testify to her innocence:

> On her face was the beauty of nature,
> Her eyes they did seem to expand;
> Her hair was so rich and so brilliant,
> Tied up in a blue velvet band.

But the girl plants a stolen diamond on him in a curiously titillating way—"in my pocket she placed her small hand"—and leaves him to the "wild scream of the siren" and to his eventual imprisonment in San Quentin. In the penultimate verse of the song the depths and heights of experience are juxtaposed as the singer, pressing his face against the bars of his cell, looks up at the night sky and fancies he can hear "her voice calling, from far out on the ocean of stars." In the concluding

verse he contemplates his eventual release, himself permanently
marked by undeserved guilt:

> I'll be out in a year, then I'm leaving;
> But I'll carry the name of the man
> Who spent ten years in prison
> For the girl in the blue velvet band.

"That's a true story," a bluegrass musician from the Clinch Mountains of Virginia once insisted to me, and of course it is—true to the
"primary laws of our nature." "The Girl in the Blue Velvet Band" is
about sexual guilt, in a tradition in which innocence is *always* symbolized by sexual purity. Even the disappointed lover in exile, however
plaintive his cry, is protected from unchastity, as well as from marriage, which would remove him from romance and place him in the
waking world of social reality. There are very few songs about wedlock
in bluegrass; two that I know of are Monroe's "A Good Woman's Love"
and the Stanley Brothers' "The Angels Are Singing." In Monroe's song
hubby has apparently repudiated his bachelor habits for the wife who
remains faithful as a housepet:

> 'Stead of roving I go home in the evening
> And she's waiting there;
> And I know that no matter what happens
> She'll always care.

In Stanley's, the woman is dead, so that their domestic life together
recedes through memory into the idyllic world, with the inevitable
promise of its restoration in the hereafter: "Sleep peacefully, darling,
I'll meet you up there."

The household itself, however, belongs by its connection with childhood to the idyllic world; though the foundation of the family is in
sexual love, that love is purified by the idyllic setting and by an emphasis upon the bond between parent and child, which is free of sexual
implication. Households can be broken up by infidelity, as in Earl
Taylor's "The Children Are Crying," or by death, which in this context
retains its old association with sin. More often, though, death is a
preserver of innocence; few motifs are more persistant in bluegrass
than the dreary and funereal landscape, a legacy of the last century's
preoccupation with the grave, where, as in these lines by John Hutchison, the grieving lover has interred his sweetheart:

> Out there in that lonely graveyard
> 'Neath the cold and silent clay,

There we laid my little darling
Just a year ago today.

Sometimes the lover speaks in anticipation of death:

Perhaps you'll plant some flowers
On my cold unworthy grave;
Come and wile away the hours
Where the roses nod and wave.

In Charlie Monroe's "Rosalie McFall," which appears to have come out of the minstrel tradition, little Rosalie, whose home is "out on a lonely hillside, in a cabin dark and small," is called by God while still a bride, her sexual purity thus fixed at its supreme moment and preserved forever; the singer undertakes a life of wandering:

I'll roam this wide world over
Through cities large and small
'Til God prepares my home in heaven
With Rosalie McFall.

This theme has its most acute expression in songs about the death of children, an obsession of the tuberculosis-haunted Victorians. In "Little Bessie," one of the loveliest, the child dies of a disease—"Something hurts me here, dear mother, like a stone upon my breast"—and wakes to a pastoral hereafter filled with singing children. In Monroe's "I Hear a Sweet Voice Calling," the sick child leaves the world with a rebuke to her parents, whose tears imply that their faith has been shaken. In Monroe's "The Little Girl and the Dreadful Snake," the child meets the Prince of Death face-to-face, in his archetypal form as serpent, her scream of terror wrought in an icy two-part harmony:

I heard the screams of our little girl far away,
"Hurry Daddy, there's an awful dreadful snake!"
I ran as fast as I could through the dark and dreary wood
But I reached our darling girl too late.

In images of death and the grave we have the romantic descent at its most literal; but the forces at work in it reveal the profound ambivalence at work in the romantic imagination, what M. H. Abrams calls "the mingling, at their highest intensity, of pleasure and pain, . . . the destructiveness of love, and the erotic quality of the longing for death."[3] It is in this ambivalence that the dynamic power of romance resides, and in its moments of "highest intensity" the possible consummation of the romantic quest.

Bill Monroe's own repertoire is made up of traditional songs, songs of love and betrayal or "heart" songs, laments of death, dissolution, or loss, nostalgic or sentimental songs which perhaps we should call idyllic songs, and gospel songs, as well as traditional and original instrumental pieces. One of the interesting aspects of Monroe's repertoire is that many of his compositions have an autobiographical basis, so that his personal life is absorbed into an essentially traditional and impersonal idiom. Traditional songs such as "Little Maggie" or "John Henry," or fiddle tunes such as "Katy Hill" or "Dusty Miller," as well as many familiar gospel songs such as "Precious Memories" are the classics of the *genre;* in singing them one is also citing them, building a scaffold of authority upon which original compositions might rest.

"Molly and Tenbrooks," a descendant of a black folk song about a horse race which actually took place in Kentucky in 1878, and which in earlier versions shows traces of the minstrel stage, is one of Monroe's most widely imitated recordings and one which vividly displays his dramatic sense.[4] We hear testimony to Tenbrooks's swiftness, how he could outrun the Memphis train; the singer calls out to the rider; even the horses speak to one another as Molly, the horse that "did as she pleased" out in California, concedes defeat. The song takes us into the midst of the excitement:

> Women all a-laughing, children all a-crying,
> Men all a-hollering, old Tenbrooks a-flying . . .

The story ends with Tenbrooks grazing contentedly in the shade, while men are preparing to bury poor Molly in a "coffin ready-made." Monroe delivers the song in a lucid and liquid calling style, brightening the scene and heightening the immediacy of the event; by featuring the banjo he not only establishes the appropriate galloping tempo but affixes to the song an authenticating historical signature: it is a kind of musical lithograph, in which we might detect, on the edge of the crowd of thirty thousand ladies and gentlemen who had come to the Louisville race track to see "the last four-mile heat in American turf history,"[5] a lone Negro banjo player, his song about the contest already half-composed.

An original song, too, can be fashioned in the traditional idiom. "When You Are Lonely," recorded on the same day in 1947 as "Molly and Tenbrooks," is in substance a love song; but its deliberate simplicity places it in a class with certain universally recognized popular songs such as "Red River Valley," to which it bears a close resemblance. Its lyrics are strictly formulaic: "Remember the heart you have broken, and the one that has loved you so true," while Lester Flatt's lead voice, always slightly off pitch and losing its balance regularly at the ends of phrases—precisely the effects for which Flatt was famous— is as ideally corny as the Pledge of Allegiance. The six-note melody hops merrily among the major triads, a devoted and indulgent fiddle at its heels; Monroe's mandolin break runs up and down the scale as pointedly as a music lesson. "When You Are Lonely" is an elegantly crafted commercial "folk song"—that is, a piece of popular art, with imaginative affinities to songbook illustrations and sheet-music covers, musically ideal for the schoolroom.

Traditional songs usually touch us at a deeper level. A traditional song most associated with Monroe, "Roane County Prison," tells the story of an irrational passion with documentary precision. It is addressed by a man in prison to a fellow prisoner who, he hopes, will send his song home in one of his letters. He tells how at the age of "about thirty years" he courted and married a young woman whose brother, "for some unknown reason," shortly stabs him; three months later, he says, "I'd taken Tom's life." He flees Roane County, "way back in old east Tennessee," and wanders over the world until he is drawn back home by an irresistible longing for the Roane County hills. Upon his return he is immediately arrested and placed before a jury removed from his case by the lapse of time—"not a man in that county would say one kind word"—and he is clapped into prison for life.

Sung in Monroe's testifying style, the song describes a dark world in which the man is no more able to influence or control the effect of his own feelings upon him than he is the weather. In this world, where most heart songs are situated, he is both betrayed and, unwittingly, a betrayer, who must not only lament his loss but solicit forgiveness. Like most love songs, Monroe's heart songs are strictly conventional, with lyrics built upon a single phrase or image: "In Despair," "Dark as the Night," or "Used to Be." When a song such as "Letter from My Darling" disturbs the conventional surface with an apparently autobiographical particularity, it risks bathos—but a revealing one. "I can't answer her letter," the song begins, "for she left me no address." The love letter is conventional enough; but the lover's account of its contents, which announce his sweetheart's departure but also declare her continuing love for him, is emotionally ambiguous. "She wrote the words she knew would hurt me," he says, "she said I never could be true," and asks in the concluding verse, "Precious one, why did we have to part?" With wailing harmonies, a complaining lead vocal, and a crying fiddle, the entire song seems to weep; and Monroe's heavy, impulsive mandolin break tears the melody apart.

By failing to acknowledge his own faithlessness, by affirming his sweetheart's enduring love for him while she permanently severs the tie between them—"The letter meant goodbye forever, though we'll have each other's heart"—the betrayed lover gains his independence. Both are, apparently, victims of a kind of fate, but one which leaves him free to forge an existence out of memory and dream, unmodified by ordinary social and practical responsibility, in the morally unimpeachable and hermetic atmosphere of offended love. Consequently the loneliness and sorrow of "that long lonesome road" are mitigated by a sense of liberation, so that emotion in songs about offended love often emerges in an ambivalent form.

"Highway of Sorrow," for instance, tells the familiar tale in a gospel idiom: he had a sweetheart, he tells us, "kind, true and sweet," but fell for another who "led my life astray":

> Down the highway of sorrow I'm traveling alone;
> I've lost all my true friends, I've lost a happy home;
> I'm headed for destruction, I'm on the wrong track;
> On the highway of sorrow there's no turning back.

But the mood of the song is far from sorrowful. It is brisk and merry, almost a jingle. Monroe sings it in an animated testifying style, offering himself as a moral exemplar, attacking each note with precision and forethought; his mandolin break is a lively flourish of light, decorative notes ascending to an ephemeral treble.

This juxtaposition of subject and mood also characterizes one of Monroe's finest songs, "On and On." We find the singer, again, "Travelin' down that long lonesome highway," but this time, as we've already seen, he feels an ennobling sense of high purpose and a kind of fate to drive him: "I have to follow you, my darling. . . . The road is clear, and that's where I'm bound." The seven-measure melody, repeated twice, opens with a note held for a full measure, the single syllable "On," stretching the three-syllable title phrase over two measures. Coupled to the song's rolling rhythm this device contributes to a sense of the journey's endlessness. Most interesting, though, is the fact that the song is done in trio, with Monroe's open calling voice at the top and Charlie Cline's warm baritone at the bottom. This gives "On and On" the conviviality of a drinking song: the very solidarity of the group insulates them from the emotion of the song and places it at a distance, in effect "dating" the song. Hence the song has what Monroe calls the "years ago" flavor, and, like "Molly and Tenbrooks," it features the banjo.

In his "I'm on My Way Back to the Old Home," one of his autobiographical songs, the wanderer finds, again, the light gone out in the home to which he's hoped to return. The song opens with Rudy Lyle's twisting, snarling banjo, and a sketch of a mountain childhood—

> Back in the days of my childhood
> In the evening when everything was still,
> I used to sit and listen to the foxhounds
> With my Dad in them old Kentucky hills.

—which Monroe sings in a dusky, passionate calling style, accompanied by a roughly-textured mandolin break. In the second verse we learn that his parents' death has left him alone in the world, while the third fixes the abandoned home place in his memory: "High in the hills of old Kentucky, stands the fondest spot in my memory." The swift pace, almost that of a breakdown, along with a falsetto harmony that nearly eclipses Martin's lead, dispels the song's emotion in the vigor of its execution.

In the movement from the second to third verse, "I'm on My Way Back to the Old Home" makes a crucial choice related to, but more deliberate than, that of the rejected lover: it rejects experience as such and turns to the inward reality, a mental world. I don't mean that it chooses fantasy over reality, for fantasy is still in thrall to actuality; I mean that it sets out to discover the inner truth of experience in the images of which the soul is constituted. This is a world of pure image, emblem, and symbol, and it is the world in which Monroe's best songs— indeed all the great traditional and bluegrass songs—are written. Whether melancholy or bright, its emotions are always emotions contemplated, so that whatever their intensity or amplitude they are released from the savage conflicts of a song like "Letter from my Darling" or the strident violence of some of Monroe's early blue yodels. In "On the Old Kentucky Shore," for example, several heterogeneous images combine in a setting over which haunting, melancholy, and somehow far-off harmonies blow, and a slow, dirge-like melody passes in procession. We are taken to a graveyard "down by the Church of God," where the singer's sweetheart is about to be laid to rest. In the second verse the angels take her; in the third she bids her last farewell to her lover and promises to meet him in the sky; but it is the chorus, which joins a visual detail to a traditional figure placed in a regional but at the same time universal setting, that secures the song's poetic status:

> Up along the Ohio River
> Over on the old Kentucky shore
> Once dwelt a fair young maiden;
> Now there's a crepe upon her door.

Often in bluegrass this contemplative distance is also a temporal one, in which nostalgia is refined by poetic economy. "When the Golden Leaves Begin to Fall" is a sentimental song in a turn-of-the-century mode, sung in Monroe's sincere pledging style, with a refined and lofty falsetto harmony. It is autumn, and when the moon "shines on the Blue Ridge mountains" the singer longs for his sweetheart, whom he pictures kneeling at her bedside with his name in her prayers. The vision prompts him to think of offering her a wedding ring, for wintertime is coming, and the "ground will soon be covered with snow." Snow has also fallen in another sentimental song, "Footprints in the Snow," where it is more directly connected to death: in this song the singer recalls his first meeting with his sweetheart who has now, many years later it seems, gone to heaven, where the happy singer will soon join her. In both songs innocence is joined metaphorically through snow to death.

Where death or the suggestion of it is absent, we are left with the eternal symbol of spotlessness, a maiden, descended in this case almost without modification from the ballad tradition and connected in Monroe's music to that complex romantic image, the rose. We meet her in a pair of songs, "My Little Georgia Rose" and its model, the rose of bluegrass songs, "My Rose of Old Kentucky," descended from a minstrel song of the same title.[6]

A popular story about Monroe claims that "My Little Georgia Rose" is about a young adolescent Monroe knew in his early manhood. The song tells a brief tale about an infant abandoned by her mother, who had planned a "carefree life." The baby has now become a lady—here stepping from the real to the ideal—"with hair of gold and a heart so true."

> Way down in the Blue Ridge mountains,
> Way down where the tall pines grow,
> Lives my sweetheart of the mountain.
> She's my little Georgia rose.

Monroe sings in a luminous, elated calling voice at a brisk, but not breakneck, tempo, accompanied by brilliant twin fiddles. In the third verse he recalls their duets together, and her sweet smile; she is somehow both girl and woman, to whom a trace of wantonness attaches through her wayward mother, faintly blushing the cheek of a child recollected at the point of her sexual blossoming.

But the purity of "My Rose of Old Kentucky" is salvaged from life and time, for the singer is joined to her through their mutual devotion and innocence:

> She bloomed for me in a little village
> In a cabin on a hill;
> We made our vows we'd love each other,
> And I know we always will.

In the chorus she becomes the universal rose, whom the singer pledges to love until he dies; but she is bound up with the past and with the entire idyllic world behind him:

> Oh in dreams I see my darling;
> In a gingham dress she looked so sweet;
> Oh I long for old Kentucky
> And my darling once more to meet.

This is one of Monroe's earliest recordings in the bluegrass style; its widely spaced melodic intervals demand agile vocal leaps through the wistful summer atmosphere of a breezy duple time. The banjo, like a running brook, sparkles in the background, behind fiddle and mandolin breaks which cheerfully repeat the unornamented melody. Monroe's voice in this recording is startlingly pure, light and accurate as a seismograph, brimming with feeling, and yet, for all its clarity and strength, somehow the voice of a very old man. He was thirty-six.

Bill Monroe's repertoire, and the bluegrass songbag generally, does not absorb everything that is in its background or in parallel popular traditions. It largely rejects the trivial or antiseptic treatments of love common in popular music and at the same time the sexual innuendo of blues or rock; it rejects, too, the tendency of contemporary country-western music to treat current social, political, or domestic problems. The reason for this is that romance, Frye tells us, always deeper than ordinary life or, with its "grave idealizing of heroism and purity," above ordinary life, is the pastime of aristocrats, or the dreams and the nightmares of peasants; it is never middle class, unless carefully disguised.[7] Bill Monroe, costumed as a prosperous southern planter, offers to his audience an image cleansed of vulgarity in which it can discern a social and economic ideal: "someone they can look up to," Bill says, "a gentleman."[8]

Like the fifteenth-century balladeers who saw the outlines of human passion in the lives of their betters, and the eighteenth-century French aristocrats who idealized the peasantry while despising the peasant, Bill Monroe has translated social distance into aesthetic distance, particularly the vast social chasms such as those opened by culture or race, which are the stuff of romance. In so doing, of course, he objectifies himself: the image we behold in Bill Monroe is beyond us whatever our social status; it is beyond us the way sculpture is beyond us. But, like a Byzantine icon, it is an image which stares back at its beholder. By placing himself dramaturgically upon an aristocratic plane, Bill Monroe climbs to a prospect from which he can contemplate his own life, and the entire way of life his own represents, at a distance. "Way down in the Blue Ridge mountains . . . ," "Back in the hills of old Kentucky . . . " The narrator of these lines has been literally and figuratively expelled from the world of which he sings. In bluegrass music, form and content meet in the principle of exile.

It is upon the fact of exile, finally, that the universe of romance is built. In separating us from our original world, it makes of that world an object of desire; we can only desire what we no longer possess. And by placing us in an alien world, *this* world, of personality and experience, it makes of it an object of loathing, for this world stands between us and our desire. Desire is the source of the romantic energy and of its differentiation into forms primitive and naive, vulgar and sophisticated, sentimental and effete, and it is the frontier upon which a conscious being first and last confronts himself. It is the essential condition of most lives, and the principal activity of the desiring imagination consists in attaching that desire to some object worthy of our striving.

Thus the romantic—yearning for whatever was or might be, despising whatever is, diving deep into experience with a self-destructive passion; or else, like the chaste medieval knight, or the John Keats who bathes and grooms himself before sitting down to write poetry, or the baseball pitcher who will not touch a woman during the baseball season, conserving through purity his strength for the ordeal of recovering or recreating the desired world. It is in the condition of exile that Bill Monroe is one in spirit with the folklorists who may study him, and with the romantic tradition to which they belong. Ever since Dryden noted "the rude sweetness of a Scotch tune" in Chaucer's verse, the underlying mood of the learned tradition from which folklore emerged is a romantic sentiment for states of society less complex than our own, in which the "primary laws of our nature" stand out more boldly and govern our existence more effectively—states of society which may be in the past, or in some isolated enclaves of the rural South, or even within our larger social order, insulated by a trade or profession, an institution, or by ties of kinship or taste.

It was a romantic impulse, certainly, which moved Cecil Sharp two generations ago to seek "the England of his dreams" in the Appalachian mountains. "He had often pictured," writes his folklorist-companion Maud Karpeles, "what it would have been like to have been born a few centuries earlier, when English folksong was the common musical expression of young and old alike."[9] "I believe so sincerely in the innate beauty and purity of folk music," Sharp had written, "that I am sure it cannot really be contaminated, but that it must and always will do good whenever it finds a resting place."[10]

"It is a paradise," Sharp wrote of Kentucky; "I don't think I have ever seen such lovely trees, ferns and wild flowers. . . . " The people, he thought, were "just exactly what the English peasant was one hundred or more years ago," except that, having owned their own land for three or four generations, "they are freer . . . there is none of the servility which is unhappily one of the characteristics of the English peasant." Indeed, Sharp believed he had encountered a lost aristocracy: "They have an easy, unaffected bearing and the unself-conscious manners of the well-bred. I have received salutations . . . such as a courtier might make to his sovereign," and found himself enamoured of the "beautiful, Madonna-like appearance" of a thirteen-year-old ballad singer, and of a young mother:

> Yesterday we called at a cabin and found such a lovely young fair-haired, blue-eyed girl, fifteen years of age with a buxom seven-months old baby in her arms. I never saw a jollier, stronger, healthier baby or mother in my life.

The world which Sharp encountered in 1916 was the same one Bill Monroe had been born into five years earlier, and it is impossible not to note in the following description of a running set Sharp saw in Harlan County echoes of Monroe's own recollections:

> It was danced one evening after dark on the porch of one of the largest houses of the Pine Mountain School with only one dim lantern to light up the scene. But the moon streamed fitfully in, lighting up the mountain peaks in the background and, casting its mysterious light over the proceedings, seemed to exaggerate the wilderness and the breakneck speed of the dancers as they whirled through the mazes of the dance . . . the air seemed literally to pulsate with the rhythms of the "patters" and the

> tramp of the dancers' feet, while over and above it all,
> penetrating through the din, floated the even, falsetto tones of
> the Caller. . . .

It is impossible, in other words, not to fall under the moonlit romantic
spell ourselves, and, forgetting the history of strife, bloodshed, poverty, ignorance, and exploitation which has marked the Appalachian
region from the Civil War to the present, imagine that at the turn of
the century in Kentucky there existed something close to the idyllic
world that Sharp and many other writers reported. For as Sharp wrote
a few years later, in 1918, "The tradition is steadily approaching destruction, owing to the establishment of schools and the contaminat-
ing influence of what is usually called modern progress."[11] Karpeles puts
it more directly: "The region is no longer the folksong collector's paradise, for the serpent, in the form of the radio, has crept in, bearing
its insidious hill-billy and other 'pop' songs."[12]

That awful dreadful snake!

However widely separated Cecil Sharp and Bill Monroe may be in
background, education, and culture, in sensibility they are very much
akin. In any case Monroe is directly connected, as we've seen, to the
learned tradition of Cecil Sharp through the participation in his career
of folk revivalists such as Ralph Rinzler, and by the influence of bluegrass upon the folk revival itself. Yet both Bill Monroe and the learned
tradition are mutually bound to a still more central European romantic
myth which, as Arthur Moore shows in *The Frontier Mind*, associated
the transmontane region, Kentucky in particular, with the Earthly
Paradise, a place "usually located to the westward of precise geographical knowledge," which only the valiant and the pure of heart,
by penetrating some perilous natural barrier such as a mountain range
or sea, might enter. From the late seventeenth century onwards, first
through the extravagant tales of Indians and wanderers, and later
through the letters, journals, chronicles, and histories of explorers and
settlers, Kentucky "acquired an enduring Paradisical character," becoming a fabled garden blessed with a temperate climate, fertile for-
ests, and boundless wildlife—ideas which Daniel Boone himself did
much to promulgate, having been himself much influenced by them.[13]
As an Ohio River boatman put it: "No, stranger, there's no place on
the universal 'erth like Old Kaintuck: she whips all 'out-west' in pret-
tiness, and you might bile down Creation and not get such another
State out of it."[14]

How can this essentially medieval idea have entered the nineteenth-
century popular imagination in America? Surely not through the *Jesuit*

Relations! As Moore points out, the paradisical tradition took the form, in popular verse, of "expressions of strong affection for Kentucky and sentimental recollections of olden times."[15] But no force in nineteenth-century popular culture more enforced the identification of the South, of which Kentucky had become a poetic symbol, with Paradise than the minstrel show, which entered the popular debate over slavery by representing the plantation as an idyll of domestic tranquillity and happiness.[16] On the plantation the Negro could survive; away from it he became ridiculous, a no-count, dandy, or fool, or else he wandered aimlessly, longing to return. Even the abolitionist side accepted a sentimentalized image of the southern black, treating the plantation cabin home as a model of Christian values and the slave himself as the patient sufferer of an unhappy lot; in *Uncle Tom's Cabin*, which the minstrel show dismantled with innumerable hilarious parodies, Harriet Beecher Stowe had represented plantation life in Old Kentucky under a benevolent master as a Christian ideal.

The grey-haired mother and dad waiting at home, the lover grieving over his sweetheart's grave, the yearning for "my dear old Southern home"—many of the motifs which now characterize hillbilly and bluegrass music were the creation of blackface minstrels; we can find them all in Stephen Foster's songs. Few were more persistant, though, than the theme of exile. As Uncle Dave Macon used to sing:

> I've worked out in the cotton, I've worked out on the river,
> I used to say if I got out I'd never go back, no never;
> But time has changed the old man, his head is hanging low,
> His heart turns back to Dixie, and I must go.

After the Civil War this theme took on an added poignancy and strength, as the minstrel stage presented the figure of the Old Darky returned to find his cottage home gone to ruin or destroyed by war—the very images that recur in "The Fields Have Turned Brown" or "Paradise." The fact is that many of the traditional songs in hillbilly and bluegrass music which touch upon these themes—many more than is immediately apparent—*are* minstrel songs, or derivatives of them, from which the element of race has evaporated. By an odd sort of historical recurrence, the blackface minstrel's characterization of nineteenth-century black experience, a characterization which oscillated between sentimentality and ridicule, had supplied the images by which the Appalachian white, himself expelled from the rural South into the urban North, himself sentimentalized in the popular imagination and at the same time despised and caricatured, himself socially and culturally set apart, might interpret his own experiences a century later.

It is a slender thread, but it is a continuous one, and it ties Bill Monroe, his audiences South and North, and bluegrass music itself to the romantic tradition that figures hugely in the settlement of the New World, in the advance of its frontiers, and in America's idea of itself.

Which brings us, at long last, to Bill Monroe's astonishing voice. It has been compared to everything from a railroad air horn to a bowl of fresh cream. Its power, like unto a jet engine, is apparent to anyone who hears it; it has set the standard for the more acute and concentrated efforts of bluegrass tenor singers, which remind us that romance, as Frye writes, "radiates a glow of subjective intensity," inclining toward the "tragic emotions of passion and fury . . . from which something nihilistic and untamable is likely to escape."[17] Not so obvious, perhaps, is the delicacy and lustre of Bill's voice. Peter Rowan, who sang next to him, calls it an oboe; Ralph Stanley says that Bill has a pearl in his voice.

High pitch, we've said, is important in bluegrass as an object of striving. But it is important in itself, too. In the psychic universe through which the romantic imagination moves, and this ought certainly to include the auditory space generated by music, heights are perennially associated with our "higher" functions: with intellect and spirit, with moral perfection, and finally, of course, with God. All organic processes, it seems, not only in our culture but in other cultures such as the Hindu as well, establish sensations in and are traditionally identified with various points in the human body, such as the genitals, the belly, the heart, and the head, seats of sexual desire, instinct, emotion, and thought. The highest operations of the soul seem to take place—or so I've heard—*above* the top of the head: "If I feel physically as if the top of my head were taken off," says Emily Dickinson, "I know that it is poetry." Southern rural culture has inherited this moral and spiritual geography too, of course; one finds it not only in the language and metaphor of the Church and in sacred song, but in the astrologic signs which the farmer uses to plant his fields and his garden, and to castrate his animals, and even to plan weddings; each sign is associated with a particular part of the body, and takes on the virtues of that part.

High pitches belong to that elevated realm which, culturally considered, is morally and spiritually above the plane of ordinary experience, a realm which in literature is metaphorically identified with the heavens, and with the mountaintops which human beings scale in order to speak with their gods. A high-pitched note, moreover, seems to concentrate sensation, removing impurities and, depending upon the degree of intensity, moving it towards the limit of sensation to the threshold of pain, the point at which the stimulus has begun to over-whelm sensation and to presage the destruction of the sensor. A soft and ineffable high note, such as that of the piano or harp, will seem light or gay, or pure and white; at the higher intensity of the violin, say, it will become sharp, keen, or piercing, and its brightness will increase—figures which, incidentally, we also apply to the human intelligence and moral sense. The soprano's effortless pure tone implies moral purity; the torch singer's breathy note implies moral sophistication. Finally, a high tone seems to come from far away.

Elevation, intensity, distance—the head-splitting note for which the jazz horn player or bluegrass singer has sold his soul moves us toward a point at the center of experience, a point without dimension and out of time which so sharply focuses the senses that it seems to reduce us to nothing. On the lofty plane to which we have ascended, this effect has a spiritual character. The horn player or singer, absorbed into his own note, recedes or even disappears into an auditory fourth dimension, freed from imperfections and lodged in a field of immensities which for a fleeting instant of psychic unity—what might be called a momentary arrest of thought—we grasp, but *from which we must depart.*

In these vocal Himalayas, where a man has to go it alone, Monroe moves about in seven-league boots. It is here that his mimetic genius shines forth most brilliantly. Other singers, perhaps, can reach their vocal *primum mobile,* and do it with ease, precision, and grace. But Bill Monroe, you might say, does it bravely—leaping, not climbing, not clinging by the fingernails but standing solidly upon two feet; only for a moment, to be sure, but long enough to breathe the air and plant a flag. Nor, having arrived, will he simply slip over the edge and be lost, or depart carelessly or in haste, but soar away like an eagle, permanently installed as a denizen of the heights. What Monroe is doing is cleaving with his voice to certain *terrestrial* laws, at once overcoming and being overcome by them, imitating, in a tour de force such as "Muleskinner Blues" or "Goodbye Old Pal" the natural decline of receding sounds—the Doppler effect—and thereby provoking an inestimable sensation of loss of the summit to which we have become, emotionally and musically, deeply committed. The feeling is a sweet bereavement, a kind of homesickness; and we find the image of it in the pearl to which Stanley referred, a vocal image which I myself have heard only in the voices of certain elderly people, and in the voice of one struggling to hold back tears, especially a child's.

What *is* the "high, lonesome sound?" There is a beauty and a power simply in the completed action of reaching the high note: it satisfies by the exhaustiveness of the effort, like a home run. And in this extraordinary effort there is something a little frightening, too, something we would not want to approach too closely, for it is a man unleashing all his energy and force upon a single object. Finally there is the sheer perfection of the tone itself, its height and its purity, with all that height and purity imply, and the emotion that arises from the embodiment of such a tone in the human voice.

I wonder if the high, lonesome sound is not a musical equivalent of that transcendentally romantic effect produced by the conjunction of beauty and terror called the Sublime. A certain kind of romantic American landscape painting comes to mind, such as that of the Hudson River school and its founder, Thomas Cole. The Hudson River painters took an interest in the wild, rustic, pastoral beauty and natural grandeur of the Catskills, which they represented in paintings characterized by lofty peaks and hanging precipices, auroral light radiating out of massive clouds or diffracted by isolated rains and lingering mists which helped to "draw a veil over the common details, the unessential parts, which shall leave the great features, whether the beautiful or the sublime, dominant in the mind."[18] All is suspended in a panoramic depth, "through the transparent abysses of which you might send an arrow out of sight,"[19] one which never fails to reveal an ethereally distant horizon. A storm-twisted tree or ancient rock might occupy the foreground, while humanity, or the signs of it, is exiled to the middle distance, where it appears as a solitary figure, tending sheep in a meadow or emerging with a hunting dog out of an autumnal wood, or as an isolated mountain cabin sending a wisp of smoke into the atmosphere: all would make excellent covers for bluegrass record albums, it seems. Or else the painter will eliminate the foreground altogether, suspending us at a carefully calculated height that is always above the plane of daily life but well below the vault of the sky and the highest peaks that reach up to it.

The familiar poignancy of this image consists in the fact that an idyllic wilderness landscape made more lovely by effects of light and color, more awesome by the presence of colossal natural features, more glorious through a figurative use of atmospheric displays, and more inscrutable through the use of grotesque or mysterious details, has at the same time been made inaccessible in all its parts by the height and distance required to present that landscape comprehensively to the eye. However ennobled or exhilarated we may feel to have the sweep of our vision expanded, in effect, supernaturally, we nevertheless behold the world before us with an acute longing that focuses upon and is intensified by the distant mountain tops and horizon we cannot reach, but especially by the tiny human figures in whom we see our own isolation and insignificance. The Sublime taxes the powers of imagination to the limits of that pleasure which can be taken in beauty, a limit at which the awful disproportion between human desire and human power seems less a source of grief than of wonder, for it has reached the point of its own extinction. With the inevitable fall of the eye from the promentory or peak, or the fall of Monroe's voice from the summit of his vocal range, and the "sweet bereavement" that follows it, comes also a blessed relief; for something that burned in us, something terrible, has been extinguished—temporarily, at least.

I confess I am at a loss to understand why the achievement of a nineteenth-century school of American pastoral painters and that of a modern hillbilly singer should, as formations of the human sensibility, so resemble one another. The pastoral ideal is of course a constant preoccupation of the American imagination, and it has never been absent, sublimely amplified, from folk song:

> Sometimes I'm cramped and crowded here and long for elbow
> room;
> I want to reach for altitude where the fairest flowers bloom;
> It won't be long before I pass into that city fair
> With fifty miles of elbow room on either side to spare.

But I will say at least that the romantic movement, in Europe and America, was a twin sun that rose out of history with the industrial age; and so I cannot but think of the Kentuckian, who left home with his family while still a boy but who nevertheless still dreams of going back, weaving his way through the Detroit traffic on a blear February morning toward his job on the assembly line, listening on the eight-track auto tapedeck he bought with the handsome salary he cannot give up, to Bill Monroe and the Blue Grass Boys, singing "I'm Going back to Old Kentucky."

I wonder, too, if the useful analogy between the pastoral painting and the high, lonesome sound is not more than merely useful. Auditory impressions are seldom unaccompanied by some phantom and fugitive visual interpolation; psychological studies have shown not only that the form of a musical composition may reflect some visual object or design that inspired the composer, but that among a number of listeners within a given culture emotional and synesthetic responses agree with a truly astonishing degree of predictability to the various elements of music such as modality, pitch, interval, tempo, and so on.[20] If, as we have suggested, music imitates the dynamic form of experience, it remains for the musician, and not merely to his audience in a state of private reverie, to articulate in a language of tones and sounds an auditory space which can be interpreted cooperatively by the senses according to the disposition of the culture.

It is plain that Bill Monroe has the landscape on his mind. His instrumental pieces often have evocative place names standing at their head, such as "Jerusalem Ridge," or "Crossing the Cumberlands," or "Roanoke," which prompt us to interpret the music with the phantasmal images of place and of the past which these titles suggest. Some of his instrumental titles glow with the radiance of that other realm "located to the westward of precise geographical knowledge," the West—"Panhandle Country," "Wheel Hoss," "Rawhide," "The Gold Rush," or "The Golden West." The carefree yodeller of "Goodbye Old Pal" or "When the Cactus Is in Bloom" is also, of course, a cowboy of the open plains. It is the landscape, too, that the bluegrass musician seems to traverse in exhilarating instrumental breakdowns such as "Orange Blossom Special," "Train 45," or "Lee Highway Blues," as if the instrumental showpiece were a form of high-speed travel.

"I don't know why," Monroe remarked one evening, "but the lay of the land does a lot to me. It touches me a lot. It's played a big part in my music."[21] Of his farm in Goodlettsville, Tennessee, Bill says, "I like to be up on the hills and mountains, and see the valleys."[22] Is it only the evocativeness of the title that gives the terrestrial quality of "Jerusalem Ridge," or a pattern of association that seems to place the high, lonesome singer in a boundless green landscape of vaulting hills and radiant sky? Or is it the music itself, imbued by culture with a specific mimetic force and by the musician with a specific mimetic form?

Let's close this discussion by looking briefly at one more tune, Monroe's instrumental "Bluegrass Breakdown," recorded with the original band in 1947. Like many traditional tunes and most of Monroe's instrumental pieces, "Bluegrass Breakdown" has a simple strophic structure in which a single pattern or idea, variously constituted, repeats itself in a series of balanced phrases, each with its own harmonic strategy. The tune has sixteen bars, the first four of which foreshadow, and the concluding four of which discharge, the exquisite tension of the tune's emotional burden, a modal contemplation of four bars, once repeated. In the opening phrase, the second bar weights the brisk movement of the first by dropping its inverted tonic chord a semitone, returning in the third and fourth bars to the tonic and resolving the phrase by shifting its dynamic balance from the octave to the root, dissolving the inversion. The second and principal phrase reverses, deepens, and expands the first by rising twice to the tonic from a major chord built upon the minor seventh below it—that is, by lifting the chord a whole tone and by assigning two bars to each chord. The musician exits from the tune by rising to the dominant chord—the only upward step from the tonic in the piece—preparing the way for harmonic resolution in the last two bars. The entire sequence returns, with the subdominant C major chord substituted for the model F major in the principal phrase.

There is very little melody as such, especially in the mandolin lead. The real interest of the tune is in the chord changes themselves, especially in the haunting Mixolydian shift in the principal phrase, which the semitone dip in the opening phrase seems to attempt imperfectly or incompletely. The genius of the tune is the poignant juxtaposition of an exhilarating rolling tempo with the strange, dolorous weight of its melodic movement, which is insistently downwards—a semitone, a modal whole tone, a major whole tone. We're traveling, but the joy of anticipation for what lies ahead is not unalloyed with regret of what has been left behind. The reprieve, which recapitulates the tune in a major tonality, seems to throw a brighter, less ambiguous light upon its melodic terrain. Its business is to fix the musical emotion in the harmonic equilibrium of the major mode, transforming it into pure design.

Scruggs's banjo break opens with the famous C#-D hammer-on which he shortly thereafter incorporated into his "Foggy Mountain Breakdown"; in fact the entire structure of "Foggy Mountain Breakdown" echoes that of "Bluegrass Breakdown," with a relative minor chord, the E minor, substituted for the modal change. Scruggs repeats his break up the neck with a shearing choke on the second string which seems to consummate the initial sally by intensifying its acoustic effects in a higher register. Wise's fiddle break is a classic, too; it ought to stand for all time as a model of great bluegrass fiddling. He enters his break, it seems, before he has decided just what to play; and so, with wistful, full-measure double stops he dreams upon the chord progression. Then, suddenly, he wakes, pursuing the tune with a wild dash of eighth and quarter notes until he has subdued it with his long, brooding bow again.

Most impressive of all, though, is Monroe's lead mandolin. He handles it as if it were alive. With a pulsing but unbroken tremolo line of double and triple stops he introduces into the tune an underlying current of force that seems to bend or twist with each chord change. In his playing hand is an energy that seems to come from some powerful mechanical engine; he makes the melody by turning the mandolin's acoustic surface against it, as a craftsman engraves a crystal bowl by turning it against a grinding wheel. He is less playing the mandolin than he is *piloting* it. A harrowing trill on the F seems to shake the entire structure of the tune, like an earth tremor, while a galloping triplet phrase causes the strings to sound together like a heavy weight, like harness bells or a drawerful of heirloom silver, or to clang with the plangency of a distant bell.

I played this recording for a group of friends one evening, asking them to write down their images and associations. Of eight, only two had any real familiarity with bluegrass music. My experiment was hardly scientific, but I am satisfied with the results. One simply felt happy, and saw the color green. One saw wagon wheels, a fence and gate, a locomotive with its cowcatcher and driving wheels. One saw distant mountains, and one a fox chase, with baying hounds. Two people saw running trains, two saw country dancing, and two saw rushing water—a river or a waterfall. And of the eight, *four* saw horses—galloping through the woods, or in a race, head-to-head at the finish line. One, an artist, drew a highly animated picture of two horses running in tandem; later he recalled a scene from his youth in South Dakota, when he and a friend, both of them cowboys in those days, had raced across the plain at a full gallop.

Speaking for myself, "Bluegrass Breakdown" commutes me to the past, thirty years back, where in some vague region of my brain an old aerodynamic sedan is rolling along a valley floor somewhere in the Blue Ridge, the telephone poles marching by as if new-made on an assembly line, on one of those old two-lane state highways, rhythmicized with strips of tar, that used to be the way we got around this country, when I was a kid. I don't know exactly where I fit into the scene or why, for me, there is something inexpressibly lonesome in it. Whether memory or dream, I frankly do not know; for I feel somehow that I am in the car, with my father, who died over twenty years ago, though the music says quite plainly that it is a vision of Bill Monroe and the Blue Grass Boys, carrying hillbilly music back to the hills from which it came.

Chapter 11

Tambo and Bones
Blackface Minstrelsy, the Opry, and Bill Monroe

. . . a vagabond with a corked face and a banjo sings a little song, strikes a wild note, and sets the heart thrilling with happy pity.—Thackeray

Acting on the strength of his own success in a commercial system which increasingly glorified the individual performer and in response to the Opry's long-standing conservative emphasis upon the traditional music of the Southeast, Bill Monroe stood between a public audience and a string band whose music, by Monroe's deliberate design, represented an archaic traditional type. By cultivating intensively certain features of that music, raising it to a level of explicitness and amplitude demanded by the occasion, Bill Monroe negotiates, in the fictional space of a musical performance, the meeting of peoples, and makes of that process an aesthetic fourth dimension alive with mimetic powers. However we may interpret it, Monroe's vivid personal presence places him, as it had just begun to do in the 1940s, in a musical and dramatic foreground to which the Blue Grass Boys provide both a background and a boundary; the consequence of this arrangement is a three-dimensional space, at once actual and fictional, which socially, psychologically, and morally resonates with the actions and interactions of the musicians.

"Nobody can say they play bluegrass," maintains banjo picker and former Blue Grass Boy Robert Black, "until they play it with Monroe."[1] That Monroe is a leader no one doubts; its impact is strong in his performances. Often he will move among individual members of the band during instrumental breaks, or drop behind to observe the whole, taking care that his contributions do not duplicate any of theirs, though they may summarize, replenish, or extend theirs. Occasionally he will address his mandolin directly to a banjo or guitar picker who has fallen off the pace, or brandish about a heavy rhythmic phrase in order to bring the band together. In harmony singing he will visibly modulate his powerful voice, in tone, timbre, volume, and phrasing, to achieve a more perfect parallel with the lead singer. At times one cannot but feel that were Monroe to relax his grip upon the operations of the band for an instant the entire phenomenon would dissolve before our eyes. "Monroe knows what everybody's doing at all times," Black goes on. "He's got a thousand ears under that hat."[2]

Monroe selects his lead singers, banjo and bass players for their musical ability, of course; a Blue Grass Boy must have complete command of Monroe's material and of the precise economy of expression designed to maintain a generally light or open sound and an overall unanimity or singularity of effect. But he chooses them, too, for their wholesome and youthful good looks, for the figurative sons of the Father of Bluegrass Music can be no less than neat, clean, well-groomed, and, by all appearances, well-bred. That a certain strict decorum reigns over the band is evident from the poker-faced expressions of the members, whose immediate audience is Monroe himself. The actual audience, whatever its character, sometimes seems to arouse terror in them. That a band member should address the audience directly, except by Bill's implicit invitation in an instrumental break, or in any other way call attention to himself, would be inappropriate and unseemly. "Being a Blue Grass Boy," Bill avers, "is like being in school."[3]

In the attention of one musician to another, in their desire to perform in a way that distinguishes them individually but at the same time wins Monroe's approval, in the necessity of holding all tightly together while keeping every part distinct, and simply in meeting the rigorous demands of Monroe's music, there is enormous tension in a performance of Bill Monroe and the Blue Grass Boys. Perhaps as a consequence of this tension, the membership of the Blue Grass Boys has been almost constantly changing. In recent years, moreover, the Blue Grass Boys have usually been young enough to be Monroe's sons or even his grandsons—"boys" in the literal sense. This flux has been explained in various ways: Bill wishes to populate the field with musicians trained in his style; or he becomes quickly dissatisfied with them; or they find life on the road too arduous; or they wish to throw off Monroe's yoke.

There is truth in all of them. But there is a sound formal explanation, too: young men, no matter how experienced or accomplished as musicians, remain in that psychosocial and aesthetic background which mimetically Monroe's music demands. Without it the negotiative process cannot take place, and one dimension of the music, so rich with implication, vanishes.

Audiences unfamiliar with bluegrass music will sometimes innocently suppose that the Blue Grass Boys, or other bluegrass musicians, are folk, not professional, musicians, and would no doubt feel betrayed to discover that in spite of all the suggestion to the contrary the bluegrass fiddler or banjo picker has not come directly from the woodshed, but from his last show date. Kenny Baker, for instance, has mined coal and been a mine inspector; but to call him a coal miner, when he has been playing country fiddle professionally for most of his life, is a bit like calling James Joyce a schoolmaster. Yet the error points to the success of the fiction. In Monroe's mastery of his music there is a peculiar kind of distance between him and it. As he plays his mandolin, with unmistakable determination and pride, his eyes fixed on the fingerboard and the instrument thrust forward or held up where we can see it, his lip noticeably tense with the concentration and effort, he actually seems to be *teaching us how* to play it; and by getting the old thing to work again he has evoked, like Aladdin rubbing the ancient lamp, the spirit of the place and time of which it is the symbol.

We have already discussed the analogy, which is far from an idle one, between Bill Monroe and the learned folklorist-antiquarian such as Bascom Lamar Lunsford or John Jacob Niles, who brings a folk song, a style, or even the folk musician himself, as the Seegers and Lomaxes have done, out of the folk community into the learned or popular one. Like them, he is an interpreter or teacher, contributing the hue of his own mind to his materials, and his art is a scholarly one:

> If you study music deep enough, old time music, why you get to
> learn what's good for it and what's not good for it. You can't
> just play it now and not pay any attention to it. . . . You've got
> to be thinking about it, maybe when you're working, doing
> other things; you've got to keep your mind on that music to
> really get deep in it. I think I've studied old time music deeper
> than anybody in the country. It all leads to where I know
> what was the foundation of a number in old time music. I know
> what's back there. . . .[4]

The important difference between Monroe and a Lomax or Seeger, though, is that this process of mediation is the subject matter of a

complex mimetic art which emphasizes the voluntary reintegration of
the mediating figure with the human order which he has transcended
but in which his whole nature and character is rooted and to which,
therefore, he must periodically return symbolically. Like Dante's Florence or Joyce's Dublin, Monroe's Kentucky is a microcosm, a well of
time from which the exile may take a spiritual draught. His symbolic
withdrawal into it is strongly archetypical in character, and like the
many political or religious rituals it resembles, it is one around which
communities of belief might form or be renewed, setting the actor at
the head of the community his action has created.

That a community *has* formed around Bill Monroe, and that he has
assumed its leadership, is obvious to anyone who follows bluegrass
music. It is vividly apparent at every bluegrass festival, especially
Monroe's own summer "celebration" at Bean Blossom, in the hills of
southern Indiana. Here, in the pastures and glades of a country music
park, bluegrass musicians and enthusiasts assemble in numbers—tens
of thousands, in recent years—to indulge in a sense of identity whose
ethnic origins, though still quite significant in themselves, have inspired the participation of people far removed from Appalachia or its
people. Mingling among them from time to time may be seen a bespectacled figure in a white cowboy hat and a sport jacket, with longish
white hair and a wide girth, attending to a variety of tasks: greeting
arrivals at the gate, pausing with a group of people to have his picture
taken, or striding out to the edge of a field with a group of young
roustabouts, all of them skinny as snakes, to sink a few new fenceposts
where cars have begun to overflow into a neighboring farm. A visitor
may recall to him some road show of twenty, thirty, even forty years
back, and the old man's memory proves exact. Or he may recall to an
enquiring youngster some detail of his boyhood in Kentucky: "Back in
them days, we had a pair of mules . . ." and you would think, the way
of life he describes is so antique, that he was not sixty-five or seventy
years old, but *one hundred* and seventy. At an afternoon workshop
he will appear in shirtsleeves to demonstrate a mandolin technique,
perhaps to retire later with another musician to exchange a few ideas,
especially if the musician happens to be black, as upon a few rare
occasions he is.[5] This same figure reappears, at sunset on the Saturday
evening of the festival—the old secular Sabbath of the rural calendar—
with the circle of his followers gathered around him, all singing and
playing the songs which everybody knows by heart. "I call you all my
children," says the man in the white hat, drawing a young boy with a
mandolin toward him on one side, grasping the hand of a blushing
matron on the other; all join the Father of Bluegrass Music in a ren-

dition of "On and On," and, just as the brimming sun dips behind the trees across the highway, the promise of an evening's frolic just ahead, the meeting will end, perhaps, as all sing "Will the Circle Be Unbroken."

With its "singing all night and dinner on the grounds," the bluegrass festival is a camp meeting, a ritual gathering in which the warmth and solidarity of the community closes around the soul stripped and wounded in its own effort to be free. Psychologically its form is precisely that of the Baptist meeting whose emotional and spiritual catharsis prepares the way for a convivial love feast of casseroles, fried chicken, and pie. For so long as we live in the world, the sublime effort, always transitory, must bring a return to social life, where the naked soul acquires a protective covering, individuated by a social mask and led in its moral confusion along the pathways of social convention. In literature, such a movement is typically the end and object of romance, symbolized, say, by the winning of a princess, whose implied marriage and ascent to the throne releases the hero from the isolation of personality and installs him in a human order metaphorically or actually connected to the divine, where he recovers his identity. This is the same "kingdom around the throne" which gospel song promises us in eternity, but we do not require the Gospel itself to feel its bouyancy. It is here, too, at Bean Blossom.

"The theme of the comic," Northrop Frye teaches, "is the integration of society."[6] This integration may take several forms: some central figure may be incorporated into the social order, or an heroic figure may emerge around whom a new order may develop, or one family or community may be integrated with another. All may of course take place at once. These processes are not "comic" because they are funny, necessarily, though it is certainly right and proper to laugh with the joy that human unanimity brings; they are comic because the comic, says Aristotle, concerns itself with characters whom we consider to be somehow inferior to ourselves. Consequently human character in society, as the satirist knows, is *inherently* comic, since as private personalities we cannot but regard our social selves—the mask we wear, the role we play—as an attenuated form of what, inwardly, we feel ourselves to be. The very idea of roles and masks as applied to society suggests its dramaturgical, and hence its artificial, character. The cheerful social harmony which prevails at the conclusion of a romantic tale or story arises from a sense that personal identity and social role have come into alignment: the kiss of a girl has released the prince from enchantment; the glass slipper has found its mate, and fits; the interloper queen has danced herself to death.

If romance obliterates identity, this consummation recovers it, and in literature is always accompanied by some festive ritual or party, usually in a pastoral setting suffused with gay spring sunshine and bursting flowers whose sympathetic magic suggests that an integrated and harmonious social order, symbolized by symmetrical patterns of paired young couples and beaming kings and queens, has its basis in Nature.[7] That is why, on the edge of this happy scene, we inevitably find the *agriokos*—the rustic, the rube, the country bumpkin. He is the bridge between society and nature, there to facilitate our acceptance of society by revealing, in his hilarious difficulties with social roles, masks, and conventions, that these *are*, after all, artificial, that beneath them lies an innocent human heart, and in them the fulfillment of human nature. Dramatically, his presence is essential, for our laughter at his expense expresses, even inspires, the immediate joy we take in the new-made human community before us.

It is a "distinctly human affair," George Hay said of the Grand Ole Opry, "which may be termed a big get-together party for those who listen in." Hay began his career as a court reporter for the Memphis *Commercial Appeal*, but transformed his column into a humorous dialogue called "Howdy, Judge" between two minstrel show stereotypes, a white judge or interlocutor who became the Opry's "Solemn Old Judge," and a series of Negro defendants.[8] These same conventions, those of the minstrel stage, George Hay adopted to produce the Grand Ole Opry, reserving the interlocutor's role for himself and placing his rural musicians in roles formerly occupied by stage representations of Negroes. When the radio program expanded into a theatrical production, first in the studio and then in the auditorium, Hay continued the theme, substituting painted barn beams, hayricks, rail fences, and the like for the minstrel show's cabin, cotton patch, levee, and riverboat and costuming his performers—tradesmen and artisans who had at first appeared at the studio in business suits—in overalls, straw hats, kerchiefs, and the like. Hay did not retain the minstrel show semicircle, which drew the audience into a closed social "circle" with the troupe; but the informality of the proceedings, with hands and musicians milling about on stage during the program, had much the same effect.

Though the minstrel show had passed its prime in the eighties, minstrel shows continued to be produced, in conjunction with ragtime and the new jazz music, well into the first decade of the new century; for Hay's generation minstrelsy was at most only a generation back, as the Big Band era is to us. Moreover the conventions and materials of the minstrel show had been drawn virtually without modification into succeeding forms of entertainment such as vaudeville, while minstrel shows proper were still being produced by amateur groups well into the 1950s. From ragtime and jazz to standup comedy and the circus ring, there are few forms of American popular entertainment that do not have a root in the minstrel show. Even the early Hollywood animations of barnyard frolics were cartoon minstrel shows; and Walt Disney's Goofy and Mickey Mouse owe at least part of their being to Jim Crow and Zip Coon.

Still more to the point, perhaps, is that blackface minstrelsy, which had enjoyed its greatest popularity in the South, endured there in a corrupt form, the medicine show, with which many hillbilly musicians had begun their professional careers.[9] Not only had mountain banjoists such as Hobart Smith and Clarence Ashley performed in blackface, but so had many country music stars, including Jimmie Rodgers, Roy Acuff, Bob Wills, even Gene Autry—men who continued to think of country music in connection with comedy and to present some form of comedy in their shows.[10] Mainer's Mountaineers, the long-lived string band whose banjoist Wade Mainer, in his eighties, still lives and performs in the Detroit area, were performing blackface skits in the South as recently as the 1960s. Bill Monroe's early career, too, shows him to have been consistently interested in comedy. Remember the jug player who had been a member of the original Kentuckians, and Stringbean, banjo player and blackface comedian. Doug Green reminds us that Monroe used to feature comic skits with the Blue Grass Boys, and in his book *Country Roots* shows us a photo of Monroe, *in an interlocutor's role*, with Stringbean and Bijou, both in blackface.[11] Monroe may even have performed in blackface himself, when at the Chicago World's Fair in 1933 he and Charlie put on a comic skit with fiddle and banjo.[12]

It was perhaps inevitable, then, that Hay should have adopted a slightly modified form of minstrelsy in order to present a musical tradition in large part descended from it. But there was considerable musicological insight in it, too, for the Opry was distinguished from other early radio barn dances for the deep Afro-American hues in its old-time music, perhaps a reflection of its setting in middle Tennessee. One wonders, indeed, if Hay was not aware that it was precisely the Afro-American element that kept the music, as he puts it, "down to earth." Deford Bailey, of course, was himself black, a harmonica player whose "Pan-American Blues" opened the Opry broadcast; both the McGee and the Delmore Brothers were blues guitarists and singers with acknowledged Negro inspiration, and both were accompanied by Arthur Smith, whose sliding single-string work on the fiddle was strongly reminiscent of the almost oriental black fiddling which might be heard in the blues and jugbands then available on race records. Even the rhythms of the Opry string bands seemed to partake of the Afro-American influence, particularly Dr. Bate's, whose sound Charles Wolfe has compared to that of the early New Orleans jazz ensemble; Bate used to tell his daughter, she later recalled, that he had learned most of his songs from an old Negro man he had known as a boy—a fact which the strongly traditional character of his repertoire, with its traces of minstrelsy in such tunes as "Hop High Ladies," "Billy in the Low Ground," "Dixie," "Uncle Joe," "Jordan Am a Hard Road to Travel" and others of obscure origin makes more intriguing. It might be said, too, that the early Opry's brightest star, Uncle Dave Macon, whom Deford Bailey called the best *white* banjo player he had ever heard, *was* a minstrel show entertainer.[13] He had been born into a theatrical boarding house in minstrelsy's last great decade, and had garnered most of his repertoire before the turn of the century; his costume and the epithet "Uncle" were both relics of the minstrel stage, and at least some Opry listeners, such as the black Virginia singer-guitarist John Jackson, thought Macon was a Negro.[14]

Minstrelsy in our civilization begins in the courts and towns of medieval Europe and continues in a variety of increasingly refined forms through the baroque and classical periods, though, for reasons which shall be apparent in a moment, the blackface minstrelsy of the nineteenth century far more resembled its medieval than its modern antecedents. As George Rehin has pointed out, the tradition of blackface is a very ancient one, and in its many forms virtually universal.[15] We find it in English mummery, where the blackfaced man, the collier, was associated with the Devil; he appears also in the May festival and Lord Mayor's pageants of the seventeenth century. In his comic guise, as Rehin suggests, the blackfaced man belongs to harlequinry, and embodies the features of the archetypical Clown—an unnerving consideration when we recall that racism in America has attempted to thrust this identity, fashioned upon the nineteenth-century minstrel stage, upon an entire race of people. At a deeper level, where our fascination with him is alloyed with fear, the blackfaced man echoes the Jungian shadow and, still more profoundly, stares back at us through the mask of his and our own mortality, a condemned man wearing the mark of his condemnation upon his face, whose antics are man's most primitive, and perhaps his best, response to the awareness of his mortal condition.

The minstrel is a servant. He amuses his master—king, court, or counsellor, landlord, alderman, or citizen—with athletic prowess such as acrobatics and juggling, narrative and wit, song and dance. About minstrelsy, then, there are these salient facts: between the minstrel and his audience there is always a social hiatus, real or apparent. The minstrel may be, in fact, like the *griot* of West Africa or the unlanded New Man of the Middle Ages, entirely outside the social order, a wise Fool whose silly antics, ludicrous costume, and grotesque mask reflect the pretensions of the society around him. The minstrel's sole occupation is to bring us pleasure, to increase our happiness, to divert us from our cares. Because he seems devoted to us, we cannot but love him—all the more so for the tremendous effort he seems to put forth for our sake. He may win us so completely that the fancy may strike us to befriend him, so guileless, carefree, and vulnerable does he seem, even somehow to become what he is, by imitation. But the social barrier is a formidable one, having been engendered by, or having itself engendered, cultural differences that baffle understanding.

It has been the point of this book to show that for better or worse such social lines as lie between the minstrel and his audience, lines which insulate one group or class from another at the same time as they lay open the life of that group to the gaze of the other, become thresholds across which romantic fictions pass back and forth, charged with romantic ambivalence. What we see influences us, and is in turn influenced by us. Minstrelsy in America stands at the Mason-Dixon line which history has drawn across the human spirit, a division so deep and persistent that its origins seem to lie less in the past than in some universal and ineradicable division in the human soul. It has no precise geographical location, and the multitude of warring forces which gather at it—urban and rural, industrial and agricultural, rich and poor, real and ideal, present and past, white and black—may confront one another anywhere in America; among them, however, there are old alliances, natural affinities, and geographical patterns from which has formed over time our great divorce between North and South.

The real history of minstrelsy in this country, were it to be honestly and comprehensively written, would touch in one way or another upon every form of popular music we have and on some part of our composed tradition—Gershwin, for example. It would begin, not with the earliest "Ethiopian Delineators," with Thomas D. Rice's "Jump Jim Crow" or George Nichols's "Corn Meal," but on board the slave ships, where the Africans were "encouraged to divert themselves with music and dancing; for which purpose such rude and uncouth instruments as are used in Africa, are collected before their departure,"[16] and thence to the plantation: "Come hither, Sambo," goes a dialogue printed in 1684, "make us *some Sport*, let us see one of your *dances*, such as are used in your own Country, with all your odd postures and tricks for Diversion; I have heard you are the best at it of all my People."[17] Slave bands performed for their masters with combinations of instruments such as the fiddle, the banjo, and percussive instruments such as the bones, the jawbone, the tamborine, and the triangle. Banjo and jawbone excepted, all these were European, and probably brought by Irishmen; the Irish *caeli* band included the fiddle, bones, and a tamborine-like instrument called the bodhran. But "the moaned and wailing notes of the bowed instruments, the rapid fingering of the lutes and harps, and the combined interweaving of melodic-rhythmic lines," all alive and well in the bluegrass band, had come from the West African savannah.[18]

The complex phenomenon of blackface minstrelsy, which began early in the nineteenth century, involves the representation of Afro-Americans by men who were principally of Irish or Irish-American background. Rice and Nichols adopted their performances from a black stableman and a street vendor respectively; their tradition continued in Elvis Presley, who tuned his ear to Arthur Crudup on Memphis radio, and his eye to Bo Diddley at the Apollo. Ry Cooder and Leon Redbone, among many others, ply the trade today. By the late nineteenth century the minstrel show had become, in one branch of it at least, a polite and highly conventionalized theatrical tradition with little connection to folk culture, black or white; but the early minstrel show, the shows of the Virginia Minstrels, of the Christys, Bryants, and Sweeneys, were simply and straightforwardly the adaptation by professional entertainers of folk material, particularly, but not exclusively, the Afro-American—a practice which continued in the rural South long after it had been abandoned in the northern theater. "Half the songs published as theirs are, as far as the words are concerned, the production of 'mean whites,'" wrote J. Kinnard, Jr. in 1845; "but the music and the dancing are all Sambo's own. No one attempts to introduce anything new there. . . ."[19] Y. S. Nathanson, recalling, in 1855, the early decades of minstrelsy, agreed. Of "Jump Jim Crow," "Zip Coon," "Long-tailed Blue," "Old Virginny Never Tire," "Settin' On a Rail," "Old Dan Tucker" and other songs he wrote: "The true secret of their favor with the world is to be found in the fact that they are genuine and real. They are no senseless and ridiculous imitations forged in the dull brain of some northern self-styled minstrel, but the veritable tunes and words which have lightened the labor of some weary negro in the cotton fields. . . . It is impossible to counterfeit, or successfully imitate, one of these songs as it would be for a modern poet to produce a border ballad like Chevy Chase or Lord Jamie Douglas."[20]

W. J. Cash has told us that in the South, where minstrelsy enjoyed its greatest and most lasting popularity, the relation between black and white on the plantation "was nothing less than organic. Negro entered into white man as profoundly as white man entered into Negro—subtly influencing every gesture, every word, every emotion and idea, every attitude."[21] But these mutual influences were not confined to the plantation. On the frontier, which in the early nineteenth century lay along the river routes between Pittsburgh and New Orleans, and spread across the Appalachians on wilderness trails to Kentucky and Tennessee, black and white folk cultures had been intermingled—on the rivers, in the growing cities to the west, in the backwoods Methodist and Baptist churches and camp meetings—wherever, in fact, social and economic marginality had created conditions favorable to cultural interpenetration. In a word, the racial barriers so familiar to us, which closed so suddenly and so resoundingly after Emancipation, had, by the middle of the nineteenth century, begun to dissolve in the American heartland. Read, for example, Lafcadio Hearn's descriptions of levee life in Cincinnati shortly after the Civil War. Black and white Ohio River boatmen shared an idiom, a dialect, a repertoire of jokes and stories, of jigs and reels.[22] The widely reported "Natchez Under the Hill," for example, was related on one side to "The Jolly Miller," an Irish reel, and on the other to the minstrels' "Zip Coon," which has become our "Turkey in the Straw." Widely disseminated along the water routes by which the minstrel shows chiefly traveled, minstrel songs reentered folk tradition, impregnating it with antebellum folksong elements still to be heard both in Afro-American and Appalachian folk music. "Travelling through the South," Kinnard went on, "you may, in passing from Virginia to Louisiana, hear the same tune a hundred times, but seldom the same words accompanying it."[23]

Even the fabled isolation of Appalachia itself was, I suspect, penetrated early on by Afro-American influences carried by eighteenth- and early nineteenth-century migrants, white and black, from the slaveholding Tidewater and Piedmont. The post-Revolutionary period, John Campbell reminds us, was characterized by the "restless movement of people of all classes";[24] the southern routes through the mountains, by land and by water, were thronged with pioneers, many of whom were small slaveholding families, setting out from Virginia and the Carolinas for frontier Tennessee, Kentucky, and Ohio. Not until the road-building decades of the mid-nineteenth century did the iso-

lation of the upland South descend in earnest. "The poorness of mountain roads was probably not as much of a deterrent to travel before
1850 as after," Campbell writes; "All travel was difficult."[25]

What magazine writers encountered in Appalachia at the end of the
nineteenth century was perhaps not so much a relic of old England,
as it pleased them to imagine, as of the post-Revolutionary backcountry
South, which in eastern Tennessee, western North Carolina, and
northern Georgia had been dominated, not of course by the baronial
planter of romantic literature, but by the small yeoman farmer, with
his subsistence grains, sorghum, and sweet potatoes, his tobacco patch
and chickens, and his one or two slaves.[26] Rare but not unknown, the
blacks of the upland region had, as Frederick Law Olmstead observed
in the 1850s, "much more individual freedom than in the rich cotton
country, and are not infrequently heard singing or whistling at their
work."[27] Much of the Negro population of the upland South was very
likely absorbed into the white over the course of the century, but not
before it had contributed the folklife of its parent and grandparent
generation. No document has surfaced, as far as I know, to confirm
the impression; but all things considered it seems at least plausible
that a certain handful of very archaic banjo tunes, with their starkly
African tonality scarcely distinguishable from the *halam* improvisations of Senegal, as well as the thoroughly rhythmicized fiddle styles
of North Carolina, north Georgia, and Virginia, were deposited there
not by blackface minstrels but by black or black-inspired pioneers
before the Civil War, and well before the arrival of black railroad
workers and miners in Appalachia in the 1870s.

Blackface minstrelsy arose out of this sociocultural ferment, and
addressed the social and psychological problems occasioned by it. By
embracing the black identity on stage, the minstrel was expressing
symbolically what had actually transpired in folk culture in the several
generations since 1660, when slavery was firmly established in Virginia. In a brilliant essay on blackface minstrelsy, German sociologist
Berendt Ostendorf calls it a "symbolic interaction ritual," by which
white society, confronting the emerging Afro-African presence in post-
Revolutionary America, developed "a symbolic language and a comic
iconography for 'intermingling' [de Tocqueville's term] culturally with
the African Caliban while at the same time 'isolating' him socially. In
blackening his face the white minstrel acculturated voluntarily to his
comic vision of blackness, thus anticipating in jest what he feared in
earnest."[28] This strategy was complicated by the fact that Afro-American culture was itself a kind of ironic reflection of white America,
which might find in it, as Harriet Martineau wrote, "a perpetual car-

icature of their own follies; a mirror of conventionalism from which they can never escape."[29]

The complex process of caricature and imitation which characterizes black-white relations today was at work between the races well before the advent of blackface minstrelsy; African slaves brought with them to America a tradition of satire, ritual put-on, verbal innuendo, and the like which in Africa had provided for the release of psychological tensions while preserving the solidarity of the community, and in America has helped to see the black man through the trials of racial oppression.[30] It has figured, too, as we've seen, in the evolution of Afro-American musical forms, which frequently rework Anglo-American forms ironically: behind the cakewalk lies the delicate minuet; behind New Orleans jazz, the pompous marching band. "Black language, black music, black dance were by 1800 neither purely African nor purely derivative Anglo-Saxon," Ostendorf reflects, "but already a pidgenized, creolized, travestied incorporation of America by blacks."[31] Hence the blackface minstrel, by taking on theatrically some form of the black image, whether rudely stereotyped or ethnographically scrupulous, had consciously or unconsciously entered upon a many-layered satire of Anglo-American life, a satire of which the minstrel himself was ultimately the object, and voluntarily so. This was one of the hidden springs of minstrelsy's popularity, both for its audiences and for the many young men who enthusiastically took it up. Here were fully four levels of reduplicated irony: behind the goofy Jim Crow and dandy Zip Coon lay the images of the ignorant southern cracker whom slavery had thrust to the bottom of the social ladder, of the booming frontiersman with his outlandish tales of eye-gouging, biting, and alligator-wrestling, and of the Broadway swell, all of whom had unwittingly contributed not only to the minstrel's "comic iconography" but to the hyperbolized Afro-American style which the minstrel meant to ridicule; at a deeper level lay the profoundly ambiguous image of the Negro original, hardly what the minstrel represented him to be, but an unknown factor, at once grotesque and beautiful, menacing and fascinating, socially, politically, and psychologically a complete enigma. Yet the deepest irony, and the deepest mystery, lay behind the black mask itself. Who *was* the man who had chosen to cork his face and imitate the Negro?

Pieced together out of a variety of Anglo-American materials but charged with the African feeling for life, Afro-American culture, then as now, was for the white man an alternative to his own. Even Randolph Jefferson, the president's brother, "used to come out among black people, play the fiddle and dance half the night," or so a Monticello slave recalled; he was "a mighty simple man."[32] The white minstrel was in effect experimenting with the black identity, "trying it on" *in the guise of parody*. Burnt cork was an attempt to resolve complicated cultural questions in the simple binary language of race; it might conceal, reveal, confuse, or falsify the identity of the minstrel who wore it, might as surely mean "white" culturally as it meant "black" theatrically. But above all it was a subterfuge by which the minstrel could indulge the exotic human mode which had touched his imagination, by which he might, as Ostendorf puts it, take "an anthropological expedition into uncharted regions, regions tabooed by his own cultural heritage."[33] In his black mask the minstrel found a kind of freedom which neither Anglo-American culture, Enlightenment philosophy, American democracy, or even frontier conditions could give him—freedom from himself. By becoming a minstrel he rebelled against the guilt and repression of Victorian society, happily sweeping away its glooms and damps and igniting what Mailer calls "the existential synapses of the Negro" in himself. "A minstrel show came to town," Ben Cotton recalled, "and I thought of nothing else for weeks."[34]

The testimony of the early minstrels suggests a guarded intimacy between the races at the lowest levels of society, where Irish-American and Afro-American culture were not so distinctly two as they were to become after emancipation; "smoked Irishman" is an old rural tag for "Negro." The early minstrels seemed to take pride in describing their affinity for the Negro, as if they detected in it the signs of a fundamental sympathy. Billy Whitlock, one of the original Virginia Minstrels, used to "steal off to some negro hut to hear the darkies sing and to see them dance, taking a jug of whiskey to make things merrier."[35] "I used to sit with them in front of their cabins," Ben Cotton recalled, "and we would start the banjo twanging, and their voices would ring out in the quiet night air in their weird melodies. . . . I was the first white man they had seen who sang as they did; but we were brothers for the time being and perfectly happy."[36]

Cotton was boasting, or course, and probably stretching the truth; nevertheless, the history of early minstrelsy abounds with hearsay regarding the relations between minstrels and their black muses. E. P. Christy is said to have learned to play the banjo on Congo Square in the 1820s; Stephen Foster is said to have attended a black church with a Negro servant as a boy, and to have listened to the songs of black stevedores on the Pittsburgh wharves. Dan Emmett, founder of the pioneer Virginia Minstrels, is said to have learned the banjo while traveling with the Cincinnati Circus Company in 1840, from a man named Ferguson: "A very ignorant person," wrote the circus manager, "and 'nigger all over' except in color."[37] Folklore in his birthplace of Mt. Vernon, Ohio, furthermore, suggests that Emmett may have absorbed much southern folklore from local Negroes, especially from the Snowden family, who had come to Knox County from Maryland in 1827. They were musicians, and earned a local reputation by playing from a stage built into the gable of their house, said to be just across a field from Emmett's. Ben and Lou, the Snowden brothers, played banjo and fiddle. Emmett is of course remembered now as the author of "I Wish I Was in Dixie's Land"; but the Snowdens' gravestone north of town proclaims: "They taught 'Dixie' to Dan Emmett."[38]

In the strange suggestiveness of the minstrel background there is also an intriguing confusion. "Uncle Dan" Emmett, as he came to be known, was the son of an Irish-American blacksmith who had come to the frontier from Virginia about 1806; his mother had come from Maryland with her family, the Zerricks, at about the same time. Daniel Zerrick was a weaver; the family claimed Indian ancestry, had the swarthy complexion which Dan inherited, and were known for their musical talents.[39] There may be nothing of particular significance in all this, of course. But it happens that during the post-Revolutionary period Irish-Americans and black Americans, slave and free, shared, in many areas of the country, the same social niche—a fact which not only inflamed racial animosities but at the same time fostered interracial friendships and even marriages. Often a journey to the frontier was a means of undertaking a new life apart from the social and racial stigmas that obtained for both groups on the eastern side of the Appalachians. The claim of Indian ancestry, moreover, had become in the seaboard states, Maryland in particular, a means of securing free status in a system of discriminatory laws designed to settle the increasingly complex question of who was white and who was black. "Hundreds of negroes," wrote Maryland's attorney general in 1797, "have been let loose upon the community by the hearsay testimony of an obscure illiterate individual."[40]

According to his old friend Al. G. Field, Emmett was "a slow study and a very indifferent reader," but showed early skill on the fiddle. "While the Negro dialect came natural to him," Hans Nathan writes, "he became self-conscious and awkward when he had to express himself in standard English."[41] When Emmett returned late in life to Mt. Vernon, taking up residence in a two-room shanty on the edge of town, raising chickens and occasionally cutting wood for his neighbors, he found himself generally acknowledged as the author of the then-famous "Dixie," but, according to still current testimony about him, repudiated by respectable people, even those related to him by blood, ostensibly on account of his association with the stage. After his death in 1904 a local committee was organized to erect a monument to Uncle Dan; but the idea foundered, and by 1912 "not even the exact location of his grave was remembered."[42] A local biographer, who recalled from his early boyhood an elderly Dan Emmett striding down the center of Main Street with a horse blanket draped over his shoulders, a long greatcoat, a heavy rope tied around his waist, and a gnarled sapling for a cane, found a good deal of conjecture among the elders of the town whom he interviewed for his biography. "Some have even maintained," he wrote incredulously, "that he was a Negro."[43]

This same claim—that he was a black—has been made by a contemporary black historian, Hildred Roach, about Joel Walker Sweeney, the man usually credited with the invention of the five-string banjo, who personally disseminated the minstrel banjo style to several of the most prominent minstrel banjoists, including the Virginia Minstrels' Billy Whitlock.[44] Sweeney had learned both banjo and fiddle from black slaves on the small family plantation in Virginia where he was raised; according to Elizabeth Baroody, Sweeney first appeared on stage with these same men, whom public opposition compelled him to replace with white performers.[45] This was apparently the troupe with which Sweeney toured the South, winning fame for himself and an eventual appearance before Queen Victoria; it consisted, wrote minstrelsy's first important chronicler, Carl Wittke, of Sweeney's brothers, one of whom, Sam, became a well-known banjoist during the Civil War.[46] When we reflect, however, that Sweeney's black*face* troupe retained the black dialect, as well as the dancing, shuffling, kicking, jumping, singing, fiddling, and banjo playing of the original slave troupe, it seems simply incredible that he could have successfully replaced the black troupe with white imitators, any more than we could replace James Brown or the Harlem Globetrotters with white imitators. Blackface theatricalized race and dispelled it as a social fact; is it not possible that Sweeney had simply corked his companions' faces?

All this is meant to suggest that the subtleties of cultural interpenetration long ago made nonsense of simple racial dichotomies, and that any attempt to understand the interchange of Irish-American or Anglo-American and Afro-American culture in America in terms of race is foolish and dangerous, even though our shorthand of "black" and "white" inclines us to do so; though racial factors certainly affect the social conditions under which cultural influence does or does not take place, race and culture are entirely independent of one another. Minstrelsy, like our own jazz, country, and rock-and-roll music, drew many of its most outstanding performers from among men who, by virtue of upbringing, background, experience, or temperament, had some feeling for Afro-American expression, not only musical and verbal, but of more ineffable kinds as well:

> He crossed that leg—well, his leg didn't do like mine does; *my* leg won't hang down . . . he put one leg over the other, and it was hangin' right down. . . . And he opened that mouth—he had a long face, you know, long jaw, like; anyhow, it just flopped! Jimmie, he reminded me more of a colored person, or a negro, or whatever you want to call 'em . . . (another voice: "he played that part a whole lot") . . . than anybody I ever saw, in a way. He had that old southern, long southern drawl, you know. . . .[47]

That's Cliff Carlisle, recalling Jimmie Rodgers; but as the strange remark of Emmett's circus manager implies, such an element in a white man's personality, whether he was a famine Irishman or a half-caste, would have placed him, as it seems to have placed Dan Emmett, in a socially marginal position from which minstrelsy offered an escape. Young European-Americans such as Benny Goodman found a similar opportunity in jazz: an opportunity to "Americanize" oneself. While burnt cork made a man theatrically "black," it made him socially "white." More importantly, the racial attitudes symbolized by blackface placed the performer, whatever his background or temperament, among his audiences, not among the people he parodied; as a matter of fact, though, the racial identity of the minstrels was apparently a matter of some confusion for northern audiences who, as Robert Toll speculates, were not entirely familiar with Afro-American manners[48]— this in spite of the fact that from the colonial period onwards Boston, Hartford, New York, and Philadelphia all had visible black populations, with visibly independent cultural traditions, such as Pinkster Day. Thus minstrel blackface, as distinct from the European blackface tradition from which it had been annexed in the 1820s, may in its American setting have been a device by which "mean whites" or "white trash" (these phrases come from writers of the period, commenting on the minstrel show) gained a place on the public stage, and thence into the society whose attitudes that stage reflected—a very different class of men, I suspect, than the "Ethiopian Delineators" of the previous generation. Many minstrel jokes and skits, as well as posters which juxtaposed images of the performers in and out of costume, were contrived to emphasize the minstrels' lily purity: "Why am I like a young widow? Because I do not stay long in black."[49]

On the cultural level, then, the entry, or rather the re-entry, of blacks into minstrelsy, *in blackface*, in the decades following emancipation may not have been so bizarre or unprecedented as appears superficially. What the emancipated slave found on the minstrel stage when he arrived there was a far more venial and vicious caricature of himself than had been promulgated in the thirties and forties, one by turns monstrously grotesque and sickeningly sentimental. The racial stereotypes which emerged in the late minstrel show—watermeloneating, chicken-stealing, foot-shuffling, you know the rap—has been, alas, one of the great disasters of American civilization, and it is altogether right and proper that we should repudiate it with all our force; it does not even warrant a nostalgic backward glance. But the virulent race hatred and fear from which these phantasms were wrought were only the diseased form of a far worthier and more wholesome impulse which lay behind the music and dance of early minstrelsy, "the golden age of negro literature," Nathanson called it, which won the world in its day as jazz has in ours. These men—Rice, Sweeney, Emmett—they were not moved by hate or fear. "I Wish I Was in Dixie" is not a song of hate or fear. It is a song of love.

The feminist of our own day, comparing the oppression of blacks to the oppression of women, correctly perceives that the white fascination with the black race, as well as white racism itself, is psychologically in the nature of romantic love, being located in the same framework of contrary attitudes which promote the attraction in a way that will guarantee the subordination of object to subject, an attraction that turns into repugnance and fear when the framework collapses. In our romantic tradition, sexual love occurs upon a psychological plane determined by three points: woman's presumed weakness or inferiority, her desirability, and her inaccessibility—the moral barrier to immediate sexual possession. Because these influences couple the most powerful human passions to the highest human motives, they prove irresistible when combined in ways sanctioned by society and thought. By its implicit appeal to elevated and noble feelings, woman's traditional role imbues an original animal attraction with all the force of pride and honor, an attraction which that very pride and honor inflames and exacerbates by frustrating it with moral principles; thus the primitive biological drive cannot find its object except among the most intractable human ideals—lifelong commitments, works of art, acts of heroism. "To desire a woman," writes John Updike, "is to desire to save her."[50]

On this same psychological plane were conducted, I suspect, the relations between white and black in the pre-Civil War South, the romantic South. In the difference between black and white was an apparent biological polarity which like the sexual polarity was implicitly challenging to imagination and thought, as the many commentaries upon Afro-American life reveal by their language and tone, all the more so because the anthropological assumptions of the period, like the racism of our own day, did not distinguish culture or class from race: the Afro-American style seemed connected to the Negro as surely as femininity was connected to woman. The inferiority of the Negro, moreover, was axiomatic, even for abolitionists, and the black man soon learned to play the role expected of him, even if he did so at times ironically; *its* appeal was to the white man's power, and perhaps to his compassion and beneficience—scarcely different psychologically from the appeal of "the womanly race."

But what of animal attraction? Did the black man display qualities which the white man would have liked for himself? Can white be said to have *desired* the black?

African civilization, and Afro-American folk culture after it, has brought into the foreground of human behavior certain habits and powers which in most Europeans and Euro-Americans are undeveloped or atrophied by reason of culture and which in certain areas of life such as the musical, not to mention the ten thousand forms of human activity such as language and bodily movement which can be said to have musical properties, plainly carry the Afro-American into a position of superiority. Quickness and acuteness of perception, especially audial perception, retentive memory, a capacity to attend to many independent processes at once, a musical and richly idiomatic speech, an integrated and expressive language of gesture and movement—these are the fruits of a lifetime of improvised social performance, formal and informal, out of which aural culture is woven. Deeper than aurality lie developmental and psychomotor traits formed in mysterious ways by tradition and custom in the organic medium of consciousness. The infant who is carried all day in a sling, or in his mother's arms, her milk never withheld, constantly stimulated by her movements, her speech and song, her love and warmth—this child will develop along different lines, and with different weaknesses and strengths, than the child left for long periods in solitude and silence, supplied and denied according to patterns which acquaint him almost from the dawn of existence with the intricate clockwork of Western life.

Culture runs deep. So far no person of Anglo-American background has stepped forward to play like Louis Armstrong, or speak like Martin Luther King, or box like Muhammad Ali. It is not that we do not have our great musicians, orators, and athletes; of course we do. But in Anglo-American culture, generally speaking, these achievements come about by dint of preparation, training, discipline, practice, concentration, effort, and will, all directed at specific objectives explicitly presented to the understanding in the form, say, of a musical score, a written text, an elapsed-time figure. Among these objectives may be, paradoxically, just that kind of performance in which the Afro-American excels, such as jazz; in this effort the Anglo-American must call upon the same discipline and dedication as he does in other enterprises, among which is the power to objectify what continually eludes objectification, the Afro-American performance itself.

> Many musicians, both accompanists and soloists, have a perfectly correct idea of tempo and phrase structure and just where the notes should go, but still cannot get across the swing because their bodies betray them. It is the American Negroes who created jazz; and the number of them who are capable of complete neuro-muscular relaxation is very remarkable. This characteristic has been demonstrated in track and field events, where colored sprinters' and jumpers' ability to relax is regarded as the principal reason for their speed and agility. Some white sprinters, by dint of much work, have managed to equal them. Similarly, if a gifted white musician works assiduously at it, he may be able to play in as relaxed a way as the great colored jazzmen. The possibility exists, but examples do not abound.[51]

The white musician's success, then, may be of precisely the same kind as that of the violinist or gymnast; or it may reveal some native power in him akin to those which originally produced the Afro-American performance. Hans Nathan points out that the Afro-American dances which were often executed in states of religious ecstacy, and were in any case usually improvised and spontaneous, became for the minstrel who imitated them exercises in "precision, speed, acrobatic flexibility and endurance," and that the minstrel show, like the circus, consequently relied heavily upon "organization, virtuosity and burlesque" for its appeal.[52] For the minstrel, becoming "black" was, like sexual possession, a kind of conquest, whose impact could be sharpened by devices such as blackface which emphasized his white identity. That is why, for example, John Diamond, the minstrel dancer, challenged other whites with wagers to excel him at the heel-and-toe: "MASTER DIAMOND, who delineates the Ethopian character superior to any other *white* person, hereby challenges any person in the world to a trial of skill at Negro dancing. . . ."[53]

But no one understood the character of racial magnetism better than the minstrels themselves. Men such as George Christy and Francis Leon became famous in minstrelsy not as buffoons but as female impersonators, crossing both racial and sexual lines to become exotic creoles and "yaller gals" upon whom men could lavish the sexual fantasies respectable women did not inspire.[54] That contemporary observers noted a natural effiminancy in these men lends credence, I think, to the idea that racial imitation, too, may have been based upon a natural affinity, and that minstrelsy offered a place in society to men with some renegade element in their natures, sexual or cultural, which on the minstrel stage might receive full and free expression. That racial fascination is charged with erotic force is hardly a new idea; such is the theme of the folklore of race hatred, whose virulence could hardly arise from any other source. If in the late minstrel show, where the caricature of the Negro was most grotesque, the possession of the black identity by the white minstrel was a kind of rape, or, on the other side, a kind of auto-eroticism where the caricature was most sentimental, it was because emancipation had broken down the fragile structure by which the white man could allow himself to love the black. For let the desirable one challenge his or her objective status; let him deny his inferiority, and stand against us demanding his rights: then he becomes a source of inestimable fear, for the very powers we have implicitly acknowledged to be superior to our own are now reared as a force against us.

Do not be misled by appearances. Bluegrass music is a form of minstrelsy in this deep sense. Like the blackface minstrel, whose burnt cork betokened a fair complexion, the bluegrass musician asserts his race and culture with mountain songs, mountain vocality, and mountain instruments, masking, but not eclipsing, the deeply Africanized manner of his execution, which we hear the instant we turn our face away. In bluegrass the theatrical role of blackface has been replaced by the hillbilly mask—precisely what George Hay did in creating the Opry, with himself as interlocutor. Monroe adopted Hay's role and introduced it into his music as a structural element supplied technologically by the broadcast mike, while in his band lay the traces of the old minstrel show endmen, the rustic plantation clowns. The early bluegrass bands without exception followed his example, presenting a central figure or figures such as Lester Flatt and Earl Scruggs, or Ralph and Carter Stanley, who stood between us and the down-home string band they had brought along—the Blue Grass Boys, the Foggy Mountain Boys, the Clinch Mountain Boys—or, as disc jockeys never tire of saying, "all" the Blue Grass Boys, or "all" the Foggy Mountain boys, as if this handful of men comprised the whole community of our friends and neighbors, "ganged around" on our doorstep for a Saturday-night play party.

Now consider Bill Monroe once again. His backwoods origins and his nineteenth-century roots; his Scots-Irish heritage; his own marginal place in society; his fascination with black people and his lifelong admiration of their music; his lasting affection, indeed his love, for the great black guitarist of central Kentucky, Arnold Shultz; and, most significantly of all, his absorption into the hillbilly string band of the dynamic form of Afro-American hot jazz—though he succeeds them by a century, Kentuckian Bill Monroe belongs, spiritually, with Sweeney, Emmett, Christy, and the rest, with the pioneers of American minstrelsy.

Like blackface minstrelsy bluegrass music emphasizes the victory of the Anglo-American musician over powerful forces in himself which would prevent his successful execution of an ensemble performance in Afro-American style. The image of Monroe, costumed as southern lawman or prosperous Kentucky planter—the symbolic planter is also, implicitly, the symbolic slaveholder—is precisely parallel to the image of the minstrel in his morning coat juxtaposed with an image of himself in motley and blackface. In bluegrass music itself this same juxtaposition rises to a level of almost painful intensity, as from the string band surges a music whose whole nature is to arouse the body to dance—a driving, pulsing, multifarious music—while the musicians themselves remain stock-still and expressionless, keeping their musical forces under strict control and implicitly demanding of their audiences that the desire to dance be suppressed—a demand which, when there is space to dance available, is not always honored.

Juxtaposition: the minstrel stage, and the Grand Ole Opry after it, achieved its comic effects by means of two related devices, burlesque and caricature. Burlesque juxtaposes opposites, comedian and straight man, in a way that brings into sharp relief the familiar or characteristic traits of each, turning them, in effect, into exaggerations of themselves. Caricature is straightforward exaggeration, usually of those stereotyped traits by which the ridiculed figure is typically identified, such as blackened teeth or ill-fitting clothes. Both devices involve exaggeration, and both have critical force: the parodist is always in effect advancing a theory of what he parodies, however shallow or deep. Both are of course instruments of ridicule, generating a mood of social solidarity by uniting the audience with the interlocutor or "straight" man socially above the ridiculed figure. Our pleasure consists not only in the sense of superiority itself but in the salutary feelings that follow from it, which include a magnanimity toward our fellow being and a conviction, as Maynard Mack puts it, "that life makes immediate moral sense."[55] For ridicule of any kind always implicitly affirms those values against which the ridiculed figure compares unfavorably; hence devices of ridicule such as burlesque and caricature are likely to be found where we require affirmation of imperiled values and conditions. Blackface minstrelsy quite obviously set out to consolidate a broad spectrum of Anglo-American values against the threat of an emerging popular culture with Afro- and Irish-American roots. The Grand Ole Opry was an attempt, an ambivalent one perhaps, to encourage acceptance of the new jazz age which World War I had ushered in by looking with gentle disparagement back upon the epoch it had succeeded. It was possible to detect the grin of parody even in the routine performances of rural musicians on the Opry simply by virtue of the implied contrast to Grand Opera on the one hand and to Dixieland jazz on the other. At the outset Hay had brought to the stage *any* kind of music—brass bands, barbershop quartets, tenors and pianists, gospel quartets, Hawaiian bands, bird imitators—which smacked of the pre-war period, keeping the sense of historical contrast alive with regular performances of jazz bands such as the "Bluegrass Serenaders."

Comedy may achieve "the integration of society" punitively, by expelling the ridiculed figure, who is understood to be a source of discord; but as Frye suggests, expulsion rattles the comic mood because it makes for pathos or even tragedy: we cannot really enjoy ourselves at somebody else's expense. The festive spirit of comedy prefers to reconcile or convert the ridiculed figure, drawing him back into the social embrace which all share. The *dramatic* end of comic ridicule, then, is to explode it with some unexpected revelation of the comic figure's essential humanity. Let the rube blow into a jug to make the sound of a bass, or imitate the sounds of a fox chase or a railroad train on his harmonica, or make his fiddle sound like a jazz clarinet, and he turns the paucity of resources which is the Opry's basic joke—which, indeed, is the basic joke of minstrelsy itself—into a display of resourcefulness and wit. That is the moment at which we break into laughter: suddenly relieved of the burden of our disdain, we take another being to ourselves in recognition of him.

It is interesting to consider, then, what an outright caricature of hillbilly string-band music might consist of, and how the caricature might be exploded. Excessively high pitches, perhaps; breakneck tempos; twanging banjos and sour, wailing fiddles; songs of unabated misery, heartbreak, and sorrow sung with exaggerated nasality by poker-faced, self-conscious men in outdated, ill-fitting suits . . . no, this does not describe bluegrass—not exactly. But we will have gone halfway toward understanding bluegrass if we regard it, for the moment, as an hyperbolized form of hillbilly music. Merely compare Monroe's recording of "Whitehouse Blues" to Charlie Poole's, and you will get the point. Monroe's early performances on the Opry were energized by an effort to combat, by means of hyperbole, the Opry's implied ridicule of hillbilly music. To have accepted passively the role which the Opry, and the country music establishment generally, had cut out for him would have meant for Bill Monroe, who had never been anything but a hillbilly musician, inevitable professional decline, as the star of old-time music waned behind the glittering singing cowboys and glamorous western swing bands. Thus with unbelievably quick tempos, frighteningly high pitches, razor-keen harmonies, and sizzling instrumental breaks Monroe pressed the Opry's engines of parody to a level of performance for which they were never intended, and did so in a deadpan serious way, itself a form of hyperbole, which directed all the force of ridicule away from hillbilly music *toward the Grand Ole Opry itself*. In all these respects Monroe's strategy was precisely that of the black musicians and dancers who came to the minstrel stage after the Civil War, who could transcend the stereotype of themselves which they found there only by exaggerating it, for this was a way to parody the *parody itself*, and through it, the parodist; by meeting the parodist's stereotyped expectations of oneself in an exaggerated way we expose *him* to ridicule and rise above his stereotype: this Chaucer's Pardonner and Wife of Bath knew very well. As Ostendorf points out, black hyperbole on the minstrel stage approached surreality, as Billy Kersands filled his mouth with billiard balls and Bert Williams moped about the stage as a man called "Nobody."[56] But something similar might be said, I think, about Monroe's early performances on the Opry, which had an undertone of rage and desperation which could never have found the repose of an achieved form without some musical and dramatic resolution.

By incorporating the *social* form of Afro-American music, which from Africa to New Orleans has ever been essentially social, into a hillbilly string band whose identity was heightened by hyperbole, Monroe converted the Opry's basic joke into a source of inexhaustible power. Listen again to those early bluegrass recordings—to "Rose of Old Kentucky" or "Sweetheart You Done Me Wrong." What could seem, on the surface, more elegantly provincial, more sweetly Appalachian, more charmingly antique, than the plunking, the strumming, the tinkling and whining of the traditional instruments, the virginal high pitches of the male singers and their chime-like harmonies, the ingenuous heart songs, the picturesque folk songs of the last century? Now listen again. Listen to that mandolin and banjo, those nimble antiphonal lines, those erupting, surging rhythms, the fiddle calling to us out of its dark mouth. Hillbillies and hayseeds they may be, but my *god*, those boys can play—just the way they do down at the Dreamland Cafe.

Instrumentally and vocally bluegrass music is a thoroughgoing "process of rhythm," an Afro-American ensemble form in the body of traditional Appalachian music. As such it brings to completion the Americanization of Appalachian music, carrying it out of the mountain fastness in which the British folk legacy had been longest perserved and into the rhythmically charged atmosphere of our native music. The minstrel tradition which shaped it had itself been the fruit of a marriage between British folk music and the African manner on the American frontier, establishing over time an identification in the American imagination of our folk music with those Afro-American influences which had severed its connection to the British Isles and rooted it in the experiences of this continent. And so it has been, from Thomas D. Rice to Bill Monroe, that wherever we hear the dislocation of rhythm and meter, the relentlessly driving beat, the play of syncopation, we hear the ring of authenticity, the heart of "the old southern sound."

Like minstrel music, jazz, and rock-and-roll, bluegrass joins what Fanny Kemble, describing the dances of southern slaves, called "languishing elegance" to "painstaking laboriousness." It shares the crazy incongruity of American music, coupling stiffness and spontaneity, formality and informality, rigorous striving and cool nonchalance, whose ultimate *musical* expression is swing, in which "the feeling of relaxation does not follow a feeling of tension but is present at the same moment." By carrying out Afro-American rhythmic processes in the traditional Appalachian medium, then, bluegrass reanimates a music whose British background and wilderness setting have made it an emblem of our folk legacy with forces emanating from the Afro-American urban subculture, where the tradition whose influence has consistently determined the special character of American music has been most fully realized. In bluegrass these forces lead a new life, with a new identity; they seem to come not from New Orleans or Kansas City or Memphis or Chicago, but from the hills of old Kentucky, the primal garden of the first frontier; they seem to authenticate again a music in which we can still detect traces of the evolution of our culture, from its remotest origins to its contemporary form. Bluegrass, then, is a kind of illusion. Though "invented" some thirty-odd years ago, it seems hoary with age, for this is how we measure its emotional depth, its erotic intensity; though replete with Afro-American influences, it wears a white, and most often an Appalachian, face. But it is an illusion we can embrace and believe in, because it pleases the imagination. In the mask and motley of the musical past bluegrass overleaps the last remaining impediment in country music to the truths of the human heart which American music has over time recovered from the Afro-American tradition, revealing them to be perennial and universal. This ought to tell us what bluegrass is, this fiction with the force of truth. It is a musical myth.

In America, where peoples strange to one another are repeatedly meeting at the ever-shifting frontiers of human understanding, where out of imitation, counterfeit, caricature, and burlesque in all their outlandish vitality civilization itself springs, minstrelsy is the very image of life. Yet minstrel Bill Monroe belongs, in a sense, to the Old World, which meant to play out in the comedy of American life—stubbornly high-minded and irrepressibly crass, shamelessly vulgar and incurably heroic, by turns sublime and grotesque, ridiculous and beautiful—the happy conclusion of its own romantic dreams.

Notes

Prologue: A New Grand Ole Opry

1. Bill C. Malone, *Country Music, U.S.A.: A Fifty-Year History* (Austin: University of Texas Press, 1968), p. 195.
2. George Vescey, "Daddy Bluegrass Comes to the City," *New York Times,* Apr. 15, 1977.
3. Kenny Baker, *Kenny Baker Plays Bill Monroe.* County 761.

Chapter 1: In the Hills of Old Kentucky: The Social Background

1. Except where noted, all biographical details come from Ralph Rinzler, "Bill Monroe," in *Stars of Country Music: Uncle Dave Macon to Johnny Rodriguez,* ed. Bill C. Malone and Judith McCulloh (Urbana: University of Illinois Press, 1975), pp. 202-19.
2. Claudia Lewis, *Children of the Cumberland* (New York: Columbia University Press, 1946), p. 54, 66.
3. Bill Monroe, interview with author, York, Pa., Apr. 1977.
4. Lewis, *Children of the Cumberland,* p. 194.
5. Ibid., pp. 70-71, 84.
6. Bill Monroe, York interview.
7. Lewis, *Children of the Cumberland,* pp. xv, 116.
8. Bill Monroe, York interview.
9. Lewis, *Children of the Cumberland,* pp. 145-46.
10. Birch Monroe, interview with author, June 1977.
11. James Rooney, *Bossmen: Bill Monroe and Muddy Waters* (New York: Hayden Book Co., 1971), p. 21.
12. Herb Wells, "Uncle Pen," *Bluegrass Unlimited* 8(Sept. 1973):15.
13. Birch Monroe, interview, June 1977.
14. See David Lamoreaux, "Baseball in the Late Nineteenth Century: The Source of Its Appeal," *Journal of Popular Culture* 11 (Winter 1977):597-613.
15. Rooney, *Bossmen,* p. 36.
16. Melvin Borstein, "Analysis of a Congenitally Blind Musician," *Psychoanalytic Quarterly* 46(1977):23-27.
17. Lewis, *Children of the Cumberland,* pp. 190-94.
18. Josiah H. Combs, *Folk-Songs of the United States.* Ed. D. K. Wilgus (Austin: University of Texas Press, 1967; originally *Folk-Songs des Midi États-Unis* [Paris: University of Paris, 1925]), pp. 100-101.

19. Alan Lomax, *The Folk Songs of North America* (Garden City, N.J.: Doubleday, 1960), p. xxiv.

20. See Archie Green and Ed Kahn, interview with Virginia Gertrude Carter Hobbs and Ruth Hobbs White, Aug. 12, 1963, Roanoake, Va. John Edwards Memorial Foundation files (hereafter abbreviated JEMF).

21. Rooney, *Bossmen*, p. 22.

22. Ibid., p. 24.

23. Ibid., p. 25.

24. Mr. Lightfoot has very kindly provided me with a copy of his paper on Arnold Schultz, delivered at the annual meeting of the American Folklore Society, Oct. 17, 1980, Pittsburgh, Pa. See also Keith Lawrence, "Arnold Shultz: The Greatest (?) Guitar Picker's Life Ended before Promise Realized," *JEMF Quarterly* 17 (Spring 1981). This article includes an extraordinary photograph of Shultz. Reprinted from Owensboro, Ky. *Messenger-Inquirer*, Mar. 2, 1980. Lawrence's research corroborates Lightfoot's conjectures. Shultz apparently died in 1931 of a mitral lesion, a heart disease.

25. Rooney, *Bossmen*, pp. 36-37.

26. Ibid., pp. 23-24.

27. Ibid., p. 28.

28. Erik Erikson, *Identity and the Life Cycle* (New York: International Universities Press, 1959).

29. Ibid., p. 70.

30. Alice Foster, "My Life in Bluegrass: An Interview with Bill Monroe," *Newport Folk Festival Program*, 1969, p. 16.

31. Bill Monroe, York interview.

32. ©1951 by Hill and Range Songs, Inc.

33. Bill Monroe, interview with author, Fairfax, Va., Apr. 1977.

34. Bill Monroe, interview with Frank W. Martin, *People* magazine.

35. Quoted by Ralph Rinzler in sleeve notes to *The High Lonesome Sound*. Decca DL7-4780.

36. Maud Karpeles, *Cecil Sharp: His Life and Work* (Chicago: University of Chicago Press, 1967), p. 151.

37. Arthur Moore, *The Frontier Mind* (Lexington: University of Kentucky Press, 1957), p. 229.

38. William Faux, *Memorable Days in America*, quoted in Moore, *The Frontier Mind*, p. 110.

Chapter 2. Hillbilly Music: The Commercial Background

1. Harold M. Mayer and Richard Wade, *Chicago: Growth of a Metropolis* (Chicago: University of Chicago Press, 1969), pp. 244-350. This book provides an excellent photographic record, as well as a narrative, of the city's growth and change.

2. Rinzler, "Bill Monroe," p. 209.

3. See *Historic City: The Settlement of Chicago* (Chicago: Department of

Development and Planning, 1976), p. 70. Figures from the 1930 census show that roughly one-tenth of the Indiana urban population, and one-twentieth of the Illinois urban population, had been born in the middle South—Kentucky, Tennessee, Alabama, and Mississippi. In urban Indiana, over 97,000 people reported Kentucky as their birthplace in 1930, as compared to roughly 26,000 from Tennessee, 6,000 from Georgia, 7,000 from Alabama and 8,000 from Mississippi. Urban Illinois figures show approximately equivalent figures for Kentucky and Tennessee (65,000 and 53,000 respectively), with much higher numbers from the deep South, reflecting the black exodus. (see U.S. Census, 1930, vol. 3, pp. 187-90.) Having grown up in the Calumet region myself I can describe it from memory; I counted many Tennesseeans and Kentuckians among my neighbors and schoolmates, while my own community was bordered on the north and west by black communities which could easily have been transplanted *in toto* from Mississippi or Alabama. Hillbilly and black gospel music divided the radio dial between them.

4. Rooney, *Bossmen*, pp. 21, 26-27.

5. With the help of Birch Monroe, whom I interviewed on July 11, 1978, I have pieced this account together from several sources: Rinzler, "Bill Monroe," p. 209; Rooney, *Bossmen*, p. 27; Malone, *Country Music, U.S.A.*, pp. 68, 72, and especially from Neil Rosenberg's biographical sketch in *Bill Monroe and His Blue Grass Boys: An Illustrated Discography* (Nashville: Country Music Foundation Press, 1974), p. 15. See also Ivan Tribe, "Charlie Monroe," *Bluegrass Unlimited* 10(Oct. 1975):12-19.

6. Malone, *Country Music, U.S.A.*, p. 36.

7. Douglas B. Green, *Country Roots: The Origins of Country Music*(New York: Hawthorn Books, 1976), p. 119. Also Rinzler, "Bill Monroe," p. 209.

8. Malone, *Country Music, U.S.A.*, pp. 68-70; Green, *Country Roots*, p. 25. I rely chiefly upon Malone's account of the Barn Dance, and my own recollection of it.

9. Sears, Roebuck and Co., "Musical Instruments," (Chicago, 1910), pp. 756-60.

10. Ivan Tribe, "The Hillbilly versus the City: Urban Images in Country Music," *JEMF Quarterly* 10(Summer 1974):41-51.

11. I have this from Neil Rosenberg, whose information is based upon an interview with Birch Monroe.

12. See Gilbert Chase, *America's Music: From the Pilgrims to the Present*, rev. 2nd ed. (New York: McGraw-Hill, 1966), pp. 481-83. The sources which trace the Chicago style are too numerous to cite here; all, or nearly all, the works I consulted will be cited elsewhere or in the bibliography. A good basic account will be found in the current edition of the *Encyclopedia Britannica*, written by the jazz critic of the *London Times*, Benny Green.

13. *Bill Monroe Sings Bluegrass, Body and Soul*. MCA 2251.

14. Chase, *America's Music*, p. 481. Nolan Porterfield informed me about the popularity of "Milneburg Joys."

15. See Lawrence W. Levine, *Black Culture and Black Consciousness: Afro-American Folk Thought from Slavery to Freedom* (New York: Oxford

University Press, 1977), pp. 30-55, 138-90. This book is unsurpassed as a history of black folk culture.

16. Rinzler, "Bill Monroe," pp. 209-10.

17. For a fascinating first-hand account of the rural medicine show, see Ralph Rinzler's notes to *Old Time Music at Clarence Ashley's*. Folkways FA 2355.

18. Rinzler, "Bill Monroe," pp. 210, 211.

19. Alice Foster, "Kenny Baker" [interview], *Bluegrass Unlimited* 3 (Dec. 1968):11.

20. This very precise word is Rinzler's.

21. Quoted in Charles K. Wolfe, "Bluegrass Touches," *Old Time Music* 16(Spring 1978).

22. If you are prepared to deal with ethnomusicological jargon, see Linda Burman-Hall, "Southern American Folk Fiddle Styles," JEMF Reprint Series, no. 32, reprinted from *Ethnomusicology* 19(Jan. 1975):58.

23. Rinzler, "Bill Monroe," p. 210.

24. "Soldier's Joy," reissued on *Ballads and Breakdowns of the Golden Era*. Columbia CS9660. Originally recorded 10/29/29, in Atlanta.

25. See Green, *Country Roots*, p. 57.

26. "Paddy, Won't You Drink Some Cider," reissued on *Ballads and Breakdowns of the Golden Era*. Originally recorded 10/26/28, in Atlanta.

27. "Bill Mason," also on *Ballads and Breakdowns*. Originally recorded 5/6/29, in New York.

28. See Robert Winans, "The Folk, the Stage, and the Five-String Banjo in the Nineteenth Century," *Journal of American Folklore* 89(1976):407-37. This remarkable piece of original scholarship, which has influenced the conception of this book more than any other single book or article, conclusively links mountain clawhammer banjo to the black-derived minstrel style, and argues persuasively that folk finger-picking styles had their origin in classical guitar styles late in the nineteenth century. Winans has mentioned to me one Dana Johnson, a white ragtime banjo player from Randleman, North Carolina, who won the banjo contest at the 1904 St. Louis World's Fair, "and who was Charlie Poole's real inspiration and idol."

29. Clifford Kinney Rorrer, *Charlie Poole and the North Carolina Ramblers*, (Eden, N.C.: privately printed, 1968), p. 1.

30. Anne and Norm Cohen, "Folk and Hillbilly Music: Further Thoughts on Their Relation," *JEMF Quarterly* 13(Summer 1977):53.

31. See Archie Green's biography and discussion of the Carter Family in *Only a Miner: Studies in Recorded Coal-Mining Songs* (Urbana: University of Illinois Press, 1972), pp. 388-98.

32. Letter from Vergie Gertrude Carter Hobbs and Mrs. Ruth Hobbs White to Archie Green and Ed Kahn, Aug. 12, 1963. JEMF files, p. 2.

33. Ibid., p. 2.

34. Rinzler, "Bill Monroe," p. 210.

35. Malone, *Country Music*, pp. 34-35.

36. Brad McKuen, "The Monroe Brothers on Record," *Country Directory*, no. 2 (n.d.), pp. 14-16. JEMF files. See also Archie Green's discussion of "Nine

Pound Hammer" and "Roll on Buddy" in *Only a Miner*, pp. 279-85, 336-39, and 344-63. Note the strong Monroe Brothers influence on an early West Virginia bluegrass band, The Lilly Brothers, on Folkways FA 2433, *Folk Songs from the Southern Mountains;* Folkways FA 2318, *Mountain Music Bluegrass Style*, and County 729, *The Early Recordings of the Lilly Brothers.*

37. Quoted in Nancy Heller and Julie Williams, *The Regionalists*, (New York: Watson-Guptill Publications, 1976), p. 136. The Benton paintings cited below, except for "The Origins of Country Music," are all reproduced in that book. For a discussion of Benton's interest in folk culture, which included his playing harmonica in an old-time band, see Archie Green, "Thomas Hart Benton's Folk Musicians," Commercial Music Graphics Series, no. 37, *JEMF Quarterly* 12(Summer 1976):74-165.

Chapter 3. Folk Music in Overdrive: The Musical Moment

1. Mayne Smith's phrase, quoted in Malone, *Country Music, U.S.A.*, p. 310.

2. Listen to the juxtaposition of these two recordings on the *Smithsonian Collection of Classic Jazz* (1973), ed. Martin Williams.

3. Alan Lomax, "Bluegrass Background: Folk Music with Overdrive," *Esquire* 52(Oct. 1959):108.

4. See Jay Bailey, "Historical Origin and Stylistic Developments of the Five-String Banjo," *Journal of American Folklore* 85(1972):58-65; and Dena Epstein, "The Folk Banjo: A Documentary History," *Ethnomusicology* 19 (Sept. 1975):347-71. JEMF Reprint, no. 33.

5. Ralph Rinzler, "Bill Monroe: The Daddy of Bluegrass Music," *Sing Out* 13 (Feb.-Mar. 1963):8 (hereafter, Rinzler, "The Daddy of Bluegrass Music").

6. William Henry Koon, "Newgrass, Oldgrass, and Bluegrass," *JEMF Quarterly* 10(Spring 1974):16.

7. Ralph Rinzler in conversation.

8. Rinzler, "Bill Monroe," p. 204.

9. Ralph Rinzler in conversation.

10. Rinzler, "Bill Monroe," p. 204.

11. James Rooney, *Bossmen*, pp. 71-81.

12. *The High Lonesome Sound.* Decca DL7-4780; also MCA 110.

13. Robert Cantwell, "Believing in Bluegrass," *Atlantic* 229(Mar. 1972):52-60.

14. Mayne Smith, "An Introduction to Bluegrass," *Journal of American Folklore* 78(1965):245-56. JEMF Reprint, no. 6. What follows is a paraphrase—I hope a fair one—of Smith's essay. For the sake of clarity I have taken considerable liberties with the organization of his essay.

15. Mike Seeger, liner notes to *Mountain Music Bluegrass Style*, Folkways FA 2178, p. 1.

16. See Robert Winans, "Early Minstrel Show Music, 1843-1852," (forthcoming). Winans notes that the minstrel banjos, with fretless necks, a larger

head diameter, and gut strings made a far mellower sound than modern banjos, especially because they were tuned at least a fourth lower, and consequently provided a richer foundation tone than is usually supposed. Winans argues convincingly that without the banjo the sound of the minstrel band would have become shallow and noisy.

17. See the highly interesting discussion of the Virginia Minstrels in Hans Nathan, *Dan Emmett and the Rise of Early Negro Minstrelsy* (Norman: University of Oklahoma Press, 1962), pp. 123-24.

18. Malone, *Country Music, U.S.A.* p. 78.

19. Ralph Rinzler played these tapes for me. Neil Rosenberg informs me that this music is available on a bootleg record album, *Bill Monroe and the Bluegrass Boys, Radio Shows, 1946-48*. Bluegrass Classics BGC 80.

20. See Green, *Country Roots*, chapt. 8, "Western Swing," pp. 131-43.

21. Malone, *Country Music, U.S.A.*, pp. 166, 170-71.

22. I have this from Neil Rosenberg.

23. Rooney, *Bossmen*, p. 32.

24. Ibid., p. 33.

25. Malone, *Country Music, U.S.A.*, pp. 75-77.

26. Ibid., pp. 205, 206.

27. See Don Rhodes, "Roy Acuff, the Real Speckled Bird," *Bluegrass Unlimited* 13 (May 1979):14-20.

28. See D. Green, "Western Swing," in *Country Roots*.

29. Neil Rosenberg, "A Brief Survey of Bluegrass Haberdashery," *Bluegrass Unlimited* 3(Mar. 1968).

30. Rooney, *Bossmen*, p. 37.

31. Reissued on *Blue Grass Music: Bill Monroe and his Blue Grass Boys*. RCA Camden CAL 719. See also Rosenberg, *Bill Monroe and his Bluegrass Boys*, p. 29.

32. Hutchinson, Justice, and Greene can be heard on *Mountain Blues*, County 511.

33. Rooney, *Bossmen*, p. 33.

34. D. Green, *Country Roots*, p. 119.

35. Rinzler, "Bill Monroe," p. 212.

36. I have heard that southern blacks used to sing this song in their funeral processions.

37. Rooney, *Bossmen*, pp. 35-36.

38. Foster, "My Life in Bluegrass." According to Neil Rosenberg, Akeman took up a two-finger style similar to Wade Mainer's shortly after joining the Blue Grass Boys, information whose original source was Clyde Moody.

39. Rosenberg has described the activity of this period closely in "From Sound to Style: The Emergence of Bluegrass," *Journal of American Folklore* 80(1967):143-50. JEMF Reprint, no. 11.

40. Rinzler, "Bill Monroe," p. 203.

41. Rooney, *Bossmen*, p. 49.

42. Ibid., p. 42.

Chapter 4. Banjo: African Rhythms and the Bluegrass Beat

1. Thomas Jefferson, *Notes on the State of Virginia, written in the year 1781.* Paris. Quoted in Epstein, "The Folk Banjo." Except where noted I am indebted to Epstein's article for the historical account of the banjo which follows.

2. Quoted in Epstein, Ibid., p. 353.

3. Winans, "The Folk, the Stage, and the Five-String Banjo in the Nineteenth Century," pp. 407-37. See also his "Early American Minstrel Music, 1843-1852" (forthcoming).

4. Henri Herz, *My Travels in America.* Trans. Henry Bertram Hall (Madison, Wis.: Historical Society, 1963). Originally published in Paris, 1866, as *Mes Voyages en Amerique.* Quoted in Epstein, "The Folk Banjo," p. 127.

5. Quoted in Winans, "The Folk, the Stage, and the Five-String Banjo in the Nineteenth Century," p. 409.

6. Richard Alan Waterman, "African Influence in the Music of the Americas," in *Acculturation in the Americas* Ed., Sol Tax (Chicago: University of Chicago Press, 1952), pp. 204-18. This seminal article has been the basis of much reflection upon the relation between African music and jazz. See also Alan Merriam, *African Music on L.P.: An Annotated Discography* (Evanston, Ill.: Northwestern University Press, 1970). Quoted in John Storm Roberts, *Black Music of Two Worlds* (New York: William Morrow, 1972), p. 11.

7. Robert Anderson, *From Slavery to Affluence: Memoirs of an Ex-Slave,* by Daisy Anderson Leonard, 1927 (reproduced in Steamboat Springs, Colo.: *Steamboat Pilot,* 1967), pp. 24-25. Quoted in Epstein, *Sinful Tunes and Spirituals,* p. 296.

8. In James Joyce, *Portrait of the Artist.*

9. Waterman, "African Influence in the Music of the Americas."

10. A. M. Jones, *Studies in African Music.* 2 vols. (London: Oxford University Press, 1959), vol. 1. My own discussion of African music has Jones's remarkable work as its foundation; I was led to it by Gunther Schuller's insightful—and I think unsurpassed—discussion of the relationships of African music to jazz in *Early Jazz: Its Roots and Musical Development* (New York: Oxford University Press, 1968). Jones's book so richly explores and illumines the nature of African music, and is so full of implication concerning Afro-American music, that I regret having to hide him back here in my notes. As regards the present point, Jones writes: *"it is the claps* [hand clapping rhythms accompanying a children's play-song] *which are the time-backbone of the song:* the bars do not exist so far as the African is concerned [p. 17]. The claps carry no accent whatever in the African mind. They serve as a yardstick, a kind of metronome which exists behind the music. Once the clap has started you can never, on any pretext whatever, stretch or diminish the clap-values. They remain constant and they *do not impart any rhythm to the melody itself"* (p. 21).

11. A. M. Jones, quoted in Paul Oliver, *Savannah Syncopators: African*

Retentions in the Blues (London: Studio Vista, 1970), p. 27. Father Jones pursues this point in *Studies*: "The melody being additive, and the claps being divisive, when put together they result in a combination of rhythms whose inherent stresses are *crossed*. This is the very essence of African music: this is what the African is after. He wants to enjoy the conflict of rhythms" (p. 21).

12. Jones, *Studies in African Music*, p. 9. Jones amplifies the point as follows: "African drum-beats vary not only in pitch but also in quality. If the wrong quality of note is played in any particular drum-pattern, that pattern is no longer what it is intended to be and becomes another pattern." Jones's informant, Ewe master drummer Desmond Tay, notes that, even in the rare cases of coinciding rhythms, "though they play the same pattern, as they each play it on a different pitch, they can be heard separately and therefore it sounds well" (p. 86). This point, which speaks directly to the character of Afro-American music, cannot be emphasized enough.

13. "We know further that he does not realize that the *number* of claps determines within fairly defined limits the length of the phrases of the song. . . ." Jones, *Studies in African Music*, p. 20.

14. "Normally speaking," Jones writes, "African music is all built up on a basis of small equal-time units . . . all rhythms are compounded of notes whose value is a simple multiple of the basic unit of time, and . . . the whole complex structure rests on this simple mathematical basis." Ibid., p. 24.

15. I adopt the term *fundamental rhythm*, which means the European meter in an explicit audible form, from Jan Slawe, *Versuch einer Definition der Jazzmusik*, quoted in Joachim Berendt, *The Jazz Book*. Trans., Dag Morgenstern (St. Albans, Herefordshire, England: Granada Publishers, 1976), p. 171.

16. This is a brief summary of Berendt's helpful discussion of jazz syncopation and swing.

17. John Work, *American Negro Songs and Spirituals* (New York: Bonanza Books, 1940), quoted in Roberts, *Black Music of Two Worlds*, p. 164. Cf. Jones's observation that "African Melodies are additive: their time-background is divisive," in *Studies in African Music*, p. 49.

18. Nathan, *Dan Emmett and the Rise of Early Negro Minstrelsy*, p. 127.

19. See Earl Scruggs, *Earl Scruggs and the Five-String Banjo* (New York: Peer International Corp., 1968), and Peter Wernick, *Bluegrass Banjo* (New York: Oak Publications, 1975). These are only two of a number of available handbooks. A careful musicological analysis will be found in James D. Green, Jr., "A Musical Analysis of the Banjo Style of Earl Scruggs: An Examination of *Country Music* (MG 20358)," in *Journal of Country Music* 5(Spring 1974). This record album, *Country Music*, includes Scruggs's classic banjo tour de force, "Foggy Mountain Breakdown."

20. Scruggs, *Earl Scruggs and the Five-String Banjo*, p. 30.

21. Jones, *Studies in African Music*, p. 102. "African phrases are built up of the numbers 2 or 3, or their multiples: or a combination of 2 and 3 or the multiples of this combination" (p. 17). "To beat 3 against 2 is to them no

different from beating on the first beat of each bar," Jones adds (p. 46), describing the 3 against 2 pattern as "part and parcel of their musical vocabulary." The rhythmic figure itself I take from Roberts, *Black Music of Two Worlds*, p. 164, who has noted the same phenomenon at work in Afro-American music. He emphasizes what he calls the "three-on-two metrical phenomenon of West African music" throughout his book, which might be described as a history of this rhythmic figure and its transformations, especially in the Caribbean.

22. Roberts, *Black Music of Two Worlds*, p. 164.

23. André Hodeir, *Jazz: Its Evolution and Essence*. Trans. David Noakes (New York: Grove Press, 1956), p. 200.

24. Frederick J. Bacon, *Seigel-Meyers Correspondence School of Music, Banjo Lesson No. 4* (Chicago, 1904). In the JEMF files.

25. Recalled by Mary A. Livermore, a Civil War nurse. Epstein, "The Folk Banjo," p. 357.

26. Epstein reproduces this picture on p. 362 of her article; it also appears in Nathan's *Dan Emmett*, p. 159. The painting was found at Columbia, South Carolina, and hangs at Colonial Williamsburg.

27. Jones, *Studies in African Music*, p. 206.

28. See Robert Toll, *Blacking Up: The Minstrel Show in Nineteenth-Century America* (New York: Oxford University Press, 1974), chap. 7, "Black Men Take to the Stage."

29. Chase, *America's Music*, pp. 438-39.

30. Winans, "Early Minstrel Show Music," p. 428.

31. C. P. Heaton, "The Five-String Banjo in North Carolina," *Southern Folklore* 35(1971), and Malone, *Country Music U.S.A.*, p. 315.

32. I have this from Sandy Rothman, banjo player and friend of Earl Scruggs.

33. Schuller, *Early Jazz*, p. 24.

34. Ibid., pp. 134-74. See also Alan Lomax, *Mister Jelly Roll: The Fortunes of Jelly Roll Morton, New Orleans Creole and "Inventor of Jazz"* (Berkeley: University of California Press, 1956).

35. On sleeve notes to *Bill Monroe with Lester Flatt and Earl Scruggs, the "Original Bluegrass Band"*, Rounder Special Series 06.

36. Rooney, *Bossmen*, p. 43.

37. Former Blue Grass Boy Peter Rowan recalls this in an interview with Doug Benson, "Bill Monroe, King of Bluegrass Music," Radio McGill interviews, 1966-67, printed in *Bluegrass Unlimited* 2(June 1968). Rowan also recalls Monroe playing his mandolin to the rhythm of horses' hooves. In my interview with Monroe at Capitol Center, April 1977, Monroe emphasized the necessity for a musician to know the rhythms of the various ballroom dances, mentioning the waltz, the fox trot, and the rhumba.

38. Eddie Condon, *We Called It Music*, quoted in Levine, *Black Culture and Black Consciousness*, pp. 294-95.

39. Schuller, *Early Jazz*, p. 7.

40. André Hodeir, *Jazz: Its Evolution and Essence*, p. 196.

41. See Mayne Smith's "An Introduction to Bluegrass," pp. 245-46.
42. Schuller, *Early Jazz*, pp.159-60.

Chapter 5. Ancient Tones: The Roots of Southern Song

1. The thirds, the sixth, and the seventh in the acoustically pure scale, which is generated out of thirds and fifths, differ by a very significant 22% from their equivalents in the Pythagorean scale, which is generated out of fifths only: the minor third sharper, the major third, sixth and seventh all flatter. This can be calculated from the actual frequencies; see the *Harvard Dictionary of Music*, under "Intervals."

2. An introduction to the modes and their history will be found in any good encyclopedia. For a fuller discussion, see Marie Pierik, *The Song of the Church* (New York: Longman's, Green, 1947), upon which part of my account is based. Willie Apel's *Gregorian Chant* (London: Burns & Oates, 1958) is an exhaustive work on the subject. Anne Dhu Shapiro offers a convenient history of the application of modal nomenclature to British-American folk song (a practice begun in earnest less than a century ago in the late 1890s by Cecil Sharp and other members of the English Folk Song Society) in "The Tune-Family Concept in British-American Folk-Song Scholarship" (Ph.D. diss., Harvard University, 1975), pp. 231-53.

3. See John Powell's preface to George Pullen Jackson's *Spiritual Folk-Songs of Early America* (Locust Valley, N.Y.: J.J. Augustin, 1937), p. vii.

4. Henry Edward Krehbiel, *Afro-American Folksongs: A Study in Racial and National Music* (New York: F. Ungar, 1913, 1974), pp. 74, 93.

5. Marshall Stearns, *The Story of Jazz* (New York: Oxford University Press, 1956), p. 138.

6. Winthrop Sargeant in *Jazz: Hot and Hybrid* (New York: DaCapo Press, 1975) describes the blues scale this way, as two tetrachords:

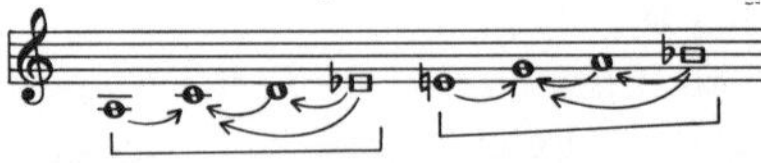

(p. 167). There is considerable general agreement as to the nature of folk tonality, especially in regard to the third and the seventh. Krehbiel notes that in all folk music the third and the seventh tend to flat, the fourth to sharp (p. 70); this sharping of the fourth is common in the blues. Nicholas G. J. Ballanta, in *Saint Helena Island Spirituals* (New York: 1925) argues that the "African" pentatonic arises from a rudimentary harmonic sense of a fifth above and a fourth below any given tone. He also notes, incidentally, that African rhythm is based on "vibration" rather than pulse, and that this explains the effect of two or four against three. Quoted in D. K. Wilgus, *Anglo-American Folksong Scholarship since 1898* (New Brunswick, N.J.: Rutgers University Press, 1959), p. 351.

7. I have this from Archie Green.

8. George Pullen Jackson, *White and Negro Spirituals: Their Life Span and Kinship* (Locust Valley, N.Y.: J.J. Augustin, 1943), p. 241. Jackson quotes Cecil Sharp, who notes that the English folksinger, too, "not having any set notion with regard to the third note of the scale, varies it according to the character of the phrase in which it happens to occur," in *English Folk Song: Some Conclusions,* in Jackson, p. 237.

9. Anton Dvorák, "Music in America," *Harper's New Monthly Magazine* 90(Feb. 1895):428-34.

10. Lomax, *Folk Songs of North America,* p. 494.

11. Quoted in Eileen Southern, *The Music of Black Americans: A History* (New York: W.W. Norton, 1971), pp. 95-96.

12. Nathan, *Dan Emmett,* p. 180.

13. Y. S. Nathanson, "Negro Minstrelsy, Ancient and Modern," *Putnam's Monthly* 5(Jan. 1855):72-79. The *Putnam's* piece appears anonymously; Bruce Jackson attributes it to Nathanson in *The Negro and His Folklore in Nineteenth-Century Periodicals* (Austin: University of Texas Press, 1967), p. 42. Apparently the essay appeared under Nathanson's name in a later collection.

14. See Nathan's excellent discussion of "Dixie" in *Dan Emmett.*

15. Nathanson, "Negro Minstrelsy," quoted in Jackson, *The Negro and His Folklore,* p. 38.

16. See D. K. Wilgus, "'Ten Broeck and Mollie': A Race and a Ballad," *Kentucky Folklore Record* 2(1956):77-89.

17. Quoted by Ralph Rinzler on sleeve notes to *The High Lonesome Sound of Bill Monroe and the Blue Grass Boys,* Decca DL 7-4780 and MCA-110.

18. A. L. Lloyd, *Folk Song in England* (St. Albans, Hertfordshire, England: Granada Publishers, Ltd., 1975), p. 165.

19. Nathan, *Dan Emmett,* p. 180.

20. Alan Lomax has made a juxtaposition of these recordings which illustrates this point very powerfully; it is of a Lousiana prison blues and a Senegalese chant, on *Roots of the Blues,* New World Records 252, part of the Rockefeller Bicentennial Series.

21. Rinzler, "Bill Monroe," p. 207.

22. Quoted in Peter Wernick, *Bluegrass Songbook* (New York: Oak Publications, 1976), p. 16.

23. Sharp, *English Folk Song.*

24. Combs, *Folk-Songs of the Southern United States,* p. 88.

25. Jean Ritchie, interview with the author, Gambier, Ohio, Oct. 1975.

26. Quoted in Southern, *The Music of Black Americans,* p. 49.

27. Quoted in Harold Courlander, *Negro Folk Music U.S.A.* (New York: Columbia University Press, 1963), p. 118.

28. Alan Lomax, *Folk Songs of North America,* p. 155.

29. For these comparisons I am indebted to English folklorist Peter Kennedy, who answered my questions with a wide variety of British folk songs recorded in the field.

30. Cecil Sharp, *English Folk Songs from the Southern Appalachians.* Ed. Maud Karpeles (London: 1932), pp. xxvi-xxvii.

31. G. B. Chambers, *Folksong-Plainsong: A Study in Origins and Musical Relationships* (London: 1956), p. 94.

32. Quoted in Ibid., p. 23.

33. Ibid., p. 33.

34. See Pierik, *The Song of the Church*, p. 54ff.

35. See Jackson, *Spiritual Folksongs*, p. 5; *White and Negro Spirituals*, pp. 251-52; and Lomax, *Folk Songs of North America*, p. 239. See also Lomax's sleeve notes to *The Gospel Ship*, New World Records 294, in the Rockefeller Series.

36. Horton Davies, *Worship and Theology in England: From Andrews to Baxter and Fox, 1603-1690*. 4 vols. (Princeton, N.J.: Princeton University Press, 1975) 3:270.

37. John C. Campbell, *The Southern Highlander and His Homeland* (Louisville, 1921, 1969), p. 162ff. Also Jackson, *Spiritual Folk Songs*, p. 6, *White and Negro Spirituals*, p. 30.

38. Quoted in Dena Epstein, *Sinful Tunes and Spirituals* (Urbana: University of Illinois Press, 1977), p. 106. This splendid book is essential for anyone interested in Afro-American and southern music.

39. Quoted in Southern, *The Music of Black Americans*, p. 59.

40. Ibid., p. 68.

41. Jackson, *White and Negro Spirituals*, pp. 248-49.

42. Morris's essay will be found in the booklet accompanying the *Smithsonian Collection of Classic Country Music* (Washington, D.C.: Smithsonian Institute, 1981).

43. Frederick Law Olmstead, *New York Daily Times* (1853), cited in Courlander, *Negro Folk Music U.S.A.*, p. 83.

44. In fact "Train on the Island," which can be heard on vol. 3 of *Anthology of American Folk Music*, Folkways FA 2953, may be descended from a plantation corn-shucking song, "Cowboy on Middle's Island," which was printed in *Putnam's Monthly* in 1855. It is related to the fiddle tune "June Apple." Also see Chase, *America's Music*, p. 280.

45. See Ruth Finnegan, "The Social, Linguistic and Literary Background," chap. 3 of her *Oral Literature in Africa* (Oxford: Oxford University Press, 1970), pp. 48-80; and also Jones's "Tone and Tune," chap. 10 of *Studies in African Music*, pp. 230-51. Jones discusses the speech-song alliance extensively, noting relationships not only in melody but in dynamics and even in breathing—the Ewe drummer plays the drum as if it had, like a speaker, only enough breath for phrases of a certain length. See also Walter Ong, "The African Talking Drum and Oral Noetics," *New Literary History* 8(Spring 1977):411-29. *Every* writer on African music emphasizes these points.

46. Quoted in Roberts, *Black Music of Two Worlds*, p. 7.

47. Mary Kingsley, *West African Studies*, pp. 53-54, quoted in Levine, *Black Culture and Black Consciousness*, p. 157.

48. Quoted in Rinzler's sleeve notes, *High Lonesome Sound*.

49. Quoted in Roberts, *Black Music of Two Worlds*, p. 189.

50. W. B. Yeats, "The Symbolism of Poetry."

51. Bill Monroe, interview with Hazel Dickens and Alice Foster, Sunset Park, West Grove, Pa., Sept. 1968.

Chapter 6. Upstairs, Downstairs, out in the Kitchen: The Tradition

1. Rosenberg, "From Sound to Style." I follow Rosenberg's account.

2. Ibid., p. 147.

3. Mike Seeger, liner notes to *Mountain Music Bluegrass Style*, p. 2.

4. Thomas Adler, "Manual Formulaic Composition: Innovation in Bluegrass Banjo Styles," *Journal of Country Music* 5(Summer 1974). Adler's Ph.D. thesis in folklore, University of Indiana, 1981, explores the acquisition of skills on the bluegrass banjo and compares it to the processes of language-learning.

5. Quoted in Wernick, *Bluegrass Songbook*, p. 8.

Chapter 7. Workin' Music: Bluegrass and Jazz

1. See chap. 4, note 38.

2. Ralph Stanley, interview with author, Columbus, Ohio, Dec. 1975.

3. Keith Whitley, interview with author, Gambier, Ohio, Oct. 1977.

4. Bill Monroe in "My Life in Bluegrass," interview with Alice Foster, Newport Folk Festival Program, 1969, p. 15.

5. Quoted in "The Rich-R-Tone Story: The Early Days of Bluegrass, Vol. 5," Rounder Records 1017. p. 8.

6. Monroe in "My Life in Bluegrass," p. 17.

7. "The Rich-R-Tone Story," p. 8.

8. Rooney, *Bossmen*, pp. 41, 61.

9. Ibid., p. 59.

10. Ibid., p. 83.

11. Quoted by Neil Rosenberg in sleeve notes to *Bill Monroe with Lester Flatt and Earl Scruggs*.

12. See Ronnie Lundy, "The New Grass Revival," *Bluegrass Unlimited* 13(Nov. 1978):10-15.

13. Ibid., 13.

14. Ibid., 14.

15. Quoted in Joachim Berendt, *The Jazz Book*, p. 168.

16. Lundy, "The New Grass revival," 14.

17. Ibid., 14.

*Chapter 8. Old Time Music: Parlor Books, the Phonograph,
and Folk Revivalism*

1. Quoted by Green in *Country Roots*, p. 57.
2. These are transcribed from Jarrell's album *Sail Away Ladies*. County
756.
3. Bob Baker, introducing "Little Willie," on *Mountain Music Bluegrass
Style*. Folkways FA 2318.
4. "How the Market Votes," transcript of television program "Wall Street
Week" with Louis Rukeyser, no. 1010, Sept. 5, 1980 (Maryland Center for
Public Broadcasting, Owings Mills, Maryland).
5. As of this writing Peter Wernick's *Bluegrass Banjo* has sold over 100,000
copies.
6. See Robert Conot, *A Streak of Luck: The Life and Legend of Thomas
Alva Edison* (New York: Seaview Press, 1979). Except where noted my account of the invention of the phonograph follows Conot's.
7. Ibid., p. 107.
8. Ibid., p. 100.
9. "Recording Industry Turns 100," *Los Angeles Times*, Nov. 16, 1977.
10. "Edison's Fabulous Phonograph," *Historical Associates*, chapbook in
JEMF files.
11. See *Virginia Traditions: Non-Blues Secular Black Music*, BRI-001.
Notes by Kip Lornell. (Blue Ridge Institute, Ferrum College, Ferrum, Va.)
p. 3.
12. For the idea that an artist must "exploit his medium" I am indebted to
Prof. Ted Cohen, of the University of Chicago, who expounded the idea in a
lecture delivered at Kenyon College in 1972. The argument I bring to bear
upon the idea, however, is my own. Prof. Cohen's highly interesting aesthetics
are based in part upon the work of the linguist A. R. Austin.
13. See Archie Green's account in *Only a Miner*, pp. 40-41.
14. I have this from Robert Winans.
15. Green, *Country Roots*, pp. 19-20.
16. Green, *Only a Miner*, p. 35.
17. See Archie Green's richly detailed and interesting "Hillbilly Music:
Source and Symbol," *JAF* 78(July-Sept. 1965):204-28. I follow him. See also
Nolan Porterfield, *Jimmie Rodgers* (Urbana: University of Illinois Press,
1979), an excellent biography of Rodgers which gives the fullest available
account of Peer's activities during these critical years and offers an unforgettable portrait of life in the South between the wars.
18. Green, "Hillbilly Music," p. 211.
19. Reproduced in Harry Smith's discographical pamphlet accompanying the
Folkways Anthology of American Folk Music. Folkways FA 2951-2953. Entry
no. 73.
20. Archie Green, "Commercial Music Graphics," No. 16, *JEMF Quarterly*
7(Spring 1971):23-26. The brochure pictures "happy darkies" in a moonlit southern setting; but the music is hillbilly music.

21. Ibid., no. 12, 4(Dec. 1968).
22. Green, "Hillbilly Music," p. 211.
23. I have this from Peter Kennedy.
24. Koon, "Newgrass, Oldgrass, and Bluegrass."
25. "The Rich-R-Tone Story," p. 4.
26. Sleeve notes to *The Hotmud Family: til we meet here again or above.* Vetco Records LP 501.

Chapter 9. The High, Lonesome Sound: Ritual, Icon, and Image

1. Rooney, *Bossmen*, p. 50.
2. Walter Ong, S.J., *The Presence of the Word: Some Prolegomena for Cultural and Religious History* (New Haven: Yale University Press, 1967), p. 118.
3. Wolfe, "Bluegrass Touches."
4. Quoted by Ralph Rinzler in the sleeve notes to *The High Lonesome Sound.*
5. Alan Lomax, *Cantrometrics: A Method in Musical Anthropology* (Berkeley, Calif.: U.C. Extension Media Center, 1976). See also *Folk Song Style and Culture* (Washington, D.C.: American Association for the Advancement of Science, 1968).
6. Johanna Stein, "Musicology for Music Therapists: The Lomax Study," *Journal of Music Therapy* 10(Sept. 1973):46-51.
7. Lomax, *Folk Songs of North America*, p. xviii.
8. Ibid., p. xvii.
9. Bill Malone, *Country Music U.S.A.*, p. 289.
10. Bill Keith, in conversation with the author.
11. Bill Monroe, interview, Apr. 1977.
12. Bill Thompson, "Country Music Portrait," radio station KGBS, Los Angeles, 1967 (interview).
13. All quoted in Peter Wernick, *Bluegrass Songbook*, pp. 104-5.
14. Martin L. Nass, "Some Considerations of a Psychoanalytic Interpretation of Music," *Psychoanalytic Quarterly* 40(1971):303-13.
15. Isador H. Coriet, "Some Aspects of a Psychoanalytic Interpretation of Music," *Psychoanalytic Review* 32(1945):408-18.
16. Northrop Frye, *Anatomy of Criticism* (Princeton, N.J.: Princeton University Press, 1957), p. 184. See also "The Context of Romance," in *The Secular Scripture* (Cambridge, Mass.: Harvard University Press, 1976), pp. 35-61.
17. Ibid., p. 35.
18. Bill Malone, *Country Music, U.S.A.* p. 306
19. Carlton Haney's "The Story of Bluegrass Music," held at Camp Springs, N.C., in 1965. I am quoting a tape, imperfectly remembered, played for me by fiddler Ed Neff, of San Rafael, Calif.
20. Columbus, Ohio *Citizen-Journal*, Apr. 21, 1981, p. 1.

21. This review is photographically reproduced in Charles Wolfe, *The Grand Ole Opry: The Early Years 1925-35* (London: Old Time Music, 1975), p. 37.

22. See Roger Smirnoff, "Gibson: The Early Years," *Pickin'* (June 1975):13, 6.

23. Ann Douglas, *The Feminization of American Culture* (New York: Alfred A. Knopf, 1977).

24. I wonder if Dolly's name is not somehow connected to the popular nineteenth-century name "Dolly Varden," which referred to "a woman's costume . . . including a flowered-trimmed, broad-brimmed hat and a dress consisting of a tight bodice and bouffant panniers in a flower print over a calf-length quilted petticoat." *(The Random House Dictionary of the English language)* The name itself originates in Dickens's *Barnaby Rudge*.

Chapter 10. Bilin' Down Creation: The Landscape of Bluegrass

1. Frye, *The Secular Scripture*, p. 53.

2. Ibid., p. 57.

3. M. H. Abrams, "The Romantic Period," in *The Norton Anthology of English Literature*, 2 vols. (New York: W.W. Norton, 1968), 2:13.

4. See Wilgus, "'Ten Broek and Mollie': A Race and a Ballad," and William Hugh Jansen, "'Ten Broek and Molly' and 'The Rose of Kentucky,'" *Kentucky Folklore Record* 4(1958):149-53.

5. Wilgus, "Ten Broek and Mollie," 77.

6. Jansen, "'Ten Broek and Molly' and 'The Rose of Kentucky,'" 152.

7. Frye, *Anatomy of Criticism*, p. 306.

8. Bill Monroe, interview with author, New York, Apr. 1977.

9. Maud Karpeles, *Cecil Sharp*, p. 140.

10. Cecil Sharp to Maud Karpeles, quoted in Ibid., p. 89.

11. Ibid., pp. 65, 145-49, 163-64.

12. Ibid., p. 170.

13. Moore, *The Frontier Mind*, pp. 3-4, 11.

14. Charles Fenno Hoffman, *A Winter in the West* (New York, 1833), quoted in Ibid., p. 17.

15. Moore, *The Frontier Mind*, p. 23.

16. See Toll, *Blacking Up*, especially chap. 4, "Minstrels Fight the Civil War."

17. Frye, *Anatomy*, pp. 304-5.

18. Thomas Cole to Asher Brown Durand, quoted in John K. Howatt, *The Hudson River and Its Painters* (New York: Viking Press, 1972), p. 37.

19. William Cullen Bryant's funeral oration for Cole, quoted in Ibid., p. 35.

20. See Alan P. Merriam, *The Anthropology of Music* (Evanston, Ill.: Northwestern University Press, 1964), pp. 88-95. Also see Bibliography.

21. Monroe, interview, York, Pa., Apr. 1977.

22. Wells, "Uncle Pen."

Chapter 11. Tambo and Bones: Blackface Minstrelsy, the Opry, and Bill Monroe

1. Quoted by Dix Hollobaugh, "Iowan Bob Black Grazes on Nashville's Bluegrass," *Des Moines Sunday Register Picture*, Sept. 19, 1976, p. 31.

2. Ibid.

3. Quoted by Richard Greene in a radio interview with Doug Bensen, "Bill Monroe, King of Bluegrass Music."

4. Quoted by Ralph Rinzler in sleeve notes to *The High Lonesome Sound*.

5. I have seen this happen on several occasions, particularly at folk festivals which include blues as well as bluegrass musicians.

6. Frye, *Anatomy of Criticism*, p. 43.

7. Ibid., p. 163ff.

8. George Hay, *Nashville Banner*, Feb. 22, 1931. Quoted in Wolfe, *The Grand Ole Opry*, pp. 18, 13.

9. For some interesting insight into this, see the photos by Ben Shahn and Walker Evans taken in Tennessee and Alabama in the thirties; these include a medicine show with a blackface comedian and a series of posters advertising "J. C. Lincoln's Mighty Minstrels," which picture a group of Negro stereotypes in a style strongly reminiscent of early Hollywood cartoons. In Hank O'Neal, *A Vision Shared: A Classic Portrait of America and Its People, 1935-43.* (New York: St. Martin's Press, 1976), pp. 40, 41, 56, 104.

10. Green emphasizes this point in *Country Roots*, p. 67.

11. Ibid., p. 76.

12. Tribe, "Charlie Monroe,"

13. Wolfe, *The Grand Ole Opry*, pp. 42, 83.

14. Quoted in Tony Russell, *Blacks, Whites and Blues* (London, 1970), p. 55.

15. George F. Rehin, "Harlequin Jim Crow: Continuity and Convergence in Blackface Clowning," *Journal of Popular Culture* 9(Winter 1975):682-701.

16. Bryan Edwards, *History, Civil and Commercial, of the British Colonies in the West Indies* (London, 1793-1801), quoted in Epstein, *Sinful Tunes and Spirituals*, p. 14.

17. [Thomas Tyron], "A Discourse in Way of Dialogue, between an Ethiopian or Negro-Slave and a Christian that was His Master in America," in *Friendly Advice to the Gentlemen Planters of the East and West Indies*, by Philotheos Physiologus [pseud.] (London, 1684). Quoted in Epstein, *Sinful Tunes and Spirituals*, p. 28.

18. Paul Oliver's description of what he heard in Senegal, in *Savannah Syncopators*, p. 43. The record album accompanying this book includes a *halam* improvisation by Thiam Sy griots which I invite the reader to compare with some of our more archaic clawhammer banjo solos, especially those in modal or nonchordal tunings. The griots' music could stow away on an album of Appalachian mountain banjo tunes virtually without detection.

19. J. Kinnard, Jr., "Who Are Our National Poets?" *Knickerbocker Magazine* 26(Oct. 1845):331-41. Quoted in Bruce Jackson, *The Negro and His Folklore in 19th Century Periodicals*, p. 29.

20. Nathanson, "Negro Minstrelsy, Ancient and Modern," quoted in Ibid., p. 38.

21. W. J. Cash, *The Mind of the South* (New York: Alfred A. Knopf, 1941), p. 51.

22. See Nathan, *Dan Emmett and the Rise of Early Negro Minstrelsy*, p. 186ff.

23. Kinnard, "Who Are Our National Poets?", in Jackson, *The Negro and His Folklore*, p. 29.

24. John C. Campbell, *The Southern Highlander and His Homeland*, p. 48.

25. "In 1825," Campbell writes:

> One Ambrose Amburgey came over from the Clinch River, Virginia, into what is now Knott County, Kentucky [southeastern Ky.] The country was exceedingly rough, but he found a couple, James and Pricilla Davis, living near the mouth of the Defeated Branch. From them he bought, for $600, the rights to over 10,000 acres of lands along Clear Creek, a narrow but fertile and lovely valley. He then went back to Virginia, gathered up his wife and two children, his parents, and brothers-in-law, together with their families and *their slaves* [my emphasis]— in all a goodly company. The next year they started for Kentucky. . . . Amburgey settled the several families along several parts of his purchase. The children were many, ten or fifteen in each household, and in a generation or so there were literally hundreds of the family in that region. Now, in this and in neighboring counties, there are thousands of their descendants."

Campbell notes, too, that the discovery of salt in eastern Kentucky brought a back-migration from the bluegrass region, bringing a slave population into the mountains; gold discovered in north Georgia in 1828 brought black and white settlers into that region as well. Ibid., pp. 42-45, 48. See note 18. Fugitive slaves probably sought refuge in the mountains, and homeless blacks after Emancipation.

26. See Hofstadter, Miller and Aaron, "The Back Country," in *The American Republic*, 2 vols. (Englewood Cliffs, N.J.: Prentiss-Hall, 1959), 1:74. Also "Dixie: The People and the Way of Life," 506ff.

27. Frederick Law Olmstead, quoted in Ibid., p. 506. This was northern Alabama.

28. Berendt Ostendorf, "Minstrelsy and Early Jazz," *The Massachusetts Review* 20(Autumn 1979):574-602.

29. Harriet Martineau, quoted in Ibid., p. 580.

30. See Levine, *Black Culture and Black Consciousness*, pp. 7-19.

31. Ostendorf, "Minstrelsy and Early Jazz," p. 578.

32. "Memories of a Monticello Slave," in *Jefferson at Monticello*. Quoted in Epstein, *Sinful Tunes and Spirituals*, p. 122.

33. Ostendorf, "Minstrelsy and Early Jazz," p. 584.

34. "Interview with Ben Cotton," *New York Mirror*, July 3, 1897, quoted in Toll, *Blacking Up*, p. 33.

35. Nathan, *Dan Emmett and the Rise of Early Negro Minstrelsy*, p. 71.

36. "Interview with Ben Cotton."

37. A statement by C. J. Rogers in the *New York Clipper*, June 20, 1874, quoted in Nathan, *Dan Emmett*, p. 110.

38. It was in the form of folklore that I first heard of the Snowdon Brothers; I suspect that their story remains in that form in Mt. Vernon because the local residents have a particular stake in protecting the reputation of Dan Emmett as the author of "Dixie," though Emmett's place in history would be assured even if he had not written the song. In fact there are few minstrel songs which warrant such an attribution in the strictest literary sense, though Nathan has made a very good case for Uncle Dan's authorship of "Dixie." Some documentation on the Snowdons will be found in the files of the Mt. Vernon Public Library, where an undated article by one Ada Bedell Wootten, which appears to have been clipped from a Columbus paper, perhaps the Sunday *Dispatch*, sometime in the fifties, describes Emmett's visits to the Snowdon household and their career in the area; this piece, "How 'Dixie's' Composer Learned About the South," includes a remarkable photograph of Ben and Lou Snowdon seated on a stage built into the gable of their house, playing fiddle and banjo. The same photograph is in the *Mt. Vernon News* files; it appeared in their Bicentennial edition.

39. See Nathan, "Dan Emmett's Youth," in *Dan Emmett*, pp. 98-106; and H. Ogden Wintermute, *Daniel Decatur Emmett* (Mt. Vernon: 1955).

40. Catterall, ed. *Judicial Cases Concerning Slavery*, 4:49-50. Quoted in Ira Berlin, *Slaves without Masters: The Free Negro in the Antebellum South* (New York: Vintage Books, 1974), p. 34. Berlin discusses the entire matter at length, p. 20ff.

41. Nathan, *Dan Emmett*, p. 284. Fields quoted from Al. G. Fields, *Watch Yourself Go By* (Columbus, Ohio: 1912), p. 485. Fields was a minstrel show producer.

42. Ibid., p. 283.

43. Wintermute, *Daniel Decatur Emmett*, p. 11.

44. Hildred Roach, *Black American Music Past and Present* (Boston: Crescendo, 1973), p. 54.

45. Elizabeth Baroody, "Banjo: The Sound of America," *Early American Life* 7(Apr. 1976).

46. Carl Wittke, *Tambo and Bones: A History of the American Minstrel Stage* (Durham, N.C.: Duke University Press, 1930), p. 218.

47. Quoted in Russell, *Blacks, Whites and Blues*, pp. 66-67.

48. Toll, *Blacking Up*, pp. 38-40.

49. Ibid., p. 40.

50. John Updike, "Lifeguard," in *Pigeon Feathers* (New York: Crest Publications, 1962).

51. Hodeir, *Jazz*, p. 207.

52. Nathan, *Dan Emmett*, pp. 71-72.

52. An 1841 playbill quoted in Ibid., p. 61.

54. Toll, *Blacking Up*, pp. 139-45.

55. Maynard Mack, "The Muse of Satire," *Yale Review*, 41(1951):80-92. In Zitner, Kissane and Liberman, eds. *The Practice of Criticism* (New York: 1966), p. 18.

56. Ostendorf, "Minstrelsy and Early Jazz," p. 590.

Selected Bibliography

The books and articles listed below are meant to introduce the reader to the key areas and concepts relevant to this book.

Folk Music and Art Music

Apel, Willi. *Gregorian Chant*. London: Burns & Oates, 1958.

Bailey, Jay. "Historical Origin and Stylistic Developments of the Five-String Banjo." *Journal of American Folklore* 85(1972):58-65.

Burman-Hall, Linda. "Southern American Folk Fiddle Styles." *Ethnomusicology* 19(Jan. 1975).

Chambers, G.B. *Folksong-Plainsong: A Study in Origins and Musical Relationships*. London: Merlin Press, 1956.

Chase, Gilbert. *America's Music: From the Pilgrims to the Present*. rev. 2nd ed. New York: McGraw-Hill, 1966.

Combs, Josiah H. *Folk-Songs of the Southern United States*. Edited by D. K. Wilgus. Austin: University of Texas Press, 1967.

Dvořák, Anton. "Music in America." *Harper's New Monthly Magazine* 90(Feb. 1895).

Epstein, Dena. "The Folk Banjo: A Documentary History." *Ethnomusicology* 19(Sept. 1975):347-71.

Green, Archie. "Thomas Hart Benton's Folk Musicians." Commercial Music Graphics no. 37, *JEMF Quarterly* (John Edwards Memorial Foundation) 12(Summer 1976):74-90.

Heaton, C. P. "The Five-String Banjo in North Carolina." *Southern Folklore* 35(1971).

Jackson, George Pullen. *White and Negro Spirituals: Their Life Span and Kinship*. Locust Valley, N.Y.: J. J. Augustin, 1943.

———. *Spiritual Folk-Songs of Early America*. Locust Valley, N.Y.: J. J. Augustin, 1937.

Jansen, William Hugh. "'Ten Broeck and Molly' and 'The Rose of Kentucky'." *Kentucky Folklore Record* 4(1958):149-53.

Karpeles, Maud. *Cecil Sharp: His Life and Work*. Chicago: University of Chicago Press, 1967.

Lloyd, A. L. *Folk Song in England*. St. Albans, Hertfordshire, England: Granada Publishers, Ltd., 1967.

Lomax, Alan. *Cantometrics: A Method in Musical Anthropology*. Berkeley: University of California Press, 1976.

———. *The Folk Songs of North America.* Garden City, N.Y.: Doubleday, 1960.

———. *Folk Song Style and Culture.* Washington, D.C.: American Association for the Advancement of Science, 1968.

———. *The Gospel Ship: Baptist Hymns and White Spirituals from the Southern Mountains.* New World Records NW 254. Brochure notes.

Pierik, Marie. *The Song of the Church.* New York: Longmans, Green, 1947.

Rinzler, Ralph. *Old-Time Music at Clarence Ashley's.* Folkways FA 2355. Brochure notes.

Sharp, Cecil. *English Folk-Song: Some Conclusions.* Edited by Maud Karpeles. New York, 1954.

Sharp, Cecil, and Maud Karpeles. *English Folk-Songs from the Southern Appalachians,* 2 vols. London: 1932.

Wilgus, D. K. *Anglo-American Folksong Scholarship since 1898.* New Brunswick, N.J.: Rutgers University Press, 1959.

———. "'Ten Broeck and Mollie': A Race and a Ballad." *Kentucky Folklore Record* 2 (1956):77-89.

African and Afro-American Music

Bebey, Francis. *African Music: A People's Art.* Translated by Josephine Bennett. New York: L. Hill, 1975.

Chernoff, John Miller. *African Rhythm and African Sensibility: Aesthetics and Social Action in African Musical Idioms.* Chicago: University of Chicago Press, 1969.

Courlander, Harold. *Negro Folk Music, U.S.A.* New York: Columbia University Press, 1963.

Epstein, Dena. *Sinful Tunes and Spirituals: Black Folk Music to the Civil War.* Urbana: University of Illinois Press, 1977.

Finnegan, Ruth. *Oral Literature in Africa.* Oxford: Oxford University Press, 1970.

James, Willis Laurence. "The Romance of the Negro Folk Cry in America." *Phylon* 16(Mar. 1955):15-30.

Jones, A. M. *Studies in African Music.* 2 vols. London: Oxford University Press, 1959.

Krehbiel, Henry Edward. *Afro-American Folksong: A Study in Racial and National Music.* New York: F. Unger, 1914.

Lawrence, Keith. "Arnold Shultz: The Greatest (?) Guitar Picker's Life Ended before Promise Realized." *JEMF Quarterly,* 17(Spring 1981):3-8.

Lomax, Alan. *Roots of the Blues.* New World Records NWR 252. Brochure notes.

Merriam, Alan. *African Music on L.P.: An Annotated Discography.* Evanston, Ill.: Northwestern University Press, 1970.

Nketia, J. H. Kwabena. *The Music of Africa.* New York: W. W. Norton, 1975.

Oliver, Paul. *Savannah Syncopators: African Retentions in the Blues.* London: Studio Vista, 1970.

Ong, Walter. "African Talking Drums and Oral Noetics." *New Literary History* 8(Spring 1977):411-29.

Ostendorf, Berendt. "Black Poetry, Blues and Folklore: Double Consciousness in Afro-American Oral Culture." *Amerikastudien* 20 (1975).

Roach, Hildred. *Black American Music Past and Present.* Boston: 1973.

Roberts, John Storm. *Black Music of Two Worlds.* New York: William Morrow, 1972.

Southern, Eileen. *The Music of Black Americans: A History.* New York: Norton, 1971.

Waterman, Richard Alan. "African Influence in the Music of the Americas." in *Acculturation in the Americas.* Edited by Sol Tax. Chicago: University of Chicago Press, 1952.

Work, John. *American Negro Songs and Spirituals.* New York: Bonanza Books, 1940.

Minstrelsy

Baroody, Elizabeth. "Banjo: The Sound of America." *Early American Life* 7 (Apr. 1976).

Callahan, Robert. "Irish Mornings and African Days on the Old Minstrel Stage: An Interview with Leni Sloan." *Callahan's Irish Quarterly* 2(Spring 1982):49-56.

Jackson, Bruce, ed. *The Negro and His Folklore in Nineteenth Century Periodicals.* Austin: University of Texas Press, 1967.

Kinnard, J., Jr. "Who Are Our National Poets?" *Knickerbocker Magazine* 26(Oct. 1845):331-41.

Nathan, Hans. *Dan Emmett and the Rise of Early Negro Minstrelsy.* Norman, Okla: University of Oklahoma Press, 1962.

[Nathanson, Y. S.] "Negro Minstrelsy, Ancient and Modern." *Putnam's Monthly* 5(Jan. 1855):72-79.

Ostendorf, Berendt. "Minstrelsy and Early Jazz." *Massachusetts Review* 20(Autumn 1979):574-602.

Rehin, George F. "The Darker Image: American Negro Minstrelsy through the Historian's Lens." *American Studies* 9(Dec. 1975):365-73.

———. "Harlequin Jim Crow: Continuity and Convergence in Blackface Clowning." *Journal of Popular Culture* 9(Winter 1975):682-701.

Rourke, Constance. "That Long-Tailed Blue." *American Humor: A Study of the National Character.* New York: Harcourt, Brace, 1947.

Simond, Ike. *Old Slack's Reminiscence and Pocket History of the Colored Profession from 1865 to 1891.* Bowling Green, Ohio: Bowling Green Popular Press, 1974. Introduction by Robert Toll.

Toll, Robert. *Blacking Up: The Minstrel Show in Nineteenth-Century America.* New York: Oxford University Press, 1974.

Winans, Robert. "The Folk, the Stage, and the Five-String Banjo in the Nineteenth Century." *Journal of American Folklore* 89(1976):407-37.
Wittke, Carl. *Tambo and Bones: A History of the American Minstrel Stage.* Durham, N.C.: Duke University Press, 1930.

Jazz

Berendt, Joachim. *The Jazz Book.* Translated by Dan Morgenstern. St. Albans, Herfordshire, England: Granada Publishers, Paladin Books, 1976.
Blesh, Rudi. *Shining Trumpets: A History of Jazz.* New York: Da Capo Press, 1946.
Condon, Eddie. *We Called It Music: A Generation of Jazz.* New York: Greenwood Press, 1947.
Hobson, Wilder. *American Jazz Music.* New York: W.W. Norton, 1939.
Hodeir, André. *Jazz; Its Evolution and Essence.* Translated by David Noakes. New York: Grove Press, 1956.
Lomax, Alan. *Mister Jelly Roll: The Fortunes of Jelly Roll Morton, New Orleans Creole and "Inventor of Jazz."* Berkeley: University of California Press, 1956.
Sargeant, Winthrop. *Jazz: Hot and Hybrid.* New York: Da Capo Press, 1946.
Schuller, Gunther. *Early Jazz: Its Roots and Musical Development.* New York: Oxford University Press, 1968.
Shapiro, Nat, and Nat Hentoff. *Hear Me Talkin' to Ya: The Story of Jazz as Told by the Men Who Made It.* New York: Rinehart, 1955.
Stearns, Marshall. *The Story of Jazz.* New York: Oxford University Press, 1956.

Country Music and Bluegrass

Adler, Thomas. "Manual Formulaic Composition: Innovation in Bluegrass Banjo Styles." *Journal of Country Music* 5(Summer 1974).
Artis, Bob. *Bluegrass.* New York: Hawthorne Books, 1975.
Benson, Doug. "Bill Monroe: King of Bluegrass Music." *Bluegrass Unlimited* 2(Dec. 1967):3-5.
Cantwell, Robert. "Believing in Bluegrass." *Atlantic* 229(March 1972):52-60.
———. "Ten Thousand Acres of Bluegrass: Mimesis in Bill Monroe's Music." *Journal of Popular Culture* 13(Spring 1980):209-20.
Cohen, Anne and Norm. "Folk and Hillbilly Music: Further Thoughts on Their Relation." *JEMF Quarterly* 13(Summer 1977):50-57.
Cohen, Norm. "The Skillet Lickers: A Study of a Hillbilly String Band and Its Repertoire." *Journal of American Folklore* 78(July-Sept. 1965):229-44.
Foster, Alice. "Kenny Baker" [interview]. *Bluegrass Unlimited* 3 (Dec. 1968).
———. "My Life in Bluegrass": An Interview with Bill Monroe." *Newport Folk Festival Program, 1969,* pp. 14-17.

Green, Archie. "Commercial Music Graphics" no. 16 ["Old Time Edison Disc Records" brochure]. *JEMF Quarterly* 7, Part 1 (Spring 1971):23-26.

——. "Hillbilly Music: Source and Symbol," *Journal of American Folklore* 78(July-Sept. 1965):204-28.

——. *Only a Miner: Studies in Recorded Coal-Mining Songs.* Urbana: University of Illinois Press, 1972.

Green, Douglas B. *Country Roots: The Origins of Country Music.* New York: Hawthorn Books, 1976.

Green, Douglas B., and George Gruhn, "Gibson Banjos." *Bluegrass Unlimited* 7(Apr. 1973):27-29.

Green, James D. "A Musical Analysis of the Banjo Style of Earl Scruggs: An Examination of *Country Music* (MG20358)." *Journal of Country Music* 5(Spring 1974):31-37.

Koon, William Henry. "Newgrass, Oldgrass, and Bluegrass." *JEMF Quarterly* 10, Part 1 (Spring 1974):15-18.

Lomax, Alan. "Bluegrass Background: Folk Music with Overdrive." *Esquire,* 52(Oct. 1959):108.

Lundy, Ronnie. "The New Grass Revival." *Bluegrass Unlimited* 13(Nov. 1978):10-15.

Malone, Bill C. *Southern Music/American Music.* Lexington: University Press of Kentucky, 1979.

——. *Country Music, U.S.A.: A Fifty-Year History.* Austin: University of Texas Press, 1968.

Malone, Bill C., and Judith McCulloh, eds. *Stars of Country Music: Uncle Dave Macon to Johnny Rodriguez.* Urbana: University of Illinois Press, 1975.

Porterfield, Nolan. *Jimmie Rodgers: The Life and Times of America's Blue Yodeler.* Urbana: University of Illinois Press, 1979.

Rhodes, Don. "Roy Acuff, the Real Speckled Bird." *Bluegrass Unlimited* 13 (May 1979):14-20.

Rinzler, Ralph. "Bill Monroe." In *Stars of Country Music.* Edited by Bill C. Malone and Judith McCulloh. Urbana: University of Illinois Press, 1975.

——. "Bill Monroe: The Daddy of Bluegrass Music." *Sing Out* 13(Feb.-Mar. 1963):5-8.

——. *The High Lonesome Sound of Bill Monroe and the Bluegrass Boys.* Decca DL7-4780 and MCA MCA-110. Liner notes.

——. "Ralph Stanley: The Tradition from the Mountains." *Bluegrass Unlimited* 8(Mar. 1974):7-11.

Rooney, James. *Bossmen: Bill Monroe & Muddy Waters.* New York: Hayden Book Co., 1971).

Rorrer, Clifford Kinney. *Charlie Poole and the North Carolina Ramblers.* Eden, N.C.: privately printed, 1968.

Rosenberg, Neil. *Bill Monroe and His Blue Grass Boys: An Illustrated Discography.* Nashville: Country Music Foundation Press, 1974.

——. *Bill Monroe with Lester Flatt and Earl Scruggs: The Original Bluegrass Band.* Rounder Records Special Series 5506. Brochure notes.

————. "A Brief Survey of Bluegrass Haberdashery." *Bluegrass Unlimited* 3(Mar. 1968):6.

————. "From Sound to Style: The Emergence of Bluegrass." *Journal of American Folklore* 80(1967):143-50.

Russell, Tony. *Blacks, Whites, and Blues*. London: Studio Vista, 1970.

Scruggs, Earl. *Earl Scruggs and the Five-String Banjo*. New York: Peer International Corp., 1968.

Seeger, Mike. *Mountain Music Bluegrass Style*. Folkways FA 2318. Brochure notes.

Smirnoff, Roger. "Gibson: The Early Years." *Pickin'* (June 1975).

Smith, Hazel. "Monroe Homecoming." *Bluegrass Unlimited* 8(Nov. 1973):245-56.

Smith, Mayne. "An Introduction to Bluegrass." *Journal of American Folklore* 78(1965):245-56.

The Smithsonian Collection of Classic Country Music. Edited by Bill C. Malone. Washington, D.C.: Smithsonian Institution, 1981. Accompanying booklet.

Tribe, Ivan. "Charlie Monroe." *Bluegrass Unlimited* 10(Oct. 1975):12-19.

————. "The Hillbilly versus the City: Urban Images in Country Music." *JEMF Quarterly* 10(Summer 1974):41-51.

Wells, Herb. "Uncle Pen." *Bluegrass Unlimited* 8(Sept. 1973):15.

Wernick, Peter. *Bluegrass Banjo*. New York: Oak Publications, 1975.

————. *Bluegrass Songbook*. New York: Oak Publications, 1976.

Wolfe, Charles K. "Bluegrass Touches." *Old Time Music* 16(Spring 1978):6-12.

————. *The Grand Ole Opry: The Early Years, 1925-35*. London: Old Time Music, 1975.

————. *Kentucky Country: Folk and Country Music of Kentucky*. Lexington: University Press of Kentucky, 1982.

————. *Tennessee Strings: The Story of Country Music in Tennessee*. Knoxville: University of Tennessee Press, 1977.

The Meaning of Music

Borstein, Melvin. "Analysis of a Congenitally Blind Musician." *Psychoanalytic Quarterly* 46(1977):23-27.

Coriet, Isadora H. "Some Aspects of a Psychoanalytic Interpretation of Music." *Psychoanalytic Review* 27(1945):408-18.

Edwards, E. M., and M. E. Smith. "The Phenomenological Description of Musical Intervals." *American Journal of Psychology* 34(1923):287-91.

Hanson, Howard. "A Musician's Point of View towards Musical Expression." *American Journal of Psychiatry* 99(1942):317-25.

————. "Some Objective Studies of Rhythm in Music." *American Journal of Psychiatry* 101(1944):364-69.

Heinlein, C. P. "The Affective Character of the Major and Minor Modes in Music." *Journal of Comparative Psychology* 8(1928):101-42.
Hevner, Kate. "The Affective Value of Pitch and Tempo in Music." *American Journal of Psychology* 49(1937):621-30.
Kohut, Heinz. "Observations on the Psychological Functions of Music." *Journal of the American Psychoanalytic Association* 5(1957):389-407.
Merriam, Alan P. *The Anthropology of Music*. Evanston, Ill.: Northwestern University Press, 1964.
Meyer, Leonard. *Emotion and Meaning in Music*. Chicago: University of Chicago Press, 1956.
Nass, Martin L. "Some Considerations of a Psychoanalytic Interpretation of Music." *Psychoanalytic Quarterly* 40(1971):303-13.
Stein, Johanna. "Musicology for Music Therapists: The Lomax Study." *Journal of Music Therapy* 10(Sept. 1973):46-51.
Stravinsky, Igor. *The Poetics of Music*. Translated by Arthur Knodel and Ingolf Dahl. Cambridge, Mass.: Harvard University Press, 1947.
Zuckerkandl, Victor. *Sound and Symbol: Music and the External World*. Princeton, N.J.: Princeton University Press, Bollinger Series, 1956.

Backgrounds

Berlin, Ira. *Slaves without Masters: The Free Negro in the Antebellum South*. New York: Vintage Books, Random House, 1974.
Campbell, John C. *The Southern Highlander and His Homeland*. 1921; rpt., Louisville: University of Kentucky Press, 1969.
Carothers, J. C. "Culture, Psychiatry, and the Written Word." *Psychiatry* 22(Nov. 1959):302-20.
Cash, W. J. *The Mind of the South*. New York: Alfred A. Knopf, 1941.
Caudill, Harry. *Night Comes to the Cumberlands*. Boston: Little, Brown, 1963.
Douglas, Ann. *The Feminization of American Culture*. New York: Alfred A. Knopf, 1977.
Erikson, Erik. *Identity and the Life Cycle*. New York: International Universities Press, 1959.
Frye, Northrop. *Anatomy of Criticism*. Princeton, N.J.: Princeton University Press, 1957.
———. *The Secular Scripture*. Cambridge, Mass.: Harvard University Press, 1976.
Hearn, Lafcadio. *Children of the Levee*. Edited by O. W. Frost. Lexington: University of Kentucky Press, 1957.
Lamoreaux, David. "Baseball in the Late Nineteenth Century: The Source of Its Appeal." *Journal of Popular Culture* 11(Winter 1977):597-613.
Levine, Lawrence. *Black Culture and Black Consciousness: Afro-American Folk Thought from Slavery to Freedom*. New York: Oxford University Press, 1977.

Lewis, Claudia. *Children of the Cumberland*. New York: Columbia University Press, 1946.
Moore, Arthur. *The Frontier Mind*. Lexington: University of Kentucky Press, 1957.
Ong, Walter, S.J., *The Presence of the Word: Some Prolegomena for Cultural and Religious History*. New Haven: Yale University Press, 1967.

Index

Note on the author

Robert Cantwell, a writer, folklorist, and bluegrass
musician, teaches English at Kenyon College. His
published work includes poetry and fiction as well as
articles on bluegrass music, which have appeared in the
Atlantic, the *Journal of Popular Culture*, and the
Kenyon Review.

Books in the series *Music in American Life*